Sharing the World Stage

VOLUME I

Sharing the World Stage: Biography and Gender in World History

Jane Slaughter

Melissa K. Bokovoy

Patricia Risso

University of New Mexico

Ping Yao

California State University, Los Angeles

HOUGHTON MIFFLIN COMPANY Boston New York

Publisher: Suzanne Jeans
Senior Sponsoring Editor: Nancy Blaine
Senior Marketing Manager: Katherine Bates
Senior Development Editor: Tonya Lobato
Senior Project Editor: Rosemary Winfield
Art and Design Manager: Gary Crespo
Cover Design Director: Tony Saizon
Photo Editor: Jennifer Meyer Dare
Composition Buyer: Chuck Dutton
New Title Project Manager: Susan Peltier
Editorial Associate: Adrienne Zicht
Marketing Assistant: Lauren Bussard

Cover design: *Rama and Sita,* Pahari style, ca. 1740. Gouache. Victoria and Albert Museum, London / Art Resource, NY.

Credits continue on page 369, which constitutes an extension of the copyright page.

Printed in the U.S.A.
Library of Congress Catalog Card number 2007922958
2 3 4 5 6 7 8 9 - EB - 11 10 09 08

Volume 1: ISBN-10, 0-618-37045-5; ISBN-13, 978-0-618-37045-0
Volume 2: ISBN-10, 0-618-37047-1; ISBN-13, 978-0-618-37047-4

CONTENTS

PREFACE

The intellectual seeds that produced this volume were gathered in many introductory civilization classes spanning almost four decades. As historians, we represent distinct generations and different training, but we share ideas and goals that we believe will resonate with other teachers of introductory history courses. The power of historical insight and the thrill of historical discovery have shaped and driven our lives. Our purpose is to share the quest and excitement with students.

Over the last thirty years, world history has expanded beyond a focus on the development of great civilizations to include comparative studies of societies and communities that were interconnected even before the rise of the West. As a result, we consider the problems that human societies have faced over time and the ingenious solutions they employed to survive and order their worlds. But the description of general patterns of human experience should not erase specific differences that give the patterns their forms and colors. The challenge of teaching world history is to provide ways for students to grasp and identify with vast and complex political, social, cultural, and religious movements. Bringing the men and women who were key players in those events onto the historical stage breathes life into these movements.

The explosion of women's history since the 1970s has given us the lives of countless ordinary and extraordinary women from all parts of the world. Comparing these individuals with other women can reveal similarities that cross classes, ethnicities, regions, and times. At the same time, grounding them in specific historical contexts avoids producing a universal female experience. Gender history recognizes that we cannot explain women's actions, status, and attitudes without understanding men's. Thus, in this volume we also consider the opportunities, expectations, and problems of being a man in historical times and places. Gender discussed in abstract terms often falls on deaf ears; our experiences have taught us that individual motives, behaviors, and goals are far more illustrative. By pairing individuals who have intimate familial or social connections or who inhabit similar chronological and geographic spaces, we introduce students to the idea that they must always consider gender as an important criterion of analysis when they assess historical significance. Moving together through time, the lives of each pair point to the facts that a man's experience is not the universal experience and that a woman's experience is not the exception. A tested mix of historical movements, biography, and gender, brought from our classrooms, is displayed in the chapters that follow.

Throughout this volume, overarching themes provide the links and connections between case studies that are chronologically and geographically diverse, while the particular subjects of the chapters provide flesh and blood to more general concepts. Among themes central to all these chapters are encounters and exchanges between people, the development of lines of authority and resistance to them, philosophical and religious systems and their transformations and transmissions, and conflicts and conquests. These are set in specific historical contexts through the consideration of such topics as the relationships between religious beliefs and political structures; issues of access to power, succession, and the ways that power is transmitted; the economic, legal, religious, and political dimensions of personal relationships; and ideal behaviors and expectations for men and women.

Each chapter focuses on one woman and one man whose lives reflect major social, cultural, political, and economic developments of the time. Often these individuals were uniquely positioned to alter the conditions of their lives or to influence the course of history, and these chapters raise important questions about differences in autonomy and power between men and women, among women, and among men.

A comparison of experiences is important, but the examples in this text also point to a comparison of sources and encourage students to ask, Whose stories are recorded, and whose records are preserved? Each chapter contains a brief introduction to the sources available for the individuals and the time period. Moving from chapter to chapter, students can begin to see how the nature of the historical record changes, as well as how the records available for men and for women vary widely. As we move forward in time, the diversity and breadth of sources for both men and women increase, and the choice of historical figures thereby expands.

The choice of individuals, of course, is dictated by their contemporaries' acknowledgment of their existence through a diverse array of sources, either written or material. In the earliest chapters, the figures discussed will be familiar and might fall into the category of great men or women, like the Roman imperial ruler Octavius and his politically astute wife, Livia. In subsequent chapters, at times one partner will be much better known than the other, for example, Ban Zhao (who wrote one of the most influential Confucian classics in Chinese history, *Lessons for Women*) and her brother, the historian and poet Ban Gu; the early church father Jerome and his spiritual partner Paula; or Chinggis (Genghis) Khan and his daughter-in-law Sorghaghtani (Sorquqtani) Beki. Even as the range of sources becomes richer, inequities and gaps in the records remain, and confronting the ways that sources shape what becomes the narrative of history remains a key contribution of this volume.

We have organized each of the chapters in *Sharing the World Stage* into six sections: Setting the Stage, the Actors, Acts, Finale, Documents, and Questions and Suggested Readings. The Setting the Stage section provides historical background on the time period and society in which the individuals lived.

The Actors section discusses the lives of the paired individuals, as well as some other figures who influenced their lives or society. The drama of these individual's lives is portrayed in the Acts section of the chapter. Here we witness how the individuals contributed to their societies and how their societies responded. The Finale section outlines the last years of the individuals' lives and attempts to provide some closure to that period of history. A collection of documents follows the narrative text at the end of each chapter. Each document opens with a brief introduction and several focus questions, and all of the documents are referenced in the narrative. At the conclusion of each chapter, suggested discussion questions ask students to pull together conflicting relationships, behaviors, and events and their historical meaning, thus allowing many possibilities for analysis and classroom discussion.

We believe that students can learn to appreciate primary documents and benefit from reading and analyzing such materials. We have selected our documents carefully to include both well-known and less famous pieces. The materials include public and private statements of the central figures in each chapter but also accounts and ideas of other men and women of the time who express different opinions and recount different experiences. This diverse documentary evidence allows the reader to discuss in detail the possible differences between men's and women's experiences and responses in each of the movements being studied. Several questions address each document; the document is placed in context and referred to in the narrative, making it both relevant and intelligible to the reader. It is our intent that this process will acquaint students with what it is that historians do and encourage them to grapple with historical problems. Ideally, after reading the text and interpreting the documents, students will learn how to construct one of the most understandable of all historical stories, the biography.

Biographies give human form to textbook narratives that often seem remote and lifeless to many students. *Sharing the World Stage: Biography and Gender in World History* is conceived to accompany the world history course and the standard textbooks used in that course. Each chapter represents a discrete historical movement or event that is easy to assign for individual reading, classroom discussion, papers, and exams. This reader complements the multifaceted ways that today's instructors teach world history. It builds on historical events and personalities familiar to instructors of the course, while offering themes suitable to teachers of history with widely ranging perspectives and interests.

Acknowledgments

Teaching introductory world civilization history survey courses is always challenging. The rewards are also manifold when students connect with events and people in the past and share our enthusiasm. Our thanks and acknowledgments in this volume must therefore begin with the wonderful students whose curiosity and intelligence have contributed unknowingly to this project. Oddly perhaps, we must thank each other as well. From quite different generations of historians, we found common ground in our passions for history and our commitment to constant revision and experimentation in our teaching. We also owe a debt to friends and colleagues who validated and encouraged our plan for the volume. Most gratefully, the volume would not exist without the enthusiasm of Jean Woy and Nancy Blaine, the editors at Houghton Mifflin who understood what we were trying to do and bought an idea that others might have found risky.

From the beginning, colleagues at the University of New Mexico—Beth Bailey, David Farber, and Virginia Scharff—were our cheerleaders, intellectual advisors, and editors. It is because of them the first volumes and now these next two have come to fruition. We, the lead authors, have been very fortunate to work with one of our UNM colleagues, Pat Risso, and with Ping Yao of Cal State Los Angeles on this project. They have brought to this project their expertise, new insights, breadth, and a willingness to take intellectual risks. We thank them for their grace, flexibility, and diligence. Our coauthors acknowledge us as well.

Over the years, we have relied very heavily on the important secondary and primary materials available at the Library of Congress. Even more important is the work that Carol Armbruster, the French area and Italian areas specialist at the Library of Congress, did for us. She came to our rescue on many occasions, finding materials and sometimes copying and sending them to us. Finally, the number of books, articles, and primary source materials necessary for this project meant ordering almost daily from our interlibrary loan department. The interlibrary loan staff worked rapidly and carefully on our requests, and without their help our project would not have been possible. Finally, the writing of *Sharing the World Stage* and *Sharing the Stage* has spanned the entire life of one patient, sweet, and loving six-year-old Kate, who watched her mother and her "niña" read books, "write pages," and drop packages off at the post office. May she one day understand why we wrote this text.

Ping Yao would like to thank her colleagues, Stanley Burstein and Scott Wells, for their constructive insights about teaching world history, her mentor, Patricia Ebrey, for inspiring her to write Asian history through global and gender perspectives, her coauthors for proofreading and commenting on her chapters, Holly Yu and Jianhua Shen for their valuable assistance during various stages of her writing, and her husband, Patrick, and daughter, Elizabeth, for their understanding and sacrifices.

We have been fortunate to have worked briefly with Katie White, Amy Gembela, and Tonya Lobato at Houghton Mifflin. However, these volumes also have benefited over the years from Julie Swasey's capable hands and creative suggestions. She helped shape the development and design of the volume at the very beginning of this project. We wish to thank the following teachers and instructors for their excellent insights, critical analyses, and meticulous reading of the chapters: Sanjam Ahluwalia, Northern Arizona

University; Jonathan Dewald, University at Buffalo, State University of New York; Alan Fisher, Michigan State University; Peter Fraunholtz, Northeastern University; Candace Gregory, California State University, Sacramento; John S. Hill, Immaculata University; Holly S. Hurlburt, Southern Illinois University, Carbondale; Mary Charlotte Safford, Western Piedmont Community College; Thomas Saylor, Concordia University; Colonel Rose Mary Sheldon, Virginia Military Institute; Steven A. Stofferahn, Indiana State University; Emily Sohmer Tai, Queensborough Community College, City University of New York; James R. Weiss, Northeastern University.

Jane Slaughter
Melissa K. Bokovoy

Sharing the World Stage

PART

I

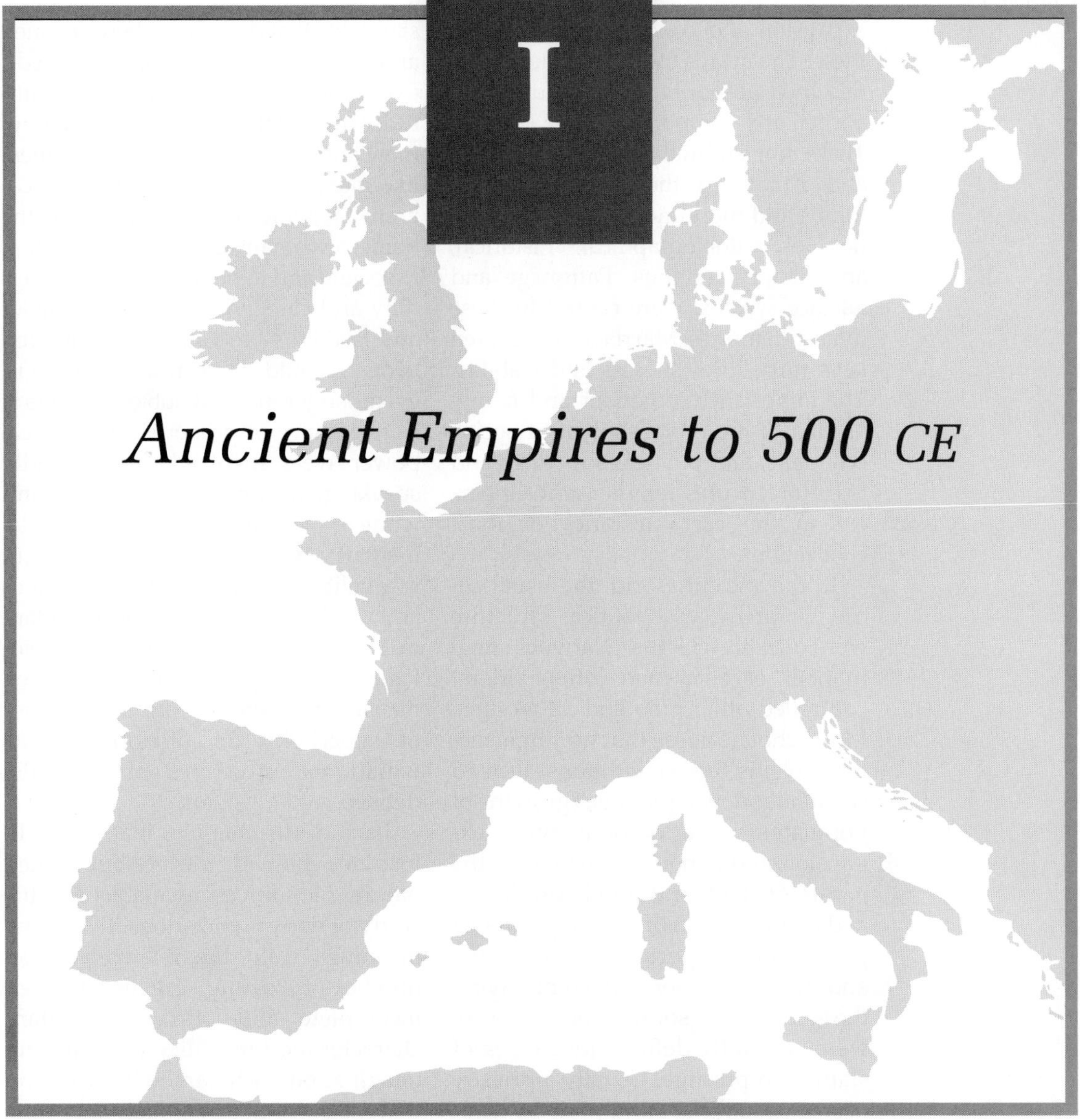

Ancient Empires to 500 CE

The first five chapters of this volume encompass the early histories of major centers of civilization, with the focus on periods in which dynastic states developed and engaged in early forms of empire building. The areas under consideration provide remarkable examples of many of the themes that are useful for the study and understanding of the earliest global civilizations. The variety of strategies and tools used to create and maintain power, the intertwining of sacred and secular authority, economic and cultural interactions, and expansion and conquest are a few of these. The means by which rulers justified their authority and conquests are particularly important to identify. These range from the use of celebration and rituals to the construction of tombs and monuments to the production of autobiographical, historical, and literary writings. Patronage and alliance systems were central to these dynastic empires. Marriages were often keys to political success and stability. The importance of gender and family or clan to the establishment of social, economic, and political structures and to cultural expressions is readily apparent in the early histories of most civilizations.

In the ancient world, the usual social hierarchy and political structure were ones in which a relatively small number of elite men (often elders) controlled other men and all women. Most scholars agree that no single factor explains these conditions. Instead economic developments, growth of populations and accompanying expansion and conquest, change in the nature of work and goods produced, and accumulation of wealth produced power and opportunities for some and not for others. Accompanying these de facto sources of authority were culturally defined ideologies of status and prestige. Usually a priestly or intellectual class and political leaders formulated and articulated values and opinions about qualities and behaviors and identified those actions or functions assumed to contribute to the public good and to ensure survival of the community.

Within this material, intellectual, and spiritual framework, it is understandable that differences between men and women, tied to survival needs, over time might produce different attitudes toward the roles and attributes of men and women. Although women, like men, engaged in a variety of economic activities inside and outside the home, a woman's greatest contribution to society and to her family was her fertility and caregiving. Female sexuality and fertility were valued, but simultaneously could be seen as mysterious, even dangerous, and subject to control if inheritance of property and political power were involved. Very broadly speaking, the different roles of men and women were thought to be complementary, but could easily result in inequality, depending on social values and material conditions. It is important to understand that transforming biological facts and differences between men and women into formal ideologies of superiority or inferiority occurs within the structures of culturally defined value systems.

Each of the chapters that follow illustrates the wide variety but limited nature of sources available for the study of early civilizations. Extracting meanings from the relatively small number of existing sources and their incomplete and often fragmentary character requires diligence, skill, and imagination. Scholars who work in materials from any place and time must ask how was a source created, for what purpose, by whom, and when? Determining the origins and purpose of many of the records of the ancient civilizations is a challenging task complicated by chance in terms of which materials survived and which did not. The dynastic rulers whose stories we consider were quite interested in creating narratives of their own successes and accomplishments, and consequently histories written for political purposes abound. Using such documents demands that we consider motives as we pull information from these documents or from many other records created for instruction or exhortation. Similarly, the fact that, with rare exception, the majority of extant materials were the work of an elite, mostly male population must always be kept in mind.

Along with questions about the nature and use of sources, readers should attempt to answer the following as they read Chapters 1 to 5:

- How and why were patronage systems and alliances created in these ancient states?
- What were the different strategies or techniques used by the rulers and their dynasties to establish imperial domination?
- How did people order their world, or what did they see as the ideally ordered society and universe?
- What are similarities and differences in status and experience between men and women?
- What sorts of power did women have? Did they have the same access to prestige and authority as men?

CHAPTER

1

City-States and Empire in Ancient Mesopotamia: King Hammurabi of Babylon (r. 1792–1750 BCE) and Queen Šibtu of Mari, Wife of Zimri-Lim (r. 1779–1761 BCE)

Setting the Stage

The city-states of Babylon and Mari occupy different yet important places in Mesopotamia's history during the second millennium. Each city and its surrounding territory was but one of the many kingdoms that dotted the banks of the Tigris and Euphrates rivers from the north to the south. Up until the eighteenth century BCE neither had played significant roles in the creation of a distinct Mesopotamian civilization or in the unification of Mesopotamia. Mari and Babylon, their rulers, and their peoples enter onto the historical stage at the beginning of the eighteenth century, each for different reasons. Babylon was a new city founded only 400 years earlier on the banks of one of the Euphrates River's many arteries. The city, situated in the geographic middle of Mesopotamia, represented the blending of three cultures: Sumerian, Akkadian, and Amorite. Under several able kings in the nineteenth century, the city expanded its territory to include some neighboring cities. Under the leadership of Hammurabi (r. 1792–1750), Babylon conquered and brought under its control the whole of Mesopotamia.

Far to the north of Babylon, one of Babylonia's principal allies and rivals, the city-state of Mari, thrived and prospered along the trade routes of northern Mesopotamia. This city-state, one of the oldest cities in the region, connected lower Mesopotamia with northwest Syria and the Mediterranean coast and was a coveted river port that taxed and facilitated the flow of goods from north to south.[1] Despite its contemporary significance, Mari's legacy rests on the 20,000 clay cuneiform tablets discovered by archeologists during the excavation of its royal palace in the 1930s, to this day the largest cache of tablets ever found. Most of the correspondence is situated chronologically in a fifty-year period, from the late nineteenth century until Mari's destruction in 1761 BCE. Much of what historians know about merchant activity in upper Mesopotamia, Hammurabi's military and diplomatic activities during his reign, relations between kingdoms, tax collection, the royal families of Mari and their allies, the position and role of imperial women, and everyday life in the eighteenth century comes from these tablets. Remarkable among these tablets are the more than 3,000 tablets that make up the royal correspondence. Contained within this archive are letters and documents written by or written for the royal women of Mari. As a result of this find, historians have been able to see that royal women held positions of status and authority.

Additional sources inform historians' understanding of Babylon and Mari. In the case of Old Babylonia and especially during Hammurabi's long reign, historians have long possessed a great variety of merchant records such as deeds of sale, receipts, and accounts as well as royal charters, inscriptions, and private letters. Scholars have discovered and used grammars that taught scribes Akkadian and the Semitic language of eastern Mesopotamia and of cuneiform tablets. Many of the grammars contained excerpts of earlier writings on law or custom. Finally, one of the most significant records of Hammurabi's reign is his code of laws—the Code of Hammurabi. A copy of these laws was found in 1901. The laws had been inscribed on an eight-foot black stone monument and were most likely displayed in public. The code details, in clear and definite language, the organization of society into three groups and the expected behaviors and responsibilities for each group. In addition, the Code of Hammurabi regulated behavior and duties according to whether a subject was a man or a woman. The code also regulated marital relations.

1. Stephanie Daly, *Mari and Karana: Two Old Babylonian Cities* (New York: Longman, 1984).

In this chapter as well as throughout the rest of this textbook, these sources and similar types of sources will be used to reconstruct the lives of two individuals, one man and one woman, who lived at the same time. The purpose of such a focus is to examine how men and women participated in their respective world societies and how they were influenced and buffeted by the social, economic, military, political, intellectual, or religious changes of their era. King Hammurabi of Babylon falls into the category of a great person of history, that is, a man or woman who was a catalyst for historical change.

Living at the same time as Hammurabi was Queen Šibtu, daughter of Yarim-lim, king of Yamhad, and wife of King Zimri-Lim of Mari (r. 1779–1761). Her historical significance is different from Hammurabi's. Šibtu and the other royal women of Mari are known to us because of letters and documents found in the ruins of the royal palace, which point to the fact that royal women held positions of status and authority in Mesopotamian society, sometimes acting on behalf or instead of the king or dedicating themselves to important religious cults. Erišti-Aya, one of Zimri-Lim's eight daughters, appears to have played a significant religious role for her father, being dedicated to a particular god and then cloistered to a religious institution.

Taken together, the stories of King Hammurabi of Babylon and Šibtu of Mari reveal the conditions of political, social, and religious life in Mesopotamia. Of course, neither was on the historical stage alone. In this chapter we will reconstruct and examine possible daily life experiences and their social and economic surroundings. The nature of documentation on each allows only a fleeting glimpse of the personal—a reported moment of aggravation, frustration, longing, or anger. These sources are limiting in another way too. Neither individual wrote about him- or herself, nor are there tell-all memoirs or contemporary biographies of those close to these powerful personages. Thus, reconstructing Hammurabi's or Šibtu's childhood or family life is impossible. All the biographer or historian can do is suggest what a common experience may have been for individuals from their class or gender. However, it is important to keep in mind throughout this chapter and those after that the lives of individuals can illustrate how political, social, economic, and religious change affects men and women differently; that a man's experience is not the norm and that a woman's experience is not the exception.

Mesopotamia provides remarkable examples of many of the themes that are useful for the study and understanding of the earlier world civilizations. The building of dynastic and territorial states, the intertwining of sacred and secular authority, the growth of urban areas, economic and cultural interactions, and expansion and conquest are a few of these themes. The importance of gender and family to initial settlement, to the establishment of social, economic, and political structures, and to cultural expressions is also readily apparent in the early histories of most civilizations.

The Actors

Hammurabi of Babylon and Šibtu of Mari

In 1792 BCE, Hammurabi became ruler of the city-state of Babylon after his father, Sinmuballit. Father and son were members of a family that ruled Babylon from the early 1900s to around 1600 BCE and is known as the First Dynasty of Babylon. Nothing is known of his mother, the year of his birth, or his childhood. Historians are confident that he was a relatively young man when he became king of Babylon. While documentation does not exist specifically for his early life, students of history can speculate about his upbringing and place within Babylonian society.

Hammurabi's family belonged to a cultural tradition that mixed Sumerian, Akkadian, and Amorite traditions and cultural practices. His family were most likely herdspeople who spoke Amorite and seized control of Babylon sometime in the early part of the second millennium. Urban dwellers like those in Babylon distrusted nomadic shepherds like Hammurabi's ancestors, the Amorites, and saw them as a threat. The Babylonians described their rural neighbors as ferocious, animal-like, and wild and complained of their lack of knowledge about the gods, improper forms of worship, and their ungovernability (**Document One**). Nomadic tribes had to range far and wide in order to find pastureland, and such wandering prevented them from being incorporated into the routines and rhythms of city life. Evidence from the Mari archives demonstrates that city officials tracked the movements of northern Amorite tribes not only to try to control them but also to employ them as laborers in the fields or on public works projects or as soldiers. Eventually, contact and familiarity with urban life caused some of the nomadic tribes and clans to settle within the boundaries of a city-state. Hammurabi's ancestors most likely followed this pattern. As they assimilated into Babylonian city life by intermarrying, adopting Akkadian as their spoken language, and forsaking their tribal ways, they eventually grabbed onto the highest rung of Babylon's social ladder and became kings.

While nothing is known about Hammurabi's early childhood or adulthood, records from Babylon and Assyria establish distinct phases of the life of a child: a child at the breast, a weaned child, a child, and an adolescent.[2] Parents held, kissed, loved, and sang lullabies to their children. There is little evidence that sons were more privileged than daughters. Sons and daughters were expected to learn behaviors, habits, and tasks from their fathers or mothers, in accordance with the gender division of labor. "Corporal punishment was sanctioned. The treatment of children had its dark side as well: deformed and handicapped children were abandoned, and others rejected by parents because of poverty or other causes. In general, though, it appears that children of both sexes were well-attended to within the material constraints of the day."[3]

2. Ibid., 131.

3. Karen Rhea Nemet-Nejat, *Daily Life in Ancient Mesopotamia* (Westport, CT: Greenwood, 1998), 132.

Education was reserved for the children of wealthy or influential parents. A young Babylonian received an education in order to become a scribe, a royal administrator, or a member of the priesthood. Boys, and possibly girls, at age eight or nine, were admitted to school. The first step was to master cuneiform, an extremely complex system of writing that involved 500 separate signs, with multiple meanings. The traditional curriculum gave central place to the lore accumulated by the Sumerians, whose civilization had flourished before 2000 BCE.

While the commonly spoken language of Babylon by the time of Hammurabi was Akkadian, tradition and practicality dictated that Sumerian still be used for nearly all texts. It was therefore necessary to train students not only in the script, cuneiform, but in the language as well. In this system, a student first had to memorize and write a sequence of sign and word lists. After this, the student had to master short sayings and proverbs, and then move on to larger texts. The mastery of these texts led to "the learning and reciting of a broader array of literature, including hymns to the king, mythic and semi-historical material, hymns, and love songs."[4] All students, whether preparing for the royal bureaucracy or the priesthood, shared common literary, moral, and religious traditions, and this curriculum helped to shape them into a coherent ruling elite. According to one historian, "Most in elite positions, whether priest or royal bureaucrat, came to possess a common store of learning, having learned both to read, recite and reproduce these ancient educational texts of diverse genres. This internalized knowledge of the ancient store of writings, seen as a divine word from before the flood, distinguished these elites from the common people."[5] One can assume that Hammurabi was fully integrated into this elite. In his late teens or early twenties, Hammurabi inherited both power and property from his father. There is nothing in the historical record to indicate that he had challenges from male siblings.

In Hammurabi's seventeenth year of rule, Mari emerged as a potential rival after it resumed its independence after several decades of rule by the Assyrian kingdom situated in upper Mesopotamia. Zimri-Lim, the son of its vanquished king, now ruled the city-state. Father and son had spent many years in exile in Yamhad, a kingdom in Syria whose center was at Aleppo. The king of Yamhad clearly saw advantage in betrothing his daughter, Šibtu, to Zimri-Lim. Marriage was seen as a link between families and larger communities as much as it was between individuals. The kingdom of Yamhad now had an important ally in northern Mesopotamia.

When Šibtu returned with Zimri-Lim to Mari, she stayed in contact with her family, providing an important link between the two kingdoms.

4. David Carr, "Wisdom and Apocalypticism: Different Types of Educational/Enculturational Literature" (paper delivered at the Society of Biblical Literature, 2004), 2; http://www.sbl-site.org/PDF/Carr_Wisdom.pdf (accessed January 7, 2006).

5. Nemet-Nejat, 147–48.

Besides her participation in statecraft, discussed below, Šibtu dutifully performed her duties as wife. She bore many children; she sent clothing that she had made to her husband when he was traveling; she maintained and managed the palace's economic activities in his absence, and she worried about her husband when he was away on campaigns. Responding to a letter that revealed her anxiousness, Zimri-Lim assured his wife that he and his troops were well (**Document Two, A**).

Both Hammurabi and Šibtu lived in a world where the "house" was the foundational building block of society. A man was expected to "build a house" by marrying, having or adopting children, and if necessary, bringing into the household unmarried sisters, widowed mothers, and underage brothers. The male head of a household was expected not only to supply the material conditions for this house and household to thrive but also to rule over all of its members.

In Mesopotamia and in Babylon, a father headed the house until he died, and his authority and actions were law. Sons and daughters as well as wives were expected to obey any decision he made. Defiance of this authority was clearly regulated in Mesopotamia law. Custom and law dictated that if a son struck his father, "they shall cut off his hand"(Hammurabi's Code, §195). If a family fell into debt, the father could sell members of his household into slavery. When a father died, sons inherited but not necessarily in equal shares. Usually the eldest son inherited a greater share. While inheritance patterns all throughout Mesopotamia were patrilineal, that is, divided among sons or to an existing male line, each city-state followed different customs for how a father's property was apportioned. In cases where the father died and left young or unmarried children, the eldest son became the head of household and administrator of the estate. Sometimes if the male heirs were too young, mothers might be given the authority of fatherhood.[6] A father provided each daughter with a dowry, and if he died before this distribution, his sons were obligated to provide one from his estate.[7]

Women were subordinate to men and the role a woman played was supportive of the family, but her role was also critical to the family's existence and success. Girls were taught at a very early age the basic skills they needed to run a household and maintain a family such as spinning, baking, and managing the house. For men and women, marriage, the formation of a household, and children were goals. Motherhood bestowed prestige on a woman, and bearing sons meant that a woman was contributing to the prosperity and continuation of the family and clan. Šibtu of Mari was an elite woman, but her responsibilities were similar to those of other Mesopotamian woman: she was expected to serve the interests of her father, through a marriage alliance, and then guarantee

6. Ibid.

7. J. N. Postgate, *Early Mesopotamia: Society and Economy at the Dawn of History* (London and New York: Routledge, 1992), 9.

the success of her husband. As we shall see in the following sections, Šibtu guarded her family's fortune and her husband's interests and kingdom in his absence. Taking on the responsibilities of rule during a husband's absence was typical of many imperial women.

ACT I

BABYLON AND HAMMURABI'S RULE

When Hammurabi ascended the throne, Babylon was one of many city-states in the region. The presence of the powerful city-state of Elam east of Babylon stifled any early military ambitions on the part of Hammurabi. Instead Hammurabi focused on domestic concerns within his modest city-state. Babylon, at the beginning of his rule, was approximately 300 square miles and was a complex urban society.

Living in a city meant that one's place in society was based on one's function within its complex economic, political, and religious structures. Hammurabi's Code divided society into three groups: the *awilum*, the *mushkenum*, and *wardum*. The *awilum* consisted of men who most likely had ancestral estates, aristocratic privileges and responsibilities and who paid taxes and provided military service. This class included government officials, priests, and soldiers. If injured, they could demand exact retaliation, "an eye for an eye." If they were found guilty of a crime, they were punished more severely or paid higher fines than members of the *mushkenum*, who were mostly merchants, shopkeepers, schoolmasters, laborers, farmers, and artisans. Many depended on this propertied class for their livelihoods. Members of this class were free and not necessarily poor or landless, but when judged, they paid smaller fines and, if injured, were awarded only monetary compensation. Slaves, or *wardum*, were the final category. One's place in society could change. A freeman could be enslaved for debt, a slave could be freed, and a landless person could become a landowner.

At the beginning of the third millennium BCE, indebtedness and debt slavery plagued Babylonian society, forcing those with very little property to use their land, their house, and even themselves and their family as collateral. By the time of Hammurabi's rule, debt slavery warranted not only legal regulation but also cancellation in order to restore social stability. Hammurabi initiated his reign with the cancellation of outstanding debt. One of Hammurabi's later ancestors, Ammisaduqu (r. 1648–1628 BCE), who followed this custom, left one of the most complete decrees:

> If an obligation has resulted in foreclosure against a citizen . . . and he placed himself, his wife, or children in debt servitude for silver, or as a pledge, he is released because the king has instituted justice in the land; his freedom is in effect.[8]

8. Ibid., 11.

Such decrees established the king as a seeker and purveyor of justice and Hammurabi was no exception. With these actions, kings set out the idea that during their reign they would free individuals from injustice.[9]

Kings were also to guarantee the protection of their peoples and lands. Hammurabi first secured this protection through strategic alliances, like the one with Mari, pacification of the gods, and just rule and then later, between the twenty-ninth and thirty-second year of his rule, through a series of aggressive military campaigns against his neighbors. After thirty years of relative peace, Hammurabi may have felt that his kingdom was being threatened by an increasingly aggressive Elam in the east and wanted to prevent its expansion westward. After his initial success against this kingdom, he may have decided that he could establish himself as the preeminent power in Mesopotamia and continue, with an experienced army, to conquer and subjugate other city-states. His final act in this drama was to defeat, sack, and destroy the kingdom of Mari.

Act II

Royal Marriages and Family in Mari

The importance of the marriage of Šibtu to Zimri-Lim cannot be underestimated. From the royal archives found at Mari, historians have found extensive correspondence between Šibtu and her husband, her father, her daughters, and official royal administrators. The letters from royal administrators detail administrative, political, legal, and military matters of importance to the kingdom. She received a report from a governor of the southern and eastern border district describing the movement of a neighbor's troops.[10] A northern governor writes to the queen about his monitoring of the activities among tribes moving along Mari's fringes. Šibtu also intervened personally in the lives of Mari subjects. Informed of the imprisonment of several women for a debt, she acted through a third party to secure their release. Of course, her ability to monitor events and intervene in the lives of individuals rested on the relationship between her and her husband.

The correspondence between Šibtu and her husband reveals that Zimri-Lim trusted his wife to look after affairs of state, especially in his absence. Since the ever-changing political alliances throughout the kingdom demanded Zimri-Lim to travel and personally oversee administrative and military affairs, much of the correspondence between husband and wife was about administration and the functioning of the palace. Royal palaces of this period were important centers for receiving raw materials such as metals, wool, stone, timber, and leather and then producing goods such as textiles, furniture inlaid with stones, armor, ornate household items, leather boots,

9. Ibid., 10.

10. P. Artzi and A. Malamat, "The Correspondence of Šibtu, Queen of Mari in Arm X," *Orientalia* 40 (1971): 75–89.

sandals, bags, harnesses, boats, carts, wagons, and many other everyday items. The letters that passed between them show Zimri-Lim depended on Šibtu to direct the labor force at the palace. In one instance, she appointed several women to oversee and work in the weaving house. In another, Zimri-Lim instructs his wife to watch over the filling of wine caskets, to send wine to Hammurabi in Babylon, and to secure a special consignment of wine from Yamhad, which was known as an exporter of excellent wine. Wine was a customary gift between royal houses.

Šibtu also played a role in the affairs of state. She wrote her husband about the current situation and welfare of the capital city and kept him abreast of developments among domestic allies. Her husband wrote her of military successes, new alliances, and his well-being. In one set of letters, Zimri-Lim instructed his wife to consult the oracles about Hammurabi's trustworthiness (**Document Two, B**). In all of the correspondence, Šibtu presented herself as a "woman of exemplary virtue," a "woman of valor," and "a true partner to her husband-king."[11] Not only did the marriage provide Mari with able and virtuous rulers, but Zimri-Lim had many daughters, some with Šibtu and others with concubines. The daughters made significant marriage alliances or played important religious roles for the dynasty. Zimri-Lim regularly used political marriage as part of his imperial policy to bind tribal rulers and leaders to him and keep their territories under his control. From surviving correspondence with his daughters, it appears that he invested his daughters with real authority, giving one daughter a mayorship in order to look over the shoulder of his son-in-law, one of his allies, and protect Mari's interest in that region, to the great annoyance of her husband[12] (**Document Three, A**).

Zimri-Lim and Šibtu also dedicated one of their daughters, Erišti-Aya, to a cloister attached to the temple of Shamash in the city of Sippar. The women living in this cloister were members of royal families or high officials. Called *naditum*, they provided a vital service to their families, praying continually for the gods to look on their families and fathers favorably. As a *naditum*, Erišti-Aya was not permitted to marry for she was deemed to be dedicated to the sun god, Shamash. She received a dowry from her family, and evidence shows that a *naditum* had some control over her dowry. Hammurabi's Code stipulated that a *naditum*'s brothers controlled the property from the dowry after the death of her father, but if they mismanaged it, she could take it away from their control. Her brothers were heirs to the land, but she could adopt a young *naditum* and cede the dowry to the younger woman. There is ample evidence of *naditums* engaging in extensive business and real estate transactions.

In Erišti-Aya's case, she felt that her father was not providing for her adequately (**Document Three, B**). She

11. Ibid., 86.

12. Bernard Frank Batto, *Studies on Women at Mari* (Baltimore, MD: Johns Hopkins Press, 1975), 53.

wrote to her father to remind him that she was dutifully performing her task, praying to the gods Shamash and Aya for his well-being, and needed to be better provisioned. She wrote, "Now your daughters of your house . . . are receiving their rations of grain, (find rest) and good beer. But even though I alone am the woman who prays for you, I am not provisioned! I dedicated a sun (disk) and my ring (money) to guard your life, but then Ermi-Addu [took] my ring (money) and the sun (disk) [for] his servant."[13] Like her sisters, Erišti-Aya played an important role in maintaining her father's and therefore her family's welfare and power.

Act III

"I am a Shepherd."

With the sack and destruction of Mari in 1761 BCE, Hammurabi had eliminated all of his nearby rivals and he now turned his attention to ruling his new empire. Even with the expansion of his state, he did not change the royal ideology inherited from other southern Mesopotamian kings and ably expressed it in the introduction to his law code: "I am a shepherd, selected by Enlil."[14] What this meant was that he had been selected by the god Enlil to provide peace, security, and prosperity to the lands over which he ruled.

Beginning in 1761 BCE, Hammurabi set out to secure the goodwill of the gods. To increase the agricultural wealth of his people, he developed and maintained irrigation canals and secured a fair distribution of land for his subjects. Another key principle of good rule was to guarantee that all people, depending on their place within society and their gender, were judged fairly and did not fear the abuse of officials in his kingdom. Drawing on earlier traditions and laws, Hammurabi had inscribed on a large black stone a set of laws that he hoped would protect all classes of Babylonian society, including women and slaves.

Almost 300 laws were carved into a black granite rock, 7 feet, 10 $^{1}/_{2}$ inches tall and 6 feet in circumference. At the top of the rock was an engraved picture of Shamash, the sun god, seated on a throne giving Hammurabi a scepter and a ring. This etching and a prologue to the laws demonstrated to the reader the divine nature of these laws and Hammurabi's connection to the gods of Babylonia (**Document Four**). At the end of the code, Hammurabi had engraved his reasons for presenting his subjects with this code. In the first part, "he focuses on his persona as a just king, one who protects his people, especially the weak among them, from injustice and abuse by the powerful"[15] (**Document Four**). He wanted the readers to find solace in the code, to know that they would be judged fairly and justly. In addition, the epilogue spoke to future

14. Marc Van de Mieroop, *King Hammurabi of Babylon* (London: Blackwell, 2005), 83.

13. Ibid., 96.

15. Ibid., 101.

kings, providing them with a guide for just rule. He claimed the title King of Justice in his epilogue, and by doing so, he hoped to inspire future rulers to be guided by a sense of justice.[16]

The code itself sought to regulate all aspects of social and economic life in Babylonian society: legal proceedings, property rights, financial transactions, marriage, family property and inheritance, assault, fees for physicians and veterinarians, professional obligations and responsibilities, agriculture, rates of hire, and treatment of slaves. Each separate law stated a hypothetical case followed by the appropriate penalty. Although clear penalties were laid out, each case had to come before a group of judges who were to mete out punishment in relation to each individual's societal rank.[17]

The largest number of laws, 127 to 195, were dedicated to marriage, family, and gender relations (**Document Five**). Marriage was a contract between two families, and fathers arranged marriages for their children. The code clearly regulated and monitored the marriage contract, from bridal payment from the husband to the woman's family, to a dowry from the woman's parents to the husband. In addition, the code spelled out a woman's responsibilities in marriage and the punishment for not fulfilling those obligations. Husbands could not simply divorce their wives without reason. If they did and no foundation was found for the divorce, the wife would receive back and control her dowry. Relations between fathers and children were also regulated. Children had to obey their fathers, and the punishment was severe for any transgressions committed by a child against his father.

Hammurabi's Code was not one that assured equality between social classes, between men and women, or between children and their parents; instead it was a code that was to protect the weak from the powerful and ensure that all people in his kingdom received similar consideration of their cases and a similar decision (**Document Six**). As he informed the reader, "Let my stela make his court case clear to him, let him see his verdict." Placing these stones in prominent places throughout his kingdom informed his subjects that in his kingdom, they would receive a verdict that was transparent, fair, and just.

Finale

The paths of Hammurabi of Babylon and Šibtu of Mari did not physically cross, but the two clearly knew of each other's place and position within their respective societies. Šibtu watched and monitored Hammurabi's actions for her husband in the years leading up to Mari's destruction. Her presence and ability to participate in the political realm differs from that of elite women in southern Mesopotamia. Why was such an arrangement possible? In the northern city-states of Mesopotamia, kingship did not rest on clearly demarcated and institutionalized offices and chains of command, mostly because of

16. Ibid., 111.
17. Ibid., 107.

the fluid and unstable political situation of tribal alliances. Mari had been ruled over the course of fifty years by three different dynasties owing allegiances to other states. As a result, political power was vested in the person of the king who personally oversaw the workings of the kingdom. As a result of this form of kingship, personal proximity to the king was the only avenue to power. Family ties and the maintenance and well-being of the dynasty allowed women greater access to power.[18] Šibtu and her daughters succeeded in providing their husband and father with skillful management of resources, reconnaissance, and loyalty.

Hammurabi ascended to the throne with hundreds of years of customary practice and law, institutions, and an ideology of kingship behind him. Kingship rested on military prowess, bringing peace and prosperity to one's subjects, and justice. Hammurabi's legacy, to a great extent, rests on his code, "an eloquent and powerful statement: the king was a man of justice, the shining example of a just ruler to be remembered for eternity."[19] However, the code also made clear that he could dispense justice in such a manner because he had pacified the world; that is, he had conquered the surrounding lands. His military prowess was justified as the means by which he brought the cause of peace and justice to all of Mesopotamia. Thus not only does Hammurabi provide an example of a just king, but his life and actions point to "an age-old belligerent ideology that military action is a justified means to bring peace and justice to the conquered lands."[20]

18. Ibid., 137.

19. Ibid., 122.

20. Ibid.

■ Documents

DOCUMENT ONE

Urban Dwellers and Tent Dwellers

A. The Marriage of Martu: c.1.7.1

The short mythological text The Marriage of Martu *describes a process of integration by a romantic marriage of an urban dweller and a tent dweller. How does the author of this text describe Martu the tent dweller? What are the tensions between the urbanites and the nomads as described in the three excerpts below?*

Now listen, their hands are destructive and their features are those of monkeys; he is one who eats what Nanna forbids and does not show reverence. They never stop roaming about . . ., they are an abomination to the gods' dwellings. Their ideas are confused; they cause only disturbance. He is clothed in sack-leather . . ., lives in a tent, exposed to wind and rain, and cannot properly recite prayers. He lives in the mountains and ignores the places of gods, digs up truffles in the foothills, does not know how to bend the knee, and eats raw flesh. He has no house during his life, and when he dies he will not be carried to a burial-place. My girlfriend, why would you marry Martu?"Adjar-kidug replies to her girlfriend: "I will marry Martu!"

B. Letter from Sîn-iddinam to the God Utu About the Distress of Larsam: c.3.2.05

Sîn-iddinam (r. 1849–1842 BCE*) was a king of Larsa, which was an important city of ancient Babylonia.*

The mountain land of Elam where there are no dead in great numbers (?) like . . ., and Subir, a heavy cloud, which knows no reverence even towards the gods—these districts have not been weakened; their time has not yet come. The Šimaškian [the ruling family of Elam, a rival to the city-states of southern Mesopotamia] knows neither his god nor those elected nugig and lukur priestesses. His soldiers are numerous like grass; his seed is widespread. He who lives in tents, who does not know of the places of the gods: like a wild beast which mounts, he knows nothing of flour and the offering of prayers.

C. "The Cursing of Agade": c.2.1.5

This poem tells of the destruction of Sargon's city, Agade, by a nomadic tribe from the mountains to the east. Around 2150 BCE*, during the rule of Sargon's* *grandson, Naramsin, a wave of nomads called Gutians, from the east, overran Agade and Sumer. Why Naramsin was unable to defeat the invaders is unknown. His empire may have been weakened by drought and famine or by plague. But like the Sumerians, the Akkadian people saw adversity as the work of displeased gods. They interpreted the Gutian invasion as the result of their goddess Inanna having left their city because of Naramsin's destruction of Enlil's temple, E-kur, when his army sacked Nippur, a rival city-state. Enlil ("lord wind"), the god of air, wind, and storms, was the foremost god of the Mesopotamian pantheon.*

Enlil, the roaring (?) storm that subjugates the entire land,
the rising deluge that cannot be confronted,
was considering what should be destroyed in return for the wrecking of his beloved E-kur.
He lifted his gaze towards the Gubin mountains,
and made all the inhabitants of the broad mountain ranges descend (?).
Enlil brought out of the mountains those who do not resemble other people,
who are not reckoned as part of the Land, the Gutians,
an unbridled people, with human intelligence but canine instincts [some manuscripts have "feelings"] and monkeys' features.
Like small birds they swooped on the ground in great flocks.
Because of Enlil, they stretched their arms out across the plain like a net for animals.
Nothing escaped their clutches,
no one left their grasp.
Messengers no longer travelled the highways,
the courier's boat no longer passed along the rivers.
The Gutians drove the trusty (?) goats of Enlil out of their folds and compelled their herdsmen to follow them,
they drove the cows out of their pens and compelled their cowherds to follow them.
Prisoners manned the watch.
Brigands occupied [one manuscript has "attacked"] the highways.
The doors of the city gates of the Land lay dislodged in [one manuscript has "were covered with"] mud, and
all the foreign lands uttered bitter cries from the walls of their cities.
They established gardens for themselves [one manuscript has "made gardens grow"] within the cities, and not as usual on the wide plain outside.
As if it had been before the time when cities were built and founded,
the large [some manuscripts add "fields and"] arable tracts yielded no grain,
the inundated [some manuscripts add "fields and"] tracts yielded no fish,
the irrigated orchards yielded no syrup or wine,
the thick clouds (?) did not rain, the macgurum plant did not grow.

DOCUMENT TWO

Queen Šibtu and King Zimri-Lim of Mari

Correspondence

Correspondence flowed back and forth between Zimri-Lim and Šibtu when he was away on campaigns. What do these excerpts reveal about their relationship? The role of an imperial woman?

Zimri-Lim Assures His Wife That He and His Army Are Safe

Perhaps you have heard some rumor and your heart is disturbed—no armed enemy has withstood me! All is well. There is no need to be concerned.

Šibtu Writes to Her Husband

May my lord conquer his enemies. And may my lord enter Mari in safety and happiness.

Zimri-Lim Asks His Wife to Consult the Oracles

Ask the oracles about Hammurabi of Babylon. Will this man ever die? Does he speak honestly with us? Will he declare war? Will he start a siege when I am on campaign in the north? Ask questions about that man. When you have done the questioning once, repeat it and write me all the answers to your questions.

Šibtu Writes Back

I have asked my questions about Babylon. That man is plotting many things against this country, but he will not succeed. My Lord will see what the god will do to him. You will capture and overpower him. His days are numbered and he will not live long. My Lord should know.

DOCUMENT THREE

ZIMRI-LIM, ŠIBTU, AND THEIR DAUGHTERS

Correspondence

What does the following correspondence between Zimri-Lim and his daughter reveal about their political and religious roles? How do their actions advance Zimri-Lim's interests?

A Daughter, Kiru, Describing an Encounter with Her Husband, Haya-Sumu When He Is Angered by Her Political Position, Which Represents the Interests of her Father, Zimri-Lim ("My Star")

Haya-Sumu arose and (spoke) thus to my face, "You exercise the mayorship here. But since I will surely kill you, let him come—your star—and take you back."

Erišti-Aya Writing to Her Parents from the Cloister

I am always, always crying out, always. . . . When I wrote to you last year, you sent me two servant girls, but one of them died, and now they have brought me two more servant girls, and one of them has died too. I am the emblem of your father's house, so why am I not provided for? They have not given me any silver or oil.

Erišti-Aya Writing to Her Mother, Šibtu

Speak to the lady my mother, thus Erišti-Aya your daughter. May my divine lord and lady grant you long life for my sake. Why didn't you ever wear my dress, but sent it back to me, and made me dishonored and accursed? I am your daughter, and you are the wife of the king. . . . Your husband and you put me into the cloister; but the soldiers who were taken captive pay me more respect than you! You should pay me respect, and them my divine lord and lady will honor you with the good opinion of the city and its inhabitants. I am sending you a nanny. Do send me something to make me happy, and then I will be happy. Don't neglect me.

DOCUMENT FOUR

HAMMURABI

Code of Hammurabi

PROLOGUE

When the lofty Anu, king of the Anunnaki, and Enlil, lord of heaven and earth, who determines the destinies of the land, committed the rule of all mankind to Marduk, the first-born son of Ea, and made him great among the Igigi; . . . at that time Anu and Enlil named me, Hammurabi, the exalted prince, the worshipper of the gods, to cause righteousness to prevail in the land, to destroy the wicked and the evil, to prevent the strong from plundering the weak, to go forth like the sun over the black-headed race, to enlighten the land and to further the welfare of the people. Hammurabi, the shepherd, named by Enlil am I, who increased plenty and abundance; who made everything complete for Nippur, the bond of heaven and earth; the exalted supporter of Ekur; the wise king, who restored Eridu to its place. . . . The ancient seed of royalty, the powerful king, the sun of Babylon, who caused light to go forth over the lands of Sumer and Akkad; the king who caused the four quarters of the world to render me to rule the people and to bring help to the land, I established law and justice in the language of the land and promoted the welfare of the people.

EPILOGUE

The righteous laws which Hammurabi the wise king established and (by which) he gave the land a firm support and a gracious rule. Hammurabi the perfect king am I. I was not careless nor was I neglectful of the black-headed (people) whom Bel presented to me and whose care Marduk gave to me. . . . The great gods have named me and I am the guardian shepherd whose scepter is righteous; my beneficent shadow is spread over the city. In my bosom I have carried the peoples of the land of Sumer and Akkad . . . that the strong might not oppress the weak, and that they should give justice to the oppressed, my weighty words I have written upon my monument, and in the presence of me, king of righteousness, have I set it up. The king who is pre-eminent among kings am I. My words are precious, my wisdom is unrivaled. . . .

Let any oppressed man who has a cause come before the image of me, the king of righteousness! Let him give heed to my weighty words! And may my monument enlighten him as to his cause and may he understand his case! May it set his heart at ease. . . . In the days to come, for all time, let the king who arises in the land observe the words of righteousness which I have written upon my monument! Let him not alter the judgments of the land which I have pronounced, the decisions of the country which I have rendered! Let him not efface my statues! . . . Let him root out the wicked and evildoer from his land! Let him promote the welfare of his people! . . . If that man give heed to my words . . ., may Shamash prolong his reign as he has mine, who am king of righteousness. If that man do not give heed to my words . . ., may the great Anu, father of the gods, who foreordained my reign, take from him the glory of sovereignty, may he break his scepter and curse his fate! May Enlil, the lord, determiner of destinies, whose word cannot be altered, who has enlarged my kingdom, kindle against him in his dwelling a revolt which cannot be controlled, the misfortune of his ruin! May he determine as his fate a reign of sighs, days few in number, years of famine, darkness without light, sudden death! . . .

May Ea, the great prince whose decrees take precedence, the leader of the gods, who knows everything, who prolongs the days of my life, deprive him of knowledge and wisdom, and bring him to oblivion. May he dam up his rivers at their sources! May he not permit corn which is the life of the people to grow in his land! May Shamash, the great judge of heaven and earth who rules all living creatures, the lord, my refuge, overthrow his dominion; may he not grant him his right! Above, may he cut him off among the living! Below, within the earth, may he deprive his spirit of water! . . . May Inanna, goddess of battle and conflict, who makes ready my weapons, my gracious protecting deity who loves my reign, curse his dominion with great fury in her wrathful heart, and turn good into evil for him! May she shatter his weapons on the field of battle and conflict! May she create confusion and revolt for him! May she strike down his warriors, water the earth with their blood! May she cast the bodies of his warriors upon the field in heaps! May she not grant his warriors mercy! May she deliver him into the hands of his enemies, and may they carry him away bound into a hostile land! . . .

May Nintu, the exalted mistress of the lands, the mother who bore me, deny him a son! May she not let him have a name, among his people create no heir! May Ninkarrasha, the daughter of Anu, who commands favor for me, in Ekur, cause to come upon his members a grievous malady, an evil disease, a dangerous sore which cannot be cured, which the physician cannot diagnose, which he cannot allay with bandages, and which like the bite of death cannot be removed; and that he, until he brings his life to an end, may lament the loss of his vigor! May the great gods of heaven and earth, the Anunnaki in their totality, the protecting deity of the temple and the walls of Ebarra, curse him, his seed, his land, his army, his people, and his troops with an evil curse. May Enlil, with his word which cannot be altered, curse him with powerful curses, and may the curse come upon him speedily!

DOCUMENT FIVE

Laws on Family
Code of Hammurabi

A significant portion of the Code of Hammurabi is dedicated to laws dictating behavior in the family. Who has authority within the family and why is the Babylonian kingdom interested in regulating and prescribing behavior?

Missing from the excerpt below are the laws on concubinage, incest, the rights of the children of concubines and slaves, and the adoption and substitution of children.

[False Accusation and Marriage]

127. If any one "point the finger" (slander) at a sister of a god or the wife of any one, and can not prove it, this man shall be taken before the judges and his brow shall be marked (by cutting the skin, or perhaps hair).

128. If a man take a woman to wife, but have no intercourse with her, this woman is no wife to him.

[Adultery]

129. If a man's wife be surprised (in flagrante delicto) with another man, both shall be tied and thrown into the water, but the husband may pardon his wife and the king his slaves.

130. If a man violate the wife (betrothed or child-wife) of another man, who has never known a man, and still lives in her father's house, and sleep with her and be surprised, this man shall be put to death, but the wife is blameless.

131. If a man bring a charge against one's wife, but she is not surprised with another man, she must take an oath and then may return to her house.

132. If the "finger is pointed" at a man's wife about another man, but she is not caught sleeping with the other man, she shall jump into the river for her husband.

[Remarriage of a Wife]

133. If a man is taken prisoner in war, and there is a sustenance in his house, but his wife leave house and court, and go to another house: because this wife did not keep her court, and went to another house, she shall be judicially condemned and thrown into the water.

134. If any one be captured in war and there is not sustenance in his house, if then his wife go to another house this woman shall be held blameless.

135. If a man be taken prisoner in war and there be no sustenance in his house and his wife go to another house and bear children; and if later her husband return and come to his home: then this wife shall return to her husband, but the children follow their father.

136. If any one leave his house, run away, and then his wife go to another house, if then he return, and wishes to take his wife back: because he fled from his home and ran away, the wife of this runaway shall not return to her husband.

[Divorce]

137. If a man wish to separate from a woman who has borne him children, or from his wife who has borne him children: then he shall give that wife her dowry, and a part of the usufruct of field, garden, and property, so that she can rear her children. When she has brought up her children, a portion of all that is given to the children, equal as that of one son, shall be given to her. She may then marry the man of her heart.

138. If a man wishes to separate from his wife who has borne him no children, he shall give her the amount of her purchase money and the dowry which she brought from her father's house, and let her go.

139. If there was no purchase price he shall give her one mina of gold as a gift of release.

140. If he be a freed man he shall give her one-third of a mina of gold.

141. If a man's wife, who lives in his house, wishes to leave it, plunges into debt, tries to ruin her house, neglects her husband, and is judicially convicted: if her husband offer her release, she may go on her way, and he gives her nothing as a gift of release. If her husband does not wish to release her, and if he take another wife, she shall remain as servant in her husband's house.

142. If a woman quarrel with her husband, and say: "You are not congenial to me," the reasons for her prejudice must be presented. If she is guiltless, and there is no fault on her part, but he leaves and neglects her, then no guilt attaches to this woman, she shall take her dowry and go back to her father's house.

143. If she is not innocent, but leaves her husband, and ruins her house, neglecting her husband, this woman shall be cast into the water.

[Inheritance and Liability for Debt]

150. If a man gives his wife a field, garden, and house and a deed therefor, if then after the death of her husband the sons raise no claim, then the mother may bequeath all to one of her sons whom she prefers, and need leave nothing to his brothers.

151. If a woman who lived in a man's house made an agreement with her husband, that no creditor can arrest her, and has given a document therefor: if that man, before he married that woman, had a debt, the creditor can not hold the woman for it. But if the woman, before she entered the man's house, had contracted a debt, her creditor cannot arrest her husband therefor.

152. If after the woman had entered the man's house, both contracted a debt, both must pay the merchant.

[Murder of a Husband]

153. If the wife of one man on account of another man has their mates (her husband and the other man's wife) murdered, both of them shall be impaled.

[Financial Arrangements at Engagement]

159. If any one, who has brought chattels into his father-in-law's house, and has paid the purchase-money, looks for another wife, and says to his father-in-law: "I do not want your daughter," the girl's father may keep all that he had brought.

160. If a man bring chattels into the house of his father-in-law, and pay the "purchase price" (for his wife): if then the father of the girl say: "I will not give you my daughter," he shall give him back all that he brought with him.

161. If a man bring chattels into his father-in-law's house and pay the "purchase price," if then his friend slander him, and his father-in-law say to the young husband: "You shall not marry my daughter," then he shall give back to him undiminished all that he had brought with him; but his wife shall not be married to the friend.

[Inheritance]

162. If a man marry a woman, and she bear sons to him; if then this woman die, then shall her father have no claim on her dowry; this belongs to her sons.

163. If a man marry a woman and she bear him no sons; if then this woman die, if the "purchase price" which he had paid into the house of his father-in-law is repaid to him, her husband shall have no claim upon the dowry of this woman; it belongs to her father's house.

164. If his father-in-law do not pay back to him the amount of the "purchase price" he may subtract the amount of the "purchase price" from the dowry, and then pay the remainder to her father's house.

165. If a man give to one of his sons whom he prefers a field, garden, and house, and a deed therefor: if later the father die, and the brothers divide the estate, then they shall first give him the present of his father, and he shall accept it; and the rest of the paternal property shall they divide.

166. If a man take wives for his son, but take no wife for his minor son, and if then he die: if the sons divide the estate, they shall set aside besides his portion the money for the "purchase price" for the minor brother who had taken no wife as yet, and secure a wife for him.

167. If a man marry a wife and she bear him children: if this wife die and he then take another wife and she bear him children: if then the father die, the sons must not partition the estate according to the mothers, they shall divide the dowries of their mothers only in this way; the paternal estate they shall divide equally with one another.

168. If a man wish to put his son out of his house, and declare before the judge: "I want to put my son out," then the judge shall examine into his reasons. If the son be guilty of no great fault, for which he can be rightfully put out, the father shall not put him out.

169. If he be guilty of a grave fault, which should rightfully deprive him of the filial relationship, the father shall forgive him the first time; but if he be guilty of a grave fault a second time the father may deprive his son of all filial relation.

[Property Rights of Remarried Women and Priestesses]

177. If a widow, whose children are not grown, wishes to enter another house (remarry), she shall not enter it without the knowledge of the judge. If she enter another house the judge shall examine the state of the house of her first husband. Then the house of her first husband shall be entrusted to the second husband and the woman herself as managers. And a record must be made thereof. She shall keep the house in order, bring up the children, and not sell the household utensils. He who buys the utensils of the children of a widow shall lose his money, and the goods shall return to their owners.

178. If a "devoted woman" or a prostitute to whom her father has given a dowry and a deed therefor, but if in this deed it is not stated that she may bequeath it as she pleases, and has not explicitly stated that she has the right of disposal; if then her father die, then her brothers shall hold her field and garden, and give her corn, oil, and milk according to her portion, and satisfy her. If her brothers do not give her corn, oil, and milk according to her share, then her field and garden shall support her. She shall have the usufruct of field and garden and all that her father gave her so long as she lives, but she cannot sell or assign it to others. Her position of inheritance belongs to her brothers.

179. If a "sister of a god," or a prostitute, receive a gift from her father, and a deed in which it has been explicitly stated that she may dispose of it as she pleases, and give her complete disposition thereof: if then her father die, then she may leave her property to whomsoever she pleases. Her brothers can raise no claim thereto.

180. If a father give a present to his daughter—either marriageable or a prostitute (unmarriageable)—and then die, then she is to receive a portion as a child

from the paternal estate, and enjoy its usufruct so long as she lives. Her estate belongs to her brothers.

181. If a father devote a temple-maid or temple-virgin to God and give her no present: if then the father die, she shall receive the third of a child's portion from the inheritance of her father's house, and enjoy its usufruct so long as she lives. Her estate belongs to her brothers.

182. If a father devote his daughter as a wife of Mardi of Babylon (as in 181), and give her no present, nor a deed; if then her father die, then shall she receive one-third of her portion as a child of her father's house from her brothers, but Marduk may leave her estate to whomsoever she wishes.

183. If a man give his daughter by a concubine a dowry, and a husband, and a deed; if then her father die, she shall receive no portion from the paternal estate.

184. If a man do not give a dowry to his daughter by a concubine, and no husband; if then her father die, her brother shall give her a dowry according to her father's wealth and secure a husband for her.

[Assault by a Son on a Father]

195. If a son strike his father, his hands shall be hewn off.

DOCUMENT SIX

"An Eye for an Eye": Justice Versus Equality
Code of Hammurabi

The Code of Hammurabi provides a clear set of consequences when a subject violates or harms another. What legal principle is represented in the laws below? Why are there different consequences for different people? What does this tell us about the nature of Mesopotamian society?

196. If a man put out the eye of another man, his eye shall be put out [An eye for an eye].

197. If he break another man's bone, his bone shall be broken.

198. If he put out the eye of a freed man, or break the bone of a freed man, he shall pay one gold mina.

199. If he put out the eye of a man's slave, or break the bone of a man's slave, he shall pay one-half of its value.

200. If a man knock out the teeth of his equal, his teeth shall be knocked out [A tooth for a tooth].

201. If he knock out the teeth of a freed man, he shall pay one-third of a gold mina.

202. If any one strike the body of a man higher in rank than he, he shall receive sixty blows with an ox-whip in public.

203. If a free-born man strike the body of another free-born man or equal rank, he shall pay one gold mina.

204. If a freed man strike the body of another freed man, he shall pay ten shekels in money.

205. If the slave of a freed man strike the body of a freed man, his ear shall be cut off.

206. If during a quarrel one man strike another and wound him, then he shall swear, "I did not injure him wittingly," and pay the physicians.

207. If the man die of his wound, he shall swear similarly, and if he (the deceased) was a free-born man, he shall pay half a mina in money.

208. If he was a freed man, he shall pay one-third of a mina.

209. If a man strike a free-born woman so that she lose her unborn child, he shall pay ten shekels for her loss.

210. If the woman die, his daughter shall be put to death.

211. If a woman of the free class lose her child by a blow, he shall pay five shekels in money.

212. If this woman die, he shall pay half a mina.

213. If he strike the maid-servant of a man, and she lose her child, he shall pay two shekels in money.

214. If this maid-servant die, he shall pay one-third of a mina.

Questions

1. What types of sources are available to study ancient Mesopotamia? Depending on the source, what type of information can they give to the historian to reconstruct the past?
2. What are the differences between urban, civilized life and nomadic life? How do Mesopotamians differentiate between the two?
3. How did Hammurabi rule? What is the basis for his kingship?
4. Describe and explain the types of roles that royal women played in the kingdom of Mari. How and why did they exercise religious or political authority?
5. How and why does Hammurabi promote his code? How does he want to be seen by his subjects and future rulers?
6. What is Babylonia's source of justice? Explain the difference between justice and equality.

Suggested Readings

Batto, Bernard Frank. *Studies on Women at Mari*. Baltimore, MD: Johns Hopkins Press, 1975.

Daly, Stephanie. *Mari and Karana: Two Old Babylonian Cities*. New York: Longman, 1984.

Kuhrt, Amélie. *The Ancient Near East*. 2 vols. New York and London: Routledge, 1995.

Lesko, Barbara, ed. *Women's Earliest Records*. Atlanta, GA: Scholars, 1989.

Nemet-Nejat, Karen Rhea. *Daily Life in Ancient Mesopotamia*. Westport, CT: Greenwood, 1998.

Van de Mieroop, Marc. *King Hammurabi of Babylon*. London: Blackwell, 2005.

Source Materials

The complete text of the Code of Hammurabi is found in *The Avalon Project at Yale Law School: Documents in Law, History, and Diplomacy*. http://www.yale.edu/lawweb/avalon/medieval/hammenu.htm

Black, J. A., G. Cunningham, J. Ebeling, E. Flückiger-Hawker, E. Robson, J. Taylor, and G. Zólyomi. *The Electronic Text Corpus of Sumerian Literature*. Oxford, UK: Oriental Institute, Oxford University, 1998. This project has made available much of the literature written in Sumerian. It includes narrative poetry, praise poetry, hymns, laments, prayers, songs, fables, didactic poems, debate poems and proverbs. Search is by key word. http://etcsl.orinst.ox.ac.uk

The Oriental Institute of the University of Chicago maintains an excellent "virtual museum." http://oi.uchicago.edu/OI/MUS/OI_Museum.html

CHAPTER

2

The Challenges of Rule in New Kingdom Egypt: Hatshepsut (1479–1458 BCE) and Tuthmosis III (1479–1425 BCE)

SETTING THE STAGE

In ancient northeastern Africa, Egyptian civilization was the most outstanding and permanent to emerge along the extensive reaches of the Nile River. By the end of the Old Kingdom (ca. 2100 BCE) Egyptian political authority, economic system, religion, law, and culture were well established. However, though remarkably stable, Egyptian civilization was not static. In fact, as dynamic rulers confronted the challenges of contact with other populations, life along the Nile was subject to considerable change.

The life histories of Hatshepsut and Tuthmosis III, members of the Eighteenth Dynasty (1550–1295 BCE), illustrate how Egyptians built and sustained their civilization in the era of the New Kingdom (1570–1085 BCE). The early rulers of the Eighteenth Dynasty reunified the Egyptian state after they expelled from their territory the western Asiatic Hykos, who had invaded and controlled the delta region of the Nile and other parts of Egypt since 1700. After the expulsion, rulers of this dynasty, especially Hatshepsut and Tuthmosis III, oversaw the resurgence of their home city, Thebes, as the center of Egyptian power. They created and maintained a powerful army, protected Egypt's borders from further invasion, changed the social and political hierarchy that had dominated Egypt under the Hykos, and extended the Egyptian Empire beyond the Nile valley.

The new dynasty that came to power after 1550 was confronted with significant social and economic chang-es and military and administrative demands. The rulers became known not just for conquests and empire building but for promoting commercial activity and economic growth, welcoming new ideas, and the vigor and success with which they faced challenges, introduced innovations of their own, and made their rule one of the last periods of great power and creativity in Ancient Egypt.[1] But as important as their unique contributions were, these rulers did not abandon centuries of historical traditions that were often the very basis for their power.

As a result of these accomplishments, the individuals and buildings of Egypt's Eighteenth Dynasty (1550–1295 BCE) have attracted popular and scholarly attention for some time. The extensive building activities of the rulers, particularly in their home region of Thebes (Luxor), reflected their wealth, power, and administrative skill. The tombs, palaces, monuments, and cities of the Eighteenth Dynasty and other dynasties of the New Kingdom (1550–1069 BCE) are among the richest sources we have for the study of ancient Egypt.

Even with these resources, tremendous difficulties exist in writing the histories of the ancient civilizations along the Nile. Three general sorts of evidence remain for Egyptian society: (1) archeological: buildings of all sorts, tombs, and monuments; (2) textual: inscriptions on walls, writings on fragments of stone or clay, and letters on papyrus; and (3) representational: statuary and paintings on a variety of surfaces. All of these must be translated or interpreted for contemporary meaning. In creating an historical narrative, the purposes for the creation of these sources must be taken into account and their creators must be identified. Most of these materials were intended to depict an ideal rather than an actual situation or person, were propaganda created to glorify their subject, or were prescriptive in the sense of providing wisdom and advice for right living. They were not supposed to express individual opinions, desires, or observations. The authors or builders were part of a very small elite—near the top of the social pyramid—who were educated, literate, and overwhelmingly male.

1. Erik Hornung, *History of Ancient Egypt* (Ithaca, NY: Cornell University Press, 1999), 75. See also Barbara Watterson, *The Egyptians* (Cambridge, MA: Blackwell, 1999), and Nicolas Grimal, *A History of Ancient Egypt* (Cambridge, MA: Blackwell, 1992), for the historical significance of this dynasty.

Occasionally, remnants of homes and everyday life, not planned to illustrate acceptable standards of behavior or ideals, give us a more intimate picture of this ancient world.

Reconstructing the Egyptian story is a challenge because sources are often fragmentary, and chance rather than intent often determined the survival of documents. A papyrus record was preserved, "not because it was kept in an archive, but . . . because no one used it to light a fire, because it was never nibbled by a passing goat."[2] Time and weather destroyed some material, but human disruption of remains—grave robbing, capture and seizure of pieces of art; and simply defacing, moving, or covering up older sources—has made scholarly inquiry even more difficult. Researchers studying the ancient Nubian civilization along the upper stretches of the Nile River face an even broader range of problems. Among these are inability to decipher the language, isolation of the area, disappearance of ruins, and plundering of cemeteries and the fact that the early excavations and surveys of the culture of the area tended "to stress the Egyptian contributions to the slighting of indigenous elements."[3] In the 1960s, when the building of the Aswan High Dam on the southern Nile was proposed, worldwide efforts salvaged threatened temples, surveyed undocumented areas, and collected inscriptions. Nevertheless, on completion, the dam created the very large Lake Nasser, which submerged many villages and some historical monuments. As a result, researching into ancient northeast Africa "is like trying to repair a tapestry with gaping holes where much of the design is lost."[4] This need to fill in the gaps has created interesting historical questions and debates, as we shall see.

The Actors

Hatshepsut and Tuthmosis III

The reigns of Hatshepsut and Tuthmosis III typify dynastic accomplishments in the areas of diplomacy and conquest, economic growth, and extensive public building. They also stand out for several reasons. First, Hatshepsut assumed the titles and authority of king in her own right, thus becoming one of only three women in ancient Egyptian history to count her own regnal years and to act as the supreme ruler. Most women who exercised political power did so as first wives or mothers of rulers and wielded power only as regents. Thus, Hatshepsut is indeed a notable historical figure. For his part, Tuthmosis became the model of the new

2. Sergio Donadoni, ed., *The Egyptians* (Chicago: University of Chicago Press, 1997), ix.

3. Edwin Yamauchi, ed., *Africa and Africans in Antiquity* (East Lansing: Michigan State University Press, 2001), intro., 4; and chap. 2, Frank Yurco, "Egypt and Nubia: Old, Middle and New Kingdom Eras," 28.

4. Gay Robins, *Women in Ancient Egypt* (Cambridge, MA: Harvard University Press, 1998), 16.

warrior king. But the lives of this pair of rulers are instructive for other reasons as well. Their royal pedigrees are complex and the nature of their personal relationship is open to question. Taken together, these factors create an interesting vantage point for a discussion of what constitutes the basis for access to royal power and of the different ways that individual rulers exercised that power.

Hatshepsut was the daughter of the first Tuthmosis, who probably ruled anywhere from 1506 to 1482 BCE.[5] Through her mother, the queen, she was descended from one of the early and most influential queens of the dynasty, Ahmose Nefertari. Hatshepsut married her half-brother, Tuthmosis II (1482–1479 BCE), the son of Tuthmosis I and a royal concubine. The only surviving child of Hatshepsut's marriage was a daughter, Neferure. Like his predecessors, Tuthmosis II had several subordinate wives, and the son of one of these women was Tuthmosis III, who was not yet ten years old when his father died. Thus Hatshepsut, his stepmother and aunt, served as regent. Familial relationships and situations such as these were not uncommon in Egyptian dynastic history. Coregencies, brother-sister unions, and marriage to multiple wives had occurred before Tuthmosis I took the throne. An especially important fact to be recognized in these historical patterns is that daughters, no matter their placement in the family lineup, were not considered legitimate heirs. Hatshepsut's blood connections to earlier pharaohs were stronger than those of either her husband or her stepson. No law explicitly forbade female rule, but since the earliest dynasties, divine rule was equated with masculine principles, and men had occupied the office of pharaoh.

ACT I

THE WORLD OF THE TUTHMOSID QUEENS AND KINGS

For centuries, unusual stability and prosperity marked the ancient Egyptian civilization that stretched along 700 miles of the Nile River. The rulers and the people of the unified state that had developed sometime after 3100 BCE believed that tranquility, continuity, and economic well-being were the will of the gods who had created order out of chaos. Although this state of harmony and balance was considered the natural order (*ma'at* in Egyptian), it always had to be protected and promoted by a divine presence on Earth that resided in the office of the king or pharaoh. Kings were mortal, born to mortal mothers, but the divine office they held had the creative powers and responsibilities of the gods, and thus kings were transformed into gods when they took office. The position they held set them apart from other humans, allowed them to communicate with the gods, and required them to mediate between the divine and human worlds.

5. Egyptians marked time by the reigns of their rulers; known birth and death dates are almost nonexistent, and even the dates of reigns are not always clear. In the case of Tuthmosis I, the start and finish dates of his rule vary among scholars.

The king sat alone at the apex of a social, political, and religious hierarchy whose "structure, order and organization . . . was symbolized in the form of the pyramid."[6] In addition to his ritual and magical duties, the king owned all the land and was the chief administrator, lawgiver, and defender of the state. In practice, the king had to delegate some of these duties, and the Egyptian kingdom developed an extensive bureaucracy. The development of writing served political, commercial, cultural, and religious purposes, but only 1 to 4 percent of the population was literate, and an elite male, scribal class held most of the bureaucratic offices (**Document One**). The highest-ranking officials usually had financial responsibilities or were first priests of the most powerful gods. One's rank in the social hierarchy depended on proximity to the king and to the functions or work one contributed to the orderly management and productivity of the society. Above all, the legitimacy of a ruler was measured by his ability to maintain prosperity and law and order—the material dimensions of *ma'at*—throughout the land. Dramatic changes in social and material conditions, and challenges to custom and tradition could be considered dangerous and evidence of the displeasure of the gods.

Egyptian women had influence beyond the household, engaged in a wide range of work and commercial activities, and could own and bequeath property. Wives of powerful bureaucrats occasionally held office, but usually as priestesses of goddesses like Hathor, who was the patron of women. Sons and daughters could inherit equally from their parents, and once married, a woman kept control of her own property. If the marriage ended by divorce or death of her husband, a woman kept her own goods and one-third of the wealth the couple had acquired during marriage. Even so, most scholars caution against overstating the freedom and equality of ancient Egyptian women. After all, women could sue and be sued, but they "were more often defendants than claimants . . . [and] men divorced women four times as often as women did men."[7] Unfortunately, since no women occupied the offices that actually governed the land, their power was limited. Most of our sources reflect the experience of elite women; their status was determined by their husbands or fathers, and even they had limited access to areas of activity like education and politics. While women shared in the same afterlife as men, were often represented in art, and were legally capable, this "should not obscure the fact that women occupied a secondary position in relation to men throughout the history of Egypt."[8]

6. Hornung, 24.

7. Andrea McDowell, *Village Life in Ancient Egypt: Laundry Lists and Love Songs* (New York: Oxford University Press, 1999), 110. See also Lynn Meskell, *Private Life in New Kingdom Egypt* (Princeton, NJ: Princeton University Press, 2002), esp. chap. 4.

8. Robins, 191. Other useful works for the history of women in Egypt are Joyce Tydesley, *Daughters of Isis: Women of Ancient Egypt* (New York: Viking, 1994); Barbara Watterson, *Women in Ancient Egypt* (Gloucester, UK: Wren's Park, 1998); and Zahi Hawass, *Silent Images: Women in Pharaonic Egypt* (New York: Abrams, 2000).

The relationships of men and women, like the absolute earthly powers of the king, were reflected in and reinforced by religious beliefs and practices. Egyptians worshiped multiple gods with various powers and responsibilities. They also accepted the supremacy of one god, while not denying the existence and functions of other deities. By the time that the Eighteenth Dynasty came to rule, the sun god Re dominated the realm of all the gods. But the new dynasty came from Thebes, where the local god Amun was prominent. Under the Theban rulers, massive building projects elevated his status, expanded his power, and eventually created a compound god, Amun-Re, the King of the Gods and Lord of the Thrones of the Two Lands (Upper and Lower Egypt). The monarchs of this dynasty also inherited the worship of brother-sister/husband-wife deities, like Isis, the ideal wife and mother, and her brother/husband Osiris, the god of the afterlife. On a practical level, this meant that interfamily marriages could be used to maintain the exclusivity of the royal line or to guarantee that royal daughters had suitable husbands. If a male successor was from a secondary family branch, he could strengthen his claim to royal power by marrying a half-sister. Many scholars have noted that, although brother-sister marriages were not particularly common in the society as a whole, there would be advantages for earthly rulers in the emulation of their divine counterparts. What was good for the gods was assumed to be advantageous for the earthly rulers as well.

Under earlier dynasties, *corvée,* or unpaid labor, was required of all peasants and other workers and could include military service. But most soldiers were not well trained and their functions were usually limited to accompanying trade missions or serving as border guards. Previous rulers had also employed foreigners in a variety of capacities, including military service, and Nubians were prominent among them.[9] In the era of the New Kingdom, defensive military actions combined with territorial expansion, and conquest led to the establishment of a regular, standing army, which was a source of national pride and often the measure of the success of the pharaoh. Positions in the army now became acceptable professions for aspiring members of the middle and upper classes, and military service joined religious and civil service in importance to the state. Foreign mercenaries and Egyptianized prisoners of war continued to do military service, but they were kept together in separate camps, commanded by Egyptians, and not included in the new army hierarchy. Nevertheless, foreign soldiers, like their Egyptian counterparts, were entitled to the use of land, and thus had a vested interest in their new home. Well-organized and trained divisions composed of thousands of infantry, chariot units, and other more specialized troops were commanded by a great army commander, or generalissimo, usually the successor to the throne,

9. See Sheikh 'Ibada al-Nubi, "Soldiers," in Donadoni, 151–84.

although the pharaoh retained absolute power over his forces.[10]

In the New Kingdom, visible and influential queens were the consorts of strong and effective warrior kings. They had a wide range of titles, owned their own estates, had administrators and servants, and wore new symbols of office. Queens had always been considered semidivine, but the Eighteenth Dynasty strengthened this claim. Like everyone else, the queen's position was defined by her relation to the pharaoh, and among her traditional titles were King's Mother and King's Wife, which reflected the veneration of motherhood common in the society but also the importance of various male-female relations in structuring the general order of the world. Ahmose Nefertari, wife (and sister or niece) of Ahmose (1550–1526 BCE), the first ruler of the New Kingdom, played a prominent role in state affairs and assumed the priestly office of God's Wife of Amun, which brought with it land, goods, and an administrative staff. She also served as regent for her young son when her husband died and after her death was deified and the object of worship throughout the land until the New Kingdom ended. Her extraordinary status is evident in the numerous inscriptions that refer to her and her activities, while the title of God's Wife was inherited and used by the women in her family line, Hatshepsut in particular.[11]

Act II

The Hatshepsut Problem: From Queen to King

Hatshepsut's public career began quite typically with her marriage to her half-brother, Tuthmosis II, when she was about fifteen. Their father (Tuthmosis I) was a successful and venerated military leader and ruler whose aggressive campaigns began the process of colonizing Upper Nubia. He pushed south into the kingdom of Kush and beyond, slaying the Kushite king and capturing his dependents, and was the first monarch to stake a claim along the Euphrates River in western Asia. He also had begun the expansion and embellishment of the Karnak temple complex near Thebes. He died when he was about fifty—an unusually long life at a time when life expectancy at birth was lower than twenty years. Those who survived birth and childhood might live to the age of thirty-five, although the elite lived slightly longer. Death in infancy and childhood was common for all social groups, including the royal family, and this helps to explain both the kings' many wives, as well as the choice of a male successor from a lesser or collateral family line if needed.

From the existing sources, Hatshepsut appears to have been a model wife. She bore the usual titles of King's Daughter, King's Wife, and King's Sister, but like Ahmose Nefertari before her, she preferred God's Wife and the

10. See Joyce Tydesley, *Hatchepsut: The Female Pharaoh* (New York: Viking, 1996), 27–29. Hornung uses the title *generalissimo*, 82.

11. See Tydesley, *Hatchepsut*, 58–62; Robins, 43–45; and Grimal, 201.

rituals and responsibilities that accompanied that position. Under the rule of Tuthmosis II and Queen Hatshepsut, Egypt prospered. Tuthmosis had to protect Egyptian territory and fortresses along the Nile from Kushite rebels, but he is thought to have suffered from ill health and was not considered an aggressive and heroic military leader like his father. In assessing his role, some caution is to be exercised. Evidence of battles can easily disappear, and burial evidence of his physical condition is fragmentary because looting and tomb robbing were fairly common after his death. Hatshepsut and Tuthmosis had a daughter, Princess Neferure, but she is typically invisible as a young child.

Tuthmosis II died in 1479 BCE; by then he had a male heir, also named Tuthmosis, whose mother was a lesser wife. Because the heir was too young to rule, Hatshepsut stepped in as regent, a common practice. An inscription in a rock tomb near Thebes describes these events: "[After the king, Tuthmosis II, died,] his son took his place as King of the Two Lands and he was the sovereign on the throne of his father. [Tuthmosis's sister], the God's Wife Hatshepsut, dealt with the affairs of the state: the Two Lands were under her government and taxes were paid to her."[12] Hatshepsut was the de facto ruler of Egypt. In the next several years, she proceeded to consolidate her position and create her own government with officials of her choosing who would be loyal to her. By the seventh year of the reign, she proclaimed herself king, was crowned king with full titles and regalia, wore the clothing and even false beard of the king, and performed the duties and rituals of the divine monarch.

This move on her part, her motives, and the possible reaction of Tuthmosis III have produced heated scholarly debates over the years. In the controversies over historical interpretation, sources again play a major role. Evidence on monuments that might have provided more clarity has disappeared, has been defaced, or was carved over with the names of other rulers and events. In addition to evidentiary problems, some scholars who simply could not understand Hatshepsut's unprecedented action have concluded that she was a greedy, even power-hungry, wicked stepmother, who usurped her stepson's birthright. In turn, they assumed that he defaced her statues, monuments, and inscriptions in acts of hatred and vengeance. Some have even argued that this animosity led him to have her assassinated. In slightly less personal interpretations, she has been assumed to have been peace loving—a characteristic often attributed to feminine nature—and he a warrior, resulting in a constant power struggle between their factions in the palace.

The use of new or different sorts of evidence and the search for other explanations has produced a slightly altered picture of the reigns of Hatshepsut and Tuthmosis III. In answering the question of why she decided to become king in her own right, it is possible that she enjoyed the exercise of power and was fairly good at it. Perhaps she thought, given high mortality rates, that Tuthmosis might not

12. Quoted in Grimal, 207.

survive, but as he came of age, it became clear that her powers as queen regent would not continue. Perhaps she also believed that, because of her family line, she had a closer connection to the divine inheritance of the pharaohs. Finally, she was able to take advantage of an old law and practice that allowed older kings to rule with younger successors as coregents. In this regard, she claimed her rule and that of Tuthmosis III to have begun in the same year; she never denied his royal status or tried to dispatch him to some obscure post. In fact, she encouraged him to train with the army and continued the tradition of the heir as commanding general.

Why did Tuthmosis not challenge his stepmother's rule? When he finally did rule alone, he was one of the most famous of the warrior-kings, so he certainly could have staged a coup. Perhaps he, too, was aware of his less glorious familial background and lacked influential male relatives to give him support. Perhaps he simply accepted the idea of coregency and assumed that he would rule eventually.[13] While there is no doubt that in later years Hatshepsut's name was erased from the legitimate royal line, it is not clear when this effort began or that it was the result of personal animosity between the two kings. Given Egyptian desires to avoid change, Hatshepsut's unusual reign might have made a number of people uncomfortable. The elimination of the record of a female pharaoh would not have been the first time that Egypt's historical narrative was reshaped to conform to tradition rather than left to depict reality.

A prevalent belief over the centuries was that legitimate rulers were gods. Thus, claims to and proof of divinity were critical dimensions of royal rule. For Hatshepsut, in particular, it was important to show her divine origins and to act in ways befitting her unique status (**Document Two**). Religious belief described the birth of a king as the miraculous result of the dominant god impregnating a mortal woman. Hatshepsut elaborated on this story, using Amun as her divine father, and had the story carved on the walls of her mortuary temple in Deir el-Bahri near Thebes. According to the story, Amun decided it was time to father a princess who would govern all of Egypt, and thus visited Hatshepsut's mother to tell her she would bear a daughter who would be "the One who is joined with Amun, [she is] the Foremost of women."[14] After her birth, Hatshepsut is presented to Amun, who calls her "daughter of my loins." During her reign, she altered one of the king's titles slightly, claiming to be the "Female Horus of Fine Gold," but both she and Tuthmosis III, when he assumed the throne, claimed to be the children of Amun and promoted his cult. Hatshepsut did not pretend to be a man; she was a woman and that was obvious to all around her. But she *was* a king with full powers and responsibilities. As she said, "none rebels against me in all lands. . . . All that the sun encompasses works for me."

13. The best discussion of these historiographical questions is in Tydesley, 77–80, 100–15.

14. Tydesley, 104.

Act III

Hatshepsut and Tuthmosis as Kings

In addition to claiming divine parentage and making such claims public in buildings, monuments, and rituals, the rulers of Egypt also proved their divinity by maintaining order and taking care of their people. From Hatshepsut's standpoint, it was very important that members of the elite classes did not oppose her rule and that Egypt was not disturbed by famines or political unrest (**Document Three**). The male elite who headed the army, civil service, and priesthood apparently accepted her. Some of the older men of the court had actually served her father and her husband and were willing to shift their loyalty to her. She also selected several new administrators who, though from humble origins, proved quite capable, and their successes no doubt enhanced her prestige.

One of the most famous of these servants was a man named Senenmut. Neither his mother nor his father had titles, but he was extremely well educated and cultured and most likely came from an upper-class family in one of the provincial cities. His education placed him in the top 10 percent of the population, and he probably moved up in either the priestly or the civilian bureaucracy of his home region. He eventually held ninety-one official titles; the most important among these were ones indicating service to Amun, and perhaps his career really began at the Karnak temple. Eventually he was known as the Overseer of all the Works of the King at Karnak.[15] As a young man he had served Queen Hatshepsut as her steward, and then later did the same for Princess Neferure. Certainly his fortunes were tied to Hatshepsut, and his able administration proved to be a major asset for her. Hatshepsut had other capable servants and officers, many of whom were also of humble or less illustrious backgrounds, but none was as prominent as Senenmut. The fact that he was in charge of the building of her mortuary temple near Thebes and that he had one of his own tombs built at that site is perhaps illustrative of his status.

By the time that the Eighteenth Dynasty took the throne, Thebes was a large and extensive city, surrounded by numerous burial grounds and temple complexes. By then, it was common to separate the burial tombs from the mortuary temples, where rulers could be served and worshiped. Reflecting the shifting centers of political power, the pharaohs were now buried in the Valley of the Kings, to the west of Thebes, while mortuary temples were built on the west bank of the Nile, directly across from the city. The increased stature of the queens by this point is evident in their burial sites at the nearby Valley of the Queens. Senenmut was in charge of building Hatshepsut's mortuary temple, the quite unusual and beautiful structure known as the Holiest of Holy Places at Deir el-Bahri. "The great originality of Hatsheptut's complex lay in its organization into a succession of terraces in

15. Descriptions of Senenmut can be found in Tydesley, chap. 7; Grimal, 209–11; and Watterson, 128–29.

which the changes in plane enabled the monument to harmonize with the natural amphitheatre of the cliffs."[16] Senenmut might not have been an architect, but he certainly had considerable organizational and administrative skills and a keen aesthetic sense.

Within the temple are many of the narratives about Hatshepsut's rule to which we already referred, but other subjects and events are also described there. One of the most prominent of these depicts the tropical scenery and exotic inhabitants of the land of Punt, which is on the Red Sea coast of Africa. Like most of her predecessors, Hatshepsut promoted trade with other kingdoms, both far and near. Trips to Punt had occurred during the Middle Kingdom and were continued by Tuthmosis III and subsequent pharaohs. Generally on these missions, the Egyptians were more interested in obtaining luxuries and exotic goods not available at home than in seeking out markets for their own goods. They were especially interested in the resins from which they made incense (myrrh and frankincense). Apparently Hatshepsut's expedition, carried out by her chancellor, also brought back bags of gold, ebony and ivory, panther skins, and even live monkeys. Such cross-cultural ventures were publicly displayed as evidence of the wealth and international prestige of King Hapshetsut, but we can also assume that she was commercially successful in less glamorous ways as Egypt remained prosperous.

16. See the description in Grimal, 211; also see Tydesley, 165–75.

Hatshepsut continued the aggressive military policies of her predecessors and with three major campaigns into Upper Nubia secured Egyptian rule there and essentially eliminated Kushite resistance. When he was king, Tuthmosis III only made one trip to the area, and that was for the purpose of inspection rather than military engagement. Fortified towns continued to be built along the river, but over time fortresses gave way to unwalled cities. While provincial governments were "pervasive and sometimes arbitrary . . . [they were] not unduly oppressive,"[17] and the colonial controls that the Egyptians established in Upper Nubia lasted until about 1000 BCE. Imperial goals in the area were protection, order, manpower, revenue from taxes and tribute, and, of course, enhancement of the status of the pharaoh as ruler of the world (**Document Four**). In the process, Egyptianization of the population, cross-cultural exchanges, and a steady flow of people back and forth, up and down the Nile resulted.[18] The Nubians adopted Egyptian writing, Egyptian-style houses, pottery, and even graves and were influenced by the dominant political ideas. Deities were sometimes merged or shared, and many of the characters and plots of popular literature were exchanged by both cultures. For their part, the Egyptians learned

17. David B. O'Connor, *Ancient Nubia: Egypt's Rival in Africa* (Philadelphia, PA: University Museum of Archaeology and Authropology, University of Pennsylvania, 1993), 61.

18. For discussions of conquest and colonialism, see O'Connor, 56–64; and Yurco, "Egypt and Nubia," in Yamauchi, 76–90. An exceptionally good discussion of cultural exchange can be found in Edda Bresciani, "Foreigner," in Donadoni, 221–53.

new techniques in glassmaking, sometimes adopted foreign clothing and hairstyles, and were especially intrigued by Nubian dancers and magicians.

The Egyptians continued to use Nubians in their army and their police forces, and the sons and daughters of Nubian princes frequently were brought to Egypt where they were raised and taught Egyptian beliefs and customs. Large numbers of foreign women were integrated into Egyptian society as weavers, singers, and dancers. In other cases, diplomatic marriages resulted as the women became the spouses of Egyptian men of rank or even lesser wives in the king's harem. The boys who attended the *kap,* or royal nursery, eventually had careers in the palace administration or army, or some returned home with positive connections to the Egyptians. The legacies of assimilation and cultural contact would be evident in northeastern Africa long after the Eighteenth Dynasty ended.

Hatshepsut used and supported the army her predecessors had founded, and it was in excellent condition, both in terms of men and material, when Tuthmosis III took over. Those who have argued that she was a pacifist, refusing to extend Egypt's power, base their conclusions on the fact that no extant records show her in the field, leading troops on aggressive military campaigns. Her diplomatic record and military policies provide a very different story, although like other dimensions of her life, how she felt about warfare will remain a mystery.

Finale

After ruling for almost twenty years Hatshepsut died in 1459 or 1458 BCE. Her daughter, Neferure, died three years earlier, and Senenmut also disappeared from the scene about the same time. Once again, we know little about how Hatshepsut died; whether, indeed, she hoped her daughter would marry her stepson or perhaps rule as a king herself; or what exactly happened to her most trusted adviser. We do know that the transition to the reign of Tuthmosis III was a smooth one and that he, in fact, kept many of Hatshepsut's advisers and officials in his government.

Like previous family members, the new pharaoh justified and legitimized his rule as Amun's wish. In an inscription in the Karnak temple to Amun, Tuthmosis explains that the great god appeared to him during a festival and appointed him king, as the living Horus, ruler of the Two Lands. Tuthmosis continued the building programs of Hatshepsut, although he revived the worship of the war god, Montu, an old Theban deity from the Middle Kingdom, by refurbishing his sanctuary and building a special chapel at the Karnak site. This change was in keeping with the new king's reputation as a great military leader and the creator of an even greater Egyptian Empire.

At the time of Hatshepsut's death, various of the Asiatic territories began to rebel against Egyptian control. During his reign, Tuthmosis carried out seventeen successful campaigns into western Asia, eventually crossing the Euphrates River north and east of Kadesh. In the process, he subdued rebellions, established provincial control or made local rulers in the area pay tribute to Egypt, and captured vast resources, war booty, and prisoners (**Document Five**). In his first campaign, after the battle at Megiddo, near the Mediterranean coast north of Joppa, he took "340 living prisoners . . . 2041 mares, 6 stallions, a chariot wrought with gold; . . . 30 chariots belonging to other chiefs plus 892 chariots belonging to the wretched army; . . . 502 bows, . . . [and numerous cattle and goats]."[19] Tuthmosis also maintained Egyptian control of the area of Nubia and extracted large amounts of gold from the mines in his African territories. Overall, Egyptian prestige was so great under his leadership that envoys came from areas as far away as Minoan Crete to bring gifts to the pharaoh of this mighty empire.

Although Thebes remained the capital and religious center of the empire, Tuthmosis III spent most of his time at Memphis, which was the center of military command and operations. Under him, the officer corps continued to expand and to gain in political importance. Eventually, under subsequent dynasties, contests between the priestly and military bureaucracies would challenge royal authority. Tuthmosis III also followed in his family's footsteps in his intellectual pursuits and cultural interests. He was well educated, and his tomb inscriptions indicate considerable interest, like Hatshepsut before him, in the flora and fauna of other areas. Finally, Tuthmosis was an excellent equestrian, archer, and athlete, but he was a modest and mild-mannered individual, not given to self-aggrandizement or bragging. This characterization would not seem to fit with that of a man driven by hatred and the desire for revenge against his stepmother. But, as already noted, the erasure of evidence of Hatshepsut's rule probably occurred late in Tuthmosis's reign or under the guidance of subsequent rulers and may well have been the result of careful political calculations designed to reshape the historical narrative by streamlining royal lineages and reinforcing connections to earlier dynasties for all male rulers.

Tuthmosis III died in 1425 BCE and was buried in a royal tomb in the Valley of the Kings. He was succeeded by a son of a second wife who proved capable of maintaining many Tuthmosid programs and goals. The Eighteenth Dynasty ended in 1295 BCE when the pharaoh, having no male lineal successor, left the throne to one of his most prominent officials, who thus became the first king of the next dynasty. By that time Egypt had an empire that included Palestine, Syria, Lebanon, and vast areas of modern Sudan. Its social fabric also had been rewoven as there was more upward mobility, and cultural and social elites were redefined. Dependent servants, workers on royal estates, and military conscripts were replaced by imported laborers, many of them slaves taken as prisoners of war

19. From the temple inscription, quoted in Watterson, 103.

or Asians bought in slave markets. Slaves now could be bought and sold by individuals, slavery itself was codified in the legal system, and the "slave becomes one of the human types" that is referred to in prescriptive literature.[20] These developments were among the permanent legacies of Hatshepsut and Tuthmosis III.

Later rulers in the Eighteenth Dynasty made names for themselves as warriors, due to the opulence of their courts, or for religious revolution (in the reign of Amenophis IV, 1352–1336 BCE, who took the name Akhenaten, meaning "pleasing to the god Aten"). And queens continued to exercise influence as de facto regents with their husbands or formal regents for their sons. But no queen or consort made good Hatshepsut's claim to rule as king in her own right.

20. Antonio Loprieno, "Slaves," in Donadoni, 189.

DOCUMENTS*

DOCUMENT ONE

"Exhortations and Warnings to Schoolboys" (New Kingdom)

Egyptian schoolboys copied out extracts from various compositions on papyri, writing boards, or pieces of soft stone or clay. The purpose was to learn to write and to learn something of ancient literature. After that initial education, a young man could become a scribe to someone in an administrative office (for example, the treasury) and there he would be trained further. The document that follows is a copying made by a schoolboy during the New Kingdom. Although its purpose was a practical one of teaching him to make his letters, it also was a piece of advice literature. Why is he encouraged to become a scribe? What criticisms are made of other occupations? Can we assume these are accurate depictions of the various careers described? Why or why not?

. . . [Do not be a soldier, a priest, or a baker.]

Be a scribe, who is freed from forced labour, and protected from all work. He is released from hoeing with the hoe, and thou needest not carry a basket.

It separateth thee from plying the oar, and it is free from vexation. Thou hast not many masters, nor an host of superiors.

No sooner hath a man come forth from his mother's womb, than he is stretched out before his superior. The boy becometh a soldier's henchman, the

*In the documents that follow in this chapter, the following symbols denote damaged, missing, or untranslatable text that archeologists were unable to read from the tablets and pillars of ancient Egypt: — or ______. Brackets [ ] denote an addition made by an editor or author for clarity.

stripling a recruit, the grown man is made into an husbandman, and the townsman into a groom. The halt (?) is made into a doorkeeper, and the (short-sighted?) into one that feedeth cattle; the fowler goeth upon the . . ., and the fisherman standeth in the wet.

The superintendent of the stable standeth at the work, while his span is left in the field. Corn is thrown down to his wife, and his daughter is on the embankment (?). If his span leaveth him and runneth away, he is carried off to the Iwai-troops.[1]

The soldier, when he goeth up to Syria, hath no staff and no sandals. He knoweth not whether he be dead or alive, by reason of the (fierce?) lions. The foe lieth hidden in the scrub, and the enemy standeth ready for battle. The soldier marcheth and crieth out to his god: "Come to me and deliver me!"

The priest standeth there as an husbandman, and the wē'eb-priest worketh in the canal[2] ______ he is drenched in the river; it maketh no difference to him whether it be winter or summer, whether the sky be windy or rainy.

When the baker standeth and baketh and layeth bread on the fire, his head is inside the oven, and his son holdeth fast his feet. Cometh it to pass that he slippeth from his son's hand, he falleth into the blaze.

But the scribe, he directeth every work that is in this land.

[Be an official.]

Let not thine heart go afluttering like leaves before the wind ______. Set not thine heart on pleasures. Alas, they profit not, they render a man no service ______. When he worketh and *it is his lot* to serve the Thirty,[3] he worketh *and* extendeth not his strength,[4] *for* evil toil lieth (yet) in front of him. No servant bringeth him water, and no women will make bread for him, whereas his companions[5] *live* according to their desire, and their servants act in their stead. (But) the man of no sense standeth there and toileth, and his eye looketh enviously at them.

Therefore give heed, thou naughty one; thou obstinate one, that will not hear when thou art spoken to. Hasten to it, the calling with the gay. . . . It is the one that directeth all Councils of Thirty and the courtiers of the (Royal) Circle. Prithee, know that.

1. Meaning probably: if during these non-military activities his horses get lost, he is put into the infantry.

2. Even the priesthood is not immune from forced labour.

3. The college of high officials.

4. He dares not sleep.

5. His erstwhile schoolfellows who have become scribes.

DOCUMENT TWO

The Birth of Queen Hatshepsut

The following excerpts have been taken from inscriptions and scenes from the king's famous temple, Deir el-Bahri. This is really a tale in which the court and higher classes heard the story of the monarch's divine origins. Beginning with her birth, it tells of the god Amun's (spelled "Amon" here) presentation of Hatshepsut to the gods and describes her coming of age, and then the coronation by her father, Tuthmosis I. (Buto is the goddess of the North; Khnum is the god who created humankind.) Why was it important for Hatshepsut to make these claims? What are the events described that give her credibility?

. . . *Words of the Queen*

Utterance by the king's-wife and king's-mother Ahmose, in the presence of the majesty of this august god, Amon, Lord of Thebes: "How great is thy fame! It is splendid to see thy front; thou hast united my majesty (fem.) with thy favors, thy dew is in all my limbs." After this, the majesty of this god did all that he desired with her.

Words of Amon

Utterance of Amon, Lord of the Two Lands, before her. "Khnemet-Amon-Hatshepsut shall be the name of this my daughter, whom I have placed in thy body, this saying which comes out of thy mouth. She shall exercise the excellent kingship in this whole land. . . .

Reply of Khnum

"I will form this [thy] daughter [Makere] (Hatshepsut), for life, prosperity and health; for offerings ______ for love of the beautiful mistress. Her form shall be more exalted than the gods, in her great dignity of King of Upper and Lower Egypt."

V. Khnum Fashions the Child

Scene

Khnum is seated before a potter's wheel, upon which he is fashioning two male (!) children.[1]

1. This would indicate that the reliefs were made according to old and traditional sketches in which, of course, a female child had no place. All the pronouns used by Khnum in addressing the child are feminine!

Words of Amon

Utterance of [Amon]. . . . . . . ______ to see his daughter, his beloved, the king, Makere (Hatshepsut), living, after she was born, while his heart was exceedingly happy.

Utterance of [Amon to] his bodily daughter [Hatshepsut]: "Glorious part which has come forth from me; king, taking the Two Lands, upon the Horus-throne forever." . . .

Words of the Gods

Utterance of all the gods, [to] Amon-[Re]: "This thy daughter [Hatshepsut], who liveth, we are satisfied with her in life and peace. She is now thy daughter of thy form, whom thou hast begotten, prepared. Thou hast given to her thy soul, thy '—', thy 'bounty', the magic powers of the diadem. While she was in the body of her that bare her, the lands were hers, the countries were hers; all that the heavens cover, all that the sea encircles. Thou hast now done this with her, for thou knowest the two aeons.[2] Thou hast given to her the share of Horus in life, the years of Set in satisfaction. We have given to her. . . .

The Queen's Growth and Beauty

Her majesty saw all this thing[3] herself, which she told to the people, who heard, falling down for terror among them. Her majesty grew beyond everything; to look upon her was more beautiful than anything; her '—' was like a god, her form was like a god, she did everything as a god, her splendor was like a god; her majesty (fem.) was a maiden, beautiful, blooming, Buto in her time. She made her divine form to flourish, 'favor of' him that fashioned her. . . .

Thutmose I's Address to the Court

Said his majesty before them: "This my daughter, Khnemet-Amon, Hatshepsut, who liveth, I have appointed [her] ______; she is my successor upon my throne, she it assuredly is who shall sit upon my wonderful seat. She shall command the people in every place of the palace; she it is who shall lead you; ye shall proclaim her word, ye shall be united at her command. He who shall do her homage shall live, he who shall speak evil in blasphemy of her majesty shall die. Whosoever proclaims with unanimity the name of her majesty (fem.), shall enter immediately into the royal chamber, just as it was done by the name of this Horus (viz., by my name). For thou art divine, O daughter of a god, for whom even the gods fight; behind whom they exert their protection every day according to the command of her father, the lord of the gods. . . .

2. An aeon is sixty years.

3. What thing is meant is not clear; possibly it refers to the preceding presentation to the gods, which she narrates now to the people. Then follow her growth into youth and beauty, and the journey.

DOCUMENT THREE

Speech of the Queen

The following speech is taken from an inscription on the obelisks at Karnak which Hatshepsut had built and dedicated to Amun. What is the purpose of the king's speech? Has she been a good king, according to this speech?

III. Base Inscription

Titulary and Encomium of the Queen

Live the female Horus . . . daughter of Amon-Re, his favorite, his only one, who exists by him, the splendid part of the All-Lord, whose beauty the spirits of Heliopolis fashioned; who hath taken the land like Irsu[1] whom he hath created to wear his diadem, who exists like Khepri[2] (*Hpry*), who shines with crowns like "Him-of-the-Horizon," the pure egg, the excellent seed, whom the two Sorceresses[3] reared, whom Amon himself caused to appear upon his throne in Hermonthis, whom he chose to protect Egypt, to 'defend' the people; the female Horus, avengeress of her father, the oldest (daughter) of the "Bull-of-his-Mother," whom Re begat to make for himself excellent seed upon earth for the well-being of the people; his living portrait, King of Upper and Lower Egypt, Makere (Hatshepsut), the electrum of kings. . . .

Speech of the Queen

"I have done this from a loving heart for my father Amon; I have entered upon his 'project' of the first occurrence, I was wise by his excellent spirit, I did not forget anything of that which he exacted. My majesty (fem.) knoweth that he is divine. I did (it) under his command, he it was who led me; I conceived not any works without his do'ing', he it was who gave the directions. I slept not because of his temple, I erred not from that which he commanded, my heart was wise before my father, I entered upon the affairs of his heart, I did not turn my back upon the city of the All-Lord, but turned to it the face. I know that Karnak is the horizon on earth, the August Ascent of the beginning, the sacred eye of the All-Lord, the place of his heart, which wears his beauty, and encompasses those who follow him."

1. A god's name, lit., "He who made him."
2. God of continued existence.
3. A divine name, lit., "two great in sorcery."

DOCUMENT FOUR

The Victorious King

This poetry is a portion of an inscription in the temple of Amun-Re at Karnak and was written to celebrate Tuthmosis's victories after his wars were over. Here the god welcomes the king as his son, gives his blessings, and promises great successes. What does this inscription tell you about the Egyptians' views of their empire and empire building?

I have come that I may cause you to trample on the great ones of Djahi[1]
That I may spread them out under your feet throughout their lands;
That I may cause them to see Your Majesty as lord of sunrays
When you shine in their faces in the likeness of me.
I have come that I may cause you to trample on the dwellers in Asia
And to smite the heads of the Amu of Retjnu;[2]
That I may cause them to see Your Majesty equipped in your panoply
When you take weapons of warfare in the chariot.
I have come that I may cause you to trample on the eastern land
And to tread down those who are in the regions of Tonuter;[3]
That I may cause them to see Your Majesty as a lightning-flash,
Strewing its levin-flame and giving its flood of water.
I have come that I may cause you to trample on the western land,
Crete and Cyprus being possessed with the awe of you;
That I may cause them to see Your Majesty as a young bull,
Firm of heart and sharp of horn, whom none can tackle.
I have come that I may cause you to trample on the 'Islanders',[4]
The lands of Mitanni[5] trembling through fear of you;
That I may cause them to see Your Majesty as a crocodile.
Lord of fear in the waters, who cannot be approached.
I have come that I may cause you to trample on the Islanders
In the midst of the sea, who are possessed with your war shout;
That I may cause them to see Your Majesty as the Protector[6]
Who appears on the back of his wild bull.

1. Palestine and part of Phoenicia.
2. The people of northern Phoenicia and Syria.
3. A name usually given to the land of Punt, possibly in Somaliland, but here apparently applied to a region in or adjoining Syria; perhaps Transjordan is meant.
4. Translation not quite certain; at any rate, a people distinct from the islanders mentioned in the next verse.
5. A people whose western border was on the Euphrates.
6. The "Protector" is Horus, the protector of his father Osiris, who is imagined as standing on the back of, i.e. subduing, a wild bull typifying Seth, the enemy of Osiris.

I have come that I may cause you to trample on Libya
And the isles of Utjena[7] through the power of your might;
That I may cause them to see Your Majesty as a fierce lion
When you make them into corpses throughout their valleys.
I have come that I may cause you to trample on the uttermost parts of the earth,
What the Ocean encircles being held in your grasp;
That I may cause them to see Your Majesty as lord of the falcon-wings
Who takes what he sees at will.
I have come that I may cause you to trample on those who are in the Southland
And to bind the Sand-dwellers as captives;
That I may cause them to see Your Majesty as a jackal of Upper Egypt,
The lord of speed, the runner who courses through the Two Lands.

7. An unknown locality.

DOCUMENT FIVE

"The Annals: First Campaign" of Tuthmosis III

The records of Tuthmosis's various campaigns come from pillars in temples built for the purpose of celebration. These particular inscriptions describe his Megiddo campaign, which lasted about 175 days. On the basis of the inscriptions, what was the purpose of this campaign? What did the Egyptian Empire gain from it? How is the king depicted?

Behold, the chiefs of this country came to render their portions, to do obeisance to the fame of his majesty, to crave breath for their nostrils, because of the greatness of his power, because of the might of the fame of his majesty ______ the country ______ came to his fame, bearing their gifts, consisting of silver, gold, lapis lazuli, malachite; bringing clean grain, wine, large cattle, and small cattle—for the army of his majesty. 'Each of the Kode (*KD-(w)* among them bore the tribute southward.[1] Behold, his majesty appointed the chiefs anew for ______.

Spoil of Megiddo

______ 340 living prisoners; 83 hands; 2,041 mares; 191 foals; 6 stallions;—young—; a chariot, wrought with gold, (its) 'pole' of gold, belonging to that foe; a beautiful chariot, wrought with gold, belonging to the chief of [Megiddo];—892 chariot[s] of his wretched army; total, 924 (chariots); a beautiful 'suit' of bronze armor, belonging to that foe; a beautiful 'suit' of bronze armor, belonging to the chief of Megiddo (*M-k-ty*); ______, 200 suits of armor, belonging to his

1. The Kode were a coastal people who probably shipped the goods. Ed.

wretched army; 502 bows; 7 poles of (*mry*) wood, wrought with silver, belonging to the tent of that foe. Behold, the army of [his majesty] took ______, 297—, 1,929 large cattle, 2,000 small cattle, 20,500 white small cattle.

Plunder of the Lebanon Tripolis, Megiddo, Etc.

List of that which was afterward taken by the king, of the household goods of that foe who was in ['the city of'] Yenoam (*Y-nw-"mw*), in Nuges (*Yn-yw-g-s'*), and in Herenkeru (*Hw-r-n-k'-rw*), together with all the goods of those cities which submitted themselves, which were brought to [his majesty: 474]—; 38 lords ([*m-r'-y-*] *n'*) of theirs, 87 children of that foe and of the chiefs who were with him, 5 lords of theirs, 1,796, male and female slaves with their children, noncombatants who surrendered because of famine with that foe, 103 men; total, 2,503. Besides flat dishes of costly stone and gold, various vessels,______, a large (two-handled) vase (*'-k'-n'*) of the work of Kharu (*H'-rw*), (*—b-*) vases, flat dishes, (*hntw-*) dishes, various drinking-vessels, 3 large kettles (*rhd't*), [8]7 knives, amounting to 784 deben. Gold in rings found in the hands of the artificers, and silver in many rings, 966 deben and 1 kidet.[1] A silver statue in beaten work______the head of gold, the staff with human faces; 6 chairs of that foe, of ivory, ebony and carob wood, wrought with gold; 6 footstools belonging to them; 6 large tables of ivory and carob wood, a staff of carob wood, wrought with gold and all costly stones in the fashion of a scepter, belonging to that foe, all of it wrought with gold; a statue of that foe, of ebony wrought with gold, the head of which ['was inlaid'] with lapis lazuli______; vessels of bronze, much clothing of that foe. . . .

1. Deben and kidet are measures of weight.

Questions

1. What made it possible for Hatshepsut to rule as a king? Why do you think she wanted that title instead of the usual ones given to women? Using Hatshepsut's experience, what general conclusions might you draw about women's access to power in the ancient world?
2. On the basis of the reigns of Hatshepsut and Tuthmosis, what were the most important qualities of a successful ruler? What did Egyptians expect of their kings?
3. In many ways Egyptian society was quite open and flexible, in others quite rigid and limiting. What sort of moral code did the Egyptians live by? What would make Egyptians follow such a code and accept divine dynastic rule?
4. All of the documents included in this chapter, as well as most of the records we have for ancient Egypt, were intended for something other than historians' examinations. Why were the records originally created, and how might their purposes affect the way we view and assess them?
5. Why and how did the Egyptians create an empire, and what were some of the consequences of those actions?

Suggested Readings

Hawass, Zahi. *Silent Images: Women in Pharaonic Egypt.* New York: Abrams, 2000.

Robins, Gay. *Women in Ancient Egypt.* Cambridge, MA: Harvard University Press, 1998.

Shaw, Ian. *The Oxford History of Ancient Egypt.* New York: Oxford University Press, 2000.

Tydesley, Joyce. *Hatchepsut: The Female Pharaoh.* New York: Penguin, 1998.

Source Materials

The two best sites for material culture as well as texts are

The Egyptian Museum in Cairo http://www.egyptianmuseum.gov.eg

The British Museum, Egyptian collection http://www.thebritishmuseum.ac.uk/world/egypt/egypt.html

Both websites are gateways to visual tours of their remarkable collections.

CHAPTER

3

The Formation of Early China: King Wu Ding (d. ca. 1189 BCE) and Lady Hao (ca. 1200) of the Shang Dynasty (ca. 1600-ca. 1050 BCE)

Setting the Stage

Compared to the other three valley civilizations (Mesopotamia, Egypt, and India), the Chinese civilization was a latecomer. Historians generally believe in the existence of an earlier dynasty, the Xia (twenty-first to seventeenth century BCE)[1], but the first archaeologically confirmed Chinese civilization is the Shang dynasty. The Shang were highly sophisticated and powerful, an indication that the people of China had long prospered before the Shang

1. In his *Historical Records*, Sima Qian of the Han dynasty presented a brief history of the Xia dynasty. Even though the Xia have not been confirmed by archaeological evidence, Chinese historians are convinced that they did exist. Aiding such a belief is the fact that Sima Qian's account of the Shang dynasty in the *Historical Records* proved to be fairly accurate when compared to archaeological discoveries.

emergence. And unlike other valley civilizations, the Chinese civilization formed by the Shang was never interrupted. Shang heritages, such as ancestor worship, kinship organization, hierarchical society, a writing system, arrays of regional identities, customs of everyday life, and, to a certain extent, a gender system, all became core components of the Chinese culture.

The Shang people were a migrant tribe from eastern China. Led by a capable king, Tang, they defeated early settlers in the Yellow River valley around seventeenth century BCE and marked the area as their territory (**Document One**). The dynasty was named after the birthplace of the tribe, a tradition that would be followed by most founding rulers in Chinese history. The Shang kingdom maintained its dominance by actively expanding alliances and fiercely conquering enemy tribal states. An important tool in forming and consolidating political alliances was marriage. Shang kings took multiple wives, the majority of whom came from other tribal states. Since the Shang were constantly at war and the size of their coalition fluctuated from time to time, the dynasty was virtually a tribal state confederation rather than a unified sovereignty. An important aspect of the Shang civilization was its mixture of political, religious, and kinship organizations. Shang kings used divination and ancestor worship to legitimize their authority. The king, as the descendent of royal ancestors, was the most qualified person to read the minds of the ancestors and to administer rituals of ancestor worship. Likewise, the degree of power he conferred to his officials was correlated with the strength of their blood ties with royal ancestors.

Several generations after settling in the Yellow River valley, the Shang suffered a series of setbacks. For a long time, kingship was passed to the deceased king's brother, rather than his son. The rationale behind this was the belief that such practice would ensure the dynasty would be in the hands of a mature and capable ruler. However, conflict frequently arose when several brothers contended for the royal seat. In the meantime, natural disasters forced the Shang to move their capital from place to place. The constant relocations depleted the dynasty's economic and human resources, providing opportunities for nominal allies to break away or even to stage attacks. Eventually the eighteenth king, Pan Geng, reversed the trend by selecting the city of Yin, a place with tremendous resources of water and forests, as the permanent capital. This marked the beginning of the Shang revival.

King Wu Ding was Pan Geng's nephew and the twenty-first king of the Shang dynasty. He set out to recover the Shang's territory of King Tang's time and was credited by the descendents of the Shang with the restoration of the dynasty. King Wu Ding also initiated the passage of the kingship to a son, a change that greatly reduced the possibility of conflicts within the royal clan. Another aspect of Wu Ding's reign was the role of women in the public sphere. A total of sixty-eight noble women appeared in oracle-bone inscriptions from the

Wu Ding era. They actively engaged in Shang state affairs. They supervised religious ceremonies, conducted divinations, took offices, commanded the royal army, and held fiefs. Among them, the most distinguished woman was Lady Hao, one of the three wives of King Wu Ding. The active roles that King Wu Ding and Lady Hao played provide modern readers a wonderful opportunity to grasp the fundamental nature of Shang society in general and the Shang gender system in particular.

There are three types of sources for piecing together the lives of King Wu Ding and Lady Hao. The first type is published oracle-bone inscriptions from Wu Ding's reign, roughly 24,000 of them. Another source of information is material artifacts from archaeological discovery. While King Wu Ding's tomb, excavated in 1935, had been badly damaged by looters, Lady Hao's tomb, excavated forty years later in 1975, was nearly intact (**Document Two**). The third type of source is early historical writings. *The Historical Records* (*Shiji*), written by Sima Qian (ca. 145–86 BCE), dedicates a chapter to the Shang, recounting the royal line and the rise and fall of its rule.[2] *The Book of Songs* (*Shijin*), a compilation attributed to Confucius (550–478 BCE), includes five hymns that were composed by descendents of the Shang.

The Actors

King Wu Ding and Lady Hao

Wu Ding was the posthumous title and the temple name for the twenty-first king of the Shang dynasty. *Wu* means "military," "force," and "courageous," signifying his character and achievements; Ding is one of the Ten Heavenly Stems, signifying the days that Wu Ding would be posthumously worshiped.[3] Wu Ding's real name was Zi Zhao. Zi was the name of his clan, and Zhao, his given name, means "bright" and "prominent." According to legend, Wu Ding's father, Xiao Yi (died around 1250 BCE), encouraged his young son to travel across the kingdom and live among the peasants and artisans. As a result, Wu Ding not only learned various work skills, but also developed a fairly realistic grasp of Shang society. Wu Ding ruled the Shang for fifty-nine years. His reign was marked by constant military actions, often led by himself, against enemy states. Under his vigorous leadership, the Shang managed to rebuild a vast confederation, rivaling that of King Tang's reign.

2. See "Basic Annals of the Yin" in Sima Qian's *Historical Records*. Yin was the name that the Shang people called themselves after they settled in the new capital, Yin.

3. The Chinese combine the Ten Heavenly Stems (namely Jia, Yi, Bing, Ding, Wu, Ji, Geng, Xin, Ren, and Gui) with the Twelve Earthly Branches (Zi, Chou, Yin, Mao, Chen, Si, Wu, Wei, Shen, You, Xu, and Hai) to designate years, months, days, and hours. Each Heavenly Stem is paired with an Earthly Branch. This practice began during the Shang dynasty and has continued to the present.

From what we can gather, Wu Ding had at least three consorts. Two of them, Ladies Hao and Jing, appear frequently in oracle-bone inscriptions; information about his third wife, known only as Spouse Gui, is rather scarce. Lady Hao's name appears in nearly 250 Shang oracle-bone inscriptions, and about fifty or so inscriptions are concerned with Lady Jing. Though much less mentioned than Lady Hao, we nevertheless learn that Lady Jing, who was from the state of Jing, was just as prominent as Lady Hao. She led battles, had fiefs, supervised agricultural activities, and hosted various religious ceremonies. Lady Jing probably died of some type of illness before the end of Wu Ding's reign. Some Shang inscriptions show that King Wu Ding had anxiously inquired about the causes of Lady Jing's disease and her imminent death. King Wu Ding appears not to have had many children. Lady Hao probably gave birth to one son and two daughters. One oracle-bone inscription recorded that she gave birth to a daughter on a Jiayin day (**Document Three**); another recorded that she started labor late at night on a Renchen day and gave birth to a daughter the next morning.[4] Her son, whose posthumous title was Xiao Ji (Filial Ji), died quite young, probably shortly after Lady Hao's death. Wu Ding's heirs, the twenty-second and twenty-third kings, were most likely sons of his other wives.

Lady Hao was probably from a Zi family, the same clan as her husband. In Chinese writing, her title was Fu Hao. *Fu* means "wife" and "lady"; the character *Hao* consists of a woman radical and the character *Zi* (meaning "child"), signifying Lady Hao's origin and heritage, the Zi clan. Lady Hao, thus, was her formal title at the Shang royal court. No information is available to pin down the exact dates of Lady Hao's birth or death. However, she must have been much younger than her husband but appears not to have lived as long as he did. The name Lady Hao first appeared in inscriptions from the ending years of Wu Ding's early reign. These divination inscriptions noted Lady Hao's pregnancy and childbirth, indicating that she had just entered the royal family as a young wife. She became very active during the mid–Wu Ding reign as a leading general of the Shang army in battles against several enemy states. However, records about her activities are absent in inscriptions belonging to the later period of Wu Ding's reign. Lady Hao may have died years before King Wu Ding.

While nurturing her children and commanding the military, Lady Hao took great care of her appearance. In her tomb archaeologists found a total of 499 bone hairpins, 47 gemstones, and 426 jade apparel accessories. Lady Hao's clothes and shoes were mostly made of silk, as at least five different types of silk fabrics were discovered in her tomb. Some of the silk fabrics were dyed with cinnabar, consistent with the scholars' speculation that red was a popular color during the Shang

4. Guo Moruo and Hu Houxuan, eds., *Jiaguwen heji* (Collection of Oracle-Bone Inscriptions) (Beijing: Zhonghua shuju, 1983), #6948.

dynasty. In traditional China, fabrics and apparel were important symbols of political and social status. The state strictly regulated types of fabrics, colors of the fabrics, and styles of the attire one could wear. Commoners, for example, were categorically forbidden to wear silk. Eventually, *Buyi*, or hemp and cotton clothes, became synonymous for commoners. The silk fabrics discovered in Lady Hao's tomb confirmed Lady Hao's privileged status within the Shang hierarchy.

Lady Hao appears to have battled numerous ailments throughout her life. At one point she had trouble breathing; another time she suffered a mysterious and lingering illness. In addition, she was constantly bothered by tooth decay. She also experienced a difficult birth, during which the infant died. The direct cause of Lady Hao's death, however, is not mentioned in oracle-bone inscriptions. Since many inscriptions about Lady Hao are concerned with her childbearing and her military battles, a modern reader cannot help but wonder if she died in a battle or during childbirth. Such consequences were certainly noted and admired in other societies. In ancient Sparta, for example, Spartans considered men who died defending Sparta and women who died giving birth to future Spartan fighters heroes. Such sacrifices were commemorated by inscribing their names on tombstones. In comparison, Lady Hao was remembered by the Shang people for her roles in both Shang victories over enemy states and birthing heirs for the royal family. Not surprisingly, buried within Lady Hao's extravagant tomb were 468 exquisite bronzes, more than half of which were weapons. In some of the bronzes, Lady Hao was revered as Mother Xin, indicating that the bronzes were dedicated to her by her children.

Act I

The Marriage of Wu Ding and Lady Hao

Lady Hao grew up in a prominent Zi family before marrying King Wu Ding. She must have had a personal name given by her parents. However, once she assumed her new identity as a royal queen, she was addressed as the Wife Who Was from the Zi Clan. The combination of the title Lady and the title of her clan seem to represent how the Shang dynasty addressed their royal wives. Similarly the Chinese title for Lady Jing was Fu Jing, consisting of *Fu* (meaning "wife" or "lady"), and *Jing*, a character that combines a woman radical and the character *Jing* (meaning "well"), a powerful tribal state during the Shang period.

The union of King Wu Ding and Lady Hao reflects several important aspects of the Shang gender system and kinship organization. First of all, the Shang developed a social system in which the father was the head of the family, men had authority over women and children, and society was governed by men. In addition, the dominant pattern of marriage at the time was *patrilocal*, which means that a woman would reside with her husband's clan. The ladies of the Shang court were selected from various clans and tribal states and married into the royal clan. Once married, they became permanent members of the royal clan and were assigned new names. Rulership and property rights were reserved exclusively for male members of the royal family. However, women were not necessarily considered weak or ignorant nor was it felt that they should be kept away from public affairs. The notion that men should dominate public affairs and that women should be confined to domestic duties and submit to men developed later with Confucian philosophy, which derived from the teachings of the scholar and philosopher Confucius (551–479 BCE) and which would be particularly influential during the Han dynasty (see Chapter Five).

Secondly, polygamy, the practice of having multiple spouses at one time, was a common practice of elite males during the Shang dynasty. King Wu Ding married Lady Hao, Lady Jing, and Spouse Gui; his father took at least two wives; and his grandfather, five wives. Shang inscriptions also show that Shang nobles who did not belong to royal clans often took multiple wives as well. It is worth noting, however, that the Shang polygamy was different from the polygamy of later periods in China when a man would take a principal wife and multiple concubines. Denoting a principal wife and then concubines enabled wealth and position to be inherited by fewer heirs and thus kept patrimonies intact. Such issues were apparently not a primary concern during the Shang dynasty.

During the Shang dynasty, the primary goal of practicing polygamy was to have more offspring, especially male offspring. Very likely the rates of maternal and infant death were quite high at the time, and polygamy provided a way to ensure the continuation of the lineage. During Wu Ding's reign, pregnancy and childbirth were among the most inquired-about topics in Shang divination. One inscription reads: "The king prayed for having offspring to ancestress Spouse Geng and Spouse Bing."[5] Another inscription recorded: "The inquiry was: 'Lady Hao will be pregnant.' The king read the crack lines and said: 'Auspicious! She will be pregnant.'"[6]

The union of Wu Ding and Lady Hao also demonstrates that multiple marriages helped the royal family to form political alliances. In fact for the entire Shang period, there are at least 120 ladies appearing in Shang oracle-bone inscriptions and the majority of them are from allied tribal states. During Wu Ding's era, most tribal states sought marriage ties with the Shang by eagerly presenting their noble daughters to the Shang royal clan. Occasionally the Shang would coerce reluctant tribes into supplying brides. The forced marriages might have helped to secure additional allies or at least to reduce the numbers of potential enemies. A state that had one of their daughters serving as a lady in the Shang court might hesitate to attack the Shang.

5. Guo and Hu, #2400.

6. Guo and Hu, #13925.

In order to marry Lady Hao, King Wu Ding probably went through the customary procedures of proposal, engagement, selecting a wedding date, fetching the bride, and wedding. Oracle-bone inscriptions reveal that before a marriage proposal, King Wu Ding would first find out whether the desired young woman was suitable to be his wife.[7] Once he was engaged, the king would select an appropriate date to report the news to his ancestors in their shrines.[8]

As a Shang practice, expanding connections and consolidating alliances through marriage became a principle of Chinese marriage practices. Such practices eventually laid the foundation for Chinese marriage customs. A chapter entitled "Meaning of Marriage" in *The Book of Rites*, one of the five Confucian classics, declared: "The purpose of marriage was intended to be a bond of love between two surnames" (**Document Four**). In believing that profound benefits could be brought by marital ties, Shang people practiced the act of marrying their deceased wife to an ancestor, hoping an afterlife marriage might bring a blessing to the living family. After Lady Hao passed away, for example, King Wu Ding conducted several divinations and pondered whether one of the past kings would take Lady Hao as a wife (**Document Five**).

Act II

Roles in Ancestor Worship and Divination

Ancestor worship was the dominant focus of Shang religious practices and pursuits. Shang people believed that whatever happened in their life in this world, whether good or bad, was at least influenced, if not entirely controlled, by their ancestors' actions. Therefore, they constantly tried to figure out which ancestor brought them harm and, more important, which ancestor to pray to for good luck.

Wu Ding was probably the most pious ancestor worshiper among the Shang kings who left divination records. He divined much more frequently than his successors and inquired about much broader topics than they did. Nearly 1,300 inscriptions from Wu Ding's era, for example, are concerned with rain; among them, many were prayers to ancestors for bringing rainfall so the Shang could have a good harvest. Besides rainfall and a good harvest, King Wu Ding also sought his ancestors' opinions about war, military levies, worship of deities, travel, feasts, pregnancy, childbirth, illness, dreams, death, selection of dates and times, climate, natural disaster, and sometimes, unusual phenomena. For example, the Shang believed that a solar eclipse

7. For example, one inscription reads: "Crack-making on Xinwei day. 'The king should marry this woman.' Crack-making on Xinwei day. 'The king should not marry this woman'" (Guo and Hu, #4923).

8. For example, one inscription reads: "Inquiry: The king received the news about the future bride and will inform the ancestors.' Inquiry: 'The king will inform them on Gengyin day, a few days from today.' Inquiry: 'The king will inform them on Jiawu day'" (Guo and Hu, #1051).

was closely related to their ancestors. Every time a solar eclipse occurred, a special ceremony would be held in an ancestor's shrine and animals would be sacrificed. One inscription reads: "Yisi day. Inquiry: 'Wine offering to Ancestor Xiao Yi.' It was completed. That day, the sun was eclipsed. In the evening, the king reported this to Shang Jia. Nine cattle were used."[9]

The Shang selection of which ancestors to communicate with was directly linked to the Shang kinship system. All male ancestors who ruled before King Tang (predynastic rulers) and all the Shang kings after the Tang (dynastic rulers) were included in the royal ancestor worship roster. In addition to male ancestors, female ancestors who produced at least one male heir were included in the worship repertoire as well. Such categorizations reinforced the Shang patriarchal system, in which the women's role as bearers of male heirs would be rewarded. In the Shang ancestor worship system, both male and female ancestors were assigned a date (which became the posthumous title and temple name of the ancestor) so they could be worshiped individually. In addition to individual worship, separate or specific ceremonies were performed for all the ancestors, ancestors of certain generations, or a male ancestor and his consorts. It is worth noting that from King Wu Ding's reign on, only royal ancestors whose son was also a king would be included in a more prestigious set of ancestors for worship. Such practice corresponds to the shift to the preference for a direct-line of inheritance which occurred during Wu Ding's reign (**Document Six**).

Shang kings regularly made important decisions, issued orders, and celebrated harvests or military successes at ancestral shrines. Ancestor worship thus served as the source of dynastic power. Shang inscriptions also reveal that, in order to maximize the ancestral blessing, King Wu Ding's royal army would carry ancestors' tablets with them during their expeditions. Makeshift rituals in the field would be held for worshipping, divination, summoning, or celebration. The king, as the host of the rites, was the center of power, and participants were invited to perform certain rites and to play specific roles according to lineage proximity and occasionally cultural and political proximity.

Shang ancestor worship was a form of food redistribution as well. The royal court routinely offered animals, grain, and wines during worships; the food used in all these rites would be consumed by the participants afterward in ceremonial banquets or dispensed among the participants. In this sense, proximity to the dynastic power was translated into proximity to a food resource. Such a connection between food and political power was an important part of Chinese tradition.

Besides royal ancestors, Wu Ding regularly made inquiry to Di, the High God, as well as various nature powers, such as gods of the Sun, wind, rain, drought, and snow. The High God not only had the power to interfere in the mundane world but also had the ability to use the power of

9. Guo and Hu, #33698. Shang Jia was a predynastic ancestor six generations before Tang.

nature to either benefit or punish the Shang. An inscription from Wu Ding's era reads:

> Crack-making on Xinwei day. Zheng was the diviner. The inquiry was: "In the next month, which is the eighth month, the High God will order to have a plenty of rainfall." The inquiry was: "In the next month, which is the eighth month, the High God will not order to have a plenty of rainfall."[10]

Clearly, it was King Wu Ding, rather than the diviners, who had the final say about the outcomes of the divination. Sometimes, King Wu Ding himself would preside over divinatory rituals to maximize his control in decision making. More interesting, all the Shang diviners were high-ranking court officials; this hints that Shang divination was closer to a cabinet meeting than a pure shaman ritual.

Archaeological evidences suggest Lady Hao was one of Wu Ding's diviners. She not only made cracks and wrote inquiries, but was also involved in ordering and preparing cattle bones and turtle shells. As a diviner, Lady Hao must have mastered the Shang written language, the early form of Chinese writing system used by more than a billion Chinese today. This writing system was invented according to the same principle of writing systems in other early civilizations, such as Egyptian hieroglyph, Mesopotamian cuneiform, and Mayan hieroglyph. Of these, only the Chinese writing system survives, and for more than 3,000 years, it has served as a key identity marker of Chinese civilization and as a unifying force among the Chinese of various regions. The fact that Lady Hao was a royal priest who mastered both writing and divinatory skills indicates that the Shang people did not consider women any less capable than men and that royal women were actively involved in the dynasty's power system.

Act III

Commanding Military Expeditions

True to his character, King Wu Ding's greatest achievement was the creation of a confederation through multiple and continuous military expeditions. Under his reign, the Shang royal army expanded to include three regiments: the Left Regiment, the Central Regiment, and the Right Regiment. Each regiment was further divided into four divisions: infantry, chariot, cavalry, and marine (or more accurately, boat unit). In addition, various Shang clans had their own militia organizations and were often ordered to participate in royal expeditions or defense. Tribal states subjected to Shang rule also had obligations to supply the royal army with troops.[11]

Historians generally divide Wu Ding's reign into three major periods, on the basis of his military expeditions. During the early era of Wu Ding's reign, the Shang army fought battles around areas east of the Shang capital. Their enemies were mostly weak tribal states; a total of more than forty such

10. Guo and Hu, #10976.

11. Guo and Hu, #5504, #5512.

states were recorded in oracle-bone inscriptions from this period. The expeditions seemed quite straightforward, as inscriptions show that King Wu Ding usually conducted one or two divinations before each battle. During this period, the most prominent general was Que, who not only commanded battles, but also actively engaged in Wu Ding's divinatory rituals.

During the middle period of Wu Ding's reign, Lady Hao became the chief general of the royal army. Very likely General Que had died. Although only ten or so tribal states were recorded as the targets of Lady Hao's and Wu Ding's expeditions, they were nevertheless powerful enemies. Shang inscriptions from this period show a lot of back and forth divinations, indicating the battles under Lady Hao's command were large scale and often prolonged. Major battles were mostly conducted in the northwest, but the Shang also engaged in small battles with states of the east and the south. One battle against the tribal state Bafang involved coordination between King Wu Ding and Lady Hao on a two-pronged front. An inscription of the middle Wu Ding period reads:

> Crack-making on Xinwei day. Zheng was the diviner. The inquiry was: "Lady Hao leads General Zhi Guo in the expedition against Bafang." The king carries out the expedition from the east . . . , and thus, force the enemy to retreat to where Lady Hao will be based.[12]

12. Guo and Hu, #6480.

Another inscription reported a joint effort between 3,000 royal soldiers commanded by Lady Hao and 10,000 militiamen in a battle against Qiangfang, from the west.[13] The biggest achievement in Lady Hao's military career was her expedition against Tufang. Tufang was located about 300 miles north of the Shang, probably a twelve- to thirteen-day travel distance. During the middle Wu Ding period, Tufang constantly harassed Shang ally tribal states, sometimes stealing their harvest and slaves but more often seizing their land. The war with Tufang probably extended over several years. Lady Hao was the chief commander who received the military orders directly from her husband.[14] The expedition was a great success: at the end of the war, Tufang surrendered and acknowledged fully the Shang's rule.[15]

During the late period of Wu Ding's reign, General Bi was the most prominent military leader. Seven tribal states are listed in inscriptions as the subjects of Shang military actions. At the beginning of this period, the Shang had largely recovered the territory of Tang's time, but two potent enemy states challenged the Shang and several states from northern and western areas took the opportunity to break away from the confederation.

13. Guo and Hu, #39902.

14. For example, one inscription recorded: "[The king] orders Lady Hao to conquer Tufang" (Guo and Hu, #6412).

15. Guo and Hu, #6454.

Finale

As prominent figures of China's first recorded civilization, King Wu Ding and Lady Hao will be forever remembered for their role in the shaping of Chinese culture and tradition. The worship of the two started immediately after their death—a normal practice among the Shang people for their ancestors. When Lady Hao passed away, she was laid to rest at a cemetery about one hundred meters southwest of Shang ancestor shrines. At least sixteen people were sacrificed, along with six dogs. After Lady Hao's death, King Wu Ding often dreamed about her and wondered whether Shang royal ancestors were fond of her. Sometimes, he would pray to her for protection and strength.

King Wu Ding died around 1189 BCE and was probably buried in the main royal cemetery. Archaeologists suspect that the occupant of a tomb in Yinxu, which they labeled Tomb 1001, might be King Wu Ding. Even though the tomb was ransacked before its rediscovery in modern times, it nevertheless yielded the remains of seventy-four human sacrifices, twelve horses, and eleven dogs, who accompanied the occupant on his journey to the next world. The arrangement of human sacrifices was a final testament to this hierarchical society: some of the followers were provided with coffins and bronze vessels or weapons of their own; some (usually female) with no coffins but with personal ornaments; yet others with no furnishings and beheaded, cut in two, or put to death in other mutilating ways.

Oracle-bone inscriptions reveal that Shang kings of the post–Wu Ding era became increasingly confident about their political power and the operation of the confederation. The pious nature that King Wu Ding had displayed was completely absent during the final reign of the Shang dynasty. King Di Xin seemed no longer interested in the birth of a male child, the choice of allies in war, or the will of the High God. To him, divination was a religious ceremony for receiving blessings, and he seemed exceedingly positive about the outcomes. Han historians, however, depicted a much more negative image of the last king of the Shang. *The Historical Records*, for example, describe King Di Xin as a ruthless tyrant who showed no interest in state affairs. He spent all his time indulging himself in bawdy music, lewd dance, exotic animals, and extravagant banquets. Sima Qian ascribed the fall of the Shang dynasty to the last king's indulgence of a woman, his consort Da Ji. Allegedly Da Ji possessed neither feminine beauty nor womanly virtues. On the contrary, she was known to be talkative and lascivious. The weak ruler Di Xin was utterly fixated on Da Ji, listening to whatever she had to say and completely ignoring his officials and allies. The tribal states were appalled and broke away from the Shang. When King Wu of the state of Zhou launched an expedition against the Shang, eight hundred states joined enthusiastically. On a Jiazi day of 1050 BCE, the coalition defeated the Shang. Di Xin committed suicide, and King Wu personally killed Da Ji. The great dynasty established by King Tang and revived by King Wu Ding finally met its brutal end.

Sima Qian apparently wrote *The Basic Annals of the Shang* with great admiration for King Wu Ding's ambition and strong abhorrence of King Di Xin's indulgence of women. Modern historians, however, are amazed at the difference a thousand years could make. From King Wu Ding's era to Sima Qian's time, a thousand years passed. Chinese civilization evolved and matured, and a patriarchy finally came to its full term. During the Shang dynasty, women were entrusted with power. By the Han dynasty, women interfering in politics had became a primary fear in a male-dominant society.

Documents

DOCUMENT ONE

"The Dark Bird" (Seventh Century BCE)

"The Dark Bird" is one of five Shang hymns contained in the Book of Songs, *compiled by Confucius. The hymns were most likely composed by the descendants of the Shang. It seems the descendents of the Shang were most nostalgic about the superiority of the Shang over other states during King Tang's time and about the mighty capability of King Wu Ding who led the Shang to glory. What does this poem tell you about the perception of the king in ancient China?*

Heaven bade the dark bird
To come down and bear the Shang,
Who dwelt in the lands of Yin so wide.
Of old God bade the warlike Tang
To partition the frontier lands.
To those lands was he assigned as their lord;
Into his keeping came all realms.
The early lords of Shang
Received a charge that was never in peril.
In the time of Wu Ding's grandsons and sons,
Wu Ding's grandsons and sons,
Warlike kings ever conquered,
With dragon-banners and escort of ten chariots.
Great store of viands they offered,
Even their inner domain was a thousand leagues;
In them the people found sure support.
They opened up new lands as far as the four seas.[1]
Men from the four seas came in homage,
Came in homage, crowd on crowd;

1. The four seas refer to the East and South China seas, the Indian Ocean, and Lake Baikal.

Their frontier was the river.
Yin received a charge that was all good;
Many blessings Yin bore.

DOCUMENT TWO

The Excavation of Lady Hao's Tomb (1975)

Lady Hao's tomb in Yinxu is located about one hundred meters southwest of Shang ancestor shrines. The pit of Lady Hao's tomb is an oblong shaft with a measurement of 5.6 meters by 4 meters at the mouth and an orientation of 10 degrees to the northeast. Toward the middle of both its eastern and western walls at a depth of about 6.2 meters is an elongated niche containing several sacrifices. The pit is provided at the bottom with secondary earthen platforms on all four sides. On the bottom of the pit is a waist-high pit with a human sacrifice and a dog. There is a wooden chamber which is 16.5 feet long, 11 to 12 feet wide, and 4.5 feet high. Inside the chamber is a lacquered coffin, now rotted. The tomb occupant was interred with at least sixteen human sacrifices (four men, two women, two children, and eight others of unknown sex and age). The burial objects were placed in the fillings of the tomb chamber, above the chamber, on the chamber top, in the space between the chamber and coffin, and inside the coffin. Among the objects buried in the tomb, there are 468 bronzes, 755 jade objects, 63 stone objects, 47 gemstone objects, 564 bone objects, 5 ivory objects, and 11 pottery objects, and there are nearly 6,900 pieces of cowry shells.

DOCUMENT THREE

King Wu Ding

"Divination on Lady Hao's Childbirth" (ca. 1200 BCE)

This is one of more than thirty Shang inscriptions concerned with Lady Hao's pregnancy and childbirth. Such divinations reflected the Shang kings' anxiety over having a male heir to continue the Shang rule. In what way does the inscription reveal the Shang gender perception?

Crack-making on Jiashen day, Qiao was the diviner. The inquiry was: "Lady Hao's childbirth will be good." The king read the cracks and said: "If it be a Ding-day childbirth, it will be good; if it be a Geng-day childbirth, there will be a prolonged luck." After thirty-one days, on Jiayin day, she gave birth. It was not good. It was a girl.

Crack-making on Jiashen day, Qiao was the diviner. The inquiry was: "Lady Hao's childbirth will not be good." After thirty-one days, on Jiayin day, she gave birth. It was not good. It was a girl.

The king read the cracks and said: "If it be a Ding-day childbirth, it will be good; if it be a Geng-day childbirth . . . luck."[1]

DOCUMENT FOUR

"Meaning of Marriage" (Second Century BCE)

"Meaning of Marriage" is one of the fifty chapters of the Book of Rites, *a collective account of ancient Chinese perceptions of proper rules and etiquette. Compiled by a group of Confucian scholars, the book covered a broad range of topics, from government regulations, religious rituals, ceremonies of passage, and household management to a calendar for farming and proper attire for various occasions. In your opinion, what was the foundation of marriage in ancient China?*

The ceremony of marriage was intended to be a bond of love between two [families of different] surnames, with a view, in its retrospective character, to secure the services in the ancestral temple, and in its prospective character, to secure the continuance of the family line. Therefore the superior men, [the

1. " . . ." part unreadable.

ancient rulers], set a great value upon it. Hence, in regard to the various [introductory] ceremonies—the proposal with its accompanying gift; the inquiries about the [lady's] name; the intimation of the approving divination; the receiving the special offerings; and the request to fix the day:—these all were received by the principal party [on the lady's side], as he rested on his mat or leaning-stool in the ancestral temple. [When they arrive], he met the messenger, and greeted him outside the gate, giving place to him as he entered, after which they ascended to the hall. Thus were the instructions received in the ancestral temple, and in this way was the ceremony respected, and watched over, while its importance was exhibited and care taken that all its details should be correct.

The father gave himself the special cup to his son, and ordered him to go and meet the bride; it being proper that the male should take the first step [in all the arrangements]. The son, having received the order proceeded to meet his bride. Her father, who had been resting on his mat and leaning-stool in the temple, met him outside the gate and received him with a bow, and then the son-in-law entered, carrying a wild goose. After the [customary] bows and yielding of precedence, they went up to the hall, when the bridegroom bowed twice and put down the wild goose. Then and in this way he received the bride from her parents.

After this they went down, and he went out and took the reins of the horses of her carriage, which he drove for three revolutions of the wheels, having handed the strap to assist her in mounting. He then went before, and waited outside his gate. When she arrived, he bowed to her as she entered. They ate together of the same animal, and joined in sipping from the cup made of the same melon; thus showing that they now formed one body, were equal rank, and pledged to mutual affection.

The respect, the caution, the importance, the attention to secure correctness in all the details, and the great points in the ceremony, and served to establish the distinction to be observed between man and woman, and the righteousness to be maintained between husband and wife. From the distinction between man and woman came the righteousness between husband and wife. From that righteousness came the affection between father and son; and from that affection, the rectitude between ruler and minister. Whence it is said, "The ceremony of marriage is the root of the other ceremonial observances."

Ceremonies [might be said to] commence with the capping; to have their root in marriage; to be most important in the rites of mourning and sacrifice; to confer the greatest honor in audiences at the royal court and in the interchange of visits at the feudal courts; and to be most promotive of harmony in the country festivals and celebrations of archery. These were the greatest occasions of ceremony, and the principal points in them.

Rising early (the morning after marriage), the young wife washed her head and bathed her person, and waited to be presented (to her husband's parents), which was done by the directrix, as soon as it was bright day. She appeared before them, bearing a basket with dates, chestnuts, and slices of dried spiced meat.

The directrix set before her a cup of sweet liquor, and she offered in sacrifice some of the dried meat and also of the liquor, thus performing the ceremony which declared her their son's wife.

The father and mother-in-law then entered their apartment, where she set before them a single dressed pig,—thus showing the obedient duty of [their son's] wife.

Next day, the parents united in entertaining the young wife, and when the ceremonies of their severally pledging her in a single cup, and her pledging them in return, had been performed, they descended by the steps on the west, and she by those on the east,—thus showing that she would take the mother's place in the family.

Thus the ceremony establishing the young wife in her position; [followed by] that showing her obedient service [of her husband's parents]; and both succeeded by that showing how she now occupied the position of continuing the family line:—all served to impress her with a sense of the deferential duty proper to her. When she was thus deferential, she was obedient to her parents-in-law, and harmonious with all the occupants of the women's apartments; she was the fitting partner of her husband, and could carry on all the work in silk and linen, making cloth and silken fabrics, and maintaining a watchful care over the various stores and depositories [of the household].

In this way when the deferential obedience of the wife was complete, the internal harmony was secured; and when the internal harmony was secured, the long continuance of the family could be calculated on. Therefore the ancient kings attached such importance [to the marriage ceremonies].

Therefore, anciently, for three months before the marriage of a young lady, if the temple of the high ancestor [of her surname] were still standing [and she had admission to it], she was taught in it, as the public hall [of the members of her surname]; if it were no longer standing [for her], she was taught in the public hall of the Head of that branch of the surname to which she belonged;—she was taught there the virtue, the speech, the carriage, and the work of a wife. When the teaching was accomplished, she offered a sacrifice [to the ancestor], using fish for the victim, and soups made of duckweed and pondweed. So was she trained to the obedience of a wife.

DOCUMENT FIVE

King Wu Ding

"Divination on Lady Hao's Afterlife Marriage" (ca. 1200 BCE)

In the following divination, King Wu Ding inquired about whether Lady Hao had become a wife of one of the past kings, and if so, which king. He suspected it would be among King Tang, the founder of the Shang dynasty; Da Jia, the third king; and Zu Yi, the twelfth king. It is clear, though, Shang people did not consider such marriage incest. On the contrary, an ancestor king taking Lady Hao as his wife would be an honor to Lady Hao and a blessing to King Wu Ding.

CHARGE: It is Zu Yi who took a wife. It is Zu Yi.
CHARGE: It is Tang who took Lady Hao as his wife. It is Tang who took Lady Hao as his wife.
CHARGE: It is Da Jia.
CHARGE: It is Da Jia who took a wife.
CHARGE: Lady Hao is married in the upper would.
CHARGE: Lady Hao is not married in the upper world.

DOCUMENT SIX

KING WU DING

"Divination on Ancestor Worship" (ca. 1200 BCE)

This inscription documents a combined rite of ancestor worship. Apparently only kings who passed down the throne to their sons were listed as subjects for this ritual. What does such restriction tell you about the kinship system during Wu Ding's era?It might be useful to, first, take a look at the Shang royal genealogy that has been reconstructed by modern historians. (P=predynastic ancestor, K=king. The ↓ indicates the main line of father-to-son descent).[1]

MODERN GENEALOGICAL RECONSTRUCTION OF SHANG ROYALTY

P1 Shang Jia
↓
P2 Bao Yi
↓
P3 Bao Bing
↓
P4 Bao Ding
↓

1. David N. Keightley, *The Ancestral Landscape: Time, Space, and Community in Late Shang China (c. 1200–1045 BC)* (Berkeley: Institute of East Asian Studies, University of California, Berkeley, 2000), 132–133.

P5 Shi Ren
↓
P6 Shi Gui
↓
K1 Da Yi
↓
K2 Da Ding
↓
K3 Da Jia → K4 Wai Bing
↓
K5 Da Geng → K6 Xiao Jia
↓
K7 Da Wu → K8 Lü Ji
↓
K9 Zhong Ding → K10 Wai Ren
↓
K12 Zu Yi → K11 Jian Jia
↓
K13 Zu Xin → K14 Qiang Jia
↓
K15 Zu Ding → K16 Nan Geng
↓
K20 Xiao Yi → K19 Xiao Xin → K18 Pan Geng → K17 Xiang Jia
↓
K21 Wu Ding
↓
K23 Zu Jia → K22 Zu Geng
↓
K25 Kang Ding → K24 Lin Xin
↓
K26 Wu Yi
↓
K27 Wen Wu Ding
↓
K28 Di Yi
↓
K29 Di Xin

Crack-making on Wei day. Charge: to offer a combined sacrifice to ten ancestors from Shang Jia, to Da Yi, Da Ding, Da Jia, Da Geng, Da Wu, Zhong Ding, Zu Yi, Zu Xin, and Zu Ding.

Questions

1. What are the characteristics of Shang civilization? What are the similarities and differences between the Shang and other valley civilizations?
2. How did the Shang contribute to the formation of Chinese civilization?
3. What does the union of Wu Ding and Lady Hao tell you about Shang society?
4. What role did Shang women play in both the public and domestic spheres? Did Shang women have equal status to men?
5. Some scholars suggested the dominance of ancestor worship in ancient China prevented Chinese civilization from developing a monotheistic and transcendental religion, such as Christianity and Islam. Do you agree?
6. What do **Documents Three, Five**, and **Six** tell you about the nature of Shang divinations?
7. Compare the Chinese interest in divination with a similar preoccupation by the Mesopotamians to know the future.

Suggested Readings

Keightley, David. *Sources of Shang History: The Oracle-Bone Inscriptions of Bronze Age China*. Berkeley: University of California Press, 1978.

———. *The Ancestral Landscape: Time, Space, and Community in Late Shang China (c. 1200–1045 BC)*. Berkeley: Institute of East Asian Studies, University of California Berkeley, 2000.

Loewe, Michael and Edward L. Shaughnessy, eds. *The Cambridge History of Ancient China: From the Origins of Civilization to 221 BC*. New York: Cambridge University Press, 1999.

Thorp, Robert L. *China in the Early Bronze Age: Shang Civilization*. Philadelphia: University of Pennsylvania, 2006.

Source Materials

Freer Gallery, Washington, DC, has online a selection of art and artifacts from the Shang period and others. http://www.asia.si.edu/collections/chineseHome.htm

The Cleveland Museum of Art also has online a selection of arts and artifacts. http://www.clemusart.com/explore/department.asp?tab=2&deptgroup=10&recNo=0&display=list

Messages from the Past. Vol. 4, *Heritage of the Wild Dragon* (Videocassette, 60 minutes). Princeton, NJ: Films for the Humanities, 2000.

CHAPTER

4

The Imperial Model: Augustus né Gaius Octavius (63 BCE–14 CE) and Livia Drusilla (58 BCE–29 CE)

Setting the Stage

Between 290 and 31 BCE, the Roman city-state expanded outward, conquering all of the Italian peninsula, substantial portions of western Europe, and territories surrounding the Mediterranean Sea from Gibraltar to the Adriatic, Aegean, and Red seas. At first, as territories came under the control of Rome, the ruling body of the city-state, the Senate, kept power exclusively in the hands of the city and its elites. Even as the Senate voted to extend various types of citizenship to others on the Italian peninsula, it jealously guarded the city-state's privileges and first-among-equals status. Beyond the peninsula, the Senate imposed Roman governors—former senators—on native populations and farmed out the collection of taxes to Roman agents. By extending the reach of the city-state and its interests and culture into the territories that it conquered, Rome, by mid–first century BCE, succeeded in centralizing power and influencing its imperial possessions in ways that earlier empires had failed to do.

As Rome expanded, however, it experienced profound changes in its political and social institutions, values, and sense of purpose. During the first century BCE, the power of the Roman state was shifting away from the Senate, which was composed of men from traditionally prominent and wealthy families of Rome, to individual senators turned military commanders and their loyal legions. In the early part of the century, these two powerful factions struggled for control of the Roman state and, with their supporters, eventually went to war against each other. After several decades of civil war, Gaius Octavius (63 BCE–14 CE), grandnephew and adopted son of Julius Caesar, defeated his opposition and stood ready to take control of the Roman state. But Octavius had a larger obstacle to conquer in order to assume power: the political traditions of the Roman Republic. He would have to find a way to concentrate power in his person, as dictator, and maintain the fiction that Rome's republican traditions were still in place.

Octavius brought to Rome a flair for reorganizing and refashioning Roman institutions and values to meet the challenge of how to rule the diverse, far-flung empire. His reforms and tactics resulted in the transformation of the fragmented, disintegrating, contentious, and overlarge republic into a well-administered, cohesive, and secure imperial state. During his rule, Octavius redefined the conception of Roman power. By the time of his death in 14 CE, Roman power no longer emanated from the Senate but from an individual and his immediate family. This transformation of the political system meant little to those outside the Roman city-state since Rome's provincial subjects already understood the source of political power as emanating from a monarch.

Octavius tamed the Roman elites by refashioning republican institutions. He also understood that the most important and persistent emblems of his authority in other parts of the empire were personal might, military victories, divinity, and cult worship. In the conquered Hellenistic East, monarchs in their kingdoms had been accorded cults as tokens of gratitude and political cohesion.[1] Augustus, therefore, pursued strategies that not only "restored" republican institutions to satisfy the elites in Rome but also appealed to Rome's conquered peoples. In this task, he was aided by his second wife, Livia Drusilla, the daughter of an illustrious Roman family with key alliances to leading senators and a woman of keen political

1. G. W. Bowersock, *Augustus and the Greek World* (Oxford, UK: Oxford University Press, 1965), 30.

acumen and savvy. The political importance of marriage and family is well exemplified in their lives and relationships. In addition, their life stories illustrate the process through which Octavius and Livia created, shaped, and stabilized imperial dynastic rule in the Roman world.

As a masterful and imaginative promoter of his own greatness, Augustus employed some of Rome's foremost writers, artisans, architects, and craftspeople to sing his praises throughout the Roman world. Rich sources exist that narrate Augustus's achievements. The writings of poets, as well as legal texts, public architecture and sculpture, and coins are good sources to see the extent to which Augustus patronized the arts and propagandized in order to reserve a place in history for himself and his family. The historical record was also augmented by the writings of two Roman historians, Suetonius (69–130/140? CE) and Tacitus (55–117? CE), and a Greek historian, Dio Cassius (155–235? CE). These historians not only provide critical assessments of Augustus's rise to imperial greatness, but note the roles that his wife, Livia, and other elite Roman women played in the founding and maintenance of the first Roman dynasty.

The historian Suetonius, writing a generation after Augustus's and Livia's deaths, had much to say about the political intrigues and personal lives of imperial Rome's rulers and their families. Suetonius and Tacitus represented Livia and other imperial women as operating capriciously and malevolently behind the political scene, abusing their power and influence over their husbands, brothers, or fathers. Both these historians exploited the existing views and prejudices against women to arouse indignation over the usurpation of power from the Senate and its families by people like Julius Caesar and Octavius. Most of the sources that detail personal conduct and public ideology carry the bias of their creators, privileged Roman males, who see imperial Roman women as disturbances and threats to Roman political order. Nonetheless, by detailing women's intrigues and political machinations, these sources reveal a political and social world where elite Roman women were socially and politically significant and often highly visible individuals.[2] The women of Augustus's family figured prominently in his ambitions and political plans for absolute power.[3]

The Actors

Augustus Né Gaius Octavius and Livia Drusilla

Gaius Octavius was born on September 23, 63 BCE, to an affluent Roman family that belonged to the equestrian, or knightly, class, the second-highest order in the Republic. This class was composed of men who possessed large tracts of land and whose family origins

2. Judith Hallett, *Fathers and Daughters in Roman Society* (Princeton, NJ: Princeton University Press, 1984), 12.

3. Susan E. Wood, *Imperial Women* (London: Brill, 1999), 27.

were outside of Rome proper. They were originally discouraged and thwarted from entering public service by men of the first order, the senatorial class. By the first century BCE, equestrians, like Octavius's father, were becoming senators. His mother, Atia, was the daughter of Julia, the sister of Julius Caesar. His mother's family belonged to the senatorial order, and young Octavius's great-uncle, Julius Caesar, was an influential senator and general.

The lives of all individuals in Roman society were structured by their social status, in other words the family, or *domus* (house), they came from, and by their legal status. It was important to have legal capacity, and this was determined by whether you were free and a citizen and influenced by age, marital status, gender, and census class. Like all members of a Roman *domus,* from the moment of birth, children were under a father's authority and rule (*patria potestas*). A son's mission in life was to obey his father, perpetuate the family line, and devote himself to the family's financial and political fortunes. However, particularly for young men of the upper classes, it was assumed they would acquit themselves well in military service and then begin to climb a ladder of public offices where they would gain power and prestige. A daughter's mission was to advantageously marry, bear and raise children, run a household, devote herself to her family's fortune and thereby contribute to the social good.

Octavius had both social and legal privilege. Like other elite Roman boys, Octavius was educated in Latin and Greek, rhetoric, and the art of politics and governance. This education tradition had begun in the second century BCE, when the ideal of general education was introduced in Rome by Greek scholars. Thus, literacy among the upper classes became common.[4] Families usually hired tutors (often Greek slaves) to train their sons in oratory, philosophy, and Greek and Latin literature, although by the end of the Republic, grammar schools also provided education. But more than education was required to ascend Rome's political ladder. A sizable fortune, civilian and military office holding, and connections with eminent men were necessary if one hoped to rise to political power in an era of civil war and political instability. According to the Greek historian Dio Cassius, Octavius's greatness was determined by both heavenly and worldly patrons.

As Octavius sought to increase his status in Rome, marriage was an important political strategy. During the decades of civil war, Octavius sought alliances with men who had noble power, influence, and wealth.[5] He gained a temporary truce with the undisputed ruler of Rome's seas, Sextus Pompeius (Pompey the Great's son) when in 40 BCE, he married Scribonia, the aunt of Pompeius's wife. At the same time, Octavius had arranged for the marriage of his sister, Octavia (69–11 BCE) to Marcus Antonius, one

4. Emily A. Hemelrijk, *Matrona Docta: Educated Women in the Roman Elite* (London: Routledge, 1999), 17–25. See as well Antony Kamm, *The Romans: An Introduction* (London: Routledge, 1995), 116–19.

5. Pat Southern, *Augustus* (New York: Routledge, 1998), 74.

of his major rivals. These marriage alliances did not spare the Romans from another ten years of civil war. Beginning in 39 BCE, Octavius waged war against his enemies and quickly vanquished Pompeius. By 36 BCE, only Antonius stood in his way for complete control of the Roman world.

In 39 BCE, while still married to Scribonia, Octavius had met and fallen in love with Livia Drusilla (58 BCE-29 CE), the pregnant wife of Tiberius Claudius Nero and daughter of another distinguished Roman, Marcus Livius Drusus Claudianus. Her mother was Alfidia, the daughter of a rich counselor from the Italian city of Fundi. Livia's father had not been a supporter of Octavius or Antonius and, indeed, had fought against both of them. Her first husband traded allegiances from Caesar to his assassins, from Pompeius to Antonius, and finally to Octavius.

Like the lives of many Roman elite women, Livia's life was shaped by laws on marriage, divorce, and transmission of property for women of her class.[6] Laws, of course, determine what one *may* do; social norms and values describe what one *should* do. But laws in Rome were subject to change or contained loopholes for alternative behaviors, and social values also shifted and included spaces where people could act and think in individual ways. Marriage required that a daughter be of age, usually between 12 and 15, and while marriages were arranged by parents, consent of the partners was mandated by law. By the first century BCE among the free, citizen classes, there were few restrictions on whom one could marry; divorce was not difficult to obtain; and adoptions, arranged to ensure the continuity of the lineage, were fairly common. Family property was also protected, and elder males were usually privileged. However, daughters were not systematically excluded from inheritance and could inherit property from fathers and husbands, transmit property to their children, and in some cases control dowries.[7] Literacy among upper-class Roman women probably was the norm, although their education was not as broad or extensive as that of their male counterparts. For elite families, education of a daughter could signify wealth and status, but it also could be controversial as some Romans saw educated women as dangerous.

Livia's family background placed her in an unusual position in Roman elite society. Consider the contrasting experiences of wives of peasant soldiers whose husbands were at home only periodically, who bore multiple children (losing many of them), and who had to figure how to plant and harvest the land and provide for the family on a daily basis. Although work and economic and living conditions separated the free women of Rome, all were expected to be fertile and virtuous mothers and modest,

6. See Hallett.

7. Mireille Corbier, "Family Behavior of the Roman Aristocracy, Second Century B.C.-Third Century A.D.," in *Women's History and Ancient History*, ed. Sarah B. Pomeroy (Chapel Hill: University of North Carolina Press, 1991), 173–96. See also Jane F. Gardner, *Women in Roman Law and Society* (Bloomington: Indiana University Press, 1986).

frugal, and chaste women who were devoted to their families. Similarly, ideologies of masculinity bound men, who were to be serious, strong, and dedicated to their families, the gods, and the state.

The affair between Livia and Octavius is well documented. Soon after their open affair began, they began to live together. Livia was pregnant by her first husband with their second son, Tiberius. Scribonia, Octavius's wife, was pregnant with their first and only child, Julia (39 BCE–4 CE?). Octavius's motivation for such a flagrant disregard for respectability remains unknown. But the fact that his marriage to Scribonia was a political match that no longer benefited him and his well-known dislike for her, combined with the prospect of marrying a woman from one of Rome's noblest families, have been cited as reasons for his conduct.[8] The circumstances of the open affair and the unorthodox events surrounding the marriage provided Octavius's opponents with ample ammunition (**Document One**).

Standards of marital honor and fidelity could become political weapons, and a marriage alliance could be a liability as Antonius discovered. During his marriage to Octavius's sister, Antonius remained politically and romantically allied with the queen of Egypt, Cleopatra VII. Cleopatra had first entered the Roman consciousness when she began a military and romantic liaison with Julius Caesar. Both the Romans and the ruling Egyptian dynasty, the Macedonian Ptolemies, were well acquainted with each other, ever since the Romans began their eastward expansion into Alexander the Great's former possessions during the third and second centuries BCE. Cleopatra, in her alliance with Caesar, continued familial political habits. In order to secure Roman acceptance of the Ptolemaic kingdom and help to defend Egypt's borders, Cleopatra first allied herself with Caesar and then with Antonius who administered the eastern provinces. Her relationship with both men brought Cleopatra into contact with the Roman public; first when she visited Rome with Caesar shortly before his murder and then when Antonius, who was still married to Octavia, decided to marry Cleopatra under Egyptian law, which permitted polygamy. Of course Antonius's brother-in-law and main rival, Octavius, did not appreciate the slight to his sister or the powerful alliance.

Octavius and his supporters used this liaison to turn Roman public opinion against Antonius. During an unsuccessful campaign against one of Rome's eastern enemies, Octavia hurried to Athens to bring reinforcements and money to her husband. Antonius did not meet her and remained in Egypt with his ally and lover. Calling this behavior mistreatment, Octavius played on the Roman Senate's disdain for Cleopatra. The Senate was suspicious of Antonius's monarchical ambitions and his liaison with a foreign queen. His public rejection of Octavia, a noble, virtuous, and loyal Roman woman, only furthered their growing distrust of Antonius. To contrast his

8. Marleen Flory, "*Abducta Neroni Uxor*: The Historiographical Tradition on the Marriage of Octavius and Livia," *Transactions of the American Philological Association* 118 (1988): 343–59, esp. 345–46.

respect for Roman women with his rival's disdain for his sister, Octavius granted to both his wife and his sister the right to be represented in public statuary, the right to control their own financial affairs, and the legal protection of their persons.[9] He made sure that public statues of these two women were quickly commissioned and displayed to publicize his respect. Antonius did not help himself when he divorced Octavia in 32 BCE and had her evicted from his house in Rome. Taking their two daughters with her, Octavia left the house with poise and dignity (**Document Two**).

Octavius's campaign of slowly sullying Antonius's reputation climaxed when he read Antonius's last will and testament to the Senate. How he obtained it or whether he forged parts of it are not known. At the meeting of the Senate, Octavius accused Antonius of harboring monarchical ambitions and wanting a separate empire in the east. He confirmed the Senate's and the public's worst fears—that a part of the Roman Empire would come under foreign and female rule. War was immediately declared against Cleopatra, not Antonius, in 32 BCE. The following year, Cleopatra and her consort were defeated at Actium. In 30 BCE Octavius conquered Egypt, making himself the undisputed leader of the Greco-Roman world.

ACT I

From Republic to Empire

The world that Octavius occupied was one that had been scarred by almost a century of war waged on behalf of aristocratic rivals for power. His faction, which slowly came together after his marriage to Livia and his successive victories over his rivals, dominated the Roman Senate, which approved all of Octavius's political reforms. He also helped his cause in the Senate by reducing the number of senators from 1,000 to 800, getting rid of those who opposed him, and distributing land to veterans of his army. Surveying all that he had conquered, Octavius believed that the empire, with its collection of lands, needed to be integrated and administered by a single, central authority instead of leaving its development to ad hoc and piecemeal decisions and edicts.[10]

During the wars, the Italian peninsula, its cities and its peoples, had suffered dearly. The countryside could not support the hungry city dwellers, and Rome in particular needed a regular and dependable supply of food. Socially, Roman customs, traditions, and religious practices had to be revived and revitalized. Politically, the vast majority of people wished for stability, security of property and person, protection from internal and external threats, and a period of peace so that they could reclaim their everyday lives.[11] To initiate reform that could address these demands, Octavius had

9. Wood, 33.

10. Southern, 102.

11. Ibid., 103–4.

to reinvent himself. The image of ruthless military commander vanquishing all who opposed him had to be shed. Accepting indefinite terms of an office or one which explicitly bestowed indefinite rule, like Perpetual Dictator, evoked images of kingship or Caesar's undisguised absolute authority, and they were not options for him (**Document Three**).

With such thoughts in mind, Octavius in 27 BCE formally announced that it was time for the Senate and the Roman people to decide the fate of the Republic. The Senate kept republican traditions and recognized Octavius's undisputed power by electing him consul yet again. In addition, the Senate conferred on him the honorary name of Augustus. From this time to his death, he was officially referred to as Augustus. Once Augustus felt that his position was secure, he declined the consulship and embraced the title of princeps, the title bestowed on the most prestigious man in the Senate, the person that other senators looked to for counsel and leadership. The actual power that Augustus held was never clarified, and the titles that he wore and then shed obscured the fact that he had established one-man rule, eviscerated the Republic's institutions, and created the Roman imperial state. In his testimonial to his accomplishments, *Res gestae,* Augustus claimed that he ruled because of his moral authority, dispensing wisdom and advice to beings of lesser experience and knowledge. Not only did he embrace the title of princeps but also the title conferred on him by the Senate in 2 BCE, *pater patriae* ("father of the country").

Claiming such authority and accepting these titles did not offend or threaten existing political traditions. The founders of the Republic had conceived the state as an extension of the Roman household, the basic unit of society and the foundation of government. In the Roman home, the adult male possessed authority over wives, children, and servants, or *patria potestas* ("power of a father"). The Republic was based on the concept that male heads of household represented their families and sat in the Senate. The senators, as the most privileged males in society, surrounded themselves with men from less powerful families—clients—and the senators held authority over these lesser males, who themselves had the power of the father in their households. The patron, the more privileged male, provided help and assistance when necessary to the client. In return, the client owed him financially and politically. A man could be both patron and client, and as a result, citizen males were connected through an intricate network of personal relationships. Thus, the Republic that Augustus inherited was a patriarchal society and to designate its most accomplished male, "father of the country" was not outside the understanding of most Romans.

Augustus's reforms went beyond changing Rome's administrative and political structures. He wished to revitalize Rome's moral and religious institutions, especially those pertaining to marriage, procreation, and the family. During his long rule, Augustus enacted extensive social legislation that attempted to restore traditional

Roman virtues, encourage thrift and stamp out corruption, secure the Roman elite's dominant position in politics, and restore the Roman family.[12] In these endeavors he was greatly aided by Livia, his wife.

Act II

Civic Morality in the Early Empire

Like other Romans, Augustus associated private and public morality with the maintenance of a well-ordered state and pleasing the gods. To appease the gods, he began a crusade to revive temperance and morality, especially among the traditional ruling families. To maintain the stability of the state, he believed that the patrician class had to be replenished and revitalized. His laws concerning marriage, procreation, and the family assumed that Rome's elites were deliberately avoiding marriage and parenthood to such an extent that the continuity of the ruling class was at risk.[13] Thus, his social legislation was as much about ensuring that the patrician class replicated itself as it was about restoring Roman values.

Noblemen appeared to be shunning legitimate marriage in favor of the single life, taking pleasure when and wherever they wished, and entertaining and cultivating rich relatives and friends while waiting for their inheritances to materialize. In addition, when elite men did marry, they did not always marry women of their class. By law, senators were prohibited from marrying outside of their class. In an argument with Augustus as reported by the historian Dio Cassius, senators maintained that Roman women were difficult and not easily controlled. Therefore, they resorted to marrying slaves whom they had freed. These slaves owed everything to them and thus would be more willing to obey them as their wives.[14]

Another symbol of social disorder and disharmony was the elite Roman woman who had moved outside the control of her father, husband, or brother and who had assumed control over her person and property, abandoned her domestic duties, and preferred childlessness to children and family. During the civil unrest, Roman noblewomen did have greater public visibility and wider roles. They gained more power over property and their persons as marriage laws and customs underwent dramatic changes during the late Republic.

Prior to the third century BCE, when women married, they were legally transferred from their father's authority to their husband's. However, "this ancient form of marriage called marriage with *manus* had been largely superseded by the so-called free marriage by the third century BCE."[15] Free marriage, or marriage without *manus*, resulted from the transformation of

12. Ibid., 146.

13. Susan Dixon, *The Roman Mother* (Norman: University of Oklahoma Press, 1988), 23.

14. Southern, 148.

15. Anne Ewing Hickey, *Women of the Roman Aristocracy as Christian Monastics* (Ann Arbor: University of Michigan Research Press, 1987), 49.

Rome from a small republic into a world empire. During the third and second centuries, female wealth increased as a result of a decrease in the male population. Because of the high casualty rates from Rome's wars of expansion, women now inherited land, property, and wealth without competition from brothers. Free marriage gave women considerable leverage against the authority of their husbands and enhanced their property rights. However, it did not make a woman legally independent. Theoretically, she was still under the authority of her father. If the father was not available, the state appointed a guardian who would perform the function of paterfamilias. The strict requirement of guardianship for women living outside male *potestas* was evaded by assertive Roman women until it became an empty form. Roman women did not have formal political rights or legal status equal to men's, but they could inherit great wealth and could therefore wield informal social and political power.

Political marriages and the absence of husbands for long periods of time meant that some women could pursue liaisons outside of marriage. Historians of the first centuries BCE and CE would have their readers believe that women of these centuries lived to feed their sexual desires and to enjoy pleasures outside of their marriages.[16] Augustus had promoted such images during his propaganda campaign against Marcus Antonius. He often depicted Antonius's ally and lover, the Egyptian queen Cleopatra, as a woman of insatiable appetites that extended from the bedroom to world domination.

Augustus's courtship of and marriage to Livia had provided fodder for their opponents during the civil war, but their indiscreet beginnings were overshadowed by their public show of marital harmony, fidelity, and proper behavior. "Ovid, the poet, justified Livia's earlier divorce by claiming that no husband but Augustus was worthy of her, while Horace describes her . . . as 'a women rejoicing in only one husband.'"[17] The only immediate flaw in this highly public marriage and perfect imperial family was the inability of Livia and Augustus to conceive a child.

Augustan laws on marriage and reproduction were a reminder to the Roman elite that marriages should be contracted between proper social groups and that their property and political power must be transferred through familial lines. The continuous presence of Rome's elite families in government had created a prosperous and formidable imperial state, and Augustus wished to maintain the moral and social structures that had brought about this success. Augustan legislation could be applied to all citizens, but the punishments were specifically designed to penalize Roman elites.[18]

Bills passed between 18 BCE and 9 CE brought into the public arena

16. Elaine Fantham et al., *Women in the Classical World* (New York: Oxford University Press, 1994), 284.

17. Wood, 76.

18. Dixon, 86.

issues of marriage and reproduction, which had been under private control and discretion. These laws penalized men who did not marry before the age of twenty-five and women who did not marry or who remained unmarried after the death of their husbands. Women were rewarded for having more than three children by bestowing on them "the right of three children." This honor allowed them to be legal persons, without a male guardian. Augustus lectured men who did not have children and spoke of the state's need for married men who had children (**Document Four**). Those who did have multiple children stood to gain a better public office, and senators and their descendants were prohibited from marrying outside their class. Ulpianus reported the spirit of this clause: "By the *lex Julia* senators and their descendants are forbidden to marry freedwomen, or women who have themselves followed the profession of the stage."[19] Women's and men's behavior within marriage became matters of state scrutiny and regulation. Adultery was made a punishable offense, although wives' indiscretions were treated quite differently from those of their husbands. These laws sought to bring women's sexual behavior in line with the standards of an idealized, traditional social order and to ensure the legitimacy of the offspring. The effect that these laws had on Roman family life is not clear. However, Augustus remained convinced of the importance of restoring Roman values and morality and used his family as examples and symbols of the desired standards.

Livia represented herself as the ideal standard for upper-class women, borrowing symbols from Roman legend and mythology. Weaving cloth for husband and children was a powerful symbol of a wife's virtue and devotion, and Livia played the role of "first lady" by weaving Octavius's garments in order to set an example for other Roman wives. Augustus appeared in public and bragged that his wife had spun and woven the clothing that he was wearing.[20] Livia participated in public displays of marital harmony and togetherness. She often accompanied her husband on trips to the provinces and sometimes took her son, Tiberius, with them. If he traveled without her, Livia made sure that her husband's homecoming was something of a public display.

Livia also used Roman religion as a platform from which to demonstrate her piety and womanly virtue; using her wealth, she sponsored the construction of the Porticus Liviae, which celebrated good wives and the virtue of marital harmony. Her private sponsorship of this public building and many others set the example of how private wealth should be used to promote public interests, an issue Augustus believed was crucial to restoring the stability of the Roman state.[21] He too used public works to provide both living and symbolic examples of his goals and values. To celebrate his great successes and Rome's new-found stability and peace, the *Ara Pacis Augustae*

19. Ulpianus, *Epitomé*, 13–14, quoted in Fantham, 305.

20. Ibid., 77.

21. Wood, 78.

("Altar of Augustan Peace") was built. On the south side of the altar, mortal women and children were represented along with men for the first time in Roman public art. Of course, the people being depicted in the relief were members of the imperial family—Livia, Julia, Julia's children, and other family members. The procession not only symbolized Augustus's bringing of peace but that his family, through the reproduction of heirs, would guarantee that the transfer of power would be done peacefully through the prolific Julio-Claudian dynasty. Adopted by Augustus, Livia's son would inherit the throne from his stepfather, thus avoiding a struggle for power. As in his legislation, Augustus sought to shape and regulate marriage, parenthood, and gender roles through public statuary and propaganda.

Livia promoted familial power in other ways. She was able to venture into nontraditional arenas, partly because of her independent holdings and partly because of the evolving nature of Roman imperial politics. She invited into her house her extended family and clients from abroad. This included her two sons, Tiberius and Drusus, and Augustus's daughter Julia and her offspring. From this set of children and their children, the Julio-Claudian dynasty would be drawn. Livia's influence was reflected in the active role that she played in Augustus's decisions concerning his heir. Suetonius remarked how this was "a clear case in which her private role as materfamilias intersected with public affairs."[22] Livia also cultivated a circle of women who had similar influence in public and private affairs. Her sister-in-law, Octavia, was one such woman, while others were clients, like the Jewish princess Salome, the sister of King Herod. Livia wielded unprecedented power for a woman, just as her husband wielded unprecedented power for a Roman man (**Document Five**). She and her husband seized the opportunities created by Rome's disintegrating social and political order, and together they created a new institution that tolerated female authority for the good of the family—the imperial family.

Finale

Livia and Augustus's relationship united family interests and the affairs of state. When Augustus fell sick in 14 CE, she used her position as wife and mother to hurry to her husband's side and to recall Tiberius from his trip to the provinces. Awaiting the arrival of her son, Livia admitted very few people to her husband's deathbed, and it was only after her son's arrival that public notice of her husband's death was announced. It is not known whether Augustus died before or after Tiberius's arrival, but Livia made sure that there would be no question concerning the transfer of imperial power. Tiberius was immediately named Augustus's successor by the Senate.

Augustus ensured his wife's continued influence and wealth in his will

22. Wood, 80.

by adopting her into the Julian family, designating her as Julia Augusta, and removing any limitations on her rights to inherit a third of his estate. When Augustus was deified after his death, Livia was made the priestess of his cult. The Senate tried to recognize her uncontested authority by conferring the title *Mater Patriae* ("Mother of her Country"), but Tiberius vetoed this bill. He wished to avoid such nontraditional titles and honors that were too extravagant and too exalted, fearing the appearance of monarchical ambitions. Even when she died in 29 CE at the age of 86, Tiberius did not attend her funeral and did not allow her to be deified. Did Tiberius resent his mother's influence? Such emotions are impossible to discern, but it was common knowledge that Tiberius owed his position to her and that until her death, her influence and authority were widely respected by members of the Senate, some of whom owed their lives to her because of her intercessions with Augustus and Tiberius on their behalf.

Augustus's initial successes rested on his ability to vanquish all of his enemies and to use his military strength to secure political rule. The Senate recognized this fact in 27 BCE when they asked him to safeguard the Republic and awarded him the title of Augustus. But raw power was not his only ambition. Augustus refashioned himself into a defender of the Republic and Roman traditions and values, and he reinforced this image with his modest behavior and restraint. He practiced patience and tact in his dealings with the Senate, giving the impression that it had important contributions, equal to his own, to make.[23] He unabashedly used his family for state and dynastic purposes, and he had help from Livia in this endeavor.

Augustus and Livia consciously and carefully cultivated the image of the Julio-Claudian clan as guarantors of peace and prosperity for the Roman state in the past, present, and future. They presented themselves as the dignified and protective father and the fertile and virtuous mother who would lead the Roman people and their children to health and happiness. This vision of the family was transmitted all over the Roman Empire through works of art, coins, shrines, ceremonies, buildings, and carefully choreographed public appearances by members of the family. Imperial family members were also expected to possess the same modesty, humility, and restraint as their parents. Later members of the Julio-Claudian dynasty who failed to follow the path set out by Augustus and Livia learned that public displays of arrogance, extravagance, and immorality could spell disaster. The goals and ideals of Augustus and Livia continued to haunt their successors in the centuries that followed.

23. Southern, 197.

Documents

DOCUMENT ONE

Suetonius
Life of Augustus

Suetonius (Caius Suetonius Tranquillus, 69–140 CE) was the private secretary of Emperor Hadrian. In this position, he was able to gather together all sorts of anecdotes and gossip about the early emperors. His biographies are not only lively and scandalous at times, but they also provide excellent insights into the thinking of Romans about the role that imperial women played in making the empire. Suetonius was taken as a model by many later biographers. In this passage, Suetonius describes Augustus's sexual and social improprieties. What acts does Augustus commit and what are their ramifications? Can such sexual and scandalous anecdotes be believed when used for political purposes?

. . . 68. As a young man Augustus was accused of various improprieties. For instance, Sextus Pompey jeered at his effeminacy; Mark Antony alleged that Julius Caesar made him submit to unnatural relations as the price of adoption; Antony's brother Lucius added that after sacrificing his virtue to Caesar, Augustus had sold his favours to Aulus Hirtius, the Governor-General of Spain, for 3,000 gold pieces, and that he used to soften the hair on his legs by singeing them with red-hot walnut shells. One day at the Theatre an actor came on the stage representing a eunuch priest of Cybele, the Mother of the Gods; and, as he played his timbrel, another actor exclaimed:

> 'Look, how this invert's finger beats the drum!'

Since the Latin phrase could also mean: 'Look how this invert's finger *sways the world*!' the audience mistook the line for a hint at Augustus and broke into enthusiastic applause.

69. Not even his friends could deny that he often committed adultery, though of course they said, in justification, that he did so for reasons of state, not simple passion—he wanted to discover what his enemies were at by getting intimate with their wives or daughters. Mark Antony accused him not only of indecent haste in marrying Livia, but of hauling an ex-consul's wife from her husband's dining-room into the bedroom—before his eyes, too! He brought the woman back, says Antony, blushing to the ears and with her hair in disorder.

Antony also writes that Scribonia was divorced for having said a little too much when 'a rival' got her claws into Augustus; and that his friends used to behave like Toranius, the slave-dealer, in arranging his pleasures for him—they would strip mothers of families, or grown girls, of their clothes and inspect them as though they were up for sale. A racy letter of Antony's survives, written before he and Augustus had quarreled privately or publicly:

> 'What has come over you? Do you object to my sleeping with Cleopatra? But we are married; and it is not even as though this were anything new—the affair started nine years ago. And what about you? Are you faithful to Livia Drusilla? My congratulations if, when this letter arrives, you have not been in bed with Tertuillia, or Terentilla, or Rufilla, or Salvia Titisenia—or all of them. Does it really matter so much where, or with whom, you perform the sexual act?'

70. Then there was Augustus's private banquet, known as 'The Feast of the Divine Twelve', which caused a public scandal. The guests came dressed as gods or goddesses, Augustus himself represented Apollo; and our authority for this is not only a spiteful letter of Antony's, which names all the twelve, but the following well-known anonymous lampoon:

Those rogues engaged the services
  Of a stage manager;
So Mallia found six goddesses
  And six gods facing her!

Apollo's part was lewdly played
  By impious Caesar; he
Made merry at a table laid
For gross debauchery.

Such scandalous proceedings shocked
  The Olympians. One by one
They quit and Jove, his thunders mocked,
  Vacates the golden throne.

What made the scandal even worse was that the banquet took place at a time of food shortage; and on the next day people were shouting: 'The Gods have gobbled all the grain!' or 'Caesar is Apollo, true—but he's Apollo of the Torments'—this being the god's aspect in one City district. Some found Augustus a good deal too fond of expensive furniture, Corinthian bronzes, and the gaming table . . .

DOCUMENT TWO

Octavia, Livia, and Cleopatra

Livia and Octavia were held up as examples of traditional matronly virtue and marital respectability; Cleopatra represented the excesses of extravagance, drunkenness, and sexual impropriety. In the passages below, one from Plutarch and the other from Horace, compare and contrast these Roman matrons and the Egyptian queen.

A. Plutarch

Life of Antony

Plutarch (?46–120 CE) was a Greek essayist and biographer who traveled extensively through the Empire in the first century CE. His work The Parallel Lives *is a series of forty-six biographies that compare one Greek life with one comparable Roman life. The purpose of these biographies was to reveal the essential character of each historical figure and to explore the moral implications of his or her actions. He uses a lot of anecdotal material and his facts are not always accurate. In the selection below, Plutarch describes Octavia's relationship with her husband Marcus Antonius (Anthony). What types of judgments does he make about each? What is his assessment of Cleopatra?*

. . . But at Rome Octavia was desirous of sailing to Antony, and Caesar gave her permission to do so, as the majority say, not as a favour to her, but in order that, in case she were neglected and treated with scorn, he might have plausible ground for war. When Octavia arrived at Athens,[1] she received letters from Antony in which he bade her remain there and told her of his expedition. Octavia, although she saw through the pretext and was distressed, nevertheless wrote to Antony asking whither he would have the things sent which she was bringing to him. For she was bringing a great quantity of clothing for his soldiers, many beasts of burden, and money and gifts for the officers and friends about him; and besides this, two thousand picked soldiers equipped as praetorian cohorts with splendid armour. These things were announced to Antony by a certain Niger, a friend of his who had been sent from Octavia, and he added such praises of her as was fitting and deserved.

But Cleopatra perceived that Octavia was coming into a contest at close quarters with her, and feared lest, if she added to the dignity of her character and the power of Caesar her pleasurable society and her assiduous attentions to Antony, she would become invincible and get complete control over her husband. She

1. In 35 B.C.

therefore pretended to be passionately in love with Antony herself, and reduced her body by slender diet; she put on a look of rapture when Antony drew near, and one of faintness and melancholy when he went away. She would contrive to be often seen in tears, and then would quickly wipe the tears away and try to hide them, as if she would not have Antony notice them. And she practised these arts while Antony was intending to go up from Syria to join the Mede. Her flatterers, too, were industrious in her behalf, and used to revile Antony as hard-hearted and unfeeling, and as the destroyer of a mistress who was devoted to him and him alone. For Octavia, they said, had married him as a matter of public policy and for the sake of her brother, and enjoyed the name of wedded wife; but Cleopatra, who was queen of so many people, was called Antony's beloved, and she did not shun this name nor disdain it, as long as she could see him and live with him; but if she were driven away from him she would not survive it. At last, then, they so melted and enervated the man that he became fearful lest Cleopatra should throw away her life, and went back to Alexandria, putting off the Mede until the summer season, although Parthia was said to be suffering from internal dissensions. However, he went up and brought the king once more into friendly relations, and after betrothing to one of his sons by Cleopatra one of the king's daughters who was still small, he returned, his thoughts being now directed towards the civil war.

B. Horace

Ode XXXVII

Horace (Quintus Horace Flaccus, 65 BCE–8 BCE) was educated in Rome and Athens and became a literary figure when his first book of satires appeared in 35 BCE. He was an unrivaled lyric poet. His poems betray the influence of Greek poets, but as his poetry matures, he displays a mastery of Latin verse. During his lifetime, he enjoyed the patronage of one of Augustus's most important allies. In the Odes, *Horace describes the fall of Cleopatra. What are his views of the Egyptian queen? Compare his views with those of Plutarch on Cleopatra and on the womanly virtues of Octavia.*

The Fall of Cleopatra

NUNC EST BIBENDUM, NUNC PEDE LIBERO. . .

Now is the time for drinking, O my friends!
Now with a free foot beating the earth in dance!
    Deck the couches of the gods
        with Salian feasts! before this day

it would have been wrong to bring forth
our Caecuban wine from the cellars of
    our ancestors, while a demented queen
        was plotting to destroy the Capitol

and lay waste the Empire
with her contaminated crew of followers
    polluted by disease—she, weak enough
        to hope for anything and drunk

with the delights of her hitherto good fortune.
But her frenzy diminished when
    but a single galley escaped the flames
        and Caesar sobered her mind,

maddened by Mareotic wine,
to the fears of harsh reality
    pursuing her in his galleys
        as she fled from Italy

as the hawk pursues the gentle dove
or the swift hunter the hare
    on the plains of snowy Thessaly
        to clap into chains the ill-fated monster.

But she, seeking a more noble death,
did not, like a woman, dread the sword,
    or search in her swift ship
        for some secret hiding place along the shore.

She even dared, with countenance serene,
to behold her palace plunged in affliction
    and she was bold enough
        to take into her hands

the irritated asps that she might absorb
the deadly venom into her body.
    So in premeditated death
        fiercer yet she became,

Scorning to be led off in triumph
on hostile Liburnian ships.
    She, no longer a queen
        but a woman unyielding, unhumbled.

DOCUMENT THREE

Augustus and Imperial Rule

A. Tacitus

The Annals, Book 1

Tacitus (Cornelius Tacitus, 55–117 CE) was a Roman historian who examined, in The Annals, *the beginnings of the Roman Empire. His account concentrates on character sketches, the transformation of Roman institutions, and morality. Only twelve of his books (chapters)—Books 1 to 6 and 11 to 16—survived. The surviving books of the* Annals *tell of the reign of Tiberius, of the last years of Claudius, and of the first years of Nero. In the selections below, Tacitus describes the process by which Augustus consolidated his power and how his stepson, Tiberius, became his heir. How does Tacitus portray Augustus's rule? Who or what affects Tiberius's ascension?*

1. Rome at the beginning was ruled by kings. Freedom and the consulship were established by Lucius Brutus. Dictatorships were held for a temporary crisis. The power of the decemvirs did not last beyond two years, nor was the consular jurisdiction of the military tribunes of long duration. The despotisms of China and Sulla were brief; the rule of Pompeius and of Crassus soon yielded before Caesar; the arms of Lepidus and Antonius before Augustus; who, when the world was wearied by civil strife, subjected it to empire under the title of "Prince. . . ."

2. When after the destruction of Brutus and Cassius there was no longer any army of the Commonwealth, when Pompeius was crushed in Sicily, and when, with Lepidus pushed aside and Antonius slain, even the Julian faction had only Cæsar left to lead it, then, dropping the title of triumvir, and giving out that he was a Consul, and was satisfied with a tribune's authority for the protection of the people, Augustus won over the soldiers with gifts, the populace with cheap corn, and all men with the sweets of repose, and so grew greater by degrees, while he concentrated in himself the functions of the Senate, the magistrates, and the laws. He was wholly unopposed, for the boldest spirits had fallen in battle, or in the proscription, while the remaining nobles, the readier they were to be slaves, were raised the higher by wealth and promotion, so that, aggrandised by revolution, they preferred the safety of the present to the dangerous past. Nor did the provinces dislike that condition of affairs, for they distrusted the government of the Senate and the people, because of the rivalries between the leading men and the rapacity of the officials, while the protection of the laws was unavailing, as they were continually deranged by violence, intrigue, and finally by corruption.

3. Augustus meanwhile, as supports to his despotism, raised to the pontificate and curule ædileship Claudius Marcellus, his sister's son, while a mere stripling, and Marcus Agrippa, of humble birth, a good soldier, and one who had shared his victory, to two consecutive consulships, and as Marcellus soon afterwards died, he also accepted him as his son-in-law. Tiberius Nero and Claudius Drusus, his stepsons, he honoured with imperial titles, although his own family was as yet undiminished. For he had admitted the children of Agrippa, Caius and Lucius, into the house of the Cæsars; and before they had yet laid aside the dress of boyhood he had most fervently desired, with an outward show of reluctance, that they should be entitled "princes of the youth," and be consuls-elect. . . .

4. Thus the State had been revolutionised, and there was not a vestige left of the old sound morality. Stript of equality, all looked up to the commands of a sovereign without the least apprehension for the present, while Augustus in the vigour of life, could maintain his own position, that of his house, and the general tranquillity. When in advanced old age, he was worn out by a sickly frame, and the end was near and new prospects opened, a few spoke in vain of the blessings of freedom, but most people dreaded and some longed for war. The popular gossip of the large majority fastened itself variously on their future masters. . . . Tiberius Nero was of mature years, and had established his fame in war, but he had the old arrogance inbred in the Claudian family, and many symptoms of a cruel temper, though they were repressed, now and then broke out. He had also from earliest infancy been reared in an imperial house; consulships and triumphs had been heaped on him in his younger days; even in the years which, on the pretext of seclusion he spent in exile at Rhodes, he had had no thoughts but of wrath, hypocrisy, and secret sensuality. . . .

B. Augustus

Res gestae

At the end of his reign, Augustus recorded the "things that he had accomplished" during his rule. He presented his rise to power in favorable terms, how he saved Rome, reestablished peace and stability, and gave the people prosperity. In this selection, Augustus describes the appreciation of the Roman people. How do they show their appreciation? How does Augustus describe his ascent to complete power? Did historians like Tacitus agree with his view?

. . . 34. In my sixth and seventh consulships, when I had extinguished the flames of civil war, after receiving by universal consent the absolute control of affairs, I transferred the republic from my own control to the will of the senate and the Roman people. For this service on my part I was given the title of Augustus by decree of the senate, and the doorposts of my house were covered with laurels by public act, and a civic crown was fixed above my door, and a golden shield was placed in the Curia Julia whose inscription testified that the senate and the Roman people gave me this in recognition of my valour, my clemency, my justice, and my piety. After that time I took precedence of all in rank, but of power I possessed no more than those who were my colleagues in any magistracy.

35. While I was administering my thirteenth consulship the senate and the equestrian order and the entire Roman people gave me the title of Father of my Country, and decreed that this title should be inscribed upon the vestibule of my house and in the senate-house and in the Forum Augustum beneath the quadriga* erected in my honour by decree of the senate. At the time of writing this I was in my seventy-sixth year.

*Chariot

DOCUMENT FOUR

Dio Cassius

Roman History, Book 56

In this selection, Dio Cassius describes Augustus's speech to the young married men and bachelors of the equestrian class who were complaining about the new laws regarding the unmarried and childless. How does Augustus justify his laws governing private conduct? What are the duties of Roman citizens, male and female?

[Augustus to Married Men]

. . . Though you are but few altogether, in comparison with the vast throng that inhabits this city, and are far less numerous than the others, who are unwilling to perform any of their duties, yet for this very reason I for my part praise you the more, and am heartily grateful to you because you have shown yourselves obedient and are helping to replenish the fatherland. For it is by lives so conducted that the Romans of later days will become a mighty multitude. We were at first a mere handful, you know, but when we had recourse to marriage and begot us children, we came to surpass all mankind not only in the manliness of our citizens but in the size of our population as well. Bearing this in mind, we must console the mortal side of our nature with an endless succession of generations that shall be like the torch-bearers in a race, so that through one another we may render immortal the one side of our nature in which we fall short of divine bliss. It was for this cause most of all that that first and greatest god, who fashioned us, divided the race of mortals in twain, making one half of it male and the other half female, and implanted in them love and compulsion to mutual intercourse, making their association fruitful, that by the young continually born he might in a way render even mortality eternal. Indeed, even of the gods themselves some are accounted male and others female; and the tradition prevails that some have begotten others and some have been begotten of others. So even among those beings, who need no such device, marriage and the begetting of children have been approved as a noble thing.

. . . For is there anything better than a wife who is chaste, domestic, a good house-keeper, a rearer of children; one to gladden you in health, to tend you in sickness; to be your partner in good fortune, to console you in misfortune; to restrain the mad passion of youth and to temper the unseasonable harshness of old age? And is it not a delight to acknowledge a child who shows the endowments of both parents, to nurture and educate it, at once the physical and the spiritual image of yourself, so that in its growth another self lives again? Is it not blessed, on departing from life, to leave behind as successor and heir to your blood and substance one that is your own, sprung from your own loins, and to have only the human part of you waste away, while you live in the child as your successor, so that you need not fall into the hands of aliens, as in war, nor perish utterly, as in a pestilence? These, now, are the private advantages that accrue to those who marry and beget children; but for the State, for whose sake we ought to do many things that are even distasteful to us, how excellent and how necessary it is, if cities and peoples are to exist, and if you are to rule others and all the world is to obey you, that there should be a multitude of men, to till the earth in time of peace, to make voyages, practise arts, and follow handicrafts, and, in time of war, to protect what we already have with all the greater zeal because of family ties and to replace those that fall by others. Therefore, men,—for you alone may properly be called men,—and fathers,—for you are as worthy to hold this title as I myself,—I love you and praise you for this; and I not only bestow the prizes I have already offered but will distinguish you still further by other honours and offices, so that you may not only reap great benefits yourselves but may also leave them to your children undiminished. . . .

[Augustus to Bachelors]

. . . A strange experience has been mine, O—what shall I call you? Men? But you are not performing any of the offices of men. Citizens? But for all that you are doing, the city is perishing. Romans? But you are undertaking to blot out this name altogether. Well, at any rate, whatever you are and by whatever name you delight to be called, mine has been an astonishing experience; for though I am always doing everything to promote an increase of population among you and am now about to rebuke you, I grieve to see that there are a great many of you. I could rather have wished that those others to whom I have just spoken were as numerous as you prove to be, and that preferably you were ranged with them, or otherwise did not exist at all. For you, heedless alike of the providence of the gods and of the watchful care of your forefathers, are bent upon annihilating our entire race and making it in truth mortal, are bent upon destroying and bringing to an end the entire Roman nation. For what seed of human beings would be left, if all the rest of mankind should do what you are doing? For you have become their leaders, and so would rightly bear the responsibility for the universal destruction. And even if no others emulate you, would you not be justly hated for the very reason that you overlook what no one else would overlook, and neglect what no one else would neglect, introducing customs and practices which, if imitated, would lead to the extermination of all mankind, and, if abhorred, would end in your own punishment? . . . For you are committing murder in not begetting in the first place those who ought to be your descendants; you are committing sacrilege in putting an end to the names and honours of your ancestors; and you are guilty of impiety in that you are abolishing your families which were instituted by the gods, and destroying the greatest of offerings to them,—human life,—thus overthrowing their rites and their temples. Moreover, you are destroying the State by disobeying its laws, and you are betraying your country by rendering her barren and childless; nay more, you are laying her even with the dust by making her destitute of future inhabitants. For it is human beings that constitute a city, we are told, not houses or porticos or marketplaces empty of men. . . .

Indeed, it was never permitted to any man, even in olden times, to neglect marriage and the begetting of children; but from the very outset, when the government was first established, strict laws were made regarding these matters, and subsequently many decrees were passed by both the senate and the people, which it would be superfluous to enumerate here. I, now, have increased the penalties for the disobedient, in order that through fear of becoming liable to them you might be brought to your senses; and to the obedient I have offered more numerous and greater prizes than are given for any other display of excellence, in order that for this reason, if for no other, you might be persuaded to marry and beget children. Yet you have not striven for any of the recompenses nor feared any of the penalties, but have shown contempt for all these measures and have trodden them all underfoot, as if you were not living in a civilized community. You talk, forsooth, about this 'free' and 'untrammelled' life that you have adopted, without wives and without children; but you are not a whit better than brigands or the most savage of beasts. For surely it is not your delight in a solitary existence that leads you to live without wives, nor is there one of you who either eats alone or sleeps alone; no, what you want is to have full liberty for wantonness and licentiousness. . . . For you see yourselves how much more numerous you are than the married men, when you ought by this time to have provided us with as many children besides, or rather with several times your number. How otherwise can families continue? How can the State be preserved, if we neither marry nor have children? . . .

DOCUMENT FIVE

Roman Historians on Livia

In the first three excerpts of this selection, Dio Cassius, Suetonius, and Tacitus discuss Livia's public role. Contrast Livia's passive image promoted by her and Augustus and the real power she enjoyed, as described by these three historians.

In the fourth excerpt, Tacitus describes a debate in the Senate concerning the issue of whether wives should accompany their husbands to the provinces. The debate reveals his attitudes toward women, their nature, and their influence and power. What are these attitudes?

A. Dio Cassius

Roman History, Book 57

For she occupied a very exalted station, far above all women of former days, so that she could at any time receive the senate and such of the people as wished to greet her in her house; and this fact was entered in the public records. The letters of Tiberius bore for a time her name, also, and communications were addressed to both alike. Except that she never ventured to enter the senate-chamber or the camps or the public assemblies, she undertook to manage everything as if she were sole ruler. For in the time of Augustus she had possessed the greatest influence and she always declared that it was she who had made Tiberius emperor; consequently she was not satisfied to rule on equal terms with him, but wished to take precedence over him. . . .

. . . Among the many excellent utterances of hers that are reported are the following. Once, when some naked men met her and were to be put to death in consequence, she saved their lives by saying that to chaste women such men are no whit different from statues. When someone asked her how and by what course of action she had obtained such a commanding influence over Augustus, she answered that it was by being scrupulously chaste herself, doing gladly whatever pleased him, not meddling with any of his affairs, and, in particular, by pretending neither to hear or nor to notice the favorites of his passion.

B. Suetonius

Life of Tiberius

. . . 50. Tiberius's first hostile action against his own family was when his brother Drusus wrote to him privately suggesting that they should jointly persuade

Augustus to restore the Republican constitution; Tiberius placed the letter in Augustus's hands. After coming to power he showed so little pity for his exiled wife Julia that he did not have the decency to confirm Augustus's decree which merely forbade her to set foot outside the town of Reggio; but restricted her to a single house where visitors were forbidden. He even deprived her of the annual sums hitherto paid her by Augustus, as both his daughter and his daughter-in-law, on the pretext that no mention of these had appeared in his will and that consequently, under common law, she was no longer entitled to draw them. Tiberius then complained that his mother Livia vexed him by wanting to be co-ruler of the Empire; which was why he avoided frequent meetings or long private talks with her. Although he did occasionally need and follow Livia's advice, he disliked people to think of him as giving it serious consideration. A senatorial decree adding 'Son of Livia' as well as 'Son of Augustus' to his honorifics so deeply offended him that he vetoed proposals to confer 'Mother of the Country' or any similarly high-sounding title on her. What is more, he often warned Livia to remember that she was a woman and must not interfere in affairs of state. He became especially insistent on this point when a fire broke out near the Temple of Vesta and news reached him that Livia was directing the civilian and military fire-fighters in person, as though Augustus were still alive, and urging them to redouble their efforts.

51. Afterwards Tiberius quarreled openly with his mother. The story goes that she repeatedly urged him to enroll in the jurors' list the name of a man who had been granted a citizenship. Tiberius agreed to do so on one condition—that the entry should be marked 'forced upon the Emperor by his mother.' Livia lost her temper and produced from a strong-box some of Augustus's old letters to her commenting on Tiberius's sour and stubborn character. Annoyance with her for hoarding these documents so long, and then spitefully confronting him with them, is said to have been his main reason for retirement to Capri. At all events he visited her exactly once in the last three years of her life, and only for an hour or two at that; and when she presently fell sick, made no effort to repeat the visit. Livia then died, and he spoke of attending her funeral, but did not come. After several days her corpse grew so corrupt and noisome that he sent it to have it buried; but vetoed her deification on the pretext that she had herself forbidden this. He also annulled her will, and began taking his revenge on all her friends and confidants—even those whom, as she died, she had appointed to take charge of her funeral rites—and went so far as to condemn one of them, a knight, to the treadmill.

C. Tacitus

The Annals, Book 1

. . . She [Livia] too, was flattered a great deal by the senate. It was variously proposed that she should be called 'parent' and 'mother' of her country; and a large body of opinion held that the words 'son of Julia' ought to form part of the emperor's name. He, however, repeatedly asserted that only reasonable honours must be paid to women—and that, in regard to compliments paid to himself, he would observe a comparable moderation. In reality, however, he was jealous and nervous, and regarded this elevation of a woman as derogatory to his own person. He would not even allow her to be allotted an official attendant, and forbade an Altar of Adoption and other honours of the kind. . . .

C. Tacitus

The Annals, Book 3

. . . 33. During this debate Severus Cæcina proposed that no magistrate who had obtained a province should be accompanied by his wife. He began by recounting at length how harmoniously he had lived with his wife, who had borne him six children, and how in his own home he had observed what he was proposing for the public, by having kept her in Italy, though he had himself served forty campaigns in various provinces. "With good reason," he said, "had it been formerly decided that women were not to be taken among our allies or into foreign countries. A train of women involves delays through luxury in peace and through panic in war, and converts a Roman army on the march into the likeness of a barbarian progress. Not only is the sex feeble and unequal to hardship, but, when it has liberty, it is spiteful, intriguing and greedy of power. They show themselves off among the soldiers and have the centurions at their beck. Lately a woman has presided at the drill of the cohorts and the evolutions of the legions. You should yourselves bear in mind that, whenever men are accused of extortion, most of the charges are directed against the wives. It is to these that the vilest of the provincials instantly attach themselves; it is they who undertake and settle business; two persons receive homage when they appear; there are two centres of government, and the women's orders are the more despotic and intemperate. Formerly they were restrained by the Oppian and other laws; now, loosed from every bond, they rule our houses, our tribunals, even our armies."

34. A few heard this speech with approval, but the majority clamorously objected that there was no proper motion on the subject, and that Cæcina was no fit censor on so grave an issue. Presently Valerius Messalinus, Messala's son, in whom the father's eloquence was reproduced, replied that much of the sternness of antiquity had been changed into a better and more genial system. "Rome," he said, "is not now, as formerly, beset with wars, nor are the provinces hostile. A few concessions are made to the wants of women, but such as are not even a burden to their husbands' homes, much less to the allies. In all other respects man and wife share alike, and this arrangement involves no trouble in peace. War of course requires that men should be unincumbered, but when they return what worthier solace can they have after their hardships than a wife's

society? But some wives have abandoned themselves to scheming and rapacity. Well; even among our magistrates, are not many subject to various passions? Still, that is not a reason for sending no one into a province. Husbands have often been corrupted by the vices of their wives. Are then all unmarried men blameless? The Oppian laws were formerly adopted to meet the political necessities of the time, and subsequently there was some remission and mitigation of them on grounds of expediency. It is idle to shelter our own weakness under other names; for it is the husband's fault if the wife transgresses propriety. Besides, it is wrong that because of the imbecility of one or two men, all husbands should be cut off from their partners in prosperity and adversity. And further, a sex naturally weak will be thus left to itself and be at the mercy of its own voluptuousness and the passions of others. Even with the husband's personal vigilance the marriage tie is scarcely preserved inviolate. What would happen were it for a number of years to be forgotten, just as in a divorce? You must not check vices abroad without remembering the scandals of the capital."

Drusus added a few words on his own experience as a husband. "Princes," he said, "must often visit the extremities of their empire. How often had the Divine Augustus traveled to the West and to the East accompanied by Livia? He had himself gone to Illyricum and, should it be expedient, he would go to other countries, not always however with a contented mind, if he had to tear himself from a much loved wife, the mother of his many children."

35. Cæcina's motion was thus defeated. . . .

Questions

1. What is the significance of family and marriage in Rome's political arena? How does family affect Augustus's rise to power?
2. What were Octavia's and Livia's duties as daughters and sisters of elite Roman men?
3. Why was it necessary to call attention to private and public behavior and to accentuate the differences between Octavia, Livia, and Cleopatra? To what extent could accusations of sexual impropriety be believed when used against political rivals?
4. Why did Augustus reform private and public behavior? How did these changes further his goals as absolute ruler of the Roman Empire?
5. What were the duties and rights of Roman men and women?
6. What was the significance of the family for the transfer of power from Augustus to his successor? To what extent was the state simply an extension of family?
7. What role did Livia play in the dynastic politics? How did she influence Augustus in policy? In what ways did she define a new role of empress?
8. Dio Cassius, Suetonius, Plutarch, and Tacitus wrote their histories several generations after Augustus and Livia died and are, in fact, secondary sources. How can we assess their historical accuracy?

Suggested Readings

Chauveau, Michel. *Cleopatra: Beyond the Myth.* Trans. David Lorton. Ithaca, NY: Cornell University Press, 2002.

Hallett, Judith. *Fathers and Daughters in Roman Society*. Princeton, NJ: Princeton University Press, 1984.

Kleinier, Diana E. *Cleopatra and Rome.* Cambridge, MA: Belknap Press of Harvard University Press, 2005.

Southern, Pat. *Augustus*. New York: Routledge, 1998.

Wood, Susan E. *Imperial Women.* London: Brill, 1999.

Source Materials

At present, one of the best digital sources for complete works and key word searches for Greek and Roman primary sources is the Perseus Digital Library. http://www.perseus.tufts.edu/cache/perscoll_Greco-Roman.html

CHAPTER

5

Historians and Empire Building Under the Han Dynasty (202 BCE–220 CE): Ban Gu (32–92 CE) and Ban Zhao (45–116 CE)

SETTING THE STAGE

The Han dynasty was established by Liu Bang (r. 202–195 BCE), who rose to prominence, reunified China, and proclaimed himself the first emperor of the Han dynasty. The dynasty embraced Confucianism, which considered state and society extensions of the hierarchical family and functioned at its best when everyone acted properly in his or her position and assigned role. Confucianism especially stressed five relations: sovereign and subject, parent and child, elder and younger brother, husband and wife, and friend and friend. In addition, it believed that these five relations should be guided by such ideals as filial piety, loyalty, benevolence, modesty, and honesty. In Confucius's view, the ruler's relationship to his subjects equaled that of parents to their children: the former, endowed with virtues and legitimacy, had absolute authority over the latter; and the latter, indebted to the benevolence and moral excellence of the former, complied with the former with unreserved devotion.

Han intellectuals used Confucianism to develop a very distinctive political ideal of sovereignty. The emperor, as the Son of Heaven, was the only agent capable of connecting heaven, Earth, and humankind. The emperor was the moral exemplar but his mandate would be taken away if his decisions and actions disrupted the natural order. Just as the emperor had responsibilities, so everyone else within this sovereignty was obliged to fulfill his or her responsibilities with diligence. Han society, which had reached a population of 58 million by the year 2 CE, consisted of four classes: (1) the elite, consisting mostly of educated landowners, who formed the ruling class; (2) the peasants who composed the social base of the agrarian empire; (3) the artisans who used their skills to provide services; and (4) the merchants who were put under the tight control of the government because Chinese culture traditionally considered them parasites who neither served society nor produced anything new. Finally, within the new concept of sovereignty the dynasty held an absolute superiority over barbarians.

In shaping its views of order and power, the Han Empire struggled to define the role of imperial consorts in particular and the role of women in general. During the Han dynasty, principal imperial consorts were often selected from prominent families in hope of cementing political connections and support for emperors. The marriage ties, in turn, brought consort families more power. Moreover, when each of several Han emperors ascended to the throne at a young age, their mothers and regents (often the emperor's maternal uncle) were able to form political cliques and assert great influence in court politics. As the first empire in Chinese history to encounter the challenge of powerful royal women, it is not surprising that scholars took the issue seriously. Several works were written addressing women's position in family and society, most of them drawing on Confucianism and arguing against women's role in the public sphere.

In the 400 years of Han history, one family stands out as the most influential force in the Han endeavor of empire building. The patriarch of the family was Ban Biao (3–54 CE), a scholar with a profound knowledge of history and a keen desire to serve the Han Empire. Ban Biao's twin sons served the empire in distinguished but different ways: Ban Gu, a staunch Confucian scholar, authored *History of the Han*, establishing the Chinese tradition of historical writing referred to as standard histories; Ban Chao (32–102), a military general, led Han forces in numerous battles against the Xiongnus and served as protector-general of the western regions (central Asia) for twenty years. Ban Biao's only daughter, Ban Zhao, was an instructor for the imperial consorts and the author of *Lessons for Women*, the first instructional book in Chinese history that was solely devoted to the role of women. These fascinating figures provide us with intimate knowledge of the goals and efforts of the Han empire builders.

Fan Ye (398–445) was the first historian to follow Ban Gu's standard history model. He wrote the *History of the Later Han*, which was the most direct source for piecing together the biographies of Ban Gu and Ban Zhao. Fan devoted two chapters of this work to the Bans and recorded Ban Zhao's life in an additional chapter entitled "Exemplary Women." These accounts, together with the Bans' own historical and literary works, have fascinated Chinese readers for nearly 2,000 years and invited heated debate and diverse interpretations about how they represented the Han dynasty as well as Chinese tradition.

The Actors

Ban Gu and Ban Zhao

The famous Ban siblings came from a prominent clan that had for several generations produced distinguished scholars, historians, poets, and writers. Their father, Ban Biao, devoted his life and writings to advocating Confucian doctrines. Ban Biao named all three of his children with great expectation: Gu means "solid," "strong" and Zhao "bright," "prominent." Gu's twin brother was named Chao, meaning "outstanding," "to excel." The father also arranged to give his children an excellent education in Confucian classics and the Six Skills. The Six Skills was a curriculum promoted by Confucius who considered rites, music, archery, driving the chariot, literacy, and mathematics as basic abilities a cultivated person should possess in order to function properly in society and in the family. During the Han dynasty, it was not uncommon for the elite families to educate both boys and girls.

At the age of nine, Ban Gu could already compose eloquent essays and fine poems. Before long, he held a reputation as one of the most well read scholars in the Han realm. Legend has it that a leading philosopher of the Han, on meeting with Ban Gu when he was only thirteen, promptly announced this prophecy: Ban Gu would have the mandate of recording the history of the Han Empire. Indeed, Ban Gu's biggest achievement was the writing of *History of the Han*. He started his writing project right after his father's death in 54 CE. While he was at home fulfilling his three-year mourning duty as required for a filial son, he undertook to expand his father's compilations.

Ban Gu's project was reported to the throne as harboring the intention of rewriting history. Soon he was arrested and thrown in jail. The crime he was accused of was indeed a serious one. At this point, the Han dynasty and its supporters sought to justify the dynasty's continuing imperial authority, especially as it conquered new territories in central Asia, and it needed the past to provide moral justification for its actions. Until his intentions were fully known, Ban Gu's historical writing presented a danger to this claim for moral authority. The Ban family was understandably worried. Ban Chao suspended his mourning duty and rushed to the capital to petition for his twin brother in front of Emperor Ming (r. 58–75 CE). At that moment, the confiscated writings arrived in the capital, along with other evidence and the local government's report on Ban Gu's case. The emperor read the writings and was profoundly impressed because of their emphasis on the legitimacy of the Han dynasty's rule. Not only did he grant Ban Gu's release, but also appointed him the head of the Imperial Library. With the throne's sanction, Ban Gu formally began his twenty-year endeavor, which established the genre of standard histories. From the Han on, each dynasty would sponsor historians to compile a history of the previous dynasty. Over time a total of twenty-four such standard histories have been compiled, all of them structured just like the *History of the Han*, with annals, tables, monographs, and biographies.

Ban Gu loved poetry and composed dozens of long poems throughout his lifetime. One of these, "Odes to the Two Capitals," recounting the fascinating history and unique characteristics of the western capital, Changan, and the eastern capital, Luoyang, came to be considered the peak of the narrative poetry, a genre developed during the Han dynasty. Both Emperor Ming and Emperor Zhang (r. 75–88 CE) were said to be extremely fond of Ban Gu's poetry, and he was often invited to join the imperial excursions and banquets, during which he would compose poems dedicated to the two emperors. Consequently, the emperors would invite Ban Gu to participate in open debates among court officials. In 79 CE, Emperor Zhang summoned scholars and princes to discuss Confucian classics, and Ban Gu was assigned to summarize the discussions. That led to the compilation of *Comprehensive Discussions in the White Tiger Hall*, the most important Confucian text of the Han dynasty.

Ban Zhao was born in 45 CE. At the age of five, her father died. Determined to raise an educated daughter, the family hired a female teacher to mentor her. At fourteen, Ban Zhao married into a Cao family from the same district. By custom, marriages were arranged by families and normally the bride and groom would have no part in the arrangements until they met on the wedding day. Ban Zhao, however, might have known her future husband, Cao Shou, quite well, considering scholars near and far visited the Ban household frequently. Cao Shou was said to be quite learned and was once summoned by Emperor Ming to compile biographies of imperial relatives and tables of administrative offices of the former Han dynasty.

Ban Gu died in the year 92 without completing the *History of the Han*. Familiar with Ban Zhao's learning, Emperor He (r. 88–105) called on her to complete the work. Ban Zhao compiled a table entitled "The Notables of the Past and the Present" and the chapter "Monograph of Astronomy." Afterward, the emperor invited her to teach the empress, Deng (81–121), and other consorts courses on Confucian classics, astronomy, and mathematics. Because of the knowledge exhibited in her chapter in *History of the Han* and the courses she provided to the palace women, Ban Zhao is widely acknowledged as the first female scientist and mathematician in Chinese history.

Ban Zhao appeared to have formed closer ties to the throne than either of her brothers, and also played an important role in court politics. At the death of Emperor He in 105, the reins of government came into the hands of Empress Deng, who was said to be strong-minded and clever, and very fond of Confucian classics. At the age of twenty-five, Deng became the regent for the infant heir apparent. A year later, the baby emperor died and was succeeded by his cousin, Emperor An (r. 106–125 CE), a boy of thirteen. The empress, however, did not relinquish her power at court until her death in 121 CE. For nearly ten years, from 105 to Ban Zhao's death in 116, Deng frequently conferred with Ban Zhao concerning state affairs. In the palace, Ban Zhao was respectfully called "Elder Aunt Mrs. Cao" and treated with high honors.

Despite her political and intellectual influence, Ban Zhao is best known as the author of *Lessons for Women* and as an advocate of female virtues. Written when she was about sixty, the book presents Ban Zhao's views of male-female relations, womanly dispositions, and wifely manners in a big household. Ban Zhao claimed that she wrote the book to give her daughters some advice before they married, so that they might avoid the uncertainty and fear she had felt in the Cao household. Historians never doubted that she had a much broader audience in her mind when she wrote it and that she most likely imparted her ideas to many imperial consorts.

Ban Gu's and Ban Zhao's legacies rest not only on their writing of history and poetry but also on their ideas and views on the organization and ordering of the Chinese state and society, based on Confucian principles. Among many views offered in their works, the most distinguished ones are about the concept of sovereignty and the role of women.

ACT I

BAN GU AND DEFINING SOVEREIGNTY

Arguably, Ban Biao composed the most influential political treatise on imperial sovereignty and the theory of the Mandate of Heaven. This essay, "The Destiny of Kings," was written by Ban Biao in 25 CE, at the very beginning of the Later Han dynasty. In it he reflects on the interruption of the Han Empire by the Xin (9–25), the short-lived dynasty established by Wang Mang (45 BCE–?), nephew of a powerful empress and the regent of two Han emperors. Ban Biao argued that the destiny of a ruler often was shown in omens and that history revealed that legitimate rulers were the ones who received charges from Heaven and whose wills represented those of the people.

Ban Gu expanded his father's ideal of Han sovereignty by establishing the ideological foundation of sovereignty, defining the role of emperor and the relationship between an emperor and his subjects, and articulating a Sino-centric world order. He did so during a period of the Han dynasty when Confucianism became firmly established as the source of resolution for all moral questions. The most distinguished contribution to the Confucian dominance was Ban Gu's compilation of *Comprehensive Discussions in the White Tiger Hall* in 79 CE. In the book, Ban Gu recorded Han scholars' understanding of Confucian classics on topics as varied as the position of an emperor and the relationship between an emperor and his subjects, the structure of the central and regional administration, education, justice, the universe, the clan system, and marriage. The book effectively reaffirmed the ideological foundation of Han sovereignty: Confucianism (**Document One**).

Ban Gu's *History of the Han* was another project reaffirming Confucian ideology and its dominance. Ban's writing of each emperor's annals looks a lot like a proclamation of the divine nature of Han sovereignty. In his view, the position of a ruler is sacrosanct regardless of his possession or lack of personal virtue; he had inherited the right to rule from the founding ancestor of his clan, who had received a mandate from Heaven to establish the dynasty. His "Biography of the Emperor Gaozu," thus, set out to prove that the founder of the Han was unanimously recognized by the kings and dukes as the one who obtained the Mandate of Heaven (**Document Two**). In his poem, "Odes to the Two Capitals," Ban Gu portrays a perfect image of the Han sovereignty that rested on the Confucian principles of filial piety, respect for ancestors, and most importantly, hierarchical social order:

> The sovereignty is based on a solid foundation of ten generations,
> And the imperial house has carried on its mission for a hundred years.
> The nobles are all from prominent families of traditional virtues;
> The peasants cultivate lands that are passed down by their ancestors;
> The merchants inherit their family business;
> And the artisans use the tools of their ancestors.
> Splendid and prosperous,
> This is a kingdom where everyone enjoys his own place.[1]

Ban Gu also argued that the Han Empire possessed cultural dominance and moral supremacy over the rest of the world. With the blessing of heaven, the ruler of such a great empire was far superior to any alien rulers. It is very likely that Ban Gu's view was somewhat influenced by his brother, Ban Chao, who spent three decades of his life as the protector-general of the western regions (central Asia), representing the Han Empire. In "The Memoir on the Western Regions," Chapter 96 of the *History of the Han*, for example, Ban Gu described the people of the states in central Asia with a condescending tone, stating that they all "have born in mind the might and morality of Han and have all rejoiced to make themselves its subjects" (**Document Three**).

During the Han dynasty, the biggest threat to its sovereignty came from the constant harassment by the Xiongnu

1. Ban Gu, "Odes to the Two Capitals" (*Liangdu fu*), in *Selections of Literary Masterpieces* (*Wenxuan*), ed. Xiao Tong (Shanghai: Shanghai guji chubanshe, 1993), 8.

(Hun) state. The Han Empire adopted various strategies to deal with the Xiongnus, but none of them effectively halted the Xiongnus' aggressions. During Emperor Zhang's reign, some officials proposed to permanently break with the Xiongnu state. Ban Gu, however, disagreed. In his opinion, the very fact of engaging the Xiongnus demonstrated the trustworthiness and generosity of the Han rulers. And only in so doing, would the Xiongnus gradually come to the realization that the saintly Han Empire held civility and principle resolutely.

Act II

Defining the Place and Roles of Women in Chinese Society

From the very beginning of the Han dynasty, imperial consorts and their families exerted great influence in court politics. Such influence was often portrayed as contrary to Confucian principles and a violation of the Mandate of Heaven. Ban Zhao's father and brother certainly contributed to this narrative in their writings about the Han dynasty (**Document Four**). In his *History of the Han*, for example, Ban Gu refused to consider Wang Mang a legitimate ruler, even though he was the founder of the Xin dynasty and emperor for fifteen years. Wang Mang's biography was listed under the section of biographies (instead of annals for emperors) and placed at the very end of the *History of the Han*. In Ban Gu's view, even though Wang Mang possessed certain virtues, he never received the mandate to start a new dynasty. Wang Mang disrupted the imperial clan's inherited rights to rule through his ties with an empress and his ruthless politicking. According to Ban Gu, from the very beginning, all the omens were against Wang Mang. In the first year of his reign, a mad girl shouted on the streets of Changan, proclaiming that the founder of the Han Empire was angered by Wang Mang's action. Next year, a severe hailstorm pounded the Zhending District where Wang Mang put down an uprising. A fortuneteller pronounced that Wang Mang's appearance resembled a man-eater's. During the fifth year into Wang Mang's reign, a comet appeared in the sky and lasted for more than twenty days. Ban Gu declared that Wang Mang was certainly "in a place that did not belong to him."

Ban Zhao's view on women's roles and her own experience as a palace instructor and the empress Deng's adviser were a departure from those of her father and brothers. Ban Zhao believed that the relationship between men and women should resemble the relationship between *yin* and *yang:* one complements the other. Since the targeted audience of the *Lessons for Women* was female, Ban Zhao mainly discussed how women should conduct themselves with humility and obedience. Confucian scholars of later times enthusiastically accepted her work as a didactic text for teaching women to be submissive. But if we examine what Confucius had to say about being a cultivated man, we find that similar attributes such as respect and caution were also expected from males. In fact, Ban Zhao stressed that to form an ideal husband-wife relationship required the efforts of both sides: "For self-culture nothing equals respect for others. To counteract firmness nothing equals compliance" (**Document Five**).

Arguably, Ban Zhao's activities and writings engaged two important themes: women's participation in politics and women's education. Even though Ban Zhao did not personally advocate women's political activity, she saw no problem in Empress Deng's exercise of power and influence in the palace; nor did she hesitate to provide advice to the empress who was in charge of the imperial court practically every day. In her essays, poems, and writing of history, Ban Zhao freely expressed her opinion on political events and historical figures (**Document Six**).

Ban Zhao's advocacy of women's education is more evident. In her view, educating women was an important step in the formation of an ideal relationship between men and women in general, and husband and wife in particular. In *Lessons for Women*, Ban Zhao lamented that the men of her time only knew that wives must be controlled and that the husband's rules of conduct manifesting his authority must be established. They therefore taught only their boys to read books and study histories. Ban Zhao argued that ignoring a girl's education was equivalent to ignoring the essential relation between men and women and, in fact, was against Confucian principles. She wrote: "According to the *Book of Rites*,[2] it is the rule to begin to teach children to read at the age of eight years, and by the age of fifteen years they ought to be ready for cultural training. Only, why should girls' education not be according to this principle?"[3]

The historical accounts of Ban Zhao changed from time to time. While Confucian scholars of later imperial periods used her as a didactic model of female virtue, Chinese intellectuals and women activists of early modern times picked up her life experience as an educator, scholar, and imperial advisor. The true legacy of Ban Zhao is that, like her brothers, she played a role in the Han endeavor of empire building.

Finale

The tale of the Ban family is fascinating, yet quite incomplete. For example, not much information about Ban Gu's mother or wife survives; we do not even know their last name or their place of origin. From what we can gather, Ban Gu's mother lived with him in Luoyang after her husband died. She probably died shortly before the emperor He's reign, and in accordance with Confucian ritual,

2. *The Book of Rites* (*Liji*), comp. Da Sheng of the former Han dynasty, is a collection of pre-Han essays concerning ancient rites and customs. Many were written by Confucius's students.

3. Nancy Lee Swann, *Pan Chao: Foremost Woman Scholar of China* (Ann Arbor: Center for Chinese Studies, University of Michigan, 2001), 84.

Ban Gu resigned from his official post to fulfill his one-year mourning period. Ban Gu's wife gave birth to several sons, none of whom grew to be as learned as their father and his siblings. In fact Ban Gu was said to be quite irresponsible as the head of his household; his sons often ran into trouble with the law, and his servants were extremely unruly. One of his servants sowed the seeds of Ban Gu's disgrace. This servant got quite drunk one day and interrupted the entourage of the Luoyang governor, Zhong Jing. When Zhong Jing's officers shouted at him, the servant responded with insulting words. The governor was terribly offended and would have held Ban Gu responsible were it not for his patron, the general Dou Xian who fought the Xiongnus. However, Zhong Jing waited for an opportunity. In 89 CE, after an unsuccessful military expedition, Ban Gu lost his powerful patron and Zhong Jing arrested Ban Gu. He died in a jail in Luoyang in 92 CE, at the age of sixty-one. Besides his *History of the Han*, Ban Gu left more than forty poems and essays.

Ban Zhao's marriage to Cao Shou produced a son, Cao Cheng, and several daughters. Cao Shou died quite young and Ban Zhao chose to remain widowed. Ban Zhao died when she was over seventy. The empress Deng mourned her in person and ordered a state mourning period. She also sent imperial officials to arrange her funeral. Ban Zhao's writings were compiled by her talented daughter-in-law, Ding, and together they made up a total of sixteen collections, ranging from narrative poems, odes, inscriptions, eulogies, argumentations, commentaries, elegies, letters, expositions, memorials, and final instructions. Ban Zhao was truly a woman of letters.

The Han dynasty represented a pinnacle of Chinese civilization, with a firm sense of moral, cultural, and economic dominance over its neighbors and a well-structured administration and society. The Ban family was, indisputably, a significant force in the Han effort of empire building. However, as much as Ban Gu wished for an everlasting sovereignty, the Han dynasty came to its end just about one hundred years after his death. What brought down the empire was not an invasion of the Xiongnus, or a usurper connected to a consort clan. Neither did an emperor disturb the balance of nature, nor did his civil officials fail to rally around him. Instead, the biggest blow to the empire was the outbreak of a large-scale rebellion staged by followers of the Yellow Turban Army, a religious cult inspired by Daoist ideas and consisting mostly of deprived peasants. The rebels invoked the idea that the heaven that blessed the Han Empire was dead, and a new era should be created by the Yellow Turbans. They predicted, "In the year of Jiazi (184 CE), the realm will be again in a great peace." The throne sent several generals to put down the rebellions, but the generals, in turn, used the armies they amassed to gain power for themselves. A civil war ensued, and Han sovereignty effectively ended when the last emperor of the Han dynasty was forced to retreat to Changan in 190.

■ Documents

DOCUMENT ONE

Ban Gu

Comprehensive Discussions in the White Tiger Hall (79 CE)

This is an excerpt from the Comprehensive Discussions in the White Tiger Hall, *the official report of Han scholars' discussions on ancient classics in* 79 CE. *Throughout Chinese history, the report has been regarded as the orthodox interpretation of Chinese classics. In reading this passage, were you able to identify the Han concept of the Mandate of Heaven?*

Why is it that a King, having received his mandate from Heaven, must alter the first month of the year? It means that he has changed the dynastic name, and indicates that he has not inherited his kingship. It means that he has received his kingship from Heaven and not from man. By this measure he changes the people's hearts and refreshes their ears and eyes, as an aid in the process of their reform. Therefore the chapter of "Important Explanations" in *The Book of Rites* says: "When a King ascends the throne he rectifies the first month of the year, he changes the color of his equipage, he transforms the emblems of the standards, he alters the vessels and instruments, and he modifies the clothing."

That is the reason why even Shun and Yu,[1] though they continued the succession in conditions of great peace, still deemed it proper to change the institutions of their predecessors, in order to respond to the will of Heaven. Why is it that the King only introduces his reforms after he has obtained Heaven's auspicious responses? To emphasize the importance of the change of the institutions. The *Explanation of the Auspicious Responses of Spring and Autumn* says: "Having reverently received auspicious responses from Heaven the King rectifies the first month of the year and the color of the equipage."[2] The *Book of Change* says: "Tang[3] and Wu[4] deprived the previous Dynasties of their mandates in accordance with the will of Heaven, and in response to the wishes of the people."[5]

1. Shun and Yu were legendary kings of ancient China. Shun ascended to the throne when the previous king, Yao, gave up the position to the more capable Shun. Later, Shun appointed Yu to be his successor because of Yu's achievements in flood control.
2. The *Explanation of the Auspicious Responses of Spring and Autumn (Chun qiu fan lu)* was written by Dong Zhongshu (*ca.* 179–104 BCE) of the Former Han dynasty. Dong, a Confucian philosopher, played a key role in reviving and expanding the theories of the Mandate of Heaven.
3. Tang was the first king of the Shang dynasty (sixteenth to eleventh centuries BCE)
4. Wu implies King Wu of the Zhou dynasty (*ca.* 1050–771 BCE). He led an alliance and overthrew the Shang dynasty.
5. *The Book of Change (Yijing)* is one of the earliest Chinese texts. While primarily a reference for divination, it nevertheless reflected early Chinese perception of the universe, society, and human relations.

DOCUMENT TWO

BAN GU

"Biography of Emperor Gaozu" (ca. 80 CE)

In this very first chapter of the History of the Han dynasty, *Ban Gu recounted how a humble, yet confident Liu Bang rose from a petty officer to the founder of one of the greatest dynasties in world history. Does this document tell you about the formation of Han imperial system? How did the Han people perceive sovereignty and the Mandate of Heaven?*

The nobles sent up a petition to the King of Han,[1] saying the King of Chu, Han Xin, the King of Han,[2] Xin, the King of Huainan, Ying Bu, the King of Liang, Peng Yue, the former King of Hengshan, Wu Rui, the King of Zhao, Zhang Ao, and the King of Yan, Zang Du, risking death and making repeated bows, say to your Majesty the great King: "In times past the Qin Dynasty acted contrary to principle and the world punished them. You, great King, were the first to capture the King of Qin and subjugate Guanzhong[3]—your achievements have been greatest in the world. You have preserved the perishing and given repose to those in danger; you have continued broken lines of descent in order to tranquilize all the people. Your achievements are abundant and your virtue is great. You have moreover granted favors to the vassal kings who have merit, enabling them to succeed in setting up their gods of the soil and grains. The division of the land has already been settled, but positions and titles are still confused with one another, without the proper division of the superior from the inferior, so that the manifestation of you, the great King's merits and virtue is not proclaimed to later generations. Risking death and making repeated bows, we offer to our superior the honorable title of Emperor."

The King of Han replied, "I, a person of little virtue, have heard that the title of emperor should be possessed by a man eminent in talent and virtue. An empty name without possessing its reality should not be adopted. Now you, vassal kings, have all highly exalted me, a person of little virtue. How could I therefore occupy such a position?"

The vassal kings all said, "You, great King, arose from small beginnings; you destroyed the seditious dynasty of Qin; your majesty stirs everything within the seas; moreover, starting from a secluded and mean region, from Hanzhong, you acted out your majesty and virtue, executing the unrighteous, setting up the

1. "The King of Han" implies Liu Bang.
2. Though pronounced "Han," the Chinese character is different from the Chinese character for the Han (dynasty).
3. Guanzhong is located in the middle section of the Yellow River valley.

meritorious, tranquilizing and establishing the empire. Meritorious officials all received territory and the income of towns; you did not appropriate them for yourself. Your virtue, great King, has been bestowed even to the borders of the four seas. We, vassal kings, find our speech inadequate to express it. For you to take the position of Emperor would be most appropriate. We hope that you, great King, will favor the world by doing so."

The King of Han replied, "Since the vassal kings would be favored by it and since they consider it to be an advantage to all the people in the world, it may be done."

Thereupon the vassal kings and the Grand Commandant and Marquis of Changan, Wan, and others, altogether three hundred persons, together with the Erudite and the Baronet of Wheat Heir, Sun Shutong, carefully selected a favorable day. In the second month, on the day of Jiawu,[4] they presented to their superior the honorable title of Emperor and the King of Han ascended the imperial throne upon the northern bank of the river Si. The Queen was honored and called "The Empress"; the Heir-apparent was called "The Imperial Heir-apparent"; the deceased old dame [the emperor's mother], was posthumously honored and called "Lady of Luminous Spirit."

4. Jiawu is a name of the Ten Celestial Stems and the Twelve Terrestrial Branches. The Chinese people combined the two systems to designate years, months, and days, in addition to the numerical counting of years, months, and days.

DOCUMENT THREE

Ban Gu

"The Memoir on the Western Regions" (ca. 80 CE)

"The Memoir on the Western Regions," the ninety-sixth chapter of the History of the Han Dynasty, *presents a general account of various small states west of the Han Empire, many of which are along the route of the Silk Road. The following excerpt is the concluding paragraph of the chapter. In what way does this passage conform to Ban Gu's view of the world order?*

The various states of the Western Regions each have their rulers and their chiefs. Their large bodies of armed men are separated and weak, with no means of united control. Although they may be subject to the Xiongnu, they are not attached to them by ties of friendship. The Xiongnu are merely able to acquire their horses, stock animals, felts and woolens, but are not able to control or lead them, or to act in concert with them. They are cut off from Han and the intervening distance is very great; if Han takes possession of them they bring no profit; if Han abandons them they constitute no loss. With us possessing great virtues, there is nothing to take from them. Hence, since the Jianwu Reign (25–55), the Western Regions have borne in mind the might and morality of Han and have all rejoiced to make themselves its subjects. Only small settlements, such as Shanshan and Jushi whose borders lie close to the Xiongnu, are still involved with them; whereas large states such as Suoju or Yutian repeatedly send envoys and lodge hostages with the Han, requesting that they be made subject to the protector general. Our saintly emperor has surveyed the circumstances of past and present; and in view of the expediency of the times he has declined their requests and withheld permission, while the bonds that relate them have not been severed. He has combined together the moral qualities shown by the Great Yu when he reduced the Western Rong to order, of the Duke of Zhou when he declined the white pheasants,[1] and of Taizong when he refused the gift of the fine horses;[2] could any conduct be more noble?

1. The duke of Zhou was the grand counselor for King Cheng of the western Zhou dynasty. He advised the king not to accept the white pheasants presented by the Zhaoshang Tribe as it was deemed not to be well governed.
2. Taizong implies Emperor Wen (r. 179–157 BCE). He declined the gift of the fine horses from a neighboring state because they were not appropriate for imperial chariots.

DOCUMENT FOUR

Ban Gu

"Lady Li, Concubine of Emperor Wu" (ca. 80 CE)

"Lady Li, Concubine of Emperor Wu" is included in the ninety-seventh chapter of the History of the Former Han Dynasty, *entitled "Account of the Families Related to the Emperors by Marriage." The story of Li reveals aspects of women's roles in imperial politics as well as Han perceptions of sibling and gender relations. Does Ban Gu's view of women differ from that of Ban Zhao?*

Lady Li, a concubine of Emperor Wu the Filial, originally entered the palace as an entertainer. Her elder brother, Li Yannian, had an innate understanding of music and was skilled at singing and dancing. The emperor Wu took a great liking to him. Whenever he presented some new song or musical composition, there were none among his listeners who were not moved to admiration. Once Li Yannian was attending the emperor, he rose from his place to dance and sing this song:

Beautiful lady in a northern land,
Standing alone, none in the world like her,

A single glance and she upsets a city,
A second glance, she upsets the state!
Not that I don't know she upsets states and cities,
But one so lovely you'll never find again!

The emperor sighed and said: "Splendid!—but I doubt there's such a beauty in the world." Princess Pingyang[1] then informed him that Li Yannian had a little sister, and he forthwith had her summoned and brought before him. She was in fact strikingly beautiful and skilled at dancing as well, and because of this she won his favor.

She bore him a son, known posthumously as King Ai of Changyi, but died shortly afterwards at a very young age. The emperor, filled with grief and longing, had a portrait of her painted at the Palace of Sweet Springs. Later Empress Wei was removed from the position of empress, and four years afterwards, when Emperor Wu passed away, the general in chief Huo Guang, following what he knew to have been the emperor's wishes, had sacrifices performed to Lady Li as though she had been his official consort, posthumously honoring her with the title "Empress of Emperor Wu the Filial."

Earlier, when Lady Li lay critically ill, the emperor came to visit in person, but she pulled the covers over her face and, apologizing, said, "I have been sick in bed for a long time and my appearance is wasted. I cannot let Your Majesty see me, though I hope to entrust Your Majesty with my son the king and my brothers."

"I know you've been very sick, and the time may come when you never rise again," said the emperor. "Wouldn't you feel better if you saw me once more and asked me face to face to take care of the king and your brothers?"

"A woman should not appear before her lord or her father when her face is not properly made up," she said. "I would not dare let Your Majesty see me in this state of disarray."

"Just let me have one glimpse of you!" said the emperor. "I'll reward you with a thousand pieces of gold and assign your brothers to high office!"

But Lady Li replied, "It is up to Your Majesty to assign offices as you please—it does not depend on one glimpse of me."

When the emperor continued to insist on one last look at her, Lady Li, sobbing, turned her face toward the wall and would not speak again. The emperor rose from his seat in displeasure and left.

Lady Li's sisters berated her, saying, "Why couldn't you let him have one look at you and entreat him face to face to take care of your brothers! Why should you anger him like this!"

"The reason I didn't want the emperor to see me," she said, "was so I could make certain he would look after my brothers! It was because he liked my looks that I was able to rise from a lowly position and enjoy the love and favor of the ruler. But if one has been taken into service because of one's beauty,

1. Princess Pingyang was the emperor Wu's elder sister.

then when beauty fades, love will wane, and when love wanes, kindness will be forgotten. The emperor thinks fondly and tenderly of me because he remembers the way I used to look. Now if he were to see me thin and wasted, with all the old beauty gone from my face, he would be filled with loathing and disgust and would do his best to put me out of his mind. Then what hope would there be that he would ever think kindly of me again and remember to take pity of my brothers?"

When Lady Li died, the emperor had her buried with the honors appropriate to an empress. After that, he appointed her eldest brother, Li Guangli, secondary general and marquis of Haixi, and Li Yannian Director of Imperial Music.

The emperor continued to think longingly of Lady Li and could not forget her. A magician from Qi named Shaoweng, announcing that he had the power to summon spirits, one night lit torches, placed curtains around them, and laid out offerings of wine and meat. He then had the emperor take his place behind another curtain and observe the proceedings from a distance. The emperor could see a fine lady who resembled Lady Li sitting down within the curtains, and then rising to walk again. But he could not move closer to get a good look and, stirred more than ever to thoughts of sadness, he composed this poem:

Is it she?
Is it not?
I stand gazing from afar:
Timid steps, soft and slow,
How long she is in coming!

He then ordered the experts of the Music Bureau to devise a string accompaniment and make it into a song. He also composed a rhyme-prose to express his grief at the loss of Lady Li. . . .

DOCUMENT FIVE

Ban Zhao

Lessons for Women (ca. 110 CE)

The full text of Lessons for Women *contains a total of seven short chapters, entitled "Humility," "Husband and Wife," "Respect and Caution," "Womanly Qualifications," "Whole-Hearted Devotion," "Implicit Obedience," and "Harmony with the Younger Brothers-Sisters-in-law." What is the basis of Ban Zhao's view of man-woman relationships?*

Chapter I

Humility

On the third day after the birth of a girl the ancients observed three customs: (first) to place the baby below the bed; (second) to give her a potsherd with which to play; and (third) to announce her birth to her ancestors by an offering. Now to lay the baby below the bed plainly indicated that she is lowly and weak, and should regard it as her primary duty to humble herself before others. To give her potsherds with which to play indubitably signified that she should practise labor and consider it her primary duty to be industrious. To announce her birth before her ancestors clearly meant that she ought to esteem as her primary duty the continuation of the observance of worship in the home.

These three ancient customs epitomize a woman's ordinary way of life and the teachings of the traditional ceremonial rites and regulations. Let a woman modestly yield to others; let her respect others; let her put others first, herself last. Should she do something good, let her not mention it; should she do something bad, let her not deny it. Let her bear disgrace; let her even endure when others speak or do evil to her. Always let her seem to tremble and to fear. (When a woman follows such maxims as these,) then she may be said to humble herself before others.

Let a woman retire late to bed, but rise early to duties; let her not dread tasks by day or by night. Let her not refuse to perform domestic duties whether easy or difficult. That which must be done, let her finish completely, tidily, and systematically. (When a woman follows such rules as these,) then she may be said to be industrious.

Let a woman be correct in manner and upright in character in order to serve her husband. Let her live in purity and quietness (of spirit), and attend to her own affairs. Let her love not gossip and silly laughter. Let her cleanse and purify and arrange in order the wine and the food for the offerings to the ancestors. (When a woman observes such principles as these,) then she may be said to continue ancestral worship.

No woman who observes these three (fundamentals of life) has ever had a bad reputation or has fallen into disgrace. If a woman fail to observe them, how can her name be honored; how can she but bring disgrace upon herself?

Chapter III

Respect and Caution

As *Yin* and *Yang* are not of the same nature, so man and woman have different characteristics. The distinctive quality of the *Yang* is rigidity; the function of the *Yin* is yielding. Man is honored for strength; a woman is beautiful on account of her gentleness. Hence there arose the common saying: "A man though born like a wolf may, it is feared, become a weak monstrosity; a woman though born like a mouse may, it is feared, become a tiger.

Now for self-culture nothing equals respect for others. To counteract firmness nothing equals compliance. Consequently it can be said that the Way of respect and acquiescence is woman's most important principle of conduct. So respect may be defined as nothing other than holding on to that which is permanent; and acquiescence nothing other than being liberal and generous. Those who are steadfast in devotion know that they should stay in their proper places; those who are liberal and generous esteem others, and honor and serve (them).

If husband and wife have the habit of staying together, never leaving one another, and following each other around within the limited space of their own rooms, then they will lust after and take liberties with one another. From such action improper language will arise between the two. This kind of discussion may lead to licentiousness. Out of licentiousness will be born a heart of disrespect to the husband. Such a result comes from not knowing that one should stay in one's proper place.

Furthermore, affairs may be either crooked or straight; words may be either right or wrong. Straightforwardness cannot but lead to quarreling; crookedness cannot but lead to accusation. If there are really accusations and quarrels, then undoubtedly there will be angry affairs. Such a result comes from not esteeming others, and not honoring and serving (them).

(If wives) suppress not contempt for husband, then it follows (that such wives) rebuke and scold (their husbands). (If husbands) stop not short of anger, then they are certain to beat (their wives). The correct relationship between husband and wife is based upon harmony and intimacy, and (conjugal) love is grounded in proper union. Should actual blows be dealt, how could matrimonial relationship be preserved? Should sharp words be spoken, how could (conjugal) love exist? If love and proper relationship both be destroyed, then husband and wife are divided.

DOCUMENT SIX

Ban Zhao

"Travelling Eastward" (113 CE)

In 113 CE, Ban Zhao accompanied her son to his new office in Chenliu, a prefecture about 180 miles east of the capital, Luoyang. Ban Zhao recounted the trip in this poem. What does this poem tell you about Ban Zhao as an intellectual?

It is the seventh year of Yung-ch'u;
I follow my son in his journey eastward.
It is an auspicious day in Spring's first moon;
We choose this good hour, and are about to start.

Now I rise to my feet and ascend my carriage.
At eventide we lodge at Yen-shih.
Already we leave the old and start for the new.
I am uneasy in mind, and sad at heart.

Dawn's first light comes, and yet I sleep not;
My heart hesitates as though it would fail me.
I pour me out a cup of wine to relax my thoughts.
Suppressing my feelings, I sigh and blame myself;
I shall not need to dwell in nests, or (eat) worms from dead trees.
Then how can I not encourage myself to press forward?
And further, am I different from other people?
Let me but hear Heaven's command and go its way.

Throughout the journey we follow the great highway.
If we seek short cuts, whom shall we follow?
Pressing forward, we travel on and on;
In abandonment our eyes wander, and our spirits roam.
We pass through the Seven Districts, watching, gazing;
At Kung Hsien we experience difficulties,
Further on we watch the Lo unite with the Great River;
We see the Ch'éng-kao's "Farewell Gate."

Just when we have left behind lofty heights.
We reach and pass Ying-yang and the nearby villages,
We find food and rest enough at Yüan-wu.
(One night) we lodge at Yang-wu, the mulberry center.
Wading (a stream near) Feng-ch'iu, again we tread the highway.
Secretly I sigh for the Capital City I love, (but)
To cling to one's native place characterizes a small nature,
As the histories have taught us.

Going forward on the highway but a little ahead,
We come to a low hill's north side.
When we enter K'uang City I recall far distant events.
I am reminded of Confucius' straitened activities
In that decadent, chaotic age which knew not the Way;
And which bound and awed even him, that Holy Man!
As I muse upon such vexing thoughts, (our train) has long halted;
Unobserved the sun has come to eventide, and dusk descends.

We arrive at the borders of Ch'ang-ÿuan,
Where we study the natives of that agricultural land.
At P'u Ch'éng we note its worn city walls

Upon which riotously thrive wild thorns.
Startled, aroused, I wake; thinking back, I wonder!
(Then) I recall the awe-inspiring spirit of Tzù-lu,
Whom the people of Wei did praise,
And to this day yet name for his brave sense of duty.
In the district southeast of this city,
The people still honor the grave of Ch'ü Yüan.

In fact genuine virtue cannot die;
Though the body decay, the name lives on.
So what the Classics always praise
And honor are truth and virtue, love and merit.
Wu Cha said this district had many princely men;
For the truth of his words there was evidence.
Afterwards came misfortune and a decadent age;
Whereupon (virtue) lapsed, and (its principle) prospered no more.
I know that man's nature and destiny rest with Heaven,
But by effort we can go forward and draw near to love.
(Muscles) stretched, head uplifted, we tread onward to the vision.
With unfailing loyalty and reciprocity, in our dealing with men,
Let us love uprightness, and turn not back.
And thus our spirits will communicate with the spirits above.
The (magic) mirror of all the Spirits of the Earth
Protects the pure and the good, and helps the faithful.

The *Luan* says:

The thoughts of the princely man
Ought to be written down.
But why not also each say one's own opinion?
As we admire the ancients, (so I attest that)
Every action of that virtuous one, (my father,)
Meant a literary creation.
Even though I am not wise,
I dare not but follow him.

Honor and dishonor, poverty and wealth,
These may not be sought.
With body erect, let us walk the Way!
And bide the proper time.
Our turn of life may be long, (or it may be) short,
The stupid and the wise are alike in this.
Let us be quietly reverential; resigned to our Destiny,
Regardless whether a good or an evil one.

Let us respect, be careful, and not be indolent;
Let us think of being humble and temperate;
Let us be pure and calm, and want little,
Like the Master Kung Ch'o.

Questions

1. What are the characteristics of the Han dynasty? Are there similarities to the Julio-Claudian dynasty? Differences?
2. Reading **Documents One** to **Three**, what is your impression of the Han concept of sovereignty? What are its key political ideas? How do these ideas compare to the Shang perception of rulership and the Roman concept of political authority?
3. How do the Bans and the Roman historians and poets depict imperial women? Do political women meet the cultural and social expectations of their respective societies?
4. Who is the intended audience of Ban Zhao's *Lessons for Women?* What are Ban Zhao's views on the relations between men and women, and men's and women's role in politics and society and in the family? Compare Chinese attitudes toward women's education and domesticity with Roman attitudes.
5. Scholars have long cited Ban Zhao's work as evidence of the oppression of women in traditional China; do you agree? Would you consider Ban Zhao an advocate for women's rights? Why or why not? Justify your answers with specific references to the reading.

Suggested Readings

Hardy, Grant, and Anne Behnke Kinney. *The Establishment of the Han Empire and Imperial China*. Westport, CT: Greenwood, 2005.

Loewe, Michael. "The Concept of Sovereignty." In *The Cambridge History of China*. Vol. 1. Ed. Denis Twitchett and Michael Loewe. Cambridge, UK: Cambridge University Press, 1986, 726–46.

Swann, Nancy Lee. *Pan Chao: Foremost Woman Scholar of China*. Ann Arbor: Center for Chinese Studies, University of Michigan, 2001.

Source Materials

A Visual Sourcebook of Chinese Civilization http://depts.washington.edu/chinaciv

The Minneapolis Institute of Arts has an excellent online tour of Asian art with a section dedicated to each dynasty. http://www.artsmia.org/art-of-asia/history/dynasty-han.cfm

PART

II

Belief Systems

The chapters in this section focus on the establishment of a number of the major religions of the world. The development of beliefs and ethical values that are expressed in rituals and ceremonies, and the creation of ever-expanding communities of individuals who identified with them constitute some of the most complex and compelling stories of early human history. Simultaneously, myth and fiction continued to exercise enduring power to describe models of human behavior and to prescribe social and political ideals. While earlier chapters have considered the role of religion, ethical values, and aesthetic sensibilities, the examples that follow provide ample material for an in-depth consideration of the personal and political dimensions of such beliefs.

Rules governing social order and behaviors are enshrined in religion, which thus becomes law and the means for governing society. Previous chapters have pointed to the fact that law and religion are not necessarily distinguishable, any more than secular and spiritual authority are separated. In the essays that follow, the development of these relationships and their human consequences are brought to light. A variety of common themes appear and reappear in the chapters that follow. The most obvious is the connection between religion and political authority and structures. The facts that religion can be a means of justifying political authority and maintaining social and political order and that religious leaders can head political states are well illustrated in all the chapters in this section. Religion can be a means of resistance as shown in the contests between Aisha bint Abi Bakr and Ali ibn Ab Talib, relatives of the prophet of Islam, Muhammed (Chapter 9), and a target of persecution as demonstrated in the discussions of religion and politics in medieval China (Chapter 8). Conflict as well as social order can accompany the growth of religious groups, and most religions from their inception include different paths to truth and ideological diversity in the face of established doctrinal authority. This point is illustrated in the lives of the individuals showcased in discussions of both Christianity and Islam in Chapters 7 and 9 respectively.

While each of the chapters speaks to the institutional and political dimensions of the major belief systems, they also consider personal dimensions of religion, especially in periods of rapid change and transformation. How are individual spiritual needs met in religious ideas, rituals and practices, and what happens when religious enthusiasm confronts orthodoxy and institutional controls? The search for religious identity and individual forms of spiritual expression appear clearly in worldwide examples of asceticism of the kind practiced by the monks and nuns of medieval China in Chapter 8 and by Christian monastics in Chapter 7. In considering these themes, each chapter also allows us to ask whether women's and men's religious longings, beliefs, and practices are similar; whether men and women have the same opportunities and occupy similar positions in religious organizations, and how religious doctrines treat women and men.

Finally, all the chapters in this section have at their core a vision of an ideal and how that ideal captures popular imaginations and satisfies spiritual and emotional needs. In the simplest terms, religions teach ethical values and moral behaviors and provide models for their followers to emulate, although the ideal virtues and prescribed comportment may differ for men and women. In a more secular realm, nowhere are the intersections between the real and the imagined more evident than in the poetry and the literature discussed in Chapter 6 about archetypal heroes Rama and Sita, and in the lives of Murasaki Shikibu and Prince Genji, the "actors" in Chapter 10. Both the *Ramayana* and the *Tale of Genji* grew from concrete historical conditions, and these love stories portray kingship and imperial systems, elite court cultures, social organization, family structures, and gender institutions of a particular time and place. However, they also place before their readers characteristics of the ideal companion and enviable relationships that served as models in rich political, literary, and cultural legacies.

Sources available for the subjects in this section are more numerous than for the earliest chapters of this volume and reflect somewhat larger literate populations. As before, however, most of the records are created by elite members of the society under discussion, although the fact that we have women as creators of some of the documents for both medieval China and Japan is noteworthy. As always knowing something about the documents, their creators, and the purpose of the creation is important. In this section we also face several specific interpretive challenges. How can we best utilize materials that evolved over many centuries, as in the case of the *Ramayana?* How reliable are accounts of individuals like Aisha and Ali that were created after the fact? What are some of the things we should be aware of when reading laudatory lives of religious figures like Jerome's account of Paula's life? And, finally, how can we best use material that is fictional, yet grounded in historical experience?

Those questions, when combined with the ones that follow, should prove a useful guide to discussions comparing beliefs and value systems in Chapters 6 to 10.

- How do belief systems affect or reflect social values and gender norms?
- What are the pathways to individual belief, and how and why do religious ideas spread?
- How do states use religion, and what is the relationship between secular and spiritual authority?
- How are ideas about gender, sexuality, reproduction, and marriage expressed in religion?

CHAPTER

6

Ancient India: Rama and Sita

■ Setting the Stage

Human spiritual needs, the development of models of human behavior, and justifications for both social order and the exercise of power combined to produce belief systems in ancient societies. One of the oldest of these traditions is the story of Rama and Sita told in an evolving epic poem of considerable length written over several centuries. The complexity of interaction between the real and the imagined is beautifully illustrated in this tale. At the same time, the messages of the poem describe the functioning of a state, the origin of royal lineages, and the responsibilities of rulers. Women are part of this world of political authority through their essential roles within the elite family structures that are central to a hierarchical social order or caste system.

Rama and Sita are ahistorical, mythological figures that pose a peculiar challenge for historians. While they are highly valued in the spiritual lives of many Hindus and, therefore, important to Indian history, their story is recorded in the *Ramayana* rather than in the chronicles, inscriptions, court records, and journals that historians normally use. While Rama and Sita are not historical figures, they represent the ideal and sometimes conflicting values of a large number of very real people.

The plot of the *Ramayana* brings Prince Rama and Princess Sita together into a royal marriage. The couple endures court intrigue, the abduction of Sita by a demon, and her ambiguous rescue by her husband. The current educated guess of when the original core story was composed is between 750 and 500 BCE, but the emergence of the full epic poem as we know it is not clear. The epic is usually divided into seven books; Books 2 through 6 are the core story; Book 1 contains both core material and additions, while the seventh book as a whole appears to be from a later time. An important historian of India's culture, A. L. Basham, who published in the 1950s, thought that India's two great epics, the *Mahabharata* and the *Ramayana,* had started out as stories of military adventure, and then had been reworked over time by priest-editors, rendering the epics more cultural in content.[1] Basham's assumption was that the poets and editors were all men.

In order to make discussing the epic's history a bit easier, most scholars agree to identify the most important editor-poet as a sage called Valmiki (ca. 200 BCE). The ancient India that Valmiki represented in the epic is itself difficult for historians to understand. Hard information on India's ancient history is limited to artifacts and inscriptions, rather than written chronicles or public records. Ironically, mythical epics may provide the best insights into this ancient past. Gods, warriors, royalty, and monsters inhabit India's ancient epics, and all the characters function in an imaginative world. Yet the epics also reflect realistic and authentic information about values, beliefs, political organization, court life, and trade. Setting the stage for Sita and Rama, therefore, involves distinguishing between Valmiki's impressions of his own historical environment and his use of mythical imagination.

Much of the Rama story takes place in the north region of India, where the sacred river Ganges made settled agriculture possible and where princely states developed, such as one called Kosala. The core *Ramayana* begins and ends in Ayodhya, capital city of this ancient kingdom. Today, the modern Indian state of Uttar Pradesh is larger than ancient Kosala and includes the city of Ayodhya, which retains the same name. Valmiki must have been familiar with both the geographic and political landscapes of northeast India because he provides considerable

1. A. L. Basham, *The Wonder That Was India* (Calcutta: Rupa, 1987 repr.), 409.

convincing detail, particularly about court life in Ayodhya. Realistic details, for example, include the information that the king had several government ministries, such as an effective police force and judiciary. On the other hand, Valmiki offers no concrete evidence about the economy of this state except to say that it was prosperous and had large stores of grain.

Valmiki generously employs his imagination. Ayodhya could not have been large enough to contain all the animals, military units, and bejeweled monumental architecture that he attributed to it (**Document One**). Other important scenes take place in a forest where magic is commonplace. The forest is dangerous, inhabited by demons, and represents external "barbarian" threats to urban civilization.[2] Much of the central action, the captivity and rescue of Sita, takes place on an island, Lanka, to the distant, vague south where a demon king, Ravana, has a massive fortress from which he claims the loyalty of a large following of lesser demons from all over India. The island may correspond to Sri Lanka (Ceylon) and could have been dimly known to Valmiki through hearsay. To those living in the northeast, Sri Lanka would have been considered a strange and exotic place.

The *Ramayana* indicates that, in Valmiki's time around 200 BCE, a social stratification, or caste system, existed, with four mutually exclusive levels. The definitions of the top two levels rest on occupations open to men, the priesthood and the military. Priests (*brahmans*), who controlled the ritual life of society and endorsed the rulers, enjoyed the highest ranking.[3] A close, competitive second were warriors (*kshatriyas*), valued for their courage and skills. Kings (*rajas*) emerged from this second group, able to carve out territory for themselves by force of arms. In practice, not all *brahman* and *kshatriya* men held the occupations indicated by their caste, but they still enjoyed the privileges of high rank. Women in the *brahman* and *kshatriya* castes were, theoretically, wives and mothers who did not need to work. The third caste level was defined as merchants and gentlemen farmers (*vaishyas*). Finally there were manual laborers (*shudras*). Common sense suggests that many women in the third and fourth category actually *did* manual labor as well as rear children. People who did work that made them ritually unclean and therefore untouchable, such as street sweepers and tanners, were outside the caste system, literally out-castes.

Occupations contribute to an explanation of caste, but it is also significant that the ancient Sanskrit word for the system is *varna,* meaning "surface color." In remote ancient times, there was a racial distinction between two broad groups. One was a shorter, darker skinned people (*dasa*), who had been living in India for many centuries. The other group consisted

2. Romila Thapar, *Early India: From the Origins to AD 1300* (Berkeley: University of California Press, 2003), 103–4.

3. All non-English terms are Sanskritic unless otherwise indicated.

of migrating or conquering Aryans, a taller, fairer-skinned people from central Asia, who monopolized the upper two tiers of the caste categories and who subjugated the *dasas*.

While caste is part of a social backdrop for the epic, *religiously sanctioned behavior* occupies center stage. The components of the religion that we now call Hinduism existed before 500 BCE and include a concept of an impersonal absolute being, an acceptance of the effects of good and bad behavior (*karma*), and a belief in rebirth of the soul. The religion of the *Ramayana* includes all these ideas but focuses on another component, *dharma*, a concept that encompasses righteousness, duty, and law, that is, religiously sanctioned behavior. At one point, Valmiki has Rama observe: "Whoever forsakes righteousness [*dharma*] and statecraft [*artha*] and follows the urgings of desire [*kama*] will soon come to grief."[4] More specifically, Rama speaks of honor, which he often defines as public approval: "I fear the danger of unrighteousness [*a-dharma*] and I fear what other people might say."[5] Rama's *dharma* also ensures that he obey his parents' wishes, those of his father first and foremost. Along with priests, he values nonviolence and spirituality, thereby establishing an unresolved tension with his warrior ideals, a reflection perhaps of tensions between the *brahman* and *kshatriya varnas*, who often vied for prestige and influence.

The concept of *dharma* extends vigorously to women in the epic as well. The status of ancient Indian women was tied to caste and wealth and therefore varied considerably, but for all women, *dharma* focused on marriage. While monogamy may have been the norm, among the powerful and wealthy were examples of both polygyny (a man having more than one wife) and, rarely, polyandry (a woman having more than one husband).[6] For example, Rama's father, the king of Kosala, had three principal wives. The elite voices in the *Ramayana* insist that a wife must regard her husband as though he were a god incarnate (**Document Two**). Valmiki, however, writing while Hinduism was still formative, qualifies this view of marriage through Sita, his most powerful female character. She participates in a discourse with Rama and others on the subject of wifely *dharma*. Rama says to his mother, "Even the most excellent of women, one who earnestly undertakes vows and fasts, will come to a bad end if she does not respect her husband's wishes."[7] Sita says to Rama's mother, her mother-in-law, "There is a limit to what a father can give, a limit to what a mother or son can give, but a husband gives without any limit. What wife would not revere him?"[8] Sita clearly expects a good return for her devotion as a wife. In a later scene in the forest, an elderly wise woman tests Sita with the suggestion

4. *The Ramayana of Valmiki: An Epic of Ancient India*, trans. Robert Goldman and Sally J. Sutherland (Princeton, NJ: Princeton University Press, 1984–1986), Bk. 2, 60.

5. Ibid., 65.

6. Thapar, 118.

7. *Ramayana*, Bk. 2, 130.

8. Ibid., 156, sec. 34, v. 26.

that every woman must obey her husband, however bad his character. Sita asks, rhetorically, "How much more readily would I obey a man praised for his virtues, a compassionate, self-disciplined, and righteous man, who is constant in his love, who defers to his mother and holds his father dear?"[9] The old sage is delighted by this response.

While the story line of the epic covers only a short span—Rama's early human adulthood—the composition of the epic itself took several centuries. During that time there were significant political, social, and religious developments witnessed by the poets and editors. The reflections on male and female *dharma* indicate that historically authentic cultural values filter through the epic. Northeastern India was in transition toward more formalized religion, including the formulation of doctrines on correct behavior. Valmiki and other *Ramayana* authors or editors use the characters to evaluate changes over the long time the epic took shape.

A mythical stage can be more elaborate than a strictly historical one, and that is certainly the case for the *Ramayana*. The stage for Rama and Sita is set with a glorious capital city under near perfect rule, a forest of powerful magic, and a beautiful but evil island. The scenes include intricate social values for groups and individuals. The plot is simple and bold, and the richest sources of information are the intimate conversations that take place.

The Actors

Rama and Sita

In the earliest version of the *Ramayana*, Rama and his brothers are born part human, part god, but they are unaware of their special status. Their divine portion is Vishnu, a universal and benevolent deity (**Document Three**). Vishnu undertakes this multiple incarnation in order to slay the dreaded demon Ravana, whose life can only be forfeited to a human. In later accretions to the story and in devotional practice, Rama came to be viewed as one of nine *avatars* (emanations or reincarnations) of Vishnu.[10] In the seventh and last book of the epic—a late addition—Rama understands his divinity and returns to heaven *as* Vishnu. In the core story, however, Rama has largely human qualities and experiences.

Rama is the son of an otherwise unknown and probably fictitious king, Dasaratha, placed in the historical kingdom called Kosala. Of his three principal wives, one is Kausayla, Rama's beloved mother. But Rama is a cultural, not a biological, phenomenon. It is likely that the poets found raw material for Rama in old ballads sung in honor of quasi-historical princes and chieftains.[11] Rama is a mixture of physical prowess, martial skills, devotion to duty (*dharma*), and divine favor. He is also "even-tempered and kind spoken."[12] All these characteristics combine into a potentially ideal ruler.

9. Ibid., 319, sec. 110, v. 4.

10. Among the other eight avatars are Lord Krishna and, from a Hindu perspective, Gautama the Buddha. A tenth avatar lies in the future. See Basham, 302–9.

11. *Ramayana*, Bk. 1, 31–32.

12. Ibid., Bk. 2, 80.

Sita was born of the earth. Her adoptive father, Janaka, finds her as an infant while he plows farmland in northeastern India, and he names her "furrow," *sita*. That he plowed his own land is a bit surprising, because Janaka is a king and, therefore, of the warrior *kshatriya varna*. The plowing detail suggests that activities associated with caste were not as inflexible in practice as they were in theory. His kingdom of Videha, like Kosala, is historical, and Janaka himself may have been based on a real king who was memorable enough to establish his identity for posterity. The poet thus gives Sita a supernatural and royal background, making her a suitable mate for the god-prince Rama.

As already indicated by her interpretation of wifely *dharma*, Sita thinks for herself, in contrast to Rama, who is bound by what others may think of him. In a late variation on the epic's conclusion, Sita *chooses* to be absorbed by the earth, her mother, in death. As we will see, she chooses this return to earth rather than submit to what she considers Rama's stifling sense of honor.[13]

Sita approaches divine status through her husband. As Rama's association with Vishnu evolved, so too Sita moved closer over time to Vishnu's consort, the goddess Lakshmi. The name Lakshmi means fortune and, in both Sanskrit and English, refers to luck as well as wealth—neither of which, we will see, apply particularly well to Sita.

Act I

Marriage and Exile

The *Ramayana*'s plot begins with a task. At the request of a holy sage, King Dasaratha reluctantly sends young Prince Rama, with an armed entourage, into the forest to destroy demons. These demons answer to the distant Ravana, evil lord of Lanka. In the forest, Rama gains allies, learns magic, and acquires supernatural weapons. Rama and his traveling party then make their way to the kingdom of Videha, ruled by King Janaka, adoptive father to the foundling Sita. Janaka is in possession of a massive archer's bow of divine origin that no one has been able to draw. Janaka has for some time offered Sita's hand in marriage to any prince able to draw it. Rama raises the bow, strings it, and positions an arrow. In drawing the bowstring, mighty Rama breaks the bow and wins Sita's hand in marriage. Rama takes Sita home to Ayodhya and they establish themselves as a happy royal couple.

King Dasaratha decides to retire and crown his eldest and highly capable son Rama as prince regent. However, a junior wife named Kaikeyi thwarts the plan. She functions in the story as something like an evil stepmother who sets things awry, a literary device probably borrowed from remotely ancient and well-known folklore. Rama's own mother, Kausalya, is alive and outranks Kaikeyi in the royal family, but Kaikeyi is able to interfere because she has the means to play on

13. See Bharati Mukherjee, *Holder of the World* (New York: Ballantine, 1994), 171–77.

the king's strong sense of honor. In the past, she had won from him two boons, that is, unrestricted, undeniable favors. Her demands are these: first, Rama must be sent back into the forest for an exile of fourteen years; second, Dasaratha's younger son by Kaikeyi, Bharata, is to be summoned to Ayodhya and placed on the throne as prince regent, apparently with the assumption that Dasaratha would die within fourteen years and Bharata would take the throne as king. Typically, succession was male, hereditary, and favored the first-born son.[14] Dasaratha had publicly made known his choice of Rama as his heir apparent, so Kaikeyi's manipulation of royal succession is highly disruptive and becomes the catalyst for the rest of the epic. Dasaratha feels compelled to honor the boons, Rama is honor bound to obey his father, and Sita wishes to stay by Rama's side, even in exile. The couple, along with Rama's brother, Lakshmana, and an entourage, sadly leave Kosala. During the period of exile, Dasaratha dies of a broken heart.

■ Act II

The Abduction and Rescue of Sita

Prince Bharata, informed of his mother's boons, is furious. He follows after his beloved half-brother Rama and finds him in the forest encamped with Lakshmana and Sita and the entourage of soldiers and servants. Bharata tries to persuade Rama to return to Kosala as ruler. Rama, however, wants to fulfill the exile for the full term in order to honor his father's wishes. Bharata reluctantly returns to Ayodhya as Rama's regent, but places his half-brother's sandals on the throne as a symbol of his awaited return.

In the forest, Rama continues to kill demons, as he had in his first task. He fights with a sister of Ravana and maims her. This last deed provokes Ravana's wrath. The evil king plots revenge: the abduction and seduction of Sita. He leaves his island fortress of Lanka and makes his way to the forest encampment in the north. Through magic and deceit, he entices Rama and his men away from their camp, leaving Sita alone. Ravana then abducts her and carries her to his island. A fallen god, Ravana has had a restriction placed on him: he cannot have sex *by force,* on pain of permanent death. Therefore, he tries first to seduce Sita, and then he threatens to eat her if she does not come to him willingly. Sita never gives in to his lust (**Document Four**).

Meanwhile, the grief-stricken Rama and his brother Lakshmana seek assistance for a rescue attempt and make their way to the citadel of a race of monkeys, led by their king, Hanuman, who offers his exceptional help. "Hanuman, born of the wind god Parvana, has the power to fly, to seize clouds, to uproot trees, to relocate mountains. He can cross the waters that separate the tip of India from Lanka in one vigorous leap."[15] Hanuman does leap to Lanka in order to locate Sita and assess the situation. He

14. Thapar, 150.
15. Mukherjee, 173.

offers to rescue Sita himself, but she insists that her rescuer must be Rama. Hanuman returns to Rama and advises an invasion. His army of monkeys constructs a stone causeway out to the island. The ensuing battle is bloody and protracted. Finally, Rama engages Ravana in single combat and, predictably, Rama slays the demon and frees Sita.

The aftermath of the rescue is not happy (**Document Five**). Rama considers Sita to be sullied because she has been under the control of another male. In the conventional value system, a woman's chastity had to remain intact in substance and perception. There was no place for even the appearance of impropriety. Perhaps not surprised but certainly distraught by her husband's attitude, Sita offers to demonstrate her innocence by undergoing trial by fire. The fire god, Agni, refuses her innocent self-sacrifice and delivers her from the fire unharmed. In the core story, Rama accepts his wife back. The fourteen years of exile are over, and they return to Ayodhya, where he is crowned the rightful king.

In the seventh book of the epic, written later than the core story, Rama remains skeptical, and the resulting alternative ending allows Sita to be seen not as a chaste, obedient wife but as a strong, self-sufficient person. In this alternative conclusion, Rama's royal spies tell him that people continue to speak unflatteringly of Sita. Divorce is not an option in their tradition. Despite his skepticism, Rama continues sexual relations with his wife. Sita becomes pregnant, and even though Rama knows of her condition, he decides that he must set a good example for his kingdom by sending his sullied wife into exile. Lakshmana, ever loyal to Rama, takes Sita into the forest and leaves her there. She gives birth to twin boys and rears them in the enchanted forest. Some years later, Rama seeks her out, wanting her and their sons to return to Ayodhya. He asks her to undergo another trial by fire, to satisfy her persistent critics. Sita refuses to do so and refuses to return to the role of an obedient wife. Instead, she consigns herself in death to her mother, the earth. Soon after, the grieving Rama dies and ascends to heaven as Vishnu.

Finale

Despite their dramatic deaths, Rama and Sita live on in literature and in faith, and so it makes sense to end this chapter with a discussion of their current roles in the imaginations and spirituality of Hindu Indians. The cult of Rama has grown dramatically in recent decades, complementary to a rise in Hindu nationalism, that is, an ideology favoring an India based on Hindu laws and culture. Rama's birthplace and capital city, Ayodhya, has become a source of contention between Hindus and the Muslim minority of India.

Islam is ardently monotheistic, placing great emphasis on the singularity of its deity. To many Indian Muslims, Hinduism is pagan polytheism, and Rama is one of many false gods and the object of idolatrous worship. For that reason, in 1528, a Muslim military commander and forerunner of the Mughal dynasty, a man called Babur, reportedly destroyed an ancient temple in Ayodhya dedicated to Rama. Babur then commissioned a mosque (Arabic *masjid*) on the same spot, for the proper worship of the one true God. Periodically, ever since, Hindus have voiced their resentment against Babur and their wish to rebuild Rama's temple.

That same edifice, the *Babri masjid,* or mosque of Babur, became known all over the world in the 1990s. In disuse and locked because of a recent (1990) resurgence of the controversy, the mosque was destroyed by a Hindu mob in December 1992. Hindu religious leaders urged the mob on by shouting that the mosque was Ravana's "dark place."[16] The crowd shouted "Ram[a], Ram[a]," as they reduced the building to rubble. The incident set off bloody conflicts between Hindus and Muslims throughout South Asia.[17] Thus, Rama has acquired a significant symbolic role in the rhetoric of Hindu nationalism. A policy paper of a Hindu nationalist party states that Rama's kingship "has always represented the ideal of governance" (**Document Six**).

Sita, too, lives on, although she has lost some of her independent spirit. She is now a role model for a virtuous wife who practices *pativrata,* husband worship. The modern interpretation of her ordeal by fire is her purification, that is, absolution from the *potential* sin of impropriety with Ravana.[18] Young Indian girls pray to be like Sita and to have a husband like Rama and a mother-in-law like Kausayla.[19] Since the two major epics of India, the *Ramayana* and the *Mahabharata,* have scriptural value, ideals that they contain have divine sanction. Words from the *Ramayana* are used, for example, in many Hindu weddings. The words are those of King Janaka, when he gives his daughter to Rama in marriage: "Here is my daughter, Sita, who will ever tread with you the path of *dharma*. Take her hand in yours. Blessed and devoted, she will ever walk with you like your own shadow."[20]

Sita's character in the Ramayana is complex and intriguing. A good illustration of this has to do with her interaction with the monkey king Hanuman. On his scouting visit to Lanka, Hanuman finds Sita and offers to fly her to safety. Sita refuses, insisting that Rama himself must come to her rescue, thus necessitating the bloody invasion.[21] The usual understanding of Sita's response is that she can touch no male except her husband and, therefore, is refusing to cling to the male monkey in flight, even to save herself. Ravana had already touched

16. Stanley Wolpert, *A New History of India,* 6th ed. (New York: Oxford University Press, 1999), 443.

17. Ibid., 436–43.

18. On *pativrata* and purification, see Rajeswari Sunder Rajan, *Real and Imagined Women: Gender, Culture, and Postcolonialism* (London: Routledge, 1993), 67, 76.

19. June McDaniels, *Making Virtuous Daughters and Wives: An Introduction to Women's Brata Rituals in Bengali Folk Religion* (New York: State University of New York Press, 2003).

20. Sara S. Mitter, *Dharma's Daughters: Contemporary Indian Women and Hindu Culture* (New Brunswick, NJ: Rutgers University Press, 1991), 82; 182, endn. 5.

21. *Ramayana,* Bk. 5, 212–15.

her, in bringing her to Lanka, but in that she had no choice. With Hanuman, however, she can decline. Sita's refusal has prompted novelist Bharati Mukherjee, writing in the 1990s, to wonder whether the character Sita fully *wanted* to be rescued. Perhaps the exotic, ten-headed Ravana held some unconventional appeal. Perhaps the poet was toying with an exciting though dangerous example of crossing a cultural border.[22] And so Sita remains, paradoxically, an obedient wife who follows her own path through fire and back into the earth.

22. Mukherjee, 173–74.

Documents

DOCUMENT ONE

Valmiki

The Ramayana (ca. 200 BCE)

The following passage from The Ramayana *is a hyperbolic description of Rama's city, Ayodhya, when it was under his father's rule. What kind of information does the poet Valmiki provide? One cannot help but note that the city approaches perfection. Why would the poet-editor want to idealize the city?*

Sarga 5

1-3. This great tale, known as the *Rāmāyana*, concerns itself with the dynasty of those great and victorious kings, the Ikṣvākus, descendants of Brahmā, lord of creatures, and those to whom this whole earth first of all belonged. Among them was Sagara, who caused the ocean to be dug and who had sixty thousand sons to form his entourage when he went abroad.

4. I will recite it from the beginning in its entirety, omitting nothing. It is in keeping with the goals of righteousness, profit, and pleasure, and should be listened to with faith.

5. There is a great, happy, and prosperous country called Kosala, situated on the banks of the Sarayū river and rich in abundance of wealth and grain.

6. There was situated the world-famous city of Ayodhyā, a city built by Manu himself, lord of men.

7. It was a great and majestic city, twelve leagues long and three wide, with well-ordered avenues.

8. It was adorned with a great and well-ordered royal highway, always strewn with loose blossoms and constantly sprinkled with water.

9. King Daśaratha, who had expanded a realm already great, dwelt in that city, like the lord of the gods in heaven. . . .

12. It was a great city filled with troops of actresses everywhere, dotted with parks and mango groves, and girdled by ramparts.

13. It was a fortress with a deep moat impossible to cross, was unassailable by its enemies, and was filled with horses, elephants, cows, camels, and donkeys.

14. Filled with crowds of neighboring kings come to pay tribute, it was likewise adorned with merchants of many different lands.

15. It was splendid with hills and palaces fashioned of jewels. Bristling with its rooftop turrets, it resembled Indra's Amarāvatī.

16. Colorful, laid out like a chessboard, and crowded with hosts of the most beautiful women, it was filled with every kind of jewel and adorned with palatial buildings.

17. Situated on level ground, its houses were built in close proximity to one another, without the slightest gap between them. It held plentiful stores of *śāli* rice, and its water was like the juice of sugar cane. . . .

SARGA 6

. . . 6. In that great city men were happy, righteous, and deeply learned. They were truthful and not covetous, for each man was content with his own property.

7. In that most excellent city there was no householder who did not have significant property, who had not accomplished his goals, or who was not possessed of cattle, horses, wealth, and grain.

8. Nowhere in Ayodhyā could one find a lecher, a miser, a cruel or unlearned man, or an agnostic.

9. All the men and women conducted themselves in accordance with righteousness and were self-controlled and joyful. In disposition and conduct they were as pure as the great seers themselves.

10. No one lacked earrings, diadem, and necklace. No one was deprived of pleasures. There was no one who was dirty or whose body lacked for ointments or perfume.

11. There was no one who had unclean food or was ungenerous. There was nobody who did not wear an armlet and a golden breastplate. No one was lacking in either rings or self-control.

12. Nor was there in Ayodhyā a single brahman who did not kindle the sacred fires, sacrifice, and donate thousands in charity. Nor were there any who indulged in mixing of the social classes.

13. The brahmans had subdued their senses and were always devoted to their proper occupation. They were given over to charity and study and were restrained in accepting gifts.

14. There were no agnostics and no liars. There was none who was not deeply learned. None was envious, incompetent, or ignorant.

15. No one was unhappy, fickle, or troubled. In Ayodhyā, one could not find a man or a woman lacking in grace or beauty, or anyone who was not devoted to the king.

16. The men of all the social classes, of which the foremost, the brahmans, makes the fourth, worshiped both gods and guests. They were long-lived, practicing truth and righteousness.

17. The kshatriyas accepted the brahmans as their superiors, and the *vaiśyas* were subservient to the kshatriyas. The *śūdras*, devoted to their proper duty, served the other three classes.

18. In short, the city was as well governed by that lord . . . as it had been long ago by the wise Manu, foremost of men. . . .

Sarga 7

1. That hero [the King] had eight renowned ministers, incorruptible and unswervingly devoted to affairs of state.

2. They were Dhṛṣti, Jayanta, Vijaya, Siddhārtha, Arthasādhaka, Aśoka, Mantrapāla, and Sumantra, who made the eighth.

3. He had also two principal officiating priests, the foremost of seers Vasiṣṭha and Vāmadeva, as well as other counsellors. . . .

9. Heroic, unflagging in energy, they put into practice the science of statecraft. They were the constant protectors of all honest inhabitants of the realm.

10. They filled the treasury without injury to the brahmans and kshatriyas and meted out strict punishment only after considering the relative gravity of a man's offense.

11. When all those honest and likeminded men sat in judgment, there was not a single man in the city or the kingdom who dared to bear false witness.

12. There was no such thing as a wicked man there, or a man who made love to another man's wife. That splendid city and, indeed, the whole country were at peace. . . .

16. Ever watchful through his secret agents, pleasing his subjects in accordance with righteousness, he found no enemy to be his equal, much less superior to him.

17. Surrounded by devoted, clever, and capable counsellors, skilled both in counsel and in strategy, the king achieved a blazing splendor, as does the rising sun surrounded by its shining rays.

DOCUMENT TWO

The Laws of Manu
(Compiled between the first and fourth centuries CE)

A corpus of Hindu values and rules is probably the work of many scholars but is attributed to one, Manu, a name suggesting "founder" or "originator." This law code, like the earlier religion of the Ramayana, *focuses on* dharma, *that is, righteousness, duty, and law. The two excerpts here convey the* dharmas *for wives and husbands, respectively. How authoritative do the* dharmas *seem to you; that is, do the passages sound like law or advice?*

Chapter 5

. . . [147]. A girl, a young woman, or even an old woman should not do anything independently, even in (her own) house. [148] In childhood a woman should be under her father's control, in youth under her husband's, and when her husband is dead, under her sons'. She should not have independence. [149] A woman should not try to separate herself from her father, her husband, or her sons, for her separation from them would make both (her own and her husband's) families contemptible. [150] She should always be cheerful, and clever at household affairs; she should keep her utensils well polished and not have too free a hand in spending. [151] When her father, or her brother with her father's permission, gives her to someone, she should obey that man while he is alive and not violate her vow to him when he is dead.

[152] Benedictory verses are recited and a sacrifice to the Lord of Creatures is performed at weddings to make them auspicious, but it is the act of giving away (the bride) that makes (the groom) her master. [153] A husband who performs the transformative ritual (of marriage) with Vedic verses always makes his woman happy, both when she is in her fertile season and when she is not, both here on earth and in the world beyond. [154] A virtuous wife should constantly serve her husband like a god, even if he behaves badly, freely indulges his lust, and is devoid of any good qualities. [155] Apart (from their husbands), women cannot sacrifice or undertake a vow or fast; it is because a wife obeys her husband that she is exalted in heaven.

[156] A virtuous wife should never do anything displeasing to the husband who took her hand in marriage, when he is alive or dead, if she longs for her husband's world (after death). [157] When her husband is dead she may fast as much as she likes, (living) on auspicious flowers, roots, and fruits, but she should not even mention the name of another man. [158] She should be long-suffering until death, self-restrained, and chaste, striving (to fulfil) the unsurpassed duty of women who have one husband. . . .

CHAPTER 9

. . . [6] Regarding this as the supreme duty of all the classes, husbands, even weak ones, try to guard their wives. [7] For by zealously guarding his wife he guards his own descendants, practices, family, and himself, as well as his own duty. [8] The husband enters the wife, becomes an embryo, and is born here on earth. That is why a wife is called a wife (*jāyā*), because he is born (*jāyate*) again in her. [9] The wife brings forth a son who is just like the man she makes love with; that is why he [husband] should guard his wife zealously, in order to keep his progeny clean.

[10] No man is able to guard women entirely by force, but they can be entirely guarded by using these means: [11] he should keep her busy amassing and spending money, engaging in purification, attending to her duty, cooking food, and looking after the furniture. . . .

DOCUMENT THREE

The Bhagavad Gita (ca. 100 BCE–100 CE)

The Bhagavad Gita (Song of the Lord) *is a scriptural story that tells of a lengthy discussion between the warrior Arjuna and his charioteer. The charioteer turns out to be Krishna, an* avatar *("reincarnation") of the deity Vishnu. Rama is an avatar of the same deity. What follows is Vishnu's description of himself, a list of characteristics that could be applied equally to Rama in his divine state. How does the human Rama measure up to the divine Vishnu?*

Now I will tell the chief of my holy powers. . . .
though there is no end to my fullness.
I am the self in the inmost heart of all that are born. . . .
I am their beginning, their middle and their end. . . .
I am the beginning, the middle, the end, of all creation,
the science of the soul among sciences,
of speakers I am the speech,
of letters I am A.[1]

I am unending time,
I am the ordainer who faces all ways,
I am destroying death,
I am the source of all that is to be. . . .
I am the dice-play of the gamester,

1. *A* is the first letter of the Sanskrit alphabet. It is also implicit in all the other letters, if they are not modified by special marks.

I am the glory of the glorious,
I am victory, I am courage,
I am the goodness of the virtuous. . . .
I am the force of those who govern,
I am the statecraft of those who seek to conquer,
I am the silence of what is secret,
I am the knowledge of those who know, and
I am the seed of all that is born. . . .

There is nothing that can exist without me.
There is no end to my holy powers. . . .
And whatever is mighty or fortunate or strong
springs from a portion of my glory.

DOCUMENT FOUR

VALMIKI

The Ramayana (ca. 200 BCE)

The monkey king, Hanuman, overhears Ravana speaking these words to an unreceptive Sita. Do you think the attempted seduction is sincere? What do you learn about Hanuman's and Ravana's values?

SARGA 18

1. Then, with honeyed words fraught with meaning, Rāvaṇa revealed his intentions to that dejected woman as she sat there surrounded, joyless and suffering.

2. "On seeing me, lady with thighs like elephants' trunks, you cover your breasts and stomach as if in your fear you wished to make yourself invisible.

3. "I long for you, wide-eyed lady. Dear lady, you are endowed with every bodily perfection. Stealer of all men's hearts, please look upon me with favor.

4. "There are no men here nor are there other *rākṣasas*, who can change their form at will. So banish your fear of me, Sītā.

5. "For, timorous woman, making love to other men's wives and even carrying them off by force is perfectly appropriate behavior for *rākṣasas*. Let there be no doubt about this.

6. "Nevertheless, Maithili, I will never touch you unless you desire it, though Kāma, the god of love, may rage through my body to his heart's content.

7. "You must trust me, dear lady. You need have no fear on this account. Give me your true love. You must not become prey to sorrow like this.

8. "This single braid, your sleeping on the ground, your brooding, your soiled garments, and your fasting at the wrong time: such things do not become you at all.

9–10. "Lovely floral garlands, sandalwood, and aloe; various garments, heavenly jewelry, costly drink, carriages, and beds; singing, dancing, and music—accept me, Maithili, and you shall have it all. . . .

24. "Consider my wealth, fortunate lady, my magnificence, and my fame. Of what use to you, my lovely, is this Rāma with his barkcloth robes?

25. "Rāma has renounced the triumph of a warrior and has lost his royal splendor to become an ascetic, a wanderer in the forest, who sleeps on the bare ground. Indeed, I doubt that he is still alive.

26. "Nor will Rāma ever get even a glimpse of you, Vaidehī, any more than he could of moonlight occluded by the dense, black storm clouds that the cranes herald.

27. "Unlike Hiraṇyakaśipu, who brought his wife back from Indra's clutches, Rāma will never be able to get you back from mine.

28. "Beautiful lady, your smile, teeth, and eyes are lovely. You carry away my heart, as Suparna would a serpent.

29. "Since first I set my eyes on you, I have taken no pleasure in my own wives, even though you are emaciated, stripped of ornaments, and clad in a garment of tattered silk.

30. "No matter how many women—replete with every virtue—I may have in my inner apartments, Jānakī, you will rule over them all.

31. "All my women—the finest in all the three worlds—will wait upon you, lady of the raven tresses, as do the *apsarases* upon Śri, the goddess of good fortune.

32. "Whatever wealth and choice things were once Vaiśravaṇa's, you will now enjoy to your heart's content, woman of lovely brows and hips, as well as all the worlds and me.

33. "Rāma cannot compare to me, my lady, in ascetic power, physical strength, valor, wealth, power, or fame.

34. "So drink, enjoy yourself, amuse yourself, take pleasure in all pleasurable things. I shall bestow heaps of wealth and even the earth itself upon you. Delight in me, delightful one, to your heart's content, and let your kinfolk join you here and delight themselves as well.

35. "In seaside forest groves—canopied with stands of flowering trees and swarming with bees—you will enjoy yourself with me, timid lady, your body ornamented with bright necklaces of gold."

DOCUMENT FIVE

The Concise Ramayana of Valmiki (ca. 200 BCE)

The encounter between Rama and Sita after the defeat of Ravana is highly dramatic. This passage comes from an abbreviated translation of a late extension of the epic. What role does the concept of honor play in this scene?

. . . Rāma said sternly: "My purpose has been accomplished, O Sītā. My prowess has been witnessed by all. I have fulfilled my pledge. Rāvaṇa's wickedness has been punished. The extraordinary feat performed by Hanumān in crossing the ocean and burning Laṅkā has borne fruit. Vibhīṣaṇa's devotion has been rewarded." Rāma's heart was in a state of conflict, afraid as he was of public ridicule. Hence, he continued: "I wish to let you know that all this was done not for your sake, but for the sake of preserving my honour. Your conduct is open to suspicion, hence even your sight is displeasing to me. Your body was touched by Rāvaṇa: how then can I, claiming to belong to a noble family, accept you? Hence I permit you to go where you like and live with whom you like—either Lakṣmaṇa, Bharata, Śatrughna, Sugrīva or even Vibhīṣaṇa. It is difficult for me to believe that Rāvaṇa, who was so fond of you, would have been able to keep away from you for such a long time."

Sītā was shocked. Rāma's words wounded her heart. Tears streamed down her face. Wiping them, she replied: "O Rāma, you are speaking to me in the language of a common and vulgar man speaking to a common woman. That which was under my control, my heart, has always been yours; how could I prevent my body from being touched when I was helpless and under another person's control? Ah, if only you had conveyed your suspicion through Hanumān when he came to meet me, I would have killed myself then and saved you all this trouble and the risk involved in the war." Turning to Lakṣmaṇa, she said: "Kindle the fire, O Lakṣmaṇa: that is the only remedy. I shall not live to endure this false calumny." Lakṣmaṇa looked at Rāma and with his approval kindled the fire. Sītā prayed: "Even as my heart is ever devoted to Rāma, may the fire protect me. If I have been faithful to Rāma in thought, word or deed, may the fire protect me. The sun, the moon, the wind, earth and others are witness to my purity; may the fire protect me." Then she entered into the fire, even as an oblation poured into the fire would. Gods and sages witnessed this. The women who saw this screamed. . . .

. . . [T]he god of fire emerged from the fire in his personal form, holding up Sītā in his hands. Sītā shone in all her radiance. The god of fire who is the witness of everything that takes place in the world, said to Rāma: "Here is your Sītā Rāma. I find no fault in her. She has not erred in thought, word or deed. Even during the long period of her detention in the abode of Rāvana, she did not even think of him, as her heart was set on you. Accept her: and I command you not to treat her harshly. . . ."

DOCUMENT SIX

Lal Krishna Advani

Preface, *White Paper on Ayodhya and Rama Temple Movement* (1993)

Lal Krishna Advani is a retired Indian politician closely associated with the movement to rebuild a temple dedicated to Rama in Ayodhya, in the modern Indian state of Uttar Pradesh. In October 1990, as a leader of the largest Hindu nationalist political party, the Bharatiya Janata Party (BJP), he began a campaign to replace a Muslim mosque, the Baburi masjid (built c. 1528) with a new Rama temple. The following is part of Advani's preface to his party's policy paper on the subject of the Baburi masjid. What is the tone of this selection?

Foreword

Sri Rama is the unique symbol, the unequalled symbol of our oneness, of our integration, as well as of our aspiration to live the higher values. As Maryada Purushottam Sri Rama has represented for thousands of years the ideal of conduct, just as Rama Rajya has always represented the ideal of governance. There is scarcely a language in our country into which the Ramayana has not been translated. There is scarcely a folk tradition, which does not celebrate the life and legend of Sri Rama. And one saint of our land after another, one saintly tradition after another has immersed itself in devotion to Him: the sacred Sri Guru Granth Sahib celebrates and invokes Sri Rama about two thousand four hundred times, Gandhiji died with His name on his lips.

It is natural therefore that the place of His birth has been an object of the deepest devotion for Hindus through the millennia — the inscription which has been found at the site and which speaks of a magnificent temple with a pinnacle of gold, dedicated to Lord Vishnu Hari who had humbled King Bali and defeated the wicked Dashanana, that is, Ravana; the record of the unremitting struggle of the Hindus to regain the site; the pathetic history of their worshipping the spot from a distance when they were denied access to it, of their circumambulating it — all these bear testimony to their deep and abiding, and indeed stirring, devotion to Sri Rama.

On the other hand, the structure which Mir Baqi put up on the orders of Babur never had any special significance from a religious point of view. It was purely and simply a symbol not of devotion and of religion but of conquest. Correspondingly, quite apart from its being an obstacle, preventing Hindus from worshipping the birthplace of their idol, Sri Rama, it was for the country the symbol of its subjugation.

As I mentioned, the Hindus had been trying for centuries to reacquire access to the spot and to reconstruct the magnificent temple. That was one stream of the

Ayodhya movement — a stream that has been unbroken through centuries, one that predates by centuries all the persons and organisations which are today associated with the Ramjanmabhoomi movement. The Sadhus and Sants who set up the Ramjanmabhoomi Nyas in 1986 — when no political party or organization was seized of the matter — represent that continuous stream in our times.

But another powerful current arose among the people, and the confluence of the two has given the power to the Sri Ramjanmabhoomi movement which we see today. The manner in which the State bent to fundamentalists and terrorists, the manner in which self-styled leaders of minorities sought to revive the politics of separatism which had led to the Partition of the country, and even more so the manner in which Prime Ministers and others genuflected to them; and the double standards which came more and more to mar public discourse in India to the point that the word "Hindu" became something to be ashamed about, to the point that nationalism became a dirty word — these ignited a great revulsion among the people. As all this was being done in the name of "Secularism," it led people to feel that what was being practised was not Secularism but a perversion. The people began to search for what true Secularism meant, they began to wonder how our country could at all survive if Nationalism was to be anathema.

Reconstructing the temple for Sri Rama became the symbol of this rising consciousness ridding the country of the perversities to which it was being subjected in the name of Secularism, forging a strong and united country. The object of the movement thus became not just to construct yet another temple, the object became to put our country back on its feet, to purify our public life, our public discourse.

This is how in 1989 the Bharatiya Janata Party formally decided to lend its shoulder to the cause — the Party was responding to the deepest urges of our people. . . .

Questions

1. Has an instructor ever asked you to read myth or fiction as a supplement to historical topics? If so, did you find the material to be frustrating or helpful? Explain why.
2. Are the values associated with marriage in the *Ramayana* and in **Document Two** consistent with the best interests of individuals? Of society as a whole? Of a specific group?
3. The information about Kosala (**Document One**) is selective and hyperbolic. What *other* information would be helpful to know?

Suggested Readings

Basham, A. L. *The Wonder That Was India* Repr., Delhi: Rupa, 1987.

Thapar, Romila. *Early India: From the Origins to AD 1300.* Berkeley: University of California Press, 2003.

Valmiki. *The Ramayana of Valmiki: An Epic of Ancient India.* 5 vols. Trans. Robert Goldman and Sally J. Sutherland. Princeton, NJ: Princeton University Press, 1984–1986.

Mukherjee, Bharati. *Holder of the World.* New York: Ballantine, 1994. A novel that makes significant reference to Sita and Rama.

CHAPTER

7

Spiritual Partners in Christian Asceticism: Jerome (?346–420 CE) and Paula (347–404 CE)

SETTING THE STAGE

By the fourth century, the Roman Empire was divided administratively into eastern and western sectors. Gradually power shifted to the eastern part of the Empire, home to multiple ethnic populations, a network of urban centers, and a still vibrant Greek and Latin cultural and intellectual life. Throughout this period, and over the next several centuries, the authorities in the East had to contend with a well-established Sasanian Persian Empire that abutted its frontiers in western Asia. In the western Mediterranean and north into Europe, Roman law, language, and social order were planted, but this was accompanied by the growth of provincial authority, increased regionalism, expanding financial burdens, and reliance on an army made up of members of assimilated Germanic tribes. Alliances with various Germanic tribes such as the Visigoths maintained peace for a time, but violent confrontations continued to occur.

Over the course of the fourth century, in both the eastern and western parts of the Empire, Christianity became legally acceptable, socially respectable, and politically powerful. In the early years of the century, the Roman emperor Constantine (r. 306–337 CE) converted to Christianity and in 313 CE issued the Edict of Milan, which gave Christians freedom to worship openly. It is important to remember that in previous centuries, persecution of Christians in the Empire had not been continuous or wholly effective, and thus by the time of Constantine's reign, important Christian centers stretched from the centers of empire, Rome and Constantinople, around the Mediterranean from the Dalmatian coast, to Syria and Egypt, to North Africa, and to Spain. As Christianity became legitimate, church authorities insisted they had brought an end to paganism, and eventually by 383, the law code of the emperor Theodosius (r. 379–395) proclaimed that all peoples in the empire must practice the Christian religion. These dramatic events were part of a dynamic process of transformation as the Roman Empire was Christianized, and as Christianity absorbed and assimilated Roman values, ideas, and administrative structures. Nevertheless, while believers and those in authority might declare Christianity universal, the geographic breadth of its sweep and the diversity of the local traditions it encompassed meant that it was hardly unified.[1] All aspects of life in the fourth century were affected by debates over beliefs and creeds, competition for authority, and tensions between civic goals and spiritual power and behaviors.

Particularly in the West, as elements of imperial structure dissolved, Christian bishops, councils, doctrine, and laws moved into the gaps and vacancies and helped to construct a distinct identity and their own claims to universal, or catholic, power. Gradually, insistence on conformity in ideas and practices, and even persecution of heretics or those who chose different teachings and behaviors, replaced an older heterodoxy that could tolerate pagans, Jews, and a variety of other spiritual expressions.

The radical promise of the early church appealed to women as it had appealed to men. Women's contributions had been welcome in the movement in its infancy, and women were among the martyrs to its cause. Legitimacy, prestige, and orthodoxy were a far cry from an era when to be Christian meant to risk one's life or when persecution and marginality served as the marks of holiness and true belief. As a result, it is important to set the institutional, legal, political, and doctrinal changes of the fourth century against their impact on individual lives and the personal responses to those changes.

1. See esp. chap. 3 in Peter Brown, *The Rise of Western Christendom* (Malden, MA: Blackwell, 2003).

The lives of Jerome and Paula allow us to consider the complex relationships between the institutional and the personal dimensions of Christianity in a period of rapid transformation. These two people were deeply involved in numerous areas of social, intellectual, and spiritual change in the fourth century, and their experiences help to illustrate why and how such changes took place. First, during this period the Roman senatorial aristocracy converted to Christianity in large numbers, or "drifted into respectable Christianity," as historian Peter Brown describes it.[2] Mothers, wives, and daughters of these families, like Paula, often led the way in the conversions and became the exemplary models of Christian devotion and morality. Second, with legalization, church offices and positions became prestigious and desirable, and a new elite of well-known specialists—intellectual men like Jerome who were well educated in philosophy and theology—helped to define what it meant to be Christian. Finally, in those years, long-existing Roman and Christian traditions of asceticism blossomed and were institutionalized in Christian monasticism, which became increasingly important in the structure and identity of Western Christendom.

The founding of affiliated holy communities in Bethlehem by Jerome and Paula typifies these developments. Their motives for founding such communities and adopting such a way of life may have been quite similar, but gender differences shaped their place in these movements, the personal meaning of their adoption of holy virginity, and the social responses to these choices. Jerome and Paula lived in similar environments and struggled with all of these issues, together and separately, in practice and in spirit.

Abundant written sources are available for the study of this era; among them are personal confessions and letters, autobiographical writings, and theoretical and moral essays. Especially popular were accounts of the lives of individuals who were models of devotion and sacrifice. In spite of their extensive size, the records from the time pose certain problems. Many accounts were written to exhort, convert, and educate, and even personal memoirs were often written long after the fact. For example, the information we have about Jerome's childhood and youth comes from documents he wrote as an adult, and thus reflect his mature interests and ideas. While Jerome's letters were preserved, none of the writings of Paula, her daughters, or their women contemporaries survived. The historical record of the Roman Empire for this era contains few examples of elite women's written work, perhaps because subsequent generations saw no reason to preserve it. And, of course, nonelite women and men left no documents of their experiences; thus "a great hole remains in our grasp of Roman actuality."[3]

2. Peter Brown, *Religion and Society in the Age of Augustine* (London: Faber and Faber, 1972), 178. This is a phrase that is often quoted by other historians. Brown's works are among the most important sources for this period.

3. Paul Halsall, "Early Western Civilization under the Sign of Gender: Europe and the Mediterranean," in *A Companion to Gender History*, eds. Teresa A. Meade and Merry Wiesner-Hanks (Malden, MA: Blackwell, 2004), 295.

The Actors

Jerome and Paula

Jerome was born in an economically comfortable family that owned valuable land in Stridon, in the northwest area of the province of Dalmatia. Uncertainty about the date of his birth plagues historians, who are forced to try to deduce when he was born from references to other people in his writing or from what others say about him.[4] His family probably immigrated from Greece, but was thoroughly Latinized by the fourth century. Jerome says little about his parents, perhaps because they were not as devout as he might have liked, although they were Christian.

Like other boys of his social class, Jerome attended an elementary school from age six or seven to age eleven or twelve. He learned to read and write, probably some basic Greek in addition to Latin, and to do elementary mathematics. When Jerome was twelve he was sent to Rome for his secondary education. This practice was common at the time because several schools in Rome offered the best possible education, which in turn could lead to lucrative and prestigious government positions. In a school run by a celebrated master, Jerome received general instruction in mathematics, science, and music, but the focus of the school program was grammar, the correct use of language, and classical literature, as it had been for centuries. Two things are important about this education. First, Jerome became familiar with a variety of classical (and pagan) authors, including Virgil, Terence, Cicero, and even the early playwright Plautus and the Stoic moralist Seneca. Later in his life, he would have to decide the value of these pagan texts in a Christian world. Second, the method of instruction, which included memorization and recitation, followed by a systematic, line-by-line analysis of the texts, made Jerome an excellent grammarian and rhetorician and one of "the finest Latin Christian writers."[5]

Jerome's life as a student in Rome was probably not greatly different from that of his fellow schoolmates. He began to buy volumes of the classics, some of which he transcribed himself. He also fully engaged in the social life of the youth of the time, including "sexual adventures" which he later regretted as failings or stumbling on "the slippery path of youth."[6] He was formally baptized at some point in his Roman sojourn, and he took advantage of Rome's history to visit the catacombs and to pay homage to earlier Christian martyrs.

Simultaneously, Paula was growing up in the conventional environment of a daughter of the Roman lower senatorial aristocracy. Later, when Jerome wrote the epitaph for Paula's tomb, he claimed she was "born from the Scipios, sprung from Pauline parents, scion of the Gracchi."[7] There is no evidence

4. J. N. D. Kelly, Jerome's major biographer, uses the earliest date, 331. See *Jerome: His Life, Writings and Controversies* (London: Duckworth, 1975), app. Peter Brown in *The Body and Society: Men, Women and Sexual Renunciation in Early Christianity* (New York: Columbia University Press, 1988), 366, uses the date 346.

5. Kelly, 13.

6. Kelly, 21.

7. Quoted in Jo Ann McNamara, "Cornelia's Daughters: Paula and Eustochium," *Women's Studies* 11 (1984): 9. This claim meant that Paula took her name from the father of Scipio Aemilianus, Aemilius Paulus.

to support this lineage, but such claims reflect the ongoing importance of family bloodlines and noble ancestry, even among Christians like Jerome. Paula's parents, Blaesilla and Rogatus, may not have had illustrious pedigrees and we don't know if they were Christians, but they were at least on the periphery of the elite, which meant they had considerable wealth.[8]

By this period of Roman history, girls of Paula's social rank were well educated in public grammar schools, where they studied Latin literary masters of the past and probably also gained some rudimentary knowledge of Greek. By the age of fifteen they were ready to be married and thus would not have had further education as Jerome did. Both the laws and actual practices regarding marriage, family, inheritance, and adultery had been in place for some time when Paula came of age. Loosening of some controls over women had given them more rights, particularly in matters of inheritance, control over property, and guardianship of minor children.

The emperor Constantine had altered some of the Augustan marriage and adultery laws (see Chapter Four)—clamping down on some behaviors and allowing others. For the topic at hand it is important that Constantine had repealed earlier legislation that had penalized celibacy. Laws providing protection for virgins and holy widows subsequently were expanded in 364 to "call for capital punishment for anyone who even 'solicited' consecrated maidens or widows."[9] Even during the centuries of Roman imperial expansion, the mixing of peoples and cultures in the Mediterranean, and the gradual assimilation of so-called barbarian populations in the frontier areas, the models of excellence and ideal comportment for men and women remained remarkably unchanged. Women were expected to follow the pattern of the Republican *matrona,* which had guided their predecessors. Marriage and motherhood were the goals; chastity, modesty, and devotion to family and community remained the desired behavior for all women of the free and freed classes. Self-discipline and order, along with civic duty and loyalty, were to guide male behavior. At the same time, the tradition of a double standard of sexual behavior persisted and allowed men, but not women, to practice marital infidelity, particularly with slaves and servants.

At the age of fifteen (ca. 362) Paula married Toxotius, who came from a senatorial family not unlike her own. We know that when she was married, Paula was a Christian, but we do not know when her conversion occurred. Mixed religious marriages were not uncommon at the time, and perhaps Toxotius was a pagan who converted

8. Among the various authors who provide details on Paula's life, and on the lives of other women who were her social equals and contemporaries, are Anne Ewing Hickey, *Women of the Roman Aristocracy as Christian Monastics* (Ann Arbor: University of Michigan Research Press, 1987); Ann Yarbrough, "Christianization in the Fourth Century: The Example of Roman Women," *Journal of Religious History* 15, no. 1 (1988): 319–35; Patricia Ranft, *Women and the Religious Life in Premodern Europe* (New York: St Martin's, 1996); and Elizabeth Clark, "Patrons, Not Priests: Gender and Power in Late Ancient Christianity," *Gender and History* 2 (1990): 253–73.

9. Hickey, 30.

after his marriage. The marriage was apparently happy and successful; they had five children, four girls and a boy, which was an unusually large family at the time. Jerome later claimed that, after Paula had finally given her husband a male heir, sexual relations between them ceased for religious reasons.[10]

As a wife and mother, Paula met the feminine ideals of the day. She probably had an active public life, using her own and her family's wealth to engage in charitable works and to meet social obligations. Somewhere around 378 Toxotius senior died, leaving Paula a widow with five children. The Romans had always been ambivalent about remarriage, as evident in the ideal of the *univira,* the woman devoted to one husband in her lifetime. Paula chose not to remarry, and instead substituted religious devotion and life in a Christian community for conventional marriage and family.

Act I

Paths to Asceticism

While Paula was embarking on a life of marriage and maternity, Jerome was completing his studies. Sometime in 367 or 368, he and a friend left Rome and traveled to Trier in northern Gaul. Why they chose this destination is not entirely clear, but Trier was the capital of the West for much of the fourth century and it was the center for a host of imperial officials and ministries. Perhaps Jerome hoped to find a lucrative position there. As it turned out, his time in Trier and then a subsequent stay in Aquileia, the military and commercial center located at the northern end of the Adriatic Sea, proved to be "of crucial importance for his personal development and for the shaping of his career."[11] During the time from 367 to 372, Jerome decided to abandon a secular career and to dedicate himself to a Christian life of contemplation and retirement from the public world.

Various factors explain Jerome's decision. Among them are the facts that both Trier and Aquileia were centers of Christian activity and energy and that both places had impressive Christian leaders, particularly in the persons of residing bishops who were engaged in heated debates over doctrinal matters. Most doctrinal controversies focused on efforts to describe the relationship between the divine and the created worlds, between spirit and body, and over how best to give expression to one's beliefs and to God's will. These questions were at the core of debates surrounding the relationship between Father, Son, and Holy Spirit. A church council meeting at Nicaea in 325 had addressed this problem and resolved that the Father and Son were of the same substance

10. See Letter 108 from Jerome to Eustochium, Paula's daughter, in *Handmaids of the Lord: Contemporary Descriptions of Feminine Asceticism in the First Six Christian Centuries,* tr. and ed. Joan H. Petersen (Kalamazoo, MI: Cistercian, 1996), 129.

11. Kelly, 25.

and time of creation. Nevertheless, treatises continued to be written on the subject and contrary views persisted, with the most heated debates continuing to focus on defining the nature of Christ, or "christology." Specifically at issue was whether the created material essence of the Son could ever be equated with the divine essence of the Father. These debates captured Jerome's intellectual and spiritual imagination, and he began a pattern of vigorous engagement in theological disputes that continued throughout his life.

Another force that would influence both Jerome and Paula in these years was the growth of asceticism, which was practiced in various forms. Ascetic behaviors in the Roman world insisted that the conquest of the body and material desires could lead to purity, enlightenment, and higher truth.[12] Christianity had established practices of self-sacrifice and self-denial as a way of escaping this world and achieving communion with God, who was the beginning and the end of human existence. Sexual abstinence in particular became a mark of holiness and an "undivided heart."[13]

The legalization of Christianity altered the status and meaning of asceticism, virginity, and celibacy in contradictory ways. For many people, legitimacy also meant secularization, and "respectable" Christianity, which seemed to have lost the inspiration and zeal of the earlier movement, offered them little satisfaction. Others who desired a "strict and simpler life" were "sickened by the hypocrisy of new recruits who joined the church only because it was now safe and fashionable to do so."[14] Jerome, for one, would frequently attack the hypocrisy and materialism of the Christian Roman elite. For some, the disappearance of persecution required a new opportunity for the sacrifices of heroic Christianity, and asceticism offered such a life and identity. Asceticism was accessible to all and provided a new sort of social ranking based on moral superiority and suffering. It offered a method for achieving the higher good that could be practiced alone or in household groups, in cities or in remote desert areas. For women, in particular those like Paula with social standing, legal autonomy, and economic resources, asceticism was available as a legitimate choice in their lives. Perhaps just as important, in theory, women were men's equals in ascetic practice and belief. In the broadest possible terms, women and men in the fourth century were both pushed and pulled into ascetic behaviors. As the century progressed, ascetic behaviors were more frequently carried out with other men and women in the Christian households of monasticism.

12. Thomas J. Heffernan, *Sacred Biography: Saints and Their Biographers in the Middle Ages* (New York: Oxford University Press, 1988), 236.

13. Quoted in Brown, *The Body and Society*, 61. See Ross Kraemer, *Her Share of the Blessings* (New York: Oxford University Press, 1992), 51–55, for a discussion of early women martyrs.

14. Peterson, 18–19. The literature of ascetism in the empire is vast; however, the following discussion relies on these most useful works: Kate Cooper, *The Virgin and the Bride* (Cambridge, MA: Harvard University Press, 1996); Susanna Elm, *"Virgins of God": The Making of Asceticism in Late Antiquity* (New York: Oxford University Press, 1994); Anne E. Hickey, *Women of the Roman Aristocracy as Christian Monastics;* and Richard Valantasis and Vincent L. Wimbush, eds, *Asceticism* (New York: Oxford University Press, 1995).

Individuals like Jerome and Paula adapted their lives and created social spaces in which they could express their religious convictions. But these decisions posed challenges to their families, social peers, and church authorities. Upper-class families in Rome feared that the individualism and otherworldliness of asceticism would undermine family lineage and destroy civic responsibility and the common good. Church leaders also had to decide how to incorporate this expanding movement into their emerging structures and how to ensure that believers stayed within the boundaries of established doctrines. Nevertheless, people like Paula and Jerome, who entered the ascetic movement at this time of flux and challenge, prevailed and helped to establish a regular tradition of religious life that has lasted into the twenty-first century.

Well before Jerome and Paula met face-to-face in Rome in the 380s, both were drawn into ascetic life. Given their social positions, intellectual standing, and the limitations or advantages of gender, their paths into dedicated, holy lives were different. For example, Jerome left western Europe in 372, heading for Jerusalem, the destination of many devout pilgrims. He visited Athens and stayed for a time with colleagues in Antioch, where he wrote some of his earliest essays. At this point, the conflict he felt between his secular training and intellectual interests on the one hand and his spiritual devotion on the other caused him great concern. Apparently in a nightmare he had at the time, Jesus appeared, rebuked him for his love of the classics, and convinced him never to read pagan works again. Encouraged by this resolution, he eventually set off for the desert near Chalcis, where numerous colonies of hermits were located. For Jerome, adopting the isolated life of the desert ascetics was not easy; he was, after all, an urban man, used to some comforts and social life. He continued to write and receive letters, and even in physical isolation he maintained ties to intellectual debates about such things as the nature of the trinity. Later Jerome remembered that throughout this period he was plagued by "sinful" thoughts. He never fit in well with the other desert dwellers, most of whom were not as educated as he. He eventually returned to Antioch in 376 or 377.

During the next five years he improved his Greek, engaged in extensive, in-depth biblical studies, and was finally ordained a priest. He also began to gain more of an intellectual reputation. Jerome was not a creative or daring thinker, but his learning was impressive and he was capable of persuasive exposition of doctrine, caustic critique of those whom he opposed, and often devastating arguments against those he judged to be heretical. In 382, Jerome had the opportunity to accompany several church leaders to a major church conference in Rome, and thus he returned to that city for the first time since his school days.

In 366, an old friend and mentor of Jerome's, Damasus, had been named pope. When they met at the conference, Pope Damasus was impressed by Jerome's scholarship and personality. He asked Jerome to help in drafting certain statements of belief and letters on church affairs. When the conference ended, Jerome remained in Rome, and his friendship and working relationship with Pope Damasus made this one of the happiest periods of his life. By 384, at Damasus's request, Jerome began a monumental project—one that he would not complete for another twenty-two years—the revision and recreation of a single standard version of the Bible out of the existing Latin translations. Jerome had never been known for his modesty, gentleness, or self-effacement, and his tendencies to exaggerate and boast of his accomplishment increased as he worked on this project. Revising the Bible was bound to displease many, and Jerome showed no tolerance for others' viewpoints. In fact, he now was able to express considerable self-confidence when he advised a group of upper-class Roman Christian women that they should "learn of me a holy arrogance; know that you are better than them all."[15]

Act II
The Founding of Women's Religious Communities

By 382, when the church council met in Rome, women throughout western Europe had established their own variations of ascetic life. A few adopted an isolated existence akin to that of the desert hermits, but many more created their own communities of women. Among the upper classes in the Roman Empire, there had been a long tradition of retreat for intellectual activity and mental rejuvenation, and both women and men, since the era of the Republic, were accustomed to urban circles of friends who gathered for reading and discussion. Christian women, including Paula, continued this sort of activity but with a spiritual or redemptive focus.

In Rome, the earliest and best known of these religious circles was that created by an upper-class woman, Marcella (325–410/411). She was raised as a Christian, and after a brief marriage left her a widow, she decided not to remarry and to create her own version of a religious life.[16] She turned her palace on the Aventine Hill into a religious household dedicated to a routine of prayer, fasting, and acts of mercy and charity. At the age of twenty-seven, she publicly pledged herself to monasticism and scriptural study, and she began to gather other women around her. Starting with her mother, her sister, and a handful of other upper-class women, she added other women to her circle. As Marcella's prominence grew, other women emulated her community. In Rome and elsewhere in the western Roman Empire, this form of expression of religious enthusiasm by women increased.

Paula became associated with Marcella's circle after she was widowed in 379. It is important to remember that, although these women from the senatorial class were well educated, their formal education had

15. Quoted in Brown, *The Body and Society*, 367.
16. Ranft, 4.

ended when they were teenagers, and opportunities for religious study were few. Thus, one of the great attractions for Paula was the opportunity to study scripture under the capable tutelage of Marcella. Paula's daughter Eustochium actually took a vow of virginity and moved into Marcella's household. Marcella, apparently knowing of Jerome's learning, enlisted Jerome as a teacher of scripture for her group. Jerome responded to her request; he did not lead or dominate the group, but instead was a tremendous resource and guide for them in their search for truth.

Pope Damasus encouraged Jerome's connections with these women throughout 383 and 384 because he supported the development of asceticism in the West. It is also important to remember that Jerome was not the only prominent leader of the fourth-century church to have close connections to women with similar religious commitments. Ambrose of Milan (340–397) had a sister, Marcellina, who was a consecrated virgin, in other words dedicated to a life of virginity from birth. After he became bishop of Milan in 374, Ambrose helped to found a community of virgins in that city. It is important to acknowledge that all of these women were from elite families and all had considerable resources at their disposal that they were willing and able to put to religious purposes.

Jerome and Paula developed an especially close relationship, often writing letters daily. She was perhaps more soft-hearted than Marcella, more focused on the moral and imaginative dimensions of Christianity, and more expressive emotionally of her faith. Paula also was a model of ascetic renunciation far more than the moderate Marcella, and perhaps Jerome admired her sense of purpose. Jerome generally did not have warm personal relationships, and perhaps he was seeking the sympathy and kindness that Paula could provide. She evidently had a great impact on him because in a later letter he wrote that there was no other Roman matron "who was able to sway me except Paula . . . [She was] the only woman who could give me delight."[17]

By early 385, Jerome's position in Rome was becoming uncomfortable for him. As already mentioned, he had antagonized numerous people with his biblical translations, and his campaign for asceticism was gaining publicity and causing concern in influential circles. The spiritual authority of devout, ascetic women posed challenges to a masculine church hierarchy, while numerous elite Roman families did not want their daughters devoted to the church. They opposed the refusal of marriage and the idea of adopting a life of virginity and were alarmed that women in their families would give away family property. Some took active steps to prevent these developments. Marcella's mother had transferred family wealth to her own brother's children so that Marcella would not give it all away. Marcella, Paula, and Melania the Elder

17. Quoted in E. Glenn Hinson, "When the World Collapsed: The Spirituality of Women During the Barbarian Invasion of Rome," *Perspectives in Religious Studies* 20 (1993): 122; and in Kelly, 109. Both are from his famous Letter 45, written to Asella (Marcella's sister) and defending his connections to the Aventine circle of women.

(342–409), who like Paula was part of the second cohort of these religious women, were widows without guardians and therefore in a better position to act independently. More unnerving to the upper-class families would be situations where daughters were pledged to virginity even before birth, thus clearly closing the doors on marital prospects and future offspring.

No doubt Jerome became a target for those fearful of the social and familial consequences of asceticism. He added fuel to the fire by writing extensively about the decadence and moral failings of the Roman upper classes, and also denounced the clergy for hypocrisy if they *didn't* adopt asceticism or encourage virginity in their congregations. The death of one of Paula's daughters, Blaesilla, in late 384 was blamed on her adoption of a severe ascetic lifestyle, and whispering increased about Jerome and Paula's relationship and his influence on her. Pope Damasus died shortly after Blaesilla, and Jerome was thus left without a powerful protector. By then Paula had decided she would embark on a pilgrimage—travel to holy places was becoming increasingly popular by this time—and spend time in Jerusalem and Bethlehem. Word circulated that Paula and Jerome were planning to go to Jerusalem together, and a church court was convened to examine Jerome's actions. Although no particular crimes were proven, his behavior was considered scandalous and he was forced to leave Rome, which he did in August 385. In the meantime, Paula made her pilgrimage plans, including giving up her young son Toxotius to other relatives to raise, and she left Rome in late September 385 with her daughter Eustochium. Jerome and Paula met in Antioch and then traveled on to the Holy Land. The first phase of their friendship and their spiritual quest was over; the second was about to begin.

Act III

Monasticism in Practice

Christianity had reached the valley of the Nile early in the millennium, and under Emperor Theodosius, Egypt became officially Christian. The area was well known for its sites of ascetic life, both of individual desert hermits and of groups of "solitaries" as they were called.[18] Paula and Jerome first traveled to Egypt because Paula was interested in visiting these sites. Apparently, she even considered joining one of the desert communities, but, given his previous experience, Jerome probably opposed that idea and within a month or so they had returned to Palestine, where they eventually settled in Bethlehem.[19] This small town with a population engaged in agriculture and sheep raising was becoming more of an attraction for pilgrims by this time. For the next three years, Paula and Jerome would make this their home, and with her money they built a hospice for travelers, and then a monastery for men

18. The Greek word for "lonely one" is *monachos,* and this radical form of religious practice became monasticism in the West. See Brown, *The Rise of Western Christendom*, 81.

19. Kelly, 124–28.

and, standing next to it, a larger, more complex convent for women. In some ways, these communities mirrored already existing institutions in Egypt and Asia Minor.

After his Christian baptism, an Egyptian, Pachomius (290–346), was drawn to the ascetic life, but he also realized that "the solitary way neglected the commandment to active charity," something he believed in deeply. He attracted followers and eventually, in 324, founded a community on the Nile river at Tabennesi. His goal was to "nourish the soul" in a community that was organized and based on firm scriptural grounds.[20] About five years after the founding of this monastery, Pachomius's sister joined them, and together they established a community for her that attracted other women.

A similar but slightly later development in Asia Minor also sustained ascetic ideals within a community and developed written precepts that they followed. Like Jerome, the individuals in this group were well trained in classical Greek language and culture, although each was "at the same time intensely critical of that tradition."[21] Basil of Caesarea (329–379) and his elder sister Macrina established both male and female communities across the river from their family's estate at Annesi in 357. The two "households" had contact with each other and lived by much the same rules, combining the contemplative life with a life of communal work and prayer. Macrina's dedication to asceticism was admired widely and her level of erudition was noteworthy. Another of her brothers, Gregory, a theologian and the bishop of Nyssa, wrote her life story, which became available to the public about 380, when Macrina died (**Document One**). Experiences such as these were well-known models in the West by the time that Jerome and Paula set out on their journey.

Another woman from Marcella's circle, Melanie the Elder, had gone to Palestine in 372 when her husband and two sons died and by 378 was in charge of a convent of fifty women on the Mount of Olives in Jerusalem. She was joined there in 381 by Rufinus, an old school friend and colleague of Jerome, who worked with Melanie and helped to supervise the men's community. Women like Melanie, Paula, and Paula's daughter Eustochium, who traveled to well-known shrines; created gathering places for holy women; often ministered to other women; and took vows of worldly renunciation, celibacy, or virginity, were well respected, even held in awe. Melanie was sometimes referred to as a "female man of God," while one of the early histories of ascetics refers to both sexes as "Fathers, male and female."[22]

Monastic communities like Paula's were modeled along the lines of the Roman households in which the women had been raised. The women

20. Elm, 288. Chap. 9 is dedicated to Pachomian monasticism, and chaps. 2 and 3 focus on Basil, bishop of Caesarea, and his family.

21. Jaroslav Pelikan, *Christianity and Classical Culture* (New Haven, CT: Yale University Press, 1993), 8.

22. See Kelly and Hinson for a discussion of Melania the Elder. The first quote that follows is in Brown, *The Body and Society*, 280. The second is in Elm, 312. Both are from Palladius's *Historia Lausiaca*.

owned their own property, strove to be economically self-sufficient, shared in the labor, followed prescribed ideals of behavior, and had an internal hierarchy.[23] Paula and the women who joined her community saw their actions as following in Jesus's footsteps by adopting celibacy and by fasting and praying together at numerous times during the day, on retiring, and then again at midnight. They had no servants and shared work assignments. They also read and sang scriptures together, attended church services together, and carried out a regular program of charity. They had little contact with men, though, again, Jerome was the exception (**Document Two**).

Jerome found this experience with asceticism much more suitable, although, even in this setting, he did not follow the rule completely, because he did not do physical labor. For him, this was a period of heightened intellectual activity. He set up a library or visited libraries close to Bethlehem, had a tutor who gave him lessons in Hebrew, and hired stenographers to copy his work. This activity, not surprisingly, was funded by Paula's wealth, although that resource eventually would run out, given her generosity. But Paula and her community were also engaged in intellectual activities, often requesting specific translations by Jerome, and some of his writings at this time are dedicated to Paula and Eustochium and acknowledge their instigation for the pieces. Jerome continued to discuss theological issues with Paula, and it appears that Paula also learned to read Hebrew at this time. One of Jerome's ongoing efforts was biblical translation, and around 390 he started the translation of a Hebrew version of the Old Testament and finally finished it in 405. He also translated into Latin Pachomius's writings, including his rules for monasticism, thus making these more available in the West, where monasticism grew as well. But Jerome could not or did not choose to adopt Paula's brand of sacrifice, and he watched her severe regimen both with awe and with fear for its devastating effects on her health.

By the 380s, when Paula and Jerome were preparing to pursue their joint spiritual lives, a whole generation of prominent church leaders were embracing the stringent spiritual goals of the desert monks. But questions about asceticism and the adoption of a virginal life were also becoming more frequent in the circles of church authority. As already noted, the purity and holiness that accompanied virginity and celibacy were admirable, but there were apparent dangers in this life if not somehow regulated and directed more officially by the recognized authorities of the church—bishops, councils, and of course the pope. Heresy was always a danger for the solitary communities, and the male-and-female-shared communities continued to present the temptation of sexual attractions and illicit behaviors. Finally at issue was the exact place holy women would have in the church hierarchy. By the fourth century, women were still not allowed to occupy official positions of authority in the Christian church, but the question remained—what should

23. Elm, 374.

be done about the *de facto* authority women like Melanie and Paula gained through their example? Jerome, for one, seemed to take for granted "the profound identity of the minds of men and women and saw no reason all aspects of intellectual and spiritual life should not be extended to women as to men."[24] Earlier in his career, Jerome had relied on the ideas of Origen (ca. 206), who had argued that the body and sexuality had little to do with defining the human spirit and that in spiritual transformation men and women overcame the physical differences that separated them.

By the early 390s, Jerome stressed the superior life of virginity and questioned the value of marriage. His essay *Against Jovinian,* written in 393, was a polemical statement of this position (**Document Three**). Within a few years, Jerome found himself in the unwelcome position of being associated with Origen, who was by that time considered a heretic by many, and under attack by other church leaders who either stressed the importance of marriage or felt it important to accept a much more skeptical view of the possibility of asexual, virginal relations between men and women. Similarly, a much more materialist approach to the body, including warnings of the dangers of sexual drives, was regaining ascendancy (**Document Four**).

Jerome backed away from association with Origen's ideas but continued to believe in the path of virginity, especially for young women. In 401 or 402, he wrote what would become a famous guide for parents who chose to dedicate their daughters to a religious life. He addressed the letter to Paula's son Toxotius and his wife Laeta, by then both devoted Christians who apparently had asked Jerome how to raise a consecrated virgin (**Document Five**). In the letter he suggested that their daughter, named Paula after her grandmother, should come to live in his and Paula's community in Bethlehem. She eventually did so, but not in time to meet her grandmother, who died in January 404. Jerome was devastated by Paula's death; for over twenty years they had followed the same path, working together and sharing visions and goals. He wrote a consolatory letter to Eustochium which is a memorial to Paula and her works. Eustochium was also inconsolable at her mother's death, but she continued the religious life they had shared, running the monasteries and giving Jerome the affection and support he needed. He was now in his seventies, and in addition to the mental strain and anger that the intellectual controversies were causing him, his physical health was failing.

FINALE

The opening years of the fifth century were unstable and threatening for all the inhabitants of the Roman Empire, as Germanic tribes moved into Italy and the Visigothic king Alaric laid siege to Rome, eventually sacking the city in 410. Marcella, the grand figure of early female ascetic

24. Brown, *The Body and Society,* 369.

communities, perished in one of those attacks. Melanie had been in Rome but returned to Jerusalem at the time of the attacks and died shortly thereafter. She, like Paula, had a granddaughter to succeed her, Melanie the Younger (385–448), who convinced her husband to live in chastity with her and to continue her grandmother's work. Jerome saw many of these events as the world was collapsing around him and interpreted them as God's punishment of a sinful society. Even so, he continued to be involved in the theological controversies of the day, usually by supporting the established orthodox positions of the church. He relied on Eustochium, but outlived her, and after her death in 418 or 419, the young Paula took on the same responsibilities. The last letter Jerome wrote expresses both his physical and mental fatigue and feebleness and indicates his willingness to have someone else take on the duties of defending the faith and protecting the true doctrine. When he died in 420, no one wrote about him, and he was buried in Bethlehem near Paula and Eustochium.

By the time of his death, the controversial Jerome probably had more enemies than friends. Over the following centuries, views of him gradually changed and he too became, along with his contemporaries Ambrose and Augustine, one of the fathers of the church. The kind of life that he and Paula had led did not disappear, and, in fact, variations of the early Christian ascetic communities formed the basis for Christian monasticism, one of the lasting achievements of the fourth century and a remarkable illustration of the changes and adaptability of the Roman Church as it was legalized.

Many issues remained unresolved after Paula and Jerome and their contemporaries died. For some, the appeal of asceticism and the growth of monasticism had its problematic side. As asceticism, virginity, and celibacy gained prestige and even became desirable prerequisites for authority in the church, other questions emerged. Because many of the participants in these movements were female, did this mean that women could occupy formal positions of power in the religious hierarchy? The answer to that question was no, but at the same time asceticism and holiness remained alternative means for the expression of female identity and of belief. The church tried to define norms of female ascetic behavior, but the very attempt to place limits on female holy charisma "could result in an expanded role for such 'holy' women," whose visions, severe fasts, and austere lives seemed to be the embodiment of saintliness. Also, as the ascetic movement strengthened the priesthood, it also created a kind of separatism that excluded those who didn't meet the new "holy" standards. "Men and women who could claim neither clerical status nor ascetic stature [were] second class citizens in the city of God."[25] Church leaders would try to lessen this division through guides for good marriages, but the message never measured up to the heroism of bodily

25. For these remarks about the legacies of asceticism, see Elm, 165–66, and Cooper, 115, 126.

renunciation, physical suffering, and self-sacrifice. Another possibility was to develop a hagiography for holy wives, perhaps modeled along the lines of Melanie the Younger, whose life was indeed added to the menu of possible behaviors for married women. The prominence and popularity of Christian asceticism, along with debates over the spiritual value of virginity versus the social, political, and moral value of marriage were a legacy of fourth-century political and religious developments. As the Roman Empire in the West came to a close, that legacy would help to define the particular identity of the Western Christian church.

Documents

DOCUMENT ONE

Gregory of Nyssa

Life of Macrina (ca. 380)

Macrina becomes a model for asceticism for Western women through her brother's narrative of her life. In what ways is Macrina a typical ascetic woman? What parts of her life became standards for women wishing to follow a religious life?

The Prospect of Marriage

Having grown up amid these and similar pursuits, especially in working with her hands at spinning, she reached her twelfth year, in which the flower of youth begins to blossom in particular splendor. Here it is appropriate for us to wonder whether or not the beauty of the young girl, though it had been kept hidden, would escape notice. Indeed there did not seem anything so marvelous throughout the whole of that region that it could be compared with her beauty and charm. The hands of painters could not do justice to her in her bloom.

Although the art of the painter is altogether ingenious and dares to confront the greatest subjects, so as to create by means of imitation images of the sun and planets themselves, it was unable to represent accurately the harmonious beauty of her form. A swarm of suitors besieged her parents on account of her beauty, but her father (a man of prudence and good judgement) chose out from the rest a well-born young man from those of his own kin, who was remarkable for his good character and had only recently completed his education. It was to him that he decided to betroth his daughter, when she had reached the appropriate age. In the meantime, the young man showed promise for the future and brought to Macrina's father, as a joyful wedding gift, a character which equalled his reputation. In the law-courts he displayed his power of speech on behalf of those who had been wronged. Yet envy cut off these promising hopes by snatching him from life at an age to arouse our pity.

Macrina's Decision to Adopt a Life of Virginity

The young girl was not unaware of her father's decision, but when the plans that had been made for her were destroyed by the death of the young man, she came to regard the marriage which her father had arranged for her as though it had actually taken place. She made up her mind to live the rest of her life on her own, and her decision was firmer than might have been expected at her age. Her parents often brought up the subject of marriage with her, because there were many men wishing to be her suitors on account of the fame of her beauty. To them she replied that it was absurd and contrary to law and custom for them not to be satisfied with the marriage which had been concluded for her by her father once and for all, but to require her to look to marriage to another; for marriage was by its nature unique, just as birth and death are unique. She strongly maintained that the man to whom she was united in accordance with the decision of her parents had not died; her judgement was that he was 'living in God' through hope of the resurrection and that he had 'gone away' and was not a corpse. It was absurd, in her opinion, not to keep faith with a bridegroom who was on a journey.

Repelling by such arguments those who tried to overrule her, she decided that the only way of safeguarding her noble resolve was never to be separated from her mother, not even for a single moment, so that her mother used to say that she carried her other children for the normal length of time, but that she carried Macrina everywhere within herself, always enclosed, so to speak, within her heart. However, living in common with her daughter was by no means burdensome or lacking in advantage for the mother, for the loving service that her daughter bestowed upon her replaced the work of several maids. There was a fruitful exchange between them: the mother cared for her daughter's soul and the daughter, her mother's body. Macrina fulfilled the service required of her in every other department; she even frequently prepared bread for her mother with her own hands. This, however, was not the principal activity in which she displayed her zeal; after she had used her hands for liturgical purposes, she then provided food for her mother by her own labors in the time that she had left, as she thought this appropriate to her way of life. Not only did she do this, but she also shared with her mother full responsibility in running the household, for her mother had four sons and five daughters and paid taxes to three rulers, because her property was scattered over as many provinces. For this reason, Macrina shared in her mother's varied concerns, for her father was already dead. In all these affairs she was the partner of her mother's labors, sharing her burdens and lightening the weight of her grief. At the same time she both retained her own purity of life through her mother's training—that life which was throughout directed and witnessed by her mother—and provided her mother with a similar ideal—I mean the ideal of philosophy—by means of her own example, drawing her gradually towards a more simple way of life, detached from material things.

Macrina's Influence over Her Brother Basil

At the time when her mother was suitably occupied in regulating the affairs of Macrina's sisters, according to what seemed to her right for each of them, the great Basil returned home. He was the brother of the aforesaid Macrina, and during all this long period, he had been receiving training in rhetoric in the schools. Macrina found that he had become excessively exalted by the idea of his own gift of oratory. He despised all those who held public office and was puffed up with pride, regarding himself as a man above the notabilities of the province. She therefore drew him too towards the ideal of philosophy, so rapidly that he renounced worldly fame. He despised the admiration which he had won through his eloquence and became, as it were, a deserter to a hard life of manual labor. Through his complete detachment from material possessions he prepared for himself a way of life in which he would be unhindered in his pursuit of virtue. However, his life and his subsequent practices, through which he became known in every country under the sun and overshadowed all those who were distinguished for their virtue with his reputation, would need a lengthy narrative and plenty of time. Let my story return once more to its point.

The Conversion of the Family Home into a Monastery

As the pretext for every kind of materialistic life had already been taken away from them, Macrina persuaded her mother to abandon the conventions of social life and the manners of a woman of the world, to give up the services of her maids, which she had been accustomed to receive up to that time, and to regard herself as being of the same rank as the mass of the people, involving herself in her personal life with all the virgins she had with her, by sharing their pursuits and making sisters and equals out of slave-women and servants. . . .

DOCUMENT TWO

Jerome

Letter to Eustochium, Letter 108

This letter is Jerome's memorial to Paula, written after her death. What are the concrete facts of Paula's life that we can glean from this letter? What aspects seem romantic idealizations and reflections of Jerome's affection for Paula?

. . . And who could find there a greater marvel than Paula? As among many jewels the most precious shine most brightly, and as the sun with its beams obscures and puts out the paler fires of the stars, so by her lowliness she surpassed all others in virtue and influence and, while she was least among all, was greater than all. The more she cast herself down, the more she was lifted up by Christ. She was hidden and yet she was not hidden. By shunning glory she earned glory; for glory follows virtue as its shadow; and deserting those who seek it, it seeks those who despise it. But I must not neglect to proceed with my narrative or dwell too long on a single point, forgetful of the rules of writing.

Being then of such parentage, Paula married Toxotius in whose veins ran the noble blood of Aeneas and the Julii. Accordingly his daughter, Christ's virgin Eustochium, is called Julia, as he is Julius, 'A name from great Iulus handed down.'

I speak of these things not as of importance to those who have them, but as worthy of remark in those who despise them. Men of the world look up to persons who are rich in such privileges. We, on the other hand, praise those who for the Saviour's sake despise them; and strangely depreciating all who keep them, we eulogize those who are unwilling to do so. Thus nobly born, Paula through her fruitfulness and her chastity alike won approval from all, from her husband first, then from her relatives, and lastly from the whole city. She bore five children: Blesilla, for whose death I consoled her while at Rome; Paulina, who has left the reverend and admirable Pammachius to inherit both her vows and property, to whom also I addressed a little book on her death, Eustochium, who is now in the holy places, a precious necklace of virginity and of the Church; Rufina, whose untimely end overcame the affectionate heart of her mother; and Toxotius, after whom she had no more children. You can thus see that it was not her wish to continue to fulfill a wife's duty, but that she only complied with her husband's longing to have male offspring.

When he died, her grief was so great that she nearly died herself; yet so completely did she then give herself to the service of the Lord, that it might have seemed that she had desired his death. In what terms shall I speak of her distinguished and noble and formerly wealthy house, almost all the riches of which she spent on the poor? How can I describe the great consideration she showed to all and her far-reaching kindness even to those whom she had never seen? What poor man, as he lay dying, was not wrapped in blankets given by her? What bedridden person was not supported with money from her purse? She would seek out such with the greatest diligence throughout the city, and would think it her loss were any hungry or sick person to be supported by another's food. She robbed her children; and, when her relatives remonstrated with her for doing so, she declared that she was leaving to them a better inheritance in the mercy of Christ.

Nor was she long able to endure the visits and crowded receptions which her high position in the world and her exalted family entailed upon her. She received the homage paid to her sadly, and made all the speed she could to shun and to escape those who wished to pay her compliments. It so happened that at that time the bishops of the East and West had been summoned to Rome by letter from the emperors to deal with certain dissensions between the churches, and in this way she saw two most admirable men and christian prelates, Paulinus, bishop of Antioch, and Epiphanius, bishop of Salamis (or, as it is now called, Constantia) in Cyprus. Epiphanius, indeed, she received as her guest; and, although Paulinus was staying in another person's house, in the warmth of her heart she treated him as if he too were lodged with her. Inflamed by their virtues, she thought every moment of forsaking her country. Disregarding her home, her children, her servants, her property, and in a word everything connected with the world, she was eager—alone and unaccompanied (if ever it could be said that she was so)—to go to the desert made famous by its Pauls and by its Antony. And at last when the winter was over and the sea was open, and when the bishops were returning to their churches, she also sailed with them in her prayers and desires. Not to prolong the story, she went down to the harbor accompanied by her brother, her kinsfolk and, above all, her own children [eager by their demonstrations of affection to overcome their loving mother]. At last the sails were set and the strokes of the oars carried the vessel into the deep. On the shore the little Toxotius stretched forth his hands in entreaty, while Rufina, now grown up, with silent sobs besought her mother to wait till she should be married. But still Paula's eyes were dry as she turned them heavenwards; and she overcame her love for her children by her love for God. She knew herself no more as a mother, that she might prove herself a handmaid of Christ. Yet her heart was rent within her, and she wrestled with her grief, as though she were being torn away from part of herself. The greatness of the affection she had to overcome made everyone admire her victory the more. Among the cruel hardships which attend prisoners of war in the hands of their enemies, there is none severer than the separation of parents from their children. Though it is against the laws of nature, she endured this trial with unabated faith; nay more she sought it with a joyful heart; and spurning her love for her children by her greater love for God, she concentrated herself quietly on Eustochium alone, the partner alike of her vows and of her voyage. Meantime the vessel ploughed onwards and all her fellow-passengers looked back to the shore. But she turned her eyes that she might not see what she could not behold without agony. No mother, it must be confessed, ever loved her children so dearly. Before setting out she gave them all that she had, disinheriting herself upon earth that she might find an inheritance in heaven. . . .

. . . [On Cyprus] she visited all the monasteries in the island, and left, so far as her means allowed, substantial relief for the brothers whom love of the holy man had brought thither from all parts of the world. Then crossing the narrow sea she landed at Seleucia, and going up thence to Antioch allowed herself to be detained for a little time by the affection of the reverend confessor Paulinus. Then, such was the ardor of her faith that she, a noble lady who had always previously been carried by eunuchs, went her way—and that in midwinter—riding on an ass. . . .

I shall now describe the order of her monastery and the method by which she turned the continence of saintly souls to her own profit. She sowed carnal things that she might reap spiritual things; she gave earthly things that she might receive heavenly things; she forewent things temporal that she might in their stead obtain things eternal. Besides establishing a monastery for men, the charge of which she left to men, she divided into three companies and monasteries the numerous virgins whom she had gathered out of different provinces, some of whom are of noble birth while others belonged to the middle or lower classes. But, although they worked and had their meals separately from each other, these three companies met together for psalm-singing and prayer. After the chanting of the Alleluia—the signal by which they were summoned to the Collect—no one was permitted to remain behind. But coming either first or among the first, she used to await the arrival of the rest, urging them to diligence rather by her own modest example than by motives of fear. At dawn at the third, sixth, and ninth hours, at evening, and at midnight they recited the Psalter each in turn. No sister was allowed to be ignorant of the psalms, and all had every day to learn a certain portion of the holy Scriptures. On the Lord's day only, they proceeded to the church beside which they lived, each company following its own mother-superior. Returning home in the same order, they then devoted themselves to their allotted tasks, and made garments either for themselves or else for others. If any was of noble birth, she was not allowed to have an attendant from home lest her maid, having her mind full of the doings of old days and of the licence of childhood, might by constant converse open old wounds and renew former errors. All the sisters were clothed alike. Linen was not used except for drying the hands. So strictly did she separate them from men that she would not allow even eunuchs to approach them, lest she should give any occasion to slanderous tongues, always ready to cavil at the religious, to console themselves for their own misdeeds. When anyone was backward in coming to the recitation of the psalms or showed herself remiss in her work, she used to approach her in different ways. Was she quick-tempered? Paula coaxed her. Was she phlegmatic? Paula chided her, copying the example of the Apostle who said: *What do you want? Shall I come to you with a rod or in the spirit of gentleness and meekness?* Apart from food and raiment she allowed no one to have anything she could call her own, for Paul had said: *Having food and raiment we are content.* She was afraid lest the custom of having more should breed covetousness in them—an appetite which no wealth can satisfy, for the more it has, the more it requires, and neither opulence or indigence is able to diminish it. When the sisters quarreled with another, she reconciled them with soothing words. If the young girls were troubled with fleshly desires, she broke their force by imposing frequent and redoubled fasts; for she wished them to be ill in body rather than to suffer in soul. If she chanced to notice any sister too attentive to her dress, she reproved her for her error with knitted brows and severe looks, saying: 'A clean body and a clean dress mean an unclean soul; a virgin's lips should never utter an improper or an impure word, for such indicate a lascivious mind, and by the outward man the faults of the inward are made manifest.' When she saw a sister verbose and talkative or forward and taking pleasure in quarrels, and when she found after frequent admonitions that the offender showed no signs of improvement, she placed her among the lowest of the sisters and outside their society, ordering her to pray at the door of the refectory and take her food by herself, in the hope that where rebuke had failed, shame might bring about a reformation. The sin of theft she loathed as if it were sacrilege; and that which among men of the world is counted little or nothing, she declared to be a crime of the deepest dye in a monastery. How shall I describe her kindness and attention towards the sick or the wonderful care and devotion with which she nursed them? Yet, although when others were sick she freely gave them every indulgence, and even allowed them to eat meat, whenever she fell ill herself, she made no concessions to her own weakness, and seemed unfair in this respect, that in her own case she exchanged for harshness the kindness which she was always ready to show to others.

No young girl of sound and vigorous constitution ever delivered herself up to a regimen so rigid as that imposed upon herself by Paula, whose physical powers age had impaired and enfeebled. I admit that in this she was too determined, refusing to spare herself or to listen to advice. . . .

DOCUMENT THREE

JEROME

Against Jovinian (393)

In this essay, Jerome takes on those individuals who were arguing that salvation didn't come from works or way of life, but was strictly spiritual. Jovinian, another Christian writer, in particular, had argued that virginity had no special place in Christian doctrine. How does Jerome defend virginity? As a result of his views on virginity, what does he say about marriage?

The battle must be fought with the whole army of the enemy, and the disorderly rabble, fighting more like brigands than soldiers, must be repulsed by the skill and method of regular warfare. In the front rank I will set the Apostle Paul, and, since he is the bravest of generals, will arm him with his own weapons, that is to say, his own statements. . . .

[Jerome then repeats Paul's statements from 1 Corinthians 7.] Let us turn back to the chief point of evidence: "It is good," he says, "for a man not to touch a woman." If it is good not to touch a woman, it is bad to touch one: for there is no opposite to goodness but badness. But if it be bad and the evil is pardoned, the reason for the concession is to prevent worse evil. But surely a thing which is only allowed because there may be something worse has only a slight degree of goodness. He would never have added "let each man have his own wife," unless he had previously used the words "but, because of fornications." Do away with fornication, and he will not say "let each man have his own wife." Just as though one were to lay it down: "It is good to feed on wheaten bread, and to eat the finest wheat flour," and yet to prevent a person pressed by hunger from devouring cow-dung, I may allow him to eat barley. "Does it follow that the wheat will not have its peculiar purity, because such an one prefers barley to excrement? That is naturally good which does not admit of comparison with what is bad, and is not eclipsed because something else is preferred. At the same time we must notice the Apostle's prudence. He did not say, it is good not to have a wife: but, it is good not to touch a woman: as though there were danger even in the touch: as though he who touched her, would not escape from her who "hunteth for the precious life," who causeth the young man's understanding to fly away. "Can a man take fire in his bosom, and his clothes not be burned? Or can one walk upon hot coals, and his feet not be scorched?" As then he who touches fire is instantly burned, so by the mere touch the peculiar nature of man and woman is perceived, and the difference of sex is understood. . . .

[Jovian argued that Solomon accomplished a great deal though he was married, and Jerome answers.] . . . [W]hen our opponent adduced Solomon, who, although he had many wives, nevertheless built the temple, I briefly replied that it was my intention to run over the remaining points. Now that he may not cry out that both Solomon and others under the law, prophets and holy men, have been dishonoured by us, let us show what this very man with his many wives and concubines thought of marriage. For no one can know better than he who suffered through them, what a life or woman is. Well then, he says in the Proverbs: "The foolish and bold woman comes to want bread." What bread? Surely that bread which cometh down from heaven: and he immediately adds "The earth-born perish in her house, rush into the depths of hell." Who are the earth-born that perish in her house? They of course who follow the first Adam, who is of the earth, and not the second, who is from heaven. And again in another place: "Like a worm in wood, so a wicked woman destroyeth her husband." But if you assert that this was spoken of bad wives, I shall briefly answer: What necessity rests upon me to run the risk of the wife I marry proving good or bad? "It is better," he says, "to dwell in a desert land, than with a contentious and passionate woman in a wide house." How seldom we find a wife without these faults, he knows who is married.

[Jerome also argued against second marriages, citing the authority of the Greek philosopher Theophrastus, who lived in the fourth century BCE and whose treatise on marriage is unknown except in Jerome's citing of it.]

. . . But what am I to do when the women of our time press me with apostolic authority, and before the first husband is buried, repeat from morning to night the precepts which allow a second marriage? Seeing they despise the fidelity which Christian purity dictates, let them at least learn chastity from the heathen.

A book *On Marriage*, worth its weight in gold, passes under the name of Theophrastus. In it the author asks whether a wise man marries. And after laying down the conditions—that the wife must be fair, of good character, and honest parentage, the husband in good health and of ample means, and after saying that under these circumstances a wise man sometimes enters the state of matrimony, he immediately proceeds thus: "But all these conditions are seldom satisfied in marriage. A wise man therefore must not take a wife. For in the first place his study of philosophy will be hindered, and it is impossible for anyone to attend to his books and his wife. Matrons want many things, costly dresses, gold, jewels, great outlay, maid-servants, all kinds of furniture, litters and gilded coaches. Then come curtain-lectures and live-long night: she complains that one lady goes out better dressed than she: that another is looked up to by all: 'I am a poor despised nobody at the ladies' assemblies.' 'Why did you ogle that creature next door?' 'Why were you talking to the maid?' 'What did you bring from the market?' 'I am not allowed to have a single friend, or companion.' She suspects that her husband's love goes the same way as her hate. There may be in some neighbouring city the wisest of teachers; but if we have a wife we can neither leave her behind, nor take the burden with us. To support a poor wife, is hard: to put up with a rich one, is torture. Notice, too, that in the case of a wife you cannot pick and choose: You must take her as you find her. If she has a bad temper, or is a fool, if she has a blemish, or is proud, or has bad breath, whatever her fault may be—all this we learn after marriage. Horses, asses, cattle, even slaves of the smallest worth, clothes, kettles, wooden seats, cups, and earthenware pitchers, are first tried and then bought: a wife is the only thing that is not shown before she is married, for fear she may not give satisfaction. Our gaze must always be directed to her face, and we must always praise her beauty: if you look at another, we must swear by her health and wish that she may survive us, respect must be paid to the nurse, to the nurse-maid, to the father's slave, to the foster-child, to the handsome hanger-on, to the curled darling who manages her affairs, and to the eunuch who ministers to the safe indulgence of her lust: names which are only a cloak for adultery. Upon whomsoever she sets her heart, they must have her love though they want her not. If you give her the management of the whole house, you must yourself be her slave. If you reserve something for yourself, she will not think you are loyal to her; but she will turn to strife and hatred, and unless you quickly take care, she will have the poison ready. If you introduce old women, and soothsayers, and prophets, and vendors of jewels and silken clothing, you imperil her chastity; if you shut the door upon them, she is injured and fancies you suspect her. But what is the good of even a careful guardian, when an unchaste wife cannot be watched, and a chaste one ought not to be? For necessity is but a faithless keeper of chastity, and she alone really deserves to be called pure, who is free to sin if she chooses. If a woman be fair, she soon finds lovers; if she be ugly, it is easy to be wanton. It is difficult to guard what many long for. It is annoying to have what no one thinks worth possessing. But the misery of having an ugly wife is less than that of watching a comely one. Nothing is safe, for which a whole people sighs and longs. One man entices with his figure, another with his brains, another with his wit, another with his open hand. Somehow, or sometime, the fortress is captured which is attacked on all sides. Men marry, indeed, so as to get a manager for the house, to solace weariness, to banish solitude; but a faithful slave is a far better manager, more submissive to the master, more observant of his ways, than a wife who thinks she proves herself mistress if she acts in opposition to her husband, that is, if she does what pleases her, not what she is commanded. But friends, and servants who are under the obligation of benefits received, are better able to wait upon us in sickness than a wife who makes us responsible for her tears (she will sell you enough to make a deluge for the hope of a legacy), boasts of her anxiety, but drives her sick husband to the distraction of despair. But if she herself is poorly, we must fall sick with her and never leave her bedside. Or if she be a good and agreeable wife (how rare a bird she is!), we have to share her groans in childbirth, and suffer torture when she is in danger. A wise man can never be alone. He has with him the good men of all time, and turns his mind freely wherever he chooses. What is inaccessible to him in person he can embrace in thought. And, if men are scarce, he converses with God. He is never less alone than when alone.

DOCUMENT FOUR

John Chrysostom

"Instruction and Refutation Directed Against Those Men Cohabiting with Virgins" and "On the Necessity of Guarding Virginity" (Probably written after 398)

In these treatises, John Chrysostom, another major church leader and thinker of the time, offers a different view of virginity and spiritual marriage. Does he oppose cohabitation of celibate men and women? What are his arguments, and how might these arguments be seen as a direct challenge to Jerome's views?

"Instruction and Refutation Directed Against Those Men Cohabiting with Virgins"

1. In our ancestors' era, two justifications were given for men and women living together. The first, marriage, was ancient, licit, and sensible, since God was its legislator. "For this reason," he said, "a man shall leave his father and mother and cleave to his wife, and the two shall be one flesh." And the other, prostitution, of

more recent origin than marriage, was unjust and illegitimate, since it was introduced by evil demons. But in our time, a third way of life has been dreamed up, something new and incredible which greatly perplexes those who wish to discover its rationale. There are certain men who apart from marriage and sexual intercourse take girls inexperienced with matrimony, establish them permanently in their homes, and keep them sequestered until ripe old age, not for the purpose of bearing children (for they deny that they have sexual relations with the women), nor out of licentiousness (for they claim that they preserve them inviolate). If anybody asks the reason for their practice, they have plenty and start rehearsing them; however, I myself think that they have not found a single decent, plausible excuse.

. . . What then is the reason? It seems to me that living with a woman entails a certain pleasure, not only in the lawful state of marriage, but also in cases which do not involve marriage and sexual intercourse.

. . . Thus [Job] says, "I mortify my body and keep it in subjection, lest in preaching to others I myself be rejected as counterfeit coin."

He made these remarks to indicate the rebelliousness of the flesh and the madness which stems from desire, to show that the battle was a constant one and his own life a contest. For this reason Christ also made clear the magnitude of the problem. He did not permit a man even to look into the eyes of a woman, but threatened those who did with the penalty laid on adulterers. When Peter commented, "It is better not to marry," Christ did not make a law prohibiting marriage but replied, indicating the importance of the subject, "He that is able to receive it, let him receive it."

We also hear in our own time that many who cover their entire bodies with iron chains and are clad in sackcloth, who have climbed the peaks of mountains and live in constant fasting accompanied by vigils and sleeplessness, who demonstrate great hardiness in every way, forbid all women to enter their chambers and cells and in this way discipline themselves—these men, we are told, scarcely prevail over the frenzy of desire.

You say, however, that if you were to see a man living with virgin, a man who is bound to her and delights in her, who would give up his life rather than his roommate and would choose to suffer and do everything than to part from his beloved, you should not believe anything evil nor view the situation as one involving lust, but rather piety. O wondrous man! . . .

Tell me, why do you live with a virgin? This cohabitation is not based on law but on love and lust. For if this reason is taken away, the need for the practice also disappears. What man, if he were free from the compulsion to have a woman, would choose to put up with the delicacy, wantonness, and all the other faults of that sex? Thus even from the beginning God endowed woman with this strength, knowing that she would be totally despicable unless she were provided with this power, that no man would choose to live with her if he were innocent of desire. For if such a necessity also presses upon us now, in addition to her many other uses (indeed we could also mention the bearing of children, taking care of the house, and the rendering of other services even loftier than these), and if even now women performing such chores for men are often easy to despise and are expelled from their homes, how would you love them if it were not for desire, especially since they cast so much reproach upon you? Now either tell us the reason for cohabitation or we will necessarily suspect that there is no other one than wanton desire and the most shameful pleasure. . . .

"On the Necessity of Guarding Virginity"

If meanwhile I ask you the pretext for this joint homesteading, what can you say? The virgin answers, "I am just a weak woman and am not capable of satisfying my own needs by myself." But when we summoned your housemates, we heard them claim the opposite, that *they* kept *you* because of *your* service to *them!* How come, then, if out of your abundant energy you can give relief to the men, you are not able to help yourselves, since you are women, but need others? For just as a man can live together easily and contentedly with a man, so also can a woman with a woman, and if you are fit for the service of men, how much more so for aiding yourselves? Tell me, how could the company of a man be beneficial and necessary? What kind of service will this man render which could be impossible for a woman to provide for one of her own sex? Can he weave at the loom and spin thread and cloth with you more ably than a woman? Just the opposite is so! For even if a man wanted to, he would not know how to put his hand to any of these tasks, not unless you have just now taught him the skill; this is the work of woman alone.

5. But to launder a cloak, kindle a fire, boil and pot—is not a woman able to manage these things not less proficiently, but even more so, than a man? In what ways, then, is the man an advantage to you, tell me? Perhaps whenever it is necessary to buy or sell something? But the woman is not inferior to the man here, as the marketplace might also testify: all who wish to buy clothes, buy most of them from women. But if it is disgraceful for a virgin to stand in the marketplace for business dealings of such a kind (and it is in truth shameful), certainly it is much more disgraceful for her to live with men. Besides, you can escape this rather minor problem more easily than that one by entrusting everything to a serving girl to minister to your needs or to older women who are useful for these purposes. . . .

. . . It is not, then, because you [the female virgin] need comfort that you drag the men inside. "Why is it, then?" someone asks. "For the sake of fornication and debauchery?" I for my part would not support that view. God forbid! Rather, I do not cease to reproach those who hold it. If only it were also possible to convince them! "Then what is the reason which makes the practice agreeable to us?" The love of vanity. Just as the men were motivated by a bleak and wretched pleasure, so also for these women this household companionship is inspired by a desire for esteem. For as it is said, the whole human race is vain, but especially the female sex. Since these women are not in need of relaxation, as has been shown, nor are they corrupted by their sexual involvement with the men, it is apparent that this reason alone remains for us to suspect. . . .

Perhaps these women themselves think this very thing, their overpowering men, is laudable. To the contrary, it is completely ridiculous; certainly only courtesans take pride in it. For it is not characteristic of free and virtuous women to be conceited about such snares. This is also another reason for dishonor: to the degree that they dominate the men and become harsher in their commandeering, to this extent they rather disgrace themselves in addition to the males. It is not the woman who brings men under her rule who is esteemed and considered remarkable by everyone, but the woman who respects them.

DOCUMENT FIVE

Jerome

Letter to Laeta, Letter 107

What guidance does Jerome offer Laeta for raising her daughter Paula, who is a dedicated virgin? These words of advice were followed by many Christian parents thereafter. What does Jerome think are the most important parts of a young virgin's life? Since you will have read two of Jerome's letters, consider also the way in which he uses personal letters to expound on themes of much broader importance. Are the letters really personal documents or something else? What might these examples illustrate about the general tradition of letter writing in the Roman world? Why do you think Jerome's letters are preserved, while the letters of his women contemporaries are not?

. . . It was my intention, in answer to your prayers and those of the saintly Marcella, to direct my discourse to a mother, that is, to you, and to show you how to bring up our little Paula, who was consecrated to Christ before she was born, the child of prayers before the hour of conception. . . .

Thus must a soul be trained which is to be a temple of God. It must learn to hear nothing and to say nothing save what pertains to the fear of the Lord. It must have no comprehension of foul words, no knowledge of worldly songs, and its childish tongue must be imbued with the sweet music of the psalms. Let boys with their wanton frolics be kept far from Paula: let even her maids and attendants hold aloof from association with the worldly, lest they render their evil knowledge worse by teaching it to her. Have a set of letters made for her, of boxwood or of ivory, and tell her their names. Let her play with them, making play a road to learning, and let her not only grasp the right order of the letters and remember their names in a simple song, but also frequently upset their order and mix the last letters with the middle ones, the middle with the first. Thus she will know them all by sight as well as by sound. When she begins with uncertain hand to use the pen, either let another hand be put over hers to guide her baby fingers, or else have the letters marked on the tablet so that her writing may follow their outlines and keep to their limits without straying away. Offer her prizes for spelling, tempting her with such trifling gifts as please young children. . . .

Her very dress and outward appearance should remind her of Him to whom she is promised. Do not pierce her ears, or paint with white lead and rouge the cheeks that are consecrated to Christ. Do not load her neck with pearls and gold, do not weigh down her head with jewels, do not dye her hair red and thereby presage for her the fires of hell. Let her have other pearls which she will sell hereafter and buy the pearl that is of great price. . . .

She should not take her food in public, that is, at her parents' guest-table; for she may there see dishes that she will crave for. And though some people think it shows the higher virtue to despise a pleasure ready to your hand, I for my part judge it part of the surer self-restraint to remain in ignorance of what you would like. Once when I was a boy at school I read this line: 'Things that have become a habit you will find it hard to blame.' Let her learn even now not to drink wine 'wherein is excess.' Until they have reached their full strength, however, strict abstinence is dangerous for young children: so till then, if needs must, let her visit the baths, and take a little wine for the stomach's sake, and have the support of a meat diet, lest her feet fail before the race begins. . . .

Let her every day repeat to you a portion of the Scriptures as her fixed task. A good number of lines she should learn by heart in the Greek, but knowledge of Latin should follow close after. If the tender lips are not trained from the beginning, the language is spoiled by a foreign accent and our native tongue debased by alien faults. You must be her teacher, to you her childish ignorance must look for a model. Let her never see anything in you or her father which she would do wrong to imitate. Remember that you are a virgin's parents and that you can teach her better by example than by words. Flowers quickly fade; violets, lilies, and saffron are soon withered by a baleful breeze. Let her never appear in public without you,. . . .

Let her learn also to make wool, to hold the distaff, to put the basket in her lap, to turn the spindle, to shape the thread with her thumb. Let her scorn silk fabrics, Chinese fleeces, and gold brocades. Let her have clothes which keep out the cold, not expose the very limbs they pretend to cover. Let her food be vegetables and wheaten bread and occasionally a little fish. I do not wish here to give long rules for eating, since I have treated that subject more fully in another place; but let her meals always leave her hungry and able at once to begin reading or praying or singing the psalms. I disapprove especially with young people, of long and immoderate fasts, when week is added to week and even oil in food and fruit are banned. I have learned by experience that the ass on the high road makes for an inn when it is weary. . . .

Questions

1. In what ways did the legalization of Christianity alter the character of the early Christian church? What was gained? What was lost?
2. What factors explain the appeal of asceticism to people in the fourth century? Were these factors the same for men and women?
3. Historians now argue that women played a much greater role in the Christianization of the Roman Empire and in the growth of monasticism than previously thought. What evidence can you cite that might support this argument?
4. Monasticism as it gained strength seemed to be a mixed blessing for the authorities of the church. Why would that be the case?
5. What factors explain the push for orthodoxy in the Christian church in the fourth century? How did the church change over the course of that century?

Suggested Readings

Bowersock, G. W., Peter Brown, and Oleg Grabar, eds. *Late Antiquity: A Guide to the Postclassical World.* Cambridge, MA: Harvard University Press, 1999.

Brown, Peter. *The Rise of Western Christendom.* 2d ed. Malden, MA: Blackwell, 2003.

Cooper, Kate. The Virgin and the Bride. Cambridge, MA: Harvard University Press, 1996.

Elm, Susanna. *"Virgins of God": The Making of Asceticism in Late Antiquity.* New York: Oxford University Press, 1994.

Salzman, Michele Renee. *The Making of a Christian Aristocracy.* Cambridge, MA: Harvard University Press, 2004.

CHAPTER

8

Religion, Politics, and Gender in Medieval China: Emperor Wuzong (r. 841–846) and Yu Xuanji (840–868) of the Tang Dynasty (618–907)

Setting the Stage

The Tang dynasty was established by Li Yuan (566–635), originally the duke of Tang and a powerful general of the short-lived Sui dynasty (581–618). Taking advantage of a political crisis in 617, Li Yuan's army captured the Sui capital, Chang'an; six months later he founded a new dynasty that would endure nearly three centuries with glories that matched the Han Empire. While the Tang dynasty represented a revival of Chinese civilization, the cultural landscape of China had indeed changed. Although

Daoist philosophy flourished during the Han dynasty, the Daoist religious movement did not begin until the last century of the dynasty. In addition, Buddhism had very little impact on Chinese society at the time. During the Tang dynasty, however, both Daoism and Buddhism were declared the state religions by the throne; underwent a full-fledged institutionalization; and became integral in every aspect of the dynasty and affected people of all walks of life.

The prominent role of religion mainly resulted from the court's enthusiastic patronage. For generations before Li Yuan, the imperial clan had intermarried widely with non-Chinese tribes. Li Yuan's mother, for example, was from a prominent Turkish clan. The tradition of intermarriage continued for a few generations after Li Yuan. The non-Chinese tribes largely embraced Buddhism because the religion provided them with a cultural identity different from that of the Chinese. Princes of the early Tang period who were raised by non-Chinese mothers naturally became either Buddhist believers or tolerant of the religion. This trend continued during the later periods of the Tang dynasty. As the imperial system matured, the princes were commonly nurtured and educated by a large staff of palace eunuchs. Unable to live a normal family life, the eunuchs tended to become followers of Buddhism, a religion that advocated asexuality. Under such circumstances many imperial princes and future rulers became quite well versed in Buddhist texts at young ages.

Of the twenty-two Tang rulers, the most fervent supporter of Buddhism, however, was the female ruler Wu Zetian (Empress Wu), who dominated the Tang court for forty-five years (660–705). It was during her rule that Buddhism became ranked higher than Daoism. Unlike Confucianism and Daoism, Buddhism was a foreign religion and, at its core, was very much against the patriarchal tradition that had dominated China for more than a thousand years. It was a convenient tool for the empress, a onetime Buddhist nun herself, to use in legitimizing her rule.

The imperial court also practiced Daoism. From the very beginning of the dynasty, Li Yuan claimed that the imperial house descended from Li Dan, or Lao Zi, as he was more commonly known, the founder of Daoism. The adoption of Daoism was apparently aimed at legitimizing the new imperial rule; nevertheless later emperors continued this tradition to glorify the dynasty. Even though some favored Buddhism, all Tang monarchs proclaimed their firm support for Daoism. With such endorsement, 17 out of 210 Tang princesses would enter the Daoist order, 11 of them lived in nunneries until the end of their lives (**Document One**).

How did people of various sectors of Tang society respond to the growth and institutionalization of Buddhism and Daoism? How did their relations to religion shape their lives? Did religion affect men and women differently during the Tang dynasty? To what extent do the religious activities of the men and women in Chinese society during this period reflect the unique dynamics of the Tang dynasty? The protagonists of this chapter, Emperor Wuzong and the poet Yu Xuanji, probably best embodied the role and impact of religion in Tang society. Although they had completely different backgrounds and never met each other, their life paths and actions show that by the mid-ninth century, religion had been tightly woven into a web of the Tang imperial system and gender institutions, as well as its distribution of power and wealth.

There are two official biographies of Emperor Wuzong, one in the *Old History of the Tang Dynasty* (*Jiu Tangshu*), compiled in the tenth century, and the other in the *New History of the Tang Dynasty* (*Xin Tangshu*), completed in the eleventh century. Major events occurring during the emperor's reign were also recorded in *Administrative Documents from the Tang* (*Tang huiyao*), a valuable collection of Tang imperial activities compiled by Wang Pu (922–982). The most detailed account of the emperor's persecution of Buddhism, however, are the diaries of Ennin (793–864), a Japanese monk who traveled to China between 838 and 847. Ennin's diaries were collected in *The Record of Pilgrimage to Tang in Search of the Law*, compiled by his disciples and translated into English by Edwin O. Reischauer in 1955.[1] The sources for reconstructing Yu Xuanji's life are twofold. The first type are various anecdotes written by Tang literati. The second are Yu's own writings. Fifty of her poems, probably a quarter of her total output, survived and were included in the *Complete Tang Poetry* (*Quan Tangshi*). The diversity of these sources enables modern historians to recover the intricate texture of the lives of these two contemporaries.

The Actors

Emperor Wuzong and Yu Xuanji

Emperor Wuzong was born to Emperor Muzong (r. 820–823) and Empress Wei in 814. His given name was Chan, the name of a river near the eastern capital, Luoyang. *Wuzong*, meaning "Fierce Ancestor," was Li Chan's temple name, given to him posthumously. As the fifth son, Li Chan grew up without much hope of ever inheriting the throne. As was the practice among princes, at the age of ten he was given a fief named Ying and was thus called the Prince of Ying. When they reached adulthood, the imperial princes were often assigned to various administrative positions and given monthly stipends just like other court officials. Li Chan was given a job as an acting minister of personnel with a prestigious title, Commander Unequalled in Honor. No sources are available to pinpoint exactly what he did in such an important court position, although most likely he was not trained for the job and day-to-day affairs were actually handled by career officials in the ministry.

By Li Chan's time, the imperial clan had ruled China for two centuries and largely lost the vigor and confidence exhibited by early emperors. Instead of growing up with non-Chinese

1. Edwin O. Reischauer, *Ennin's Diary: The Record of a Pilgrimage of China in Search of the Law* (New York: Ronald, 1955). Reischauer also wrote a companion volume discussing Ennin's journey, Tang society, and major events that Ennin witnessed. See Reischauer, *Ennin's Travels in T'ang China* (New York: Ronald, 1955).

mothers, the princes were now raised by palace eunuchs and often suffered at the whim of these eunuchs. Li Chan's eldest brother, Emperor Jingzong (r. 824–825), for example, was murdered on his return from a drunken excursion at the order of eunuchs who deemed him too wayward. The eunuchs then intervened in the succession to pick his half-brother, Li Ang, on whom they had already exerted great influence, as the dynasty's fifteenth emperor. When Li Ang was dying, he appointed his nephew as the heir apparent. However, confident that he would have more influence over Li Chan, Protector Qiu Shiliang (781–843), a powerful eunuch, forged a decree naming Li Chan as the emperor. Li Chan became the sixteenth emperor of the Tang dynasty in the first month of 840 and, after a brief mourning period, officially started his reign in 841. The auspicious name of his reign, *Huichang,* meant "Converging Prosperity" and was collectively selected by a group of highest-ranking court officials. This term, however, would soon become synonymous with catastrophe in Chinese history.

Yu Xuanji was born in 840 to a poor scholarly family in Chang'an. Her father named her Youwei, meaning "young rose." Xuanji, meaning "profound and mysterious truth," was the religious name she took after she entered the Daoist order. Yu's courtesy name, usually received on a girl's engagement, was Huilan, or Gracious Orchid. Failing repeatedly on the Civil Service Examinations, Yu's father devoted his energy to educating his only daughter. With this attention, she was able to recite hundreds of poems at the age of five, was able to compose poetry at seven, and was known to Chang'an literati as an extremely talented young poet at twelve. Yu's father probably died before she reached her teenage years. By then she was said to be so beautiful that her appearance alone could "topple a kingdom."[2]

Yu's first love interest was poet Wen Tingyun (812–866), who also failed the Civil Service Examinations. When they met in 856, she was probably living in the Pingkang Ward, an entertainment district that largely catered to Civil Service Examination candidates. The literary exchange between the two appears quite flirtatious, but Wen never took the step to marry her and she continued her life as a courtesan. The constant contact with the examination candidates and the memory of her father's disappointment often reminded Yu of how unfortunate she was to be born a woman. Even though she was as talented as the examination candidates, she could never fulfill her father's dream and sit behind an examination desk. One day, while accompanying some literati to visit a Daoist temple, Yu encountered a group of new examination graduates who were writing poems on the walls to commemorate their success. In emulating these graduates, Yu wrote the following lines to express her aspiration and regrets:

2. For a study of Yu Xuanji's life and writing, see Suzanne Cahill, "Resenting the Silk Robes That Hide Their Poems: Female Voices in the Poetry of Tang Dynasty Daoist Nuns," in *Women and Society in Tang-Song China* (*Tang Song nüxing yu shehui*). ed. Deng Xiaonan, Gao Shiyu, and Rong Xinjiang (Shanghai: Shanghai cishu chubanshe, 2003), 563.

Cloudy peaks fill the eye, releasing spring's brightness;
One after another, silver hooks arise beneath their fingers.
Involuntarily I resent the silk netted-gauze robes that hide my lines of poetry;
Lifting my head, I vainly envy the names on the plank.[3]

Yu met Li Yi, her future husband, when he lived in Chang'an around 865. He was then twenty-one years old. Born to a privileged family in eastern China, Li Yi never took the Civil Service Examination. He received the appointment of Rectifier of Omissions at Left, an administrative position in the court, through so-called protection, a limited quota for high-ranking officials' descendents. Li Yi knew Yu through Wen and was very attracted to her beauty, literary talent, and musical skill. He rescued her from her entertainment house and set up a residence with her in Linting, about 10 miles west of Chang'an. Now legally married to Li Yi as a concubine, Yu seemed to be quite happy with her new life and in love with Li Yi. A poem entitled "Sent to Zi'an" expressed her longing and passion for Li when he took a five-month journey to bring his family back from the east: "Drunk at parting; a thousand goblets of wine won't wash away my sorrows; My heart in separation tied into a hundred knots—no way to undo them."[4]

Before coming to the capital, Li Yi had already married Pei, a woman from a prominent family in eastern China, as his principal wife. Once settled into her husband's new residence, Pei could not tolerate the fact that her husband had taken a charming concubine. She often physically abused Yu and forced Li Yi to divorce her. The eight-month marriage between Li and Yu ended in 866. After being expelled from the Li household, Yu entered a monastery named Belvedere of Universal Propriety. There, Yu was given a new identity: she was named Profound and Mysterious Truth by the abbot, signifying her status as a Daoist nun. However, Yu Xuanji would soon be remembered by the society and in history by another identity: criminal.

ACT I

THE HUICHANG PERSECUTION

The Huichang Persecution of Buddhism was probably the result of about 800 years of suspicion, resistance, and transformation of this foreign religion. Buddhism, which reached China in the first century CE, had a quite different value system from that of Confucianism. Buddhism

3. Yu Xuanji, "Wandering to the South Tower of the Belvedere for Venerating the Perfected, Then Viewing the Place Where Names of New Exam Graduates are Inscribed," trans. Suzanne Cahill, in Cahill, 546. "Silk netted-gauze robes" represents the calligraphy of the successful candidates.

4. Trans. Jennifer Carpenter. See Kang-i Sun and Haun Saussy, eds., *Women Writers of Traditional China: An Anthology of Poetry and Criticism* (Stanford. CA: Stanford University Press, 1999), 70. Zi'an was Li Yi's courtesy name.

advocated celibacy and the goal of reaching nirvana, while Confucianism stressed the individual's duty to ancestors, family, and society. To convert the Chinese masses, Buddhist apologists argued that becoming a Buddhist monk or nun was even more meritorious and filial than having family, because devoting one's life to Buddhism enabled the individual to accumulate karma and thus accelerate the progress of his or her living relatives and ancestors toward the eternal bliss. Not surprisingly Chinese Buddhists translated the term *karma* into *ye,* which means one's entire life circumstances, understood in the Chinese context as a life centered on family. Such understanding was the foundation of the Sinification of Buddhism, which was com- pleted in the Tang dynasty. During the Tang dynasty, four major Buddhist schools (Tiantai, Pure Land, Chan, and Huayan) arose and interpreted Buddhist insights and practices as relevant to the Chinese way of life. This marked the Tang dynasty as the pinnacle of Buddhism in Chinese history. In the domestic sphere, women, especially widowed mothers, played an important role in the spread of Buddhism. Along with the Confucian ideal of female chastity, women were drawn to Buddhist teachings of emptiness and asexuality, finding solace in religion for facing a lonely life without any hope for marital happiness.

Buddhism's initial foothold in China was the beginning of the process of its becoming an institutionalized religion. With the support of the throne, during the Tang dynasty basic forms of meditation practice, the structure of the liturgy, ordination procedure, daily regime of monastic life, administrative framework of the monastic organization, nature of the state-church relation, and the role of the Buddhist estate all came into being. The dynasty also witnessed the highest increase in the number of new monasteries and priests. The *New History of the Tang Dynasty* records that around 720, the dynasty had listed 75,525 Buddhist monks and 50,576 Buddhist nuns nationwide. A century later, the total number of monks and nuns reached more than 260,500. We do not know the total number of monasteries during the Tang dynasty, but in a letter sent to the emperor Wuzong congratulating him on the success of the persecution, the chief minister Li Deyu (784–850) recounted that nationwide a total of 46,600 Buddhist monasteries and shrines were destroyed.

The process of institutionalizing Buddhism apparently brought the Buddhist estates and the clergy tremendous wealth and power. This was probably the major cause of the Huichang Persecution. Scholars estimate that during the Tang dynasty, the yield of lands owned by the Buddhist establishments, all exempted from taxation, may have exceeded 10 percent of the total of land used for cereal and garden produce. Furthermore, as monks and nuns were not obliged to pay tax, this resulted in the loss of additional government revenue and was felt to be a great strain on the currency-starved economy. In addition to producing agricultural and forestry products, enterprising abbots also used the Buddhist establishment and laborers to manufacture crafts, carry out trade, host religious festivals and fairs, and even conduct money-lending businesses. Tang monasteries routinely used part of their establishments' permanent assets to provide loans at high interest. Lands, commodities, and money were sometimes donated by lay followers or by the monks themselves expressly for that purpose. The interest rate was always set at 50 percent, due at the time of the harvest (**Document Two**).

In addition to the loss of revenue, court politics likely played an important role in leading to Emperor Wuzong's decision. The emperor apparently exploited the resentment of scholar-officials and intellectuals toward the eunuchs' growing power. In addition to their tremendous influence in court politics, the eunuchs amassed huge wealth through selling ordination quotas at high prices, as the management of Buddhist affairs was entrusted to the eunuchs. Even though Emperor Wuzong ascended to the throne with eunuch Qiu Shiliang's help, he nevertheless wanted his independence. To curb Qiu Shiliang's power and influence, the emperor relied on Li Deyu, the chief minister and a political opponent of Qiu Shiliang, for decision making. Li Deyu grew up in a very privileged environment and received an excellent education in Confucian classics. He was appointed to various administrative positions before he became the chief minister in 840. During his tenure as a regional official, he was said to have witnessed in person how "Buddhist magicians" used religion to enrich themselves. Not surprisingly Li Deyu, sharing the scholar-officials' attitudes toward eunuchs and their enrichment through Buddhism, played a key role in launching the persecution.

The Huichang Persecution began gradually in 842 and peaked in 845. The first sign of attacks on Buddhism was the so-called Wei Zongqing Incident. Wei was a court official who had been working on the compilation of Buddhist works for a while. Just before the emperor's birthday on the twelfth day of the sixth month in 842, Wei presented him with two completed editions. The emperor was enraged and took immediate action to punish Wei. He issued an edict condemning Buddhism's "evil doctrines" and the Buddha as "a western barbarian in origin" and demoted Wei to be a low-ranking official in a remote region (**Document Three**).

About four months after the incident, the emperor Wuzong intensified his political assault on Buddhism. The first imperial edict that was directly aimed at the Buddhist church was issued on the ninth day of the tenth month in 842. Shocked by the event, the Japanese monk Ennin copied the edict verbatim in his diary four days later, and this became the only surviving copy of this edict:

> On the 9th Day of the Tenth Moon an Imperial edict was issued [to the effect that] all monks and nuns of the empire who understand alchemy, the art of incantations, and magic, who

5. See Jacques Gernet, *Buddhism in Chinese History: An Economic History from the Fifth to the Tenth Centuries* (New York: Columbia University Press, 1995), 139.

have fled from the army, who have on their bodies the scars of flagellations or tattoo marks [for former offenses, who have been condemned to] various forms of labor, who have formerly committed sexual offenses or maintain wives, or who do not observe the Buddhist rules, should all be forced to return to lay life. If monks and nuns have money, grains, fields, or estates, these should be surrendered to the government. If they regret [the loss of] their wealth and wish to return to lay life [in order to retain it], in accordance with their wishes, they are to be forced to return to lay life and are to pay the "double tax" and perform the corvée. The text of the Imperial edict is separately [recorded].[6]

Emperor Wuzong's last edict on the persecution of Buddhism was issued in the eighth month of 845. This was often regarded as the official edict of the persecution and was thus included in Wang Pu's *Administrative Documents from the Tang*. The edict stressed again that Buddhism was the worst religion with a barbarian origin. It had "corrupted the morals of our land," exhausted "men's strength in construction work," robbed men for their own golden and jeweled adornments, and so on. The edict then declared that "more than 4,600 monasteries are being destroyed throughout the empire; more than 260,000 monks and nuns are being returned to lay life and being subjected to the double tax; more than 40,000 temples and shrines are being destroyed; several hundred million acres of fertile lands and fine fields are being confiscated; 150,000 slaves are being taken over to become payers of the double tax." Wuzong's fears and destruction show that by his times, the imperial strengths and characteristics that brought the dynasty to glory were all but gone.

Act II

Becoming a Daoist Master

When Li Yi's principal wife joined him and forced Yu Xuanji out of the household, Yu entered the Daoist order as a last resort. The Belvedere of Universal Propriety was located in a quiet corner of the capital, Chang'an. Yu's status in the monastery was refined master, indicating that her main duty was to concentrate on refining the Daoist lifestyle and that she did not have to take on administrative responsibilities or labor in the monastery. It was during her life there that Yu transformed herself from an abandoned victim to a strong-willed individual. Such a possibility for Yu and other Tang women was brought about by the institutionalization of Daoism during the Tang dynasty.

As China's indigenous religion, Daoism was first developed during the sixth century BCE as a philosophical interpretation of the universe and the relations between humans and the

6. Trans. James R. Hightower, in Reischauer, 321–23.

universe.[7] While Daoist philosophy continued to flourish, a Daoist religious movement, the Way of the Celestial Masters (*Tianshi dao*), took shape during the second century. The movement stressed moral principles such as filial piety, obedience, and loyalty and advocated "nourishing life" and "sloughing the corpse" so one would go to heaven at the moment of death. The fourth and fifth centuries were the formative period of Daoism. Important Daoist texts were gradually codified during this period, and the goals of Chinese Daoists, individual immortality and universal salvation, were further clarified. Undoubtedly, this quest was very much influenced by Buddhist ideas of nirvana.

The institutionalization of Daoism occurred during the Tang dynasty. This was brought about by two factors. First the Tang imperial house practiced Daoism to bolster its dynastic prestige, and consequently became heavily involved in Daoist church organization. Second, the spread of Buddhism, a much more sophisticated and complex religion, provided Daoists with a model to emulate. By the end of the seventh century, a network of state-sponsored monasteries had been established throughout the empire; and the *Daodejing* was assigned as a required text for the Civil Service Examination. Just as with Buddhist monasteries, the Tang court was heavily involved with regulating Daoist monasteries, especially the ordination practices.

Presumably, when Yu was ordained, she took a vow to pledge her lifelong spiritual pursuit. As a Daoist nun, her goal was to attain higher states of transcendence and salvation. In doing so, she was required to observe strict celibacy, remain in seclusion, and pursue a life of fasting, meditation, and charity. However, her experience in the Belvedere of Universal Propriety as well as stories of other Daoist nuns show that in practice this was not always the case. The most intriguing example might be Yang Guifei's (719–756) brief stint as a Daoist nun. Yang, the famed consort of Emperor Xuanzong (r. 712–756), first became the bride of the emperor's eighteenth son in 736. However, her charm captivated the emperor himself, and she was then ordained as a Daoist nun and moved into a monastery. This arrangement allowed her to leave her first marriage and paved the way for her to be remarried. In 745 Yang left the monastery, entering the palace to become the Precious Consort of the emperor. Infatuated with her, the emperor neglected state affairs and allowed her family to gain unprecedented influence. An Lushan, whose rebellion eventually would devastate the Tang dynasty, was Yang's adopted son.

When Yu Xuanji entered the Belvedere of Universal Propriety, apparently she was still in love with Li Yi, for several times she would send a poem to Li professing her feeling for him and hoping he would visit. But Li Yi never once made an effort to contact Yu, and just a few months after

7. For a brief account of the history of Daoism, see Peter N. Gregory and Patricia Buckley Ebrey, "The Religious and Historical Landscape," in *Religion and Society in T'ang Sung China*, ed. Ebrey and Gregory (Honolulu: University of Hawaii Press, 1993), 1–44.

Yu left the household he took his wife and family to Yongzhou in eastern China for a newly appointed official position. As she resigned herself to her abandonment, Yu gradually learned to appreciate the tranquility and freedom of her life. In a poem titled "Handing over My Feelings," she depicted her daily life in the Belvedere of Universal Propriety:

> Swallows and sparrows I simply treat as nobles;
> Gold and silver I willingly forsake.
> The spring wine filling my cup is green;
> At night the window facing the moon is dark.
> I circle stepping-stones around the clean clear pool,
> Pluck out my hairpin to shine in slender currents.
> I lie in bed, texts and fascicles all around me,
> Then half drunk, get up to comb my hair.[8]

Living at the monastery allowed Yu to enjoy more freedom than most Tang women. It seems she left her residence quite often and had broad contact with various people. Her poems "I Pay a Visit to Refined Master Zhao Without Meeting Her" (**Document Four**) and "Poem Composed Following the Rhyme Words of Three Sisters" (**Document Five**) show that she formed strong bonds with neighboring women. Another poem, titled "Following the Rhymes of My Western Neighbor Who Is Newly Settled In, and Begging for Barley Wine," shows that Yu was not afraid of making an overture to a newly arrived male neighbor as well:

> One poem comes and I chant it a hundred times;
> Renewing my passions: each word resonates like gold.
> Looking west, I already had plans to climb your fence;
> Gazing far off, how can my heart not turn to stone? [9]

During this time Yu also resumed her contact with Chang'an literati, of whom some were her pen friends, others apparently intimate. One such intimate friend was the poet· Zuo Mingchang. In a poem titled "Hearing that Zuo Mingchang Arrived the Capital from Zezhou, Sent Someone to Pass on My Message," Yu recalled, "In a raining night, I accompanied you in a merry-making feast." In the poem, Yu also expressed her excitement about their imminent tryst "in a tiny house in a neighboring lane."[10] In a poem that was said to be dedicated to her last lover, possibly a male musician named Chen Wei, Yu confessed, "I entrusted my bitterness to a lute's crimson strings, Hold back passion—my thoughts unbearable." She then explicitly conveyed her desire to meet her lover in the convent: "The moon's hue is pure on mossy steps, soon comes from deep within the bamboo garden. Before my gate—ground

8. Trans. Suzanne Cahill. See Cahill, 556–57.

9. Yu, "Following the Rhymes of My Western Neighbor Who Is Newly Settled In, and Begging for Barley Wine." trans. Suzanne Cahill. See Cahill, 543.

10. Cao Ying, ed. *Complete Tang Poetry (Quan Tangshi)* (Shanghai: Shanghai guji chubanshe, 1986), 1973.

covered with red leaves, I don't sweep them away, waiting for one who understands me."[11]

Li Jinren was another intimate male friend of Yu Xuanji. In the poem "Welcoming Director Li Jinren," Yu expressed her delight at seeing Li back home from an official journey: "Burning incense, I step out to welcome my Pan Yue. Content, I do not envy Herding Boy and Weaving Maid's household." Pan Yue (247–300), a handsome and talented poet, was said to be the most sought-after young man in ancient China; Herding Boy and Weaving Maid were a happily married couple in Chinese myth. It seems that, by then, Yu was resigned to the fate that she could have love, but would never become a wife and mother.

Finale

In the beginning of the third month of his fifth year's reign, Emperor Wuzong became gravely ill. Now a fanatic Daoist, he issued a proclamation to name himself Yan. Yan is a character combining two fire symbols with the meanings "inflammation" and "hot." Convinced that the element of water in his name (the River Chan) disturbed the balance of his organism, the emperor desperately hoped that the element of fire would change his fate. The emperor also took medicines prescribed by Daoist magicians. He soon went insane and lost the ability to speak, possibly due to the effect of these medications. On the twenty-third day of the third month, the emperor passed away. Buried in the imperial cemetery, his tomb site was named Duan, meaning "proper," "right." Alongside his coffin rested the coffin of his late concubine, Lady Wang. He left five sons and seven daughters.

Before his last breath, his uncle, Li Chen, handpicked by the eunuchs, was named heir apparent; he became the emperor Xuanzong (r. 847–860). The new regime quickly took steps to reverse the Huichang rule: Buddhist monasteries were restored; monks and nuns were encouraged to resume their religious identities. The Huichang Persecution nonetheless permanently crippled Buddhism and the religion never recovered its former glory. The Huichang political crisis, however, continued: eunuchs and factions of civil officials plotted against one another; regional generals fought wars among themselves. The dynasty soon disintegrated.

Yu Xuanji's life ended in 868 when she was convicted of murder and swiftly executed. The incident was recorded in a short biography, written by a male literati of her time named Huangfu Mei.[12] It reads like a modern tale of sex, lies, murder, and revenge.

11. Yu, "Deeply Moved, I Send This to Someone," in Sun and Saussy, 69.

12. For a full translation of the biography, see Cahill, 563–66.

Yu had a beautiful maidservant named Lüqiao who had served her for years in the convent. One day in the spring, Yu went to a neighboring convent for a gathering and returned to find Lüqiao acting quite suspicious. Convinced that the maid was having an affair with one of her lovers, Yu stripped her naked and gave her over a hundred lashes. Before her death, the maid reportedly scolded at Yu: "You Refined Master want to see the three clear realms of Daoist heavens and the way of prolonging life, yet you cannot forget the pleasures of releasing your sash and offering to share a pillow. On the contrary, through your deep suspicions you heap up false accusations against one who is chaste and righteous!" Yu buried Lüqiao's body in the backyard of the convent and told everyone that the maid had run way.

A guest feasting in Yu's convent found traces of blood in the backyard and told his servant who later told his older brother. The older brother, a prefectural watchman, had long harbored resentment against Yu because she once refused to loan him money. The watchman gathered some people, and they forced their way into Yu's convent and uncovered Lüqiao's body. A city official interrogated Yu and quickly obtained a confession. Yu was convicted immediately and put to death in the fall. Before her execution, she composed a farewell poem, declaring: "It's easy to find a priceless treasure, much harder to get a man with a heart!" (**Document Six**).

No legal documents concerning her murder case survived. One can imagine that a free-spirited woman such as Yu would be tried quite harshly by the court, considering how the male literati of her time judged the incident in their writings. Her life and her tragic death nevertheless exemplify the intersection of religion, gender, and personal life in a unique period of Chinese history.

Documents

DOCUMENT ONE

Diagram of Capital Chang'an

In the early eighth century Chang'an had a total of ninety-one Buddhist monasteries, sixteen Daoist abbeys, two Nestorian Christian churches, and four Zoroastrian shrines.

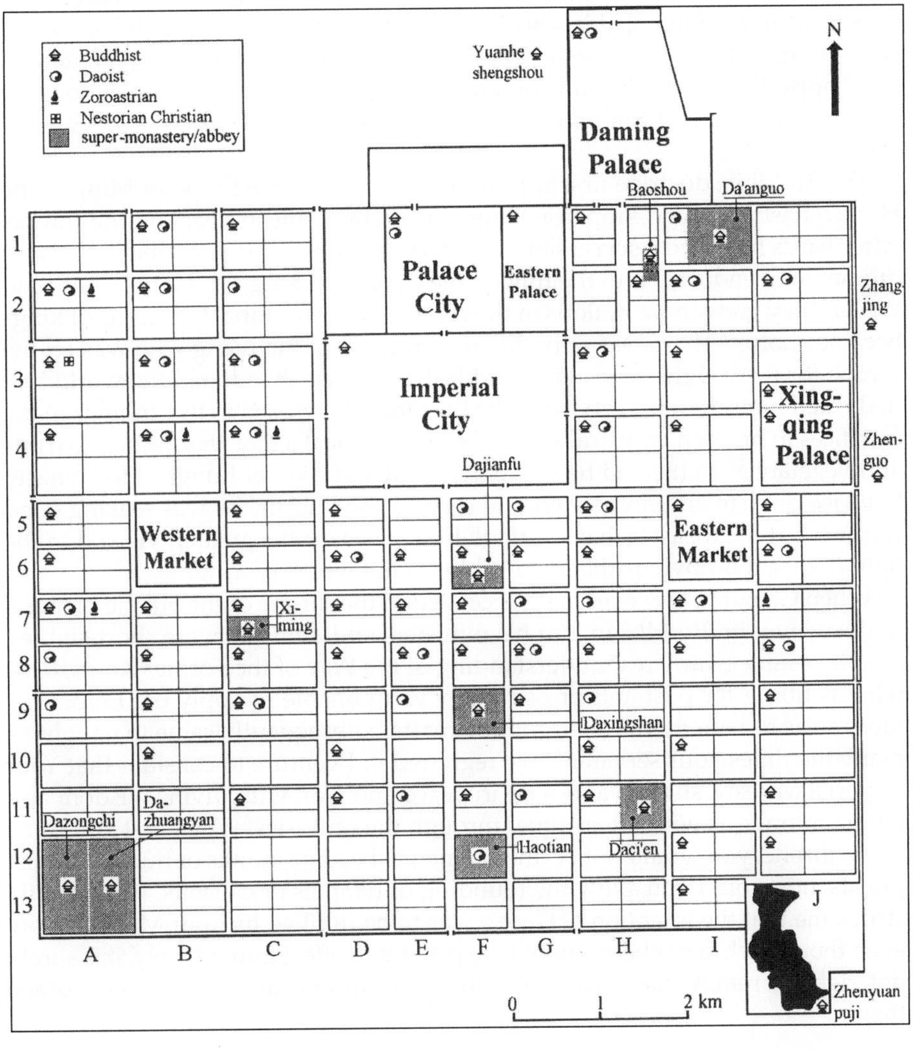

DOCUMENT TWO

Han Yu

Memorial on Buddhism (819)

Han Yu (770–824) was a Confucian scholar, court official, and renowned writer. His memorial, considered a literary masterpiece in China, best represented Tang scholar-officials' sentiments against Buddhism. What are the bases of Han Yu's anti-Buddhist stand?

Your servant submits that Buddhism is but one of the practices of barbarians which has filtered into China since the Later Han. In ancient times there was no such thing. . . . In those times the empire was at peace, and the people, contented and happy, lived out their full complement of years. . . . The Buddhist doctrine had still not reached China, so this could not have been the result of serving the Buddha.

The Buddhist doctrine first appeared in the time of the Emperor Ming of the Han Dynasty, and the Emperor Ming was scant eighteen years on the throne. Afterwards followed a succession of disorders and revolutions, when dynasties did not long endure. From the time of the dynasties Song, Qi, Liang, Chen, and Wei, as they grew more zealous in the service of the Buddha, the reigns of kings became shorter. There was only the Emperor Wu of the Liang who was on the throne for forty-eight years. First and last, he thrice abandoned the world and dedicated himself to the service of the Buddha. He refused to use animals in the sacrifices in his own ancestral shrine. His single meal a day was limited to fruits and vegetables. In the end he was driven out and died of hunger. His dynasty likewise came to an untimely end. In serving the Buddha he was seeking good fortune, but the disaster that overtook him was only the greater. Viewed in the light of this, it is obvious that the Buddha is not worth serving.

When Gaozu (r. 618–626) first succeeded to the throne of the Sui, he planned to do away with Buddhism, but his ministers and advisors were short-sighted men incapable of any real understanding of the Way of the Former Kings, or of what is fitting for past and present; they were unable to apply the Emperor's ideas so as to remedy this evil, and the matter subsequently came to naught — many the times your servants have regretted it. I venture to consider that Your Imperial Majesty, shrewd and wise in peace and war, with divine wisdom and heroic courage, is without an equal through the centuries. When first you came to the throne, you would not permit laymen to become monks or nuns or Daoist priests, nor would you allow the founding of temples or cloisters. It constantly struck me that the intention of Gaozu was to be fulfilled by Your Majesty. Now even though it has not been possible to put it into effect immediately, it is surely not right to remove all restrictions and turn around and actively encourage them.

Now I hear that by Your Majesty's command a troupe of monks went to Fengxiang to get the Buddha-bone, and that you viewed it from a tower as it was carried into the Imperial Palace; also that you have ordered that it be received and honored in all the temples in turn. Although your servant is stupid, he cannot help knowing that Your Majesty is not misled by this Buddha, and that you do not perform these devotions to pray for good luck. But just because the harvest has been good and the people are happy, you are complying with the general desire by putting on for the citizens of the capital this extraordinary spectacle which is nothing more than a sort of theatrical amusement. How could a sublime intelligence like yours consent to believe in this sort of thing?

But the people are stupid and ignorant; they are easily deceived and with difficulty enlightened. If they see Your Majesty behaving in this fashion, they are going to think you serve the Buddha in all sincerity. All will say, "The Emperor is wisest of all, and yet he is a sincere believer. What are we common people that we still should grudge our lives?" Burning heads and searing fingers by the tens and hundreds, throwing away their clothes and scattering their money, from morning to night emulating one another and fearing only to be last, old and young rush about, abandoning their work and place; and if restrictions are not immediately imposed, they will increasingly make the rounds of temples and some will inevitably cut off their arms and slice their flesh in the way of offerings. Thus to violate decency and draw the ridicule of the whole world is no light matter.

Now the Buddha was of barbarian origin. His language differed from Chinese speech; his clothes were of a different cut; his mouth did not pronounce the prescribed words of the Former Kings, his body was not clad in the garments prescribed by the Former Kings. He did not recognize the relationship between prince and subject, nor the sentiments of father and son. Let us suppose him to be living today, and that he come to court at the capital as an emissary of his country. Your Majesty would receive him courteously. But only one interview in the audience chamber, one banquet in his honor, one gift of clothing, and he would be escorted under guard to the border that he might not mislead the masses.

How much the less, now that he has long been dead, is it fitting that his decayed and rotten bone, his ill-omened and filthy remains, should be allowed to enter in the forbidden precincts of the Palace? Confucius said, "Respect ghosts and spirits, but keep away from them." The feudal lords of ancient times, when they went to pay a visit of condolence in their states, made it their practice to have exorcists go before with rush-brooms and peachwood branches to dispel unlucky influences. Only after such precautions did they make their visit of condolence. Now without reason you have taken up an unclean thing and examined it in person when no exorcist had gone before, when neither rush-broom nor peachwood branch had been employed. But your ministers did not speak of the wrong nor did the censors call attention to the impropriety; I am in truth ashamed of them. I pray that Your Majesty will turn this bone over to the officials that it may be cast into water or fire, cutting off for all time the root and so dispelling the suspicions of the empire and preventing the befuddlement of later generations. Thereby men may know in what manner a great sage acts who a million times surpasses ordinary men. Could this be anything but ground for prosperity? Could it be anything but a cause for rejoicing?

If the Buddha has supernatural power and can wreak harm and evil, may any blame or retribution fittingly fall on my person. Heaven be my witness: I will not regret it. Unbearably disturbed and with the utmost sincerity I respectfully present my petition that these things may be known.

Your servant is truly alarmed, truly afraid.

DOCUMENT THREE

Ennin

Diary (842)

This diary entry was registered on the eleventh day of the sixth month in 842, the eve of Emperor Wuzong's twenty-eighth birthday. Ennin recorded the imperial edict word by word, and it is now the only surviving copy of the so-called Wei Zongqing Incident edict. What was Wei's offense? What was Emperor Wuzong's purpose in issuing this edict?

Wei Zongqing . . . stands among those of honorable degree and should conform to the Confucian way of life, but he is drowned in evil doctrines, which stir up depraved customs. He has opened the door to delusions and has gone completely against the doctrines of the sages. How deep is the depravity among those of high office. How much more should Wei proscribe that is not the words of the sages. Why should foreign religions be propagated?

We should like to overlook [his offense], but this may do injury to public morality. He is to be demoted, and Wei are still to be called magnanimous [in doing this]. He is to be made the Prefect of Chengdufu and is to be rushed there by post stations.

[Wei] Zongqing . . . has presented to the throne *The Three Virtues as Culled from the Buddhist Nirvana Sutra* in twenty scrolls and *An Abstract of the Imperially Commissioned Complete Mirror to the Letter "I"*[1] in twenty scrolls. They have been carefully examined.

The Buddha was a western barbarian in origin, and his teachings spread the doctrine of "non-birth." Confucius, however, was a Chinese sage, and the Classics provide words of profit. Wei Zongqing, while being an ordinary Confucianist, a scholar, an official, and [a man of] distinguished family, has not been able to spread [the teaching of] Confucius and Mozi, but, on the contrary,

1. A letter in the Sanskrit alphabet.

believes blindly in Buddhism and has foolishly made compilations from barbarian writings and has rashly presented them. How much more have the common people of China been steeped for long in these ways! In truth, their delusions should all be stopped, and they should be made to return to their pristine simplicity. But [Wei Zongqing] assembles mystical falsehoods and in turn misleads the stupid people. Ranking as he does among the courtiers, should he [not] be ashamed of himself?

The scriptures he resented have already been burned in the Palace. The Imperial Secretariat and Imperial Chancellery are commissioned to find the original drafts and burn them, so that he cannot pass them on to others.

DOCUMENT FOUR

Yu Xuanji

"I Pay a Visit to Refined Master Zhao Without Meeting Her" (ca. 866)

This poem describes Yu Xuanji's feeling on visiting a Daoist nun's residence. In expressing her appreciation of Zhao's simple, aesthetic, and peaceful lifestyle, Yu Xuanji creates a harmonious realm without the existence of men. What other messages do you think the poem conveys?

Where are you and your transcendent companions?
Your green-clothed servant rests alone in the household.
On the warm stove: remains of your steeped herbs,
In the adjoining courtyard: boiling tea.
Painted walls, dim in the lamps' radiance;
Shadows from banner's poles slant.
Anxiously I turn my head back again and again,
At numerous branches of blossoms outside your walls.

DOCUMENT FIVE

Yu Xuanji

"Poem Composed Following the Rhyme Words of Three Sisters" (ca. 866)

This poem celebrates women's beauty, talent, free spirit, and friendship. It conveys a feeling of Chinese women's self-assurance, sexuality, and power. In your opinion, what are the factors that contributed to this rare presentation of Chinese women?

Preface: Guang, Wei, and Pou are three sisters, orphaned when young and accomplished from the beginning. Now they have written these poems, so essential and pure that they are hard to match. How could even the linked verses from the Xie household [i.e., by Xie Daoyun][1] add to them? There was a stranger coming from the capital city who showed them to me. Consequently, I put these rhymes in order.

Formerly I heard that in the southern nations flowery faces were few,
But today my eastern neighbors are three sisters.
In their dressing room, gazing upon one another: the "Rhapsody on the Parrot";
At their cyan window they must be embroidering phoenix slips.
Pink fragrant plants fill the courtyard, ragged and jaggedly broken off;
Green strained wine fills our cups; one after another we put them to our mouths.
I suspect they once served as girl attendants at the Turquoise Pond (Yaochi);
Coming in exile to this dusty world, they did not become males.
I finally venture to compare them to the appearance of Lady Wenji;
Little Xi would be speechless before them; I am still more mortified.
A single tune of ravishing song—the zither seems far away and indistinct;
While the four-strings are lightly strummed, they talk, murmuring unclearly.
Facing the mirror stand, they compete equally with their blue-glinting silk-thread hair.
Opposite the moon, they vie in showing off their white jade hairpins.
In the midst of the Lesser Existence Grotto (Xiaoyou dong), pine dew drops;
Above the Great Veil Heaven (Daoluo tian), willow mist is contained.
If only they were able to tarry on account of the rain,
They need not fear that matters of "blowing the syrinx" are not yet understood.
How many times has the Amah scolded them for talking beneath the flowers?
Lord Pan [Pan Yue] consulted them once in a meeting in a dream.
When I temporarily grasp their pure sentences, it's as if my cloud-soul were cut off;
If I were looking at their pink faces, even dying would be sweet.
Despondently I look afar for those delightful people; where are they?
Traversing the clouds, I return home to the north while they return to the south.

1. Xie Daoyun (fl. 400) was one of most talented female writers in Chinese history. Ed.

DOCUMENT SIX

Yu Xuanji

"Given to a Neighbor Girl" (868)

This is Yu's most famous poem, allegedly written on the morning of her execution. What is the theme of this poem? Some scholars argue the poem reflects Yu's defiant optimism; do you agree with that assessment?

Shamed before the sun, I shade myself with my netted gauze silk sleeve,
Depressed by the spring, reluctant to rise and put on make-up.
It's easy to find a priceless treasure,
Much harder to get a man with a heart!
On my pillow, secretly flow my tears;
Amidst the flowers, silently my guts are sliced.
Since I will soon personally be able to peek at Song Yu,[1]
Why regret Wang Chang?[2]

1. Song Yu was a handsome writer who lived during the third century BCE.
2. Wang Chang, a desirable bachelor, was a fictional character in Chinese literature.

Questions

1. How was Buddhism introduced to China? What aspects of Buddhism attracted the Chinese people?
2. Raised as a Buddhist believer, Emperor Wuzong eventually became a fervent Daoist. What does this transformation tell you about religion and politics in the Tang dynasty? In reading **Documents Two** and **Three,** what led to Emperor Wuzong's decision to attack Buddhism?
3. What impact did the Huichang Buddhist Persecution have on Tang society? What are the similarities and differences among the Huichang incident and other religious persecutions in world history?
4. Who was Yu Xuanji? In your opinion, what was her real identity?
5. What does Yu Xuanji's life experience tell you about women's position in the Tang dynasty? What does it tell you about religion and gender at the time?
6. Who is the intended audience of Yu Xuanji's poetry? Justify your answer with specific reference to the reading.

Suggested Readings

Benn, Charles. *China's Golden Age: Everyday Life in the Tang Dynasty*. Oxford, UK: Oxford University Press, 2002.

Gernet, Jacques. *Buddhism in Chinese History: An Economic History from the Fifth to the Tenth Centuries*. Trans. Franciscus Verelien. New York: Columbia University Press, 1995.

Reischauer, Edwin O. *Ennin's Travels in T'ang China*. New York: Ronald, 1955.

Twitchett, Denis. *The Cambridge History of China*. Vol. 3, *Sui and T'ang China, 589–906*, Pt. 1. Cambridge, UK: Cambridge University Press, 1979.

Source Material

A Visual Sourcebook of Chinese Civilization
http://depts.washington.edu/chinaciv

CHAPTER

9

The Foundations of Islam: Aisha bint Abu Bakr (614–678) and Ali ibn Abu Talib (599–661)

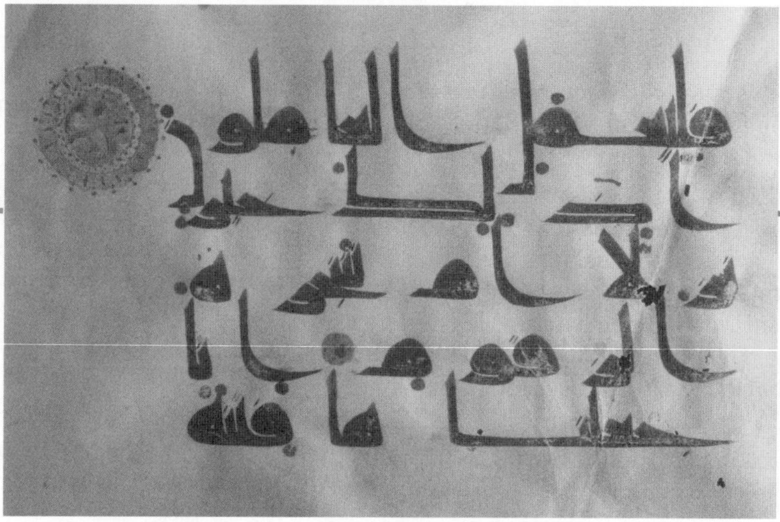

Nearly all the pairs in this book are represented in images at the beginning of each chapter, but the illustration for this chapter is a single page from a ninth century Qur'an fragment. *Not* providing illustrations of Ali and Aisha[1] is in keeping with an important point: in orthodox Islam, it is considered inappropriate to depict humans, an act that usurps the creative power of God. This helps explain why nonfigural art, especially calligraphy and abstract design, was favored in Islam. However, in cultures where there was a well-developed artistic tradition before the Islamic conquests, such as Persia and India, human depiction did continue. Even then, in a respectful nod to the strict avoidance of human depiction in the core Arabic-speaking regions of Islam, Persian

1. Her personal name was Aisha; *bint* means daughter (of). His personal name was Ali; *ibn* means son (of). Birth and death dates are from the foundation story.

(and later also Ottoman) artists usually painted Muhammad and members of his family with white veils over their entire faces.

Setting the Stage

Before the rise and spread of Islam, the Middle East was divided between two expansive imperial powers, Greek-speaking East Roman Byzantium and Persian-speaking Sasanid Persia. Over the course of several centuries, these two empires exhausted themselves and their subject populations with warfare, competing for territory and access to trade. In the course of the long struggle, both imperial powers had intruded into the Arabian Peninsula, especially in the Yemen. Agriculture was feasible in parts of the peninsula due to underground aquifers. Yemeni ports enjoyed a thriving trade because of their access to the Red Sea, Persian Gulf, and western Indian Ocean. Silver mines in southeastern Arabia were also attractive, particularly to the Sasanids, who had merely to cross the gulf to reach them. Some historians argue that these imperial interests in Arabia provide a partial explanation of the rise of a unified, anti-imperial Arabian state.

The founder of the Islamic state, the Prophet Muhammad (d. 632 CE), was from a significant tribal group, the Quraysh, who dominated the town of Makka (or the less accurate transliteration, Mecca) in west central Arabia. The tribe was subdivided into several clans. Muhammad's clan, the Hashimi, was less wealthy and prestigious than others, although its fortunes rose along with his. The most powerful clan, the Umayya, plays a major role in the story that follows. This tribal structure would, however, give way to something a bit different, a state in which loyalty to Muhammad and his prophetic role were crucial.

Many if not all religions produce debate and conflict at the time of their establishment. For Islam, the stories of Aisha bint Abu Bakr and Ali ibn Abu Talib illustrate this tension. Both were close to the Prophet Muhammad and instrumental in the formation of Islam. Ali was a cousin and son-in-law to Muhammad and served as the fourth successor (caliph) to the Prophet. Aisha was Muhammad's youngest wife and was politically active long after his death, resisting the caliphate of Ali. While Aisha and Ali are part of Islam's *seventh*-century-CE foundation story, they have come to us in *ninth*-century literary representations, in which they symbolize competing religious-political tendencies that were in the process of crystallizing into the Sunni and Shi'i branches of Islam.

The traditional or conventional account of Islam's foundation comes to us through pious, internal sources. According to this widely repeated account, Muhammad was a spiritually sensitive man who worked as a caravan manager. While on retreat in a mountain cave, he received revelations which he believed were from Allah (God) and which he recited to his family and followers. The revelations were starkly poetic and called on listeners to be grateful to Allah for creation and to stand in awe of final judgment. Not all Makkans were pleased by this message because it conflicted with the town's polytheism. The Umayya clansmen in particular worried that his message would interfere with their control over a long-standing, lucrative pilgrimage to a polytheistic shrine in Makka. Their opposition to Muhammad sometimes turned violent.

The conventional account emphasizes the year 622, when Muhammad and his followers moved to the more hospitable town of Yathrib, later referred to as *al-Madina*, "the town" of the Prophet, and he established there the core of his new state. At first, he functioned as a respected mediator, settling disputes among the various clans, tribes, and religious groups represented in Yathrib. Many in the town also came to accept him as a prophet and as a political and military leader, signaling the start of an Islamic state. The revelation process that had begun in Makka continued, but the style and content of the message changed. Revelations were no longer poetic but more like prose, and they contained abbreviated stories of biblical figures, such as Abraham, Moses, and Jesus and also set out laws and precepts for the community. (Both Makkan and Madinan revelations were later collected into a holy book, *al-Qur'an*, "the Recitation" or "the Reading.") Muhammad expanded his new political order and gained control over Arabian tribes, through treaties and conquest. Before his death in 632, Muhammad brought nearly the entire Arabian Peninsula under his control, including his hometown, Makka, where the defeated Umayya finally converted.

When Muhammad died, his successors (caliphs) reasserted control over Arabia and also expanded their conquest outside Arabia, deep into the territories of the East Romans and Sasanids and beyond. Although the state grew rapidly, it did so without full agreement about how succession should be handled, a tension that is crucial to this chapter.

The sources for this foundation period are controversial. The pious story is based largely on a biography of Muhammad, originally written around the middle of the eighth century CE, but lost to us. We do have a copy of this biography edited by Ibn Hisham, from the early part of the ninth century CE. This edition fleshes out passages in the Qur'an that Ibn Ishaq and Ibn Hisham believed were allusions to events in Muhammad's life. Muslim chronicles or digests of early politics and military campaigns date from the late ninth and tenth centuries. Sources that are contemporary with very early Islam are few and written by outsiders who are not helpful for information about either Aisha or Ali.

The Actors

Muhammad, Khadija, Ali, and Aisha

According to the conventional account of Islam, Muhammad was born in 570 CE. His father died before he was born, and his mother died when he was about six. He lived with his grandfather until he, too, passed away, and then with his uncle, Abu Talib (d. 619). The fact that Muhammad was an orphan has large symbolic power for Muslims, who stress the importance of helping widows, orphans, and all those who find themselves in unfortunate circumstances.

Muhammad's life is closely interwoven with that of his younger cousin, Ali, since the two grew up together in the household of Ali's father, Abu Talib. As a mature adult, Muhammad shared with his family and clan the revelations he believed were from Allah. The first person to believe him was his wife, Khadija (d. 619). The second person was Ali. Early acceptance of Muhammad's message was later considered a badge of honor and prestige (**Document One**).

In the foundation story, the match between Muhammad and Khadija was their mutual choice, not an arranged marriage. Khadija was a widow who had inherited a caravan business from her first husband. She hired Muhammad as a caravan manager and came to admire his abilities. Though she was older than Muhammad, by as much as fifteen years, they married in about 596. Khadija's situation indicates that a pre-Islamic woman *could* be independent, but she also may represent the exception.

We know relatively little about pre-Islamic Arabian social norms. In a nomadic situation, men were the warriors who defended the tribe's arid, scrub-growth territories; conquered new pastures; and raided villages for booty. Women moved the campsites, prepared food, and, together with the children, managed the herds of sheep and goats. The tribe was the survival unit, and people identified themselves by their tribal affiliation rather than as individuals. Nomadic society was not static, but it avoided rapid changes that might endanger the tenuous balance between humans and a brutal environment. The foundation story places Islam in settled, urban settings, Makka and Madina, where tribal society was evolving more quickly. Individuals and clans within the Quraysh tribe came to vary in socioeconomic status, and the tribe no longer functioned as a survival unit but more as a network for business and social support.

Issues addressed in early Islam indicate societal complexities and a strong sense of transition to a new order. Islamic law protected private property and articulated rules of inheritance, making it important for society to regulate reproduction. The Qur'an allows a man to have up to four legal wives on condition that he treat them equally. Custody of children goes to the father, either after they are weaned or after they reach a certain age, such as seven. The Qur'an forbids infanticide. Early Islamic attention to family law indicates that previous rules concerning family and reproduction may not have been uniform. An urban tribal society was establishing standards and values and placing all that under the authority of a single deity.

The union between Muhammad and Khadija lasted approximately thirteen years. The couple had no surviving sons, but most notable of their daughters was Fatima, who later married Ali. Both Khadija and Ali's father, Abu Talib, died in 619, causing deep grief for the family, particularly for Muhammad and Ali.

The cousins Muhammad and Ali also shared the experience of persecution at the hands of Umayya clansmen, who did not appreciate Muhammad's monotheistic message. In 622, Muhammad and his followers left Makka for Yathrib (later Madina), an emigration that marks the beginning of the Muslim lunar calendar. The emigrants included, among others, Muhammad's new wife Sawda, his daughters by Khadija, his close friend Abu Bakr along with Abu Bakr's family, and Ali.

About two years after settling in the new town, Muhammad arranged a marriage between Ali and Fatima. The symbolic value of this union is strong because, although the traditional account gives Muhammad at least eleven wives over the course of his life, he had no male heir. Having a son and heir was extremely important in this as in many societies, in order to sustain the family name and any fortune. Muhammad's cousin and now son-in-law filled a crucial void.

From later sources, a personal description of Ali emerges. He was stout but broad shouldered, and bald but with a long white beard. His manner was brusque and his religious observance quite rigid.[2] Fatima complained to her father that Ali treated her harshly. Out of concern for his daughter's feelings, Muhammad persuaded Ali not to take other wives. After Muhammad died, however, Ali married eight more women and took a number of concubines, all within the bounds of the cultural tradition and Islamic rules, but clearly not what Muhammad would have wanted. Of all Ali's many children, the most famous was Fatima's son, Husayn, who later in the seventh century would become the preeminent martyr of the Shi'i Muslim tradition.[3]

Ali himself has a revered place in both Sunni and Shi'i Islam, based not only on his close association with Muhammad but also on his piety and skill in battle. In the Shi'i tradition, he has acquired elevated status, nearly equal to and occasionally exceeding the status of Muhammad (**Document Two**). A supporter of Ali claimed to "seek God at the future abode [paradise] through my love for Ali."[4] Muhammad is credited with saying that "Ali is never separated from the Truth, nor the Truth from Ali," Truth being used here as a name for God. From an early point in Islamic history,[5] it appears that Ali had supporters who viewed him as specially blessed. One early Muslim who did not share that view was a relative by marriage, Aisha.

Aisha was a child of nine when her father, Abu Bakr, arranged her marriage with Muhammad, who was then about fifty-three.[6] The story goes

2. L. Veccia Vaglieri, "'Ali ibn Abi Talib," in *Encyclopedia of Islam,* 2d ed. (Leiden, The Netherlands: Brill, 1960), 385.

3. In 680, despite no chance of success, Husayn led a small loyal band against a large tribal force of the Umayyad caliph, Yazid. The battle and Husayn's death are reenacted by Shi'i communities every year.

4. Fazlur Rahman, *Islam,* 2d ed., (Chicago: University of Chicago Press, 1979) 171; see also **Document Two**.

5. 'Allamah Sayyid Muhammad Husayn Tabataba'i, *Shi'ite Islam* (Albany: State University of New York Press, 1975), 192.

6. I am highly indebted to Denise A. Spellberg for her excellent and readable book on Aisha, titled *Politics, Gender, and the Islamic Past: The Legacy of 'A'isha bint Abi Bakr* (New York: Columbia University Press, 1994).

that she brought her toys with her to her husband's home—interpreted as sweet innocence in their relationship. The marriage took place in Yathrib (Madina) in 623, one year into Muhammad's career in that town. Aisha's extreme youth and the large age difference are very strange to us now, but at that time and place, the arrangement was acceptable. In fact, Muhammad particularly favored Aisha because she was his youngest wife and the only one who was a virgin at the time of their marriage (the others all being divorcées or widows). Aisha is described as beautiful and petite. Like all the wives of Muhammad, she was referred to as a "mother of the believers." As a rhetorical device, "mother of" anything indicates high significance, as in the expression, "mother of all battles." The title was particularly poignant in her case because she remained childless.

Aisha's identity was partly formed by an unfortunate incident during her married life that is related in Ibn Ishaq's biography of the prophet (**Document Three**). Muhammad's military entourage, including the wives and concubines of the men, was encamped, on its way home from a raid in 627. Aisha, then fourteen, went beyond sight of the group in order to relieve herself. While she was gone, the order came to break camp. Aisha's litter bearers did not notice her absence, since the palanquin was closed and she weighed very little. By the time she returned to the spot, the group had left her far behind. A young, handsome man who had been assigned to guard the rear of the caravan came to her rescue and accompanied her back to Madina. A scandal ensued. Some assumed that Aisha and her rescuer had committed adultery, thereby dishonoring both her husband and father. Soon after, Muhammad proclaimed that he had received a revelation that exonerated Aisha and blamed her accusers for lying (**Document Four**). The vindication of Aisha reflects well not only on her, but also, in a sense, on God (for timely intervention) and on Muhammad (for backing his wife) and on the Muslim community (for punishing those who lied). One reaction stands apart, and that is the reaction of Ali, who did not understand what all the fuss was about. Before the exonerating revelation came, he advised Muhammad that "women are plentiful, and you can easily change one for another."[7] Later writers who were sympathetic to Ali and his descendents may well have attributed these words to Ali in order to express their own scorn for Aisha, who, as we will see, would later oppose Ali.

While the "account of the lie" sticks to Aisha like glue, other factors crucial to her *identity* are the reputations of both her husband and her father, just as her reputation was important to their *honor*. Her husband was a prophet of Allah and soon recognized as the political and military leader of a tribal confederation based on his prophetic authority. Her father was Abu Bakr of the Hashimi clan, a close friend of Muhammad and

7. Ibn Ishaq, *The Life of Muhammad: A Translation of Ishaq's Sirat Rasul Allah*, ed. Ibn Hisham, trans. and introd. Alfred Guillaume (London: Oxford University Press, 1955), 496. Ibn Ishaq (d. 767 CE) wrote a very early version of Muhammad's biography. This version is not directly available to us, but Ibn Hisham (d. 834 CE) left us his edited version.

an early convert who had also migrated to Yathrib. After Muhammad's death in 632, when Aisha was only eighteen, her father was selected as the first caliph, and he successfully moved the state beyond the death of its founder. Abu Bakr's reign was only a brief two years before his natural death in 634. These two male relatives had allowed Aisha to enjoy status and protection within the community.

Certainly Aisha's situation changed after the deaths of Muhammad and Abu Bakr. According to inheritance verses in the Qur'an, the deaths would have resulted in her receiving a portion from each man's estate. Each of Muhammad's surviving wives would have received a year's maintenance and, as a daughter, Aisha would have received from Abu Bakr's estate one-half of what any brother received.[8] Financially, then, Aisha was probably modestly comfortable. However, she no longer had a prestigious male protector. She seems to have been undaunted, and boldly participated in the political life of the community, reworking her own identity. When eventually Ali's supporters claimed for him the fourth caliphate, Aisha tried to stop them, for reasons to be introduced soon. Together with others of like mind, she gathered a force of several hundred men and led them toward Ali's defending forces in southern Mesopotamia. Her attempt failed, but she won for herself a unique position in Islamic tradition that contrasts with the position enjoyed by Khadija, Muhammad's first wife. Khadija stands as an independent and self-sufficient businesswoman of the pre-Islamic period, while Aisha has status as a political activist in early Islam. In Aisha's case, however, her independence and strength are not necessarily viewed as positive traits. The assessment depends, we will see, on the political persuasion of the assessor.

■ Act I

The Conventional Story of the First Four Caliphs

Before Muhammad died, he left no generally agreed on instructions about succession. His revelations held no blueprint for government. As Ali prepared Muhammad's body for burial, the leaders of the Quraysh tribe discussed succession. Who was qualified to rule the Muslim state? What type of authority should he have?

The council of elders selected one of their own number, Abu Bakr, as the first successor to Muhammad. In justification of this tribal practice, Qurayshi leaders later argued that Muhammad had expressed a preference for Abu Bakr as his successor. Their argument rested largely on a significant incident: when ill, the prophet had enlisted Abu Bakr to lead the community in prayer in his stead. Another obvious token of Muhammad's favor was his marriage to Abu Bakr's daughter, Aisha. It seemed logical to the council that Abu Bakr had been Muhammad's tacit choice. In retrospect, the position taken by this group of Quraysh confirmed the

8. *The Qu'ran*, sura 2, aya 240; sura 4, aya 11. Later, different schools of jurisprudence refined inheritance law.

status quo that historians call proto-Sunnism.

The prefix *proto-* indicates a tendency toward a Sunnism that was unself-conscious and still forming. The term *sunni* is the adjectival form of the noun *sunna*, meaning "custom" and referring to the customary practice of Muhammad, established by the accounts (*hadith*s) of things he did or said. Muhammad's request to Abu Bakr to lead prayers is an example of information from a particular *hadith*. The customs of the prophet provide additional guidelines for life, alongside those in the Qur'an. While all early Muslims respected the *sunna*, the term was most closely associated with the majority who emphasized its authority. The more obvious issue that set the proto-Sunnis apart was their understanding of leadership, an understanding that relied heavily on the practices of a tribal council. In the ninth century, the ideological descendents of these men became self-conscious of themselves as a group and as a majority; they then articulated Sunni Islam in law and theology.

In contrast stood the proto-Shi'is, precursors of the Shi'i branch of Islam. The nickname derives from the expression *shi'at Ali*, the "faction of Ali." While the faction did not clarify its ideology until the tenth and eleventh centuries, some earlier proto-Shi'is argued that Muhammad had publicly designated Ali as his successor. Shi'i Muslims interpreted a controversial *hadith* as Muhammad's designation of Ali. Further, they said that the designation was ignored by the proto-Sunnis, perhaps because the latter considered thirty-something Ali to be too young to be considered for tribal-style leadership. One version tells of the newly selected caliph, Abu Bakr, approaching Ali's home, seeking Ali's oath of loyalty to him as caliph. Ali came out to meet him with his sword in hand and refused to make an oath. Some sources contend that Ali staunchly refused to swear allegiance to the new caliph for six months, long enough to make his point. Aisha probably held his stubbornness toward her father against Ali.

For twenty-five years after the death of Muhammad, Ali left center stage and stood modestly to the side as the tribal councils chose the next three successors, Abu Bakr, Umar, and Uthman. In 656, discontented Muslims assassinated Uthman. His death threw the Muslim community into a leadership crisis once again. The supporters of Ali, concentrated in southern Mesopotamia in the town of Kufa, appear to have been stronger and more vocal than advocates for any other individual candidate. Ali's supporters proclaimed him to be the fourth caliph.

Act II

Emerging Factions and Branches of Islam

Uthman was of the Umayya clan, the last clan of the Quraysh tribe to accept Muhammad's leadership and, therefore, the first to draw resentment from the other clans. Uthman was a controversial caliph partly because he was Umayyad and partly because he blatantly engaged in nepotism, appointing members of his clan to important positions. One such appointment was of his cousin, Mu'awiya, to be military governor of geographic Syria, a large and potentially powerful province in the new Islamic order.

However unpopular Uthman may have been, his assassination was still considered regicide, a high crime. Even those who may have applauded the act *said* they wanted to avenge it. The new caliph, Ali, from his capital at Kufa, said that he had tried but failed to find the killers, an admission that played into the hands of Uthman's cousin Mu'awiya in Damascus. Mu'awiya could now seek clan vengeance and at the same time criticize Ali for ineffectiveness. He could also begin his own bid for the caliphate. Worried, Ali did try to appoint a replacement as governor of Syria, but Mu'awiya held his ground and kept his job.

Opposition to Ali in Makka and Madina began to coalesce as well. The leader of this opposition, at least symbolically, was Muhammad's young widow, Aisha. She was joined by two men who had been companions of the late prophet and former friends of Ali, Talha and Zubayr. The latter was Aisha's nephew and the former was related to her by marriage. Some sources say that the two men manipulated her, while others suggest that Aisha's involvement was proactive and even insistent.

Why would Aisha be so insistent in opposing Ali? As Abu Bakr's daughter, she would have resented Ali's slow and reluctant tolerance of her father's caliphate. Ali's alleged advice to Muhammad to dismiss Aisha after the adultery accusation would give her a strong motive to oppose him. Another explanation, plausible to historians even without reference to the conventional story of Muhammad's extended family, is that the conflict mirrored a power struggle between two geographic strongholds. Ali and his faction represented southern Mesopotamia, an upstart political center, while Aisha, Talha, and Zubayr symbolized west central Arabia and the political status quo. The geographic factor seems to have outweighed even *tribal* politics, since many of those involved on both sides were of the same Hashimi clan.

The fight between the factions of Aisha and Ali took place in southern Mesopotamia and was dubbed the Battle of the Camel, so called because of an ingrained literary image of Aisha riding in a howda, atop a camel in the middle of the fray. Ali's forces won the battle, while Talha and Zubayr died. Aisha was captured, but Ali allowed her to live out the rest of her long life in Madina, under conditions similar to house arrest, a time during which she transmitted many *hadith*s, that is, accounts, of what Muhammad used to do and say. Her status as a transmitter of such important traditions ensured her legacy.

With Aisha safely under house arrest in Madina, Ali had to turn his full attention to Mu'awiya of Syria, who now sent out an army to challenge Ali's rule. The result was the Battle at Siffin, in Syria, in 657. The long, bloody battle was inconclusive, and so the two sides agreed to arbitration. While the appointed negotiators conferred, Mu'awiya reinforced his military strength. Ali, however, lost a contingent of followers who were angry about his consent to arbitration. These renegades wanted to continue the military encounter until a clear victory for one side indicated God's will. One of the renegades assassinated Ali in 661, unwittingly making it much easier for Mu'awiya to claim the caliphate and establish the Umayyad dynasty, named for his clan. Ali's burial place was kept a secret for fear that his enemies would desecrate his grave. Later, and to this day, Shi'i Muslims accepted the southern Mesopotamian town of Najaf as the correct location of Ali's tomb and the object of pious pilgrimage.

Early proto-Shi'is regarded Ali as a rightful but dispossessed ruler, their first imam, the true leader of the entire Islamic community.[9] Ali was now a martyr in their cause, more influential dead than alive. Later, Shi'i Muslims would make Ali the subject of prayerful reverence, an example of which is given in **Document Two**, and would also, during the tenth and eleventh centuries, fully articulate the doctrine of the imamate. After the death of Ali, in the next period of Islamic development, both geographic expansion and new leadership produced cultural shifts in the Islamic world. One of the most obvious changes was the disappearance of women from the chronicles. Some modern Muslim scholars, like Moroccan sociologist Fatima Mernissi, argue that the fluidity and even instability of early Islam had provided women with an agency and opportunity that challenged earlier, more rigid roles assigned to women. This argument continues that with Muhammad's death and the institutionalization of Islam, male religious leaders imposed narrower roles and stricter rules for women through law.[10]

Finale

The debate that had framed the hostility between Ali and Aisha came to a head in the mid-ninth century CE, by which time a new regime, the Abbasids, had moved the capital city from Damascus to Baghdad, not far from Kufa. The Abbasids, named for one of Muhammad's uncles, started with support from many proto-Shi'is, and the regime paid at least lip service to the idea of imamate leadership.

In 833, the Abbasid administration imprisoned a prominent scholar named Ahmad ibn Hanbal over a doctrinal dispute. The public outcry in Baghdad and beyond was large and unexpected. Ibn Hanbal was of the proto-Sunni persuasion, and the swell of support he received indicated clearly that a significant majority agreed with him. In 847, the Abbasid regime made an about-face, embracing the popular doctrinal positions of Ibn Hanbal and outlawing all others, including the Shi'is. For both groups, at this juncture, historians can drop the prefix *proto-*. The Sunni majority began to articulate its doctrines and laws. Shi'is, who now quickly

9. The term *imam* can also be a generic term of respect, often for the prayer leader of a mosque.

10. Fatima Mernissi, *Beyond the Veil: Male-Female Dynamics in Modern Muslim Society*, rev. ed. (Bloomington: Indiana University Press, 1987).

realized their minority status, were left to regroup in the tenth and eleventh centuries and consolidate their own tradition under conditions of persecution.

On the issues of leadership and authority, the Sunnis had a distinctive position. They believed that the caliph must be an upright man from Muhammad's extensive tribe, the Quraysh. Prophecy had ended with Muhammad's death, and his successor should have only worldly (not divine) authority and be responsible for mediating internal disputes, administering Islamic law, and leading men in battle. Sunnis believed that the successions of the first four caliphs were legitimate and in accordance with Allah's will, even if they held Uthman's personal character in question. The Sunni paradigm was dominant throughout most of caliphal history, and today Sunni Muslims constitute at least an 85 percent majority in the entire Muslim community of approximately 1 billion people. However, as the Ottoman Empire fell apart at the end of World War I, so did the caliphate. There has been no caliph, and no serious aspirant to the job, since then.

When Shi'is articulated their doctrines, they argued that, since Allah had bothered to establish a Muslim state and society, He would not leave it undirected. God had entrusted special divine knowledge to Muhammad who had passed it on to Ali. Divine knowledge would be passed along through the descendents of the household of the prophet, and each caretaker of that knowledge, with the title imam, would have the capacity to interpret Islam and the Qur'an perfectly. Those interpretations were collected as the teachings of the imams, and they had great authority, virtually equal to the sayings and actions of Muhammad, contained in the *sunna*. The Shi'i minority took particular comfort in a verse in the Qur'an that warns against following the lead of the majority: "If you were to follow the majority on earth, they would lead you astray from the path of God. They follow only conjecture and they lie."[11]

The official decision by the Abbasid regime to sponsor Sunni Islam was a blow to Shi'i political aspirations. Open persecution made it virtually impossible to make concrete efforts to reclaim the caliphate and blend it into the imamate. The mainstream group of Shi'is pragmatically put the imamate on hold. A doctrine emerged saying that, in 873 CE, the twelfth imam had passed into a state of occultation, that is, existing but not accessible to human beings. These *Twelver* Shi'is, now heavily dominant in Iran, a majority in Iraq, and significant in Lebanon and Bahrain, await the return of the Twelfth Imam, a messianic figure, who will establish an era of perfect rule before the end of the world.

Ali was elevated to a lofty position in the Shi'i tradition, as its first rightful imam. Even among Sunnis, he remained respected for his personal qualities and for his association with Muhammad. Aisha, however, did not enjoy the same immunity from character assassination. The object of an adultery allegation, she was also a touchstone for Sunni and Shi'i allegiance. For Sunnis, caretakers of the status quo, Aisha stood exonerated of

11. *The Qu'ran*, sura 6, aya 116.

all charges; she was often praised—or at least excused—for her role in the Battle of the Camel. She was valued for her transmission of hadiths. This relatively positive assessment must be qualified by the fact that Aisha did not provide a precedent for other women to take leadership roles in Islam; rather, her position as a wife of the prophet and a "mother of the believers" set her apart. For Shi'is, her virtue remained questionable, and her opposition to Ali was anathema. A twelfth-century Shi'i Muslim writer elaborated on the Battle of the Camel. In his version, he has Ali chide Aisha in a letter: "You went out from your home in disobedience to Allah and his Prophet. . . . Then you pretend that you want peace between Muslims. . . . So tell me how can a woman incite armies and the establishment of peace between people? . . . Fear Allah, O 'A'isha, and return to your dwelling and cover yourself with your veil."[12]]

12. Quoted in Spellberg, 31. See also *The Qu'ran*, sura 33, ayas 32–33: "O women of the Prophet! You are not like other women. . . . Stay quietly in your homes."

Documents

DOCUMENT ONE

Ibn Ishaq, Edited By Ibn Hisham

The Life of Muhammad Apostle of Allah (Early ninth century CE)

In this selection, Ali ibn Abu Talib has already accepted Muhammad's revelation of a new faith. The conversions of Ali's father, Abu Talib, and Aisha's father, Abu Bakr, are mentioned here. The Arabic word for making such a conversion is aslama, *"he submitted" [himself to God]. This verb has the same three-consonant roots (*s-l-m*) as the nouns* Islam *("submission") and* Muslim *("one who submits"). During the conquest period, booty was distributed on the basis of early conversion to Islam: the earlier the conversion, the larger the share.*

Ali remained with the apostle of Allah and followed him, believed in him, and accepted the truth of his doctrines. When the time of prayer was at hand, the apostle of Allah habitually went out to the valleys of Mecca, and took Ali with him, unknown to his father Abu Talib or to his people; and they prayed together and returned in the evening. This continued for some time, until one day Abu Talib happened to discover them at prayer and asked the apostle of Allah, 'What religion is this I see you practising?' He replied, 'This is the religion of Allah, and of His angels, of His apostles, and of our father Abraham. Allah has sent me with this religion, as an apostle to His servants; and you, my uncle, are the most worthy on whom I could bestow advice and invitation to guidance; you are the most worthy to comply in it and to aid me therein.' But Abu Talib said, 'I cannot abandon the religion of my forefathers and what they believed in; but no harm shall be done to you as long as I live.' It is also said that he asked Ali, 'What religion is this thou believest in?' and Ali replied, 'I believe in the apostle of Allah, and that his revelation is true. I pray with him, and I follow him.' His father said, 'He has called thee only to what is good; therefore obey him.'

Now Abu Bakr, called *Assidiq* ('The True'), made his profession of Islam, confessing it publicly. The apostle of Allah later said, 'I have preached Islam to no one who did not hesitate, consider, and contradict, save Abu Bakr, who neither hesitated nor was perplexed.' Abu Bakr invited the people to believe in Allah the most high and glorious, and in His apostle. He was popular with his people, amiable, and compassionate, and was unusually well acquainted with Quraysh genealogy, and with whatever was good or evil therein. He was a merchant, of humane and kindly disposition, so that the people of his tribe sought after his company more than that of any other man, on account of his knowledge, his scrupulous honesty, and his friendly conversation. He now invited to Islam all the people who trusted in him, and associated with him.

At his invitation Uthman made profession of Islam, as well as al-Zubayr, Abdul-Rahman, Sad b. Abu Waqqas, and Talha. Abu Bakr went with them to the apostle of Allah and they made their profession of Islam and prayed. These eight men preceded all others in Islam; they prayed, they believed in the apostle of Allah, and accepted as true the revelation which had come to him from Allah.

DOCUMENT TWO

From a Shi'i Prayer Book

Here is a prayer addressed to God meant to be recited at the tomb of Ali, in Najaf, Iraq. The pronouns his *and* him *refer to Ali.* Lord *and the familiar forms* Thou *and* Thy *refer to God (Allah). What might Ali's "protection" or "intercession" mean to someone saying this prayer in faith?*

Facilitate my visit to him, O my Lord, through his goodness. And as Thou hast not deprived me of a visit to him, so let me not be deprived of his protection; but continue Thy gifts of grace to me O God, and as Thou hast given me the grace of knowing him, so make me of his party (*shī'a*) and bring me into Paradise through his intercession.

DOCUMENT THREE

Ibn Ishaq Edited By Ibn Hisham

The Life of Muhammad Apostle of Allah (Early ninth century CE)

This selection covers the "account of the lie," that is, the accusation of infidelity against Aisha. Note that Aisha is the speaker for most of this selection. What elements of the story make it human and compelling? Compare this to Document Four, which contains the exonerating revelation. Remember that the story of the lie, as we have it, long postdates the Qur'an.

According to Aisha, 'When the apostle of Allah was about to depart on a journey, he used to throw lots to decide which of his wives he would take with him. Before an expedition against the Banu Mustaliq, my lot came out; so the apostle of Allah took me with him. In those days women used to eat only the necessities of life, and did not become strong and heavy on meat. When my camel was ready, I would seat myself in the howdah, which my attendants would then lift on to the back of the camel; then they would attach it to the beast and we could set off.

'During our return from the Mustaliq expedition we paused to rest for a night. Before the company set off again, I withdrew for a moment; but I was wearing a string of Yemeni beads and when I returned I found they had fallen from my neck. Although the people were about to start I went back to the place where I had been and searched until I found them. The attendants who were in the habit of saddling my camel had meanwhile done so and had taken up the howdah (thinking that I was in it as usual) and tied it upon the camel; then they had led the camel off. When I returned to the camp not a soul was there, so I wrapped myself in my cloak and laid myself down, for I knew that they would miss me and come to seek me.

'While I was thus reclining, Sufwan—who had fallen behind the company for some reason, and had not spent the night with them—passed by and observed me. He exclaimed, "To Allah we belong, and to Him we must return! This is the wife of the apostle of Allah!" and he brought his camel near and said, "Mount!" He withdrew a little and I mounted, then he took hold of the camel's head and advanced rapidly, being anxious to overtake the company; but we neither overtook them, nor did they miss me, until they again encamped. When Sufwan arrived, leading me on his camel, slander was uttered against me although I knew nothing of it.

'I became very ill when we arrived in Medina and so I still did not hear the slanders, but they were communicated to the apostle as well as to my parents. They did not speak of it to me, but I observed the absence of that kindliness which the apostle of Allah used always to show me when I was ill. This I thought strange on his part. However, I knew nothing of the matter until I had recovered from my illness, after more than twenty days.

'At that time we still lived like true Arabs and had no privies in our houses as the Persians did, because we despised and disliked such luxuries. Instead, we went out to an open plain in Medina, the women going at night. Thus I walked out one night, and the woman who walked with me stumbled over the hem of her skirt and cursed, saying "Let Auf perish!" "By Allah!" I exclaimed. "That seems to me an evil wish, since it concerns a Believer who has fought at Badr." The woman asked, "Has not the news reached thee, o daughter of Abu Bakr?" and when I asked what news she told me of the slanders. I could scarce believe it and fled to the house of my mother, weeping so that I thought my heart would break. I said to my mother, "May Allah forgive thee; the people slander me and you have said nothing of it to me!" and she replied, "Do not be unhappy. There are but few handsome women—who are loved by their husbands, and have rivals—who escape false imputations and slander."

'Meanwhile, unknown to me, the apostle of Allah addressed the people, glorified and praised Allah, and said, "How do you dare to insult me by insulting my family, and by saying things about them which are not true? By Allah, I know nothing but good of them." [The lies were spread by some of the Khazraj and by the sister of another wife of the apostle.] When the apostle of Allah had finished, Usayd, one of the Aus, rose and said, "If the slanders are spoken by the Aus, we shall silence them; and if they be spoken by our brothers, the Khazraj, say the word and we shall punish them!" Then one Sad b. Ubada, who had hitherto seemed a true Believer, said, "You lie. By Allah, you have suggested this punishment only because you know the slanderers are of the Khazraj; had they been of your tribe you would not have suggested it." Usayd retorted, "*You* lie, by Allah! You are a Hypocrite and give your support to the Hypocrites!" Then the people assailed each other, and it would have taken little for evil to come to pass between the two tribes.

'The Apostle of Allah now consulted Ali and Usama, and Usama spoke only what was good, saying, "O apostle of Allah. We know only good of Aisha, and thou knowest only good of her, and these are merely false and idle rumours!" But Ali said, "There are many women! Thou canst take another! Ask her slave and she will tell thee the truth." So the apostle of Allah summoned my slave to examine her. Ali rose and struck the woman a violent blow, and said, "Tell the truth to the apostle of Allah", and she replied, "I know only what is good; and I cannot say ill of Aisha, save that one day I was kneading my dough and asked her to watch it, but she fell asleep and a sheep came and ate it up."

'After this, the apostle came to me, while both my parents were with me; and I wept. He sat down, glorified and praised Allah, and then said, "Thou must have heard what the people are saying. Fear Allah! If thou hast done wrong, then repent, for Allah accepts the repentance of his servants." While he spoke thus, my tears ceased to flow. I waited for my parents to reply to the apostle, but neither of them spoke; and I entertained too low an opinion of myself to hope that Allah would reveal verses of the Koran about me. But I hoped the apostle might have a vision in his sleep, in which Allah would expose the liars, or justify me, or tell the apostle the truth. When I saw that my parents did not speak, I asked, "Will you not reply to the apostle of Allah?" They said, "We know not what to say to him!"

'When I saw my parents thus estranged from me my tears flowed once more, and I cried, "I shall never repent to Allah for what I am accused of, because Allah knoweth I should be repenting something which did not occur, and thus I should speak untruth. But if I deny the charges, you will not believe me."

'And the apostle of Allah had not yet left us when he lost consciousness, as always happened before a revelation; then I neither feared nor cared, for I knew that I was innocent, and that Allah would do no injustice to me. But my parents seemed about to die for fear, lest Allah might send a revelation confirming the words of the slanderers.

'The apostle of Allah came back to consciousness and sat up, and the perspiration trickled like pearls from his forehead, although it was a winter day. Then he wiped it away, and said, "Allah has revealed thy innocence", and I replied, "Allah be praised!" After that, he went out to the people and recited to them verses of the Koran revealed to him by Allah, and he ordered the slanderers to be scourged.'

Sufwan, who had been slandered with Aisha, met one of the worst slanderers, the poet Hassan, and struck him with his sword. Another man, Thabit, hastened to assist Hassan, grasping Sufwan, and tying his hands to his neck with a rope; he then took him to the dwelling of one of the Khazraj, where Abdullah b. Rawaha met them. He asked, 'What is this?' and Thabit replied, 'Are you displeased? He struck Hassan with a sword and, by Allah, he might have killed him.' Abdullah asked, 'Does the apostle of Allah know of this?' and when Thabit said he did not, Abdullah told him, 'You have been presumptuous! Let the man go.'

When the apostle heard of this, he had Sufwan and Hassan brought before him, and Sufwan explained, 'He offended and mocked me; anger overcame me, and I struck him.' Then the apostle said to Hassan, 'Why do you malign my people when Allah has given them enlightenment? I think you deserved the blow.' However, the apostle soothed the poet by presenting him with a fortress in Medina, and a Coptic slave girl. Then Hassan composed verses complimentary to the chastity and beauty of Aisha.

DOCUMENT FOUR

The Qur'an (Seventh century CE)

These verses constitute the exoneration of Aisha. Notice that there is no mention of her by name. Verses 2 through 10 are generically legal but clearly related. That probably explains the juxtaposition of them with verses 11 through 15, which can be linked to the story in the biography of Muhammad. Repetitive portions are omitted and indicated by ellipses. What are society's motivations for regulating sexual behavior?

CHAPTER (SURA) 24, VERSES (AYAS) 2–15

Verse 2

The female fornicator/adulterer and the male fornicator/adulterer, lash each of them one hundred times.[1] Do not allow compassion to keep you from the religion of God, if you believe in God and the Last Day. And let a party of believers witness their punishment.

Verse 3

The male fornicator/adulterer must not marry any except a female fornicator/adulterer or a female unbeliever (ingrate). . . .

Verse 4

And those who lie about good women and do not produce four witnesses, flog them eighty lashes and reject their witness. . . .

Verse 5

. . . except those who repent afterward. . . . For God is forgetful [of wrongdoing], and merciful. . . .

Verse 11

Those came forward with the lie are a clique among all of you. . . . To each of them will come what he deserves. . . .

1. The Arabic words, feminine *al-zaniya* and masculine *al-zani*, refer to both fornicators and adulterers, with no legal distinction.

Verse 12

Why did not the believers, men and women . . . say, "This is a clear lie?"

Verse 13

Why did they not bring in four witnesses? . . .

Verse 14

Except for the generosity of God toward you, and His mercy, in this world and the hereafter, a great foment would have befallen you in that you rushed into it [rushed to judgment]. . . .

Verse 15

Indeed, you whispered it with your tongues and spoke without knowledge; you considered it minor but God (considered) it serious.

Questions

1. How might historians explain the gap between the time Ali and Aisha lived (seventh century CE) and the time they are written about (ninth century CE)?
2. What role does geography play in this chapter? Think about Madina, an Arabian town; Damascus, an eastern Roman city; and Kufa, established in southern Mesopotamia.
3. It was acceptable in seventh-century Arabia for Muhammad to take a child bride when he was in his fifties. Ancient global history provides many examples of such marriages. Can you think of reasons why this is the case?

Suggested Readings

Crone, Patricia. *Meccan Trade and the Rise of Islam.* Princeton, NJ: Princeton University Press, 1987.

Ibn, Ishaq. *The Life of Muhammad: A Translation of Ishaq 's* Sirat Rasul Allah, ed. Ibn Hisham, trans. Alfred Guillaume. London: Oxford University Press, 1955.

Spellberg, Denise A. *Politics, Gender, and the Islamic Past: The legacy of 'A'isha bint Abi Bakr.* New York: Columbia University Press, 1994.

Watt, William Montgomentry. *Muhammad: Prophet and Statesman.* Oxford: Oxford University Press, 1961.

CHAPTER

10

The Formation of Japanese Identity: Prince Genji and Murasaki Shikibu (973–1014?) of Heian Japan (794–1185)

■ SETTING THE STAGE

Overcome with gloom,
I suffer agonies
In my inmost heart,
For nobody cares to ask,
"Come, now, how is it with you?"[1]

After several failed attempts to meet the Lady Akashi, Genji, the Shining

1. Helen and Craig McCullough, trans., *Genji & Heike: Selections from The Tale of Genji and The Tale of the Heike* (Stanford, CA: Stanford University, 1994), 202.

Prince, sent her this poem, expressing his desire to be with her. The verse was written in a beautiful hand on a piece of elegant paper, and the prince believed that "no girl could have looked at it with indifference." Prince Genji, whose refined styles and courtly love conquered numerous women, was a fictional character in Murasaki Shikibu's masterpiece, *The Tale of Genji*. Yet, for nearly a thousand years, his life stories were read and savored, and this fictional prince and his creator, Lady Murasaki, have forever become the embodiment of Heian Japan.

The Heian era began in 794 with the transfer of the capital to Heian-kyō and ended in 1185 when Shogun Minamoto no Yoritomo (1147–1199) seized power. Prior to Heian, the Nara court had embraced the Chinese civilization with great enthusiasm, adopting the Chinese writing system, bureaucratic structure, legal code, arts, and lifestyles, as well as religious institutions. Buddhism, introduced to Japan through China and Korea, became a dominant religious force during the Nara period. Historians believe that Emperor Kanmu moved the capital to Heian to free his administration from political interference by Buddhist clergy.

Kanmu's intention of breaking away from the past launched a unique period in Japanese history: an effort to neutralize Chinese civilization and fashion a Japanese identity. In 894 the Japanese court closed its embassies to Tang China, hoping to separate itself from Chinese cultural influences. Beginning in the 900s, the Japanese produced literary texts in their own writing styles. Educated women undoubtedly played a key role in this nativist literary movement. During the Heian period the Chinese writing system was the official written language used at the imperial court and in schools for men. Discouraged from learning men's writing (Chinese), Heian women used *hiragana*, a writing system that was developed during the ninth century to convey emotions and observations. In the Heian period, *hiragana* was, thus, called *onna-de*, or "women's writing." The Heian *hiragana* texts proved to be a quite subtle, sophisticated, yet unrestrained self-expression.

The Heian period is also known as the Fujiwara period. Fujiwara is the name of a family clan whose northern branch intermarried with the imperial clan throughout the Heian period. Bringing land and resources more valuable than those of the imperial clan, the Fujiwara ensured that one of its daughters would bear the next crown prince. Heian emperors were often persuaded to officially abdicate in favor of a young son. The maternal grandfather of the Fujiwara family would then rule as regent.

Murasaki Shikibu, the creator of Genji, was born to a minor Fujiwara branch that produced a long line of literary talents. The *Tale of Genji* consists of 54 chapters, covering about 75 years and encompassing nearly 500 characters, and includes 800 poems. It was at first circulated as a serial at the court of Emperor Ichijō (r. 986–1011) around the beginning of the eleventh century. Readers at the time were so captivated by the story that drafts of the *Tale of Genji* were stolen from

Murasaki Shikibu's room. It has since become the pillar of Japanese literary tradition. Westerners first became aware of the existence of such a novel in the late nineteenth century. Today at least three English translations are available.[2] In addition, court records, court histories, and Murasaki Shikibu's own diary and poetry collection are wonderful sources for reconstructing the life and times of the first novelist in world history.[3]

Genji and Murasaki Shikibu are both the product of Heian Japan, during which time gender norms, social order, kinship system, literary trends, and cultural life were all unique and yet central to the formation of Japanese tradition.

The Actors

Prince Genji and Murasaki Shikibu

The fictional Prince Genji was born to the emperor and Lady Kiritsubo, a concubine who died when Genji was two. His father soon took a new consort who strongly resembled Genji's mother. The loss of his mother and his father's new consort were significant factors in the development of his emotional life and in his involvement with women throughout his life. Genji fell in love with his father's new consort, Lady Fujitsubo, who later became pregnant by Genji. Guilt-ridden, Lady Fujitsubo converted to Buddhism and lived the rest of her life as a nun.

At the age of twelve, Genji married his first official wife, Aoi, the daughter of the minister of the left. Coming from a high-ranking noble family, Aoi often put on arrogant airs and seldom showed affection for Genji. At eighteen, Genji met the love of his life, Murasaki, the daughter of Lady Fujitsubo's elder brother. Genji kidnapped Murasaki who was barely ten and molded her into his ideal woman. The two consummated the unofficial marriage when she reached fourteen. A vulnerable young girl and without a powerful father, Murasaki was considered not the best choice for an official wife.

Genji's intimate marital life with Murasaki was interrupted when he was reprimanded by the court for a political error. He went into exile first at Suma and then at Akashi, and the couple endured a long and painful separation (**Document One**). The former governor of Akashi, however, determined that Genji provided him with an opportunity to move up socially. He pressed Genji to marry his daughter, Lady Akashi, who gave birth to Genji's daughter. Murasaki discovered Genji's affair with Lady Akashi three years after the girl's birth. Even though she was heartbroken, she nevertheless was content that Lady Akashi did not intend to move to the capital. Unable to bear children herself, she eventually adopted the girl. Murasaki was happy that Genji returned to her after three years of exile and that his son, now emperor,

2. *The Tale of Genji: A Novel in Six Parts*, trans. Arthur Waley (Boston: Houghton Mifflin, 1935); trans. Edward G. Seidensticker (New York: Knopf, 1976); and trans. Royall Tyler (New York: Penguin, 2001).

3. See Richard Bowring, trans., *Murasaki Shikibu, Her Diary and Poetic Memoirs: A Translation and Study* (Princeton, NJ: Princeton University Press, 1982); and Richard Bowring, rev. trans., *Diary of Lady Murasaki.* (New York: Penguin, 2005).

rewarded him with a key position at court, the palace minister.

At about the same time, Genji became determined to use his charm on women to move up even more quickly. He first set his sights on Lady Asagao, daughter of a prince who was the minister of ceremonial. At forty, Genji married the thirteen-year-old Onna Sannomiya (the third princess) and made her his second official wife. Genji believed he had achieved everything he could possess as a man: women possessing every possible desirable quality. In his late years, Genji rose to the most powerful level that a prince could achieve. He was made chancellor and then finally attained the position called "equal to a retired emperor." He was the father of both an emperor and an empress who later gave birth to the crown prince, and his adopted daughter became the favorite consort of the emperor.

The life of Murasaki Shikibu is one of the most studied subjects in Japanese literature and Japanese history. Born to the Fujiwara clan, she was at first known as Tō no Shikibu. *Tō* is an abbreviation of Fujiwara in Japanese, *no* means "of," *Shikibu,* means "secretary at the ministry of Ceremonial" and was the official title of her father. Later she was given the name Murasaki Shikibu, most likely because the principal female character in the *Tale of Genji,* Murasaki, was so well known that her contemporaries bestowed the name on the author.

Both of Murasaki's parents traced their ancestry through the prominent Fujiwara clan. Just like Ban Zhao (45–116) of the Han dynasty of China (Chapter 5), Murasaki's literary talent was largely a consequence of her family heritage. Her great-grandfather, her grandfather, his younger brother, and her uncle were all famed poets whose poems were collected in various imperial anthologies. Growing up in a learned household, Murasaki picked up reading and writing easily and demonstrated very early her literary talent. Chinese learning was not encouraged for girls, and her father lamented that she had not been born a boy (**Document Two**). Murasaki frequently accompanied her father on his travels for the court or as governor. Leaving her familiar household and friends behind, she often succumbed to loneliness on such trips and would fill her days by corresponding and exchanging poems with her female friends. The exchange of poetry seems to have been quite common among Heian elite women. Some of them would keep their writings in a safe place and compile them into anthologies in their late years.

In 998, at age twenty-five, Murasaki married forty-seven-year-old Fujiwara Nobutaka (d. 1001), a well honored and highly positioned royal official and governor. Murasaki and Nobutaka probably knew each other from the time they were young, and allegedly had begun a relationship before they married. Poems by Murasaki to Nobutaka show that the two quarreled with each other during the period when Nobutaka courted her. Nobutaka had already had several wives and concubines and at least three children when he married Murasaki. From the evidence we have, however, Murasaki's married life was a happy one. Not long after their marriage, a daughter and their only child, Kenshi, was born (999).

Murasaki's married life was cut short when Nobutaka died in an epidemic in 1001. Devastated by the loss, Murasaki seriously considered becoming a Buddhist nun but might have been dissuaded by the fact that early Heian Buddhism regarded a woman's body as a major handicap in achieving nirvana[4] (**Document Three**).

Five years after her husband's death, Murasaki was appointed as a lady in waiting serving Fujiwara Shōshi, empress to Emperor Ichijō, and moved to the imperial palace. Here, Murasaki's literary talent won the affection of the empress and her father, Fujiwara Michinaga (966–1027). Such favor apparently caused great enmity and jealousy among the other ladies in waiting, and her frustration over such intrigues was one of the themes of her diary (**Document Two**). The year of Murasaki's death is a matter of disagreement. Some scholars suggest 1014, others 1025. No information is available to pinpoint the exact cause of her death either. She was said to be buried in the cemetery of a Buddhist temple named Unrin near Kyoto.

■ Act I

The Pursuit of Refinement

The Heian dynasty was a period of cultural refinement and the creation of Prince Genji perfectly captured the qualities and the essence of such a distinct tradition. Genji was an excellent scholar of Chinese classics, well versed in history and politics; he was a brilliant poet, calligrapher, painter, dancer, and musician. These were considered the most important accomplishments for courtiers at the time.

In the story, Prince Genji not only spent his life pursuing the ideals of beauty and elegance, he was also endowed with perfect qualities. He was astonishingly beautiful as an infant and instantly became the emperor's favorite. Growing up, Genji developed all the skills that were essential to becoming a man of culture and refinement. In Heian Japan, a courtier's skills in poetry and handwriting were closely related to his standing. As symbols of the highborn, these skills also became a man's weapon to conquer women. Genji, for example, equated the amount of effort he was willing to put into writing a poem to his lover with how highly he regarded her. Painting ability as well as the capacity to appreciate a masterpiece were both critical signs of refinement and reflections of a courtier's status. In the chapter "A Picture Contest" in the *Tale of Genji*, Murasaki Shikibu used the ranks of paintings, judged and placed by the emperor, to represent the political standing of various factions in the court. Genji's paintings of the remote provinces of Suma and Akashi triumphed over all others, signifying his ultimate political success over his rivals.

In Heian Japan, paintings were also often combined with poems to convey the artist's *mono no aware* ("aesthetic of sensibility"). This was the ability to be touched by nature, to convey its beauties, and to realize the tyranny of time and the impermanence of things. Probably recalling her own experiences of traveling and being away from the

4. Bowring, 2005, 59, n. 78.

capital, Murasaki Shikibu's description of Genji's *mono no aware* during his exile at Suma is one of the most profound scenes in the *Tale of Genji*:

> With the arrival of the new year, the days grew tediously long at Suma. The newly planted cherry saplings put forth their first hesitant blossoms, the air was balmy, and Genji often found himself in tears, his mind full of sad memories. With an aching heart, he remembered the pathetic figures of those who had mourned his departure from the capital late in the second month of last year.[5]

This Heian aesthetic of sensibility reflected the early stage of the Japanese religio-aesthetic tradition and its role in everyday life. Genji's life and his personalities exemplify the Shinto perception of *mono no aware* ("standing in awe before the wonder of things") and *makoto no kokoro* ("pure and sincere heart"). On the one hand, Genji was always drawn to everything beautiful and elegant. On the other hand, he was constantly saddened by the realization that everything is uncertain and transient, as in the Buddhist perception of the universe.

Dance and music, as expressions of such an aesthetic of sensibility, were central to Heian culture as well. By the age of eighteen, Genji was already a master dancer whose skill surpassed that of everyone at the court. The role of music in the Heian pursuit of refinement is most clearly reflected in how Genji judged women by their musical skill and how he used his own musical skills to advance himself. In Heian Japan, music was not just for pleasure, but was a reflection of one's upbringing, a vehicle of emotion, thoughts, and most important, one's *mono no aware*.

The pursuit of refinement reflects Heian Japan's quest for its own identity. However, as Murasaki Shikibu demonstrates throughout the *Tale of Genji*, the Heian court did not completely break away from Chinese culture, and the very definition of cultural refinement also included the ability to appreciate things Chinese. Indeed, Heian Japan's devotion to beauty and elegance was very much enriched by Chinese tradition. The very word for elegance, *fūryū*, for example, was directly borrowed from the Chinese word, *fengliu*, often used in Chinese literature to describe poets who loved verses, beautiful women, music, and nature and who were constantly reminded of the passing of things.

ACT II

HEIAN JAPAN AND GENDER

If the Heian pursuit of cultural refinement was more or less influenced by China, the Heian gender system certainly demonstrates its native roots. Genji officially married two wives. Like all other noblemen of the Heian period, Genji's first marriage was arranged by his family and the family of the bride when he was only

5. Helen and Craig McCullough, 185.

twelve. This practice of child marriage was very common among the Heian aristocrats, as it was perceived as a perfect way to form alliances between the fathers-in-law. Fujiwara Michinaga, father of the empress Shōshi, for example, arranged Shōshi's marriage to Emperor Ichijō when she was only eleven. Such an arrangement helped pave the way for Michinaga's forty-year dominance in Heian court politics. In the novel, Genji's father-in-law, the minister of the left, bypassed the crown prince and married his daughter to Genji. This was because Genji was the emperor's favorite son and possessed the qualities of culture and refinement admired by the court. The bride, Aoi, however, was unimpressed, if not embarrassed, by Genji's young age. Having no say in such an arrangement, she was quite unhappy throughout their marriage.

During the Heian period, the most common arrangement of marital residence was uxorilocal, that is, a man and his wife residing at the house of the wife's parents. As an imperial prince, however, Genji did not permanently move in with Aoi's family. After their wedding, Aoi continued to reside at her parents' mansion, just like most young wives at the time, but Genji remained at his own residence and commuted to Aoi's. Genji and Aoi's son, Yūgiri, was born in Aoi's father's mansion and had a very close relationship with Aoi's parents. Close ties of this sort between maternal grandparents and their grandchildren were the norm of the time and are well documented in Heian literature and histories.[6] It certainly was the most important factor in the Heian imperial succession and regent system. As a lady in waiting for Empress Shōshi, for example, Murasaki witnessed the birth of Prince Atsuhira who later reigned as Emperor Go-Ichijō (r. 1016–1036) (**Document Four**). Atsuhira was born in the residence of his maternal grandfather, who made the event a great public affair. Scholars believe that uxorilocal marriage and the birth of a child into his or her maternal grandfather's household played an important role in neutralizing and stabilizing power.[7]

Another aspect of Heian marriage practices was polygamy and concubinage. This is clearly demonstrated in both the actual experiences of Murasaki and the fictional life of Genji. Genji's second official wife, Princess Nyosan, was a daughter of the Suzaku emperor and sister of the last emperor. She represented another dimension of Heian marriage institutions: acquiring prestige or moving up the social ladder through marriage ties. Unlike his first official marriage, this time Genji himself was in total control of the process. The wedding did not take place at the third princess's residence; instead, Genji received her at the Rokujō Mansion. The possession of the third princess reflected Genji's quest to display his power and glory. The marriage

6. William H. McCullough, "Japanese Marriage Institutions in the Heian Period," *Harvard Journal of Asiatic Studies* 27 (1967): 144.

7. Peter Nickerson, "The Meaning of Matrilocality: Kinship, Property and Politics in Mid-Heian," *Monumenta Nipponica* 48, no. 4 (1993): 465.

certainly demonstrates that Genji had finally reached the pinnacle of his political power.

Even though Genji married twice in an official capacity, which was quite close to the norm for Heian nobles who chose polygamy,[8] what is unusual about the *Tale of Genji*, was Genji's lifelong love of Murasaki, who represented what Heian men considered ideal femininity. She was pleasant and lively, yet shy and compliant. "Incomparably superior to all the others in appearance, she showed promise of developing into a remarkable woman,"[9] and Genji took it on himself to mold her into this perfect woman. Murasaki Shikibu might have created this love story to satisfy Heian readers' desire for a romance, which rarely existed in Heian society. Marriages in the Heian court were about alliance, wealth, influence, prestige, and political advantage, and pursuit of a woman out of romantic love is a denial of all that.[10]

Act III

In Search of Women's Voice

The position of Murasaki Shikibu in Japanese literary tradition is often considered equal to that of Homer in Greek culture and Shakespeare in English literature.[11] Such success was, nevertheless, partly a result of the new literary movement propelled by Heian Japan's desire to establish its own cultural identity. While Japanese men, confined by their Chinese learning, were hesitant writers, educated Japanese women prospered, expressing themselves through *hiragana* writings. The freedom accorded to women contributed to the development of a unique literary genre: narrative prose, which was considered more suitable for feminine readership. As a result of this cultural movement, the single most impressive accomplishment of Heian civilization was Murasaki Shikibu's *Tale of Genji*.

As talented as she was, Murasaki Shikibu was not an isolated case in Heian Japan. While she alone was able to create a fictional tale that has withstood the test of time, many other noblewomen were just as accomplished in literature, music, and calligraphy. In a sense, the *Tale of Genji* is a celebration of both Genji's accomplishments as a courtier and a group of extremely gifted Heian women represented in fictional characters, such as Lady Fujitsubo, who possessed a refined manner and musical talent; Princess Asagao, who was unusually erudite and intuitive; and Murasaki, who cultivated the finest ability of *mono no aware*. Murasaki Shikibu bestowed more talents on Lady Akashi than any of Genji's other women, probably because there is a close resemblance

8. McCullough, 144.

9. Helen and Craig McCullough, 87.

10. See Nickerson, 462; and William H. McCullough, 115.

11. See Doris G. Bargen, *A Woman's Weapon: Spirit Possession in the Tale of Genji* (Honolulu: University of Hawaii Press, 1997), xv.

between the characters of Lady Akashi and Murasaki Shikibu herself. Both had inferior social positions as daughters of powerless provincial governors. There are certainly more highly talented women than men in the *Tale of Genji*.

Another contributing factor to the development of women's writings and women's learning was the lady-in-waiting service. During the Heian period, the need for ladies in waiting was at its peak largely due to the intense internecine struggles between different parts of the Fujiwara clan. Powerful Fujiwara families competed with each other to have their daughters be the first to marry a crown prince, and then through that marriage ultimately become empress. To help their daughters succeed in court life, Fujiwara fathers tried to attract learned women to serve as their daughters' ladies in waiting. These ladies in waiting not only assisted the royal women in daily life, but also instructed them on literature, the arts, and manners. Women chosen to be a lady in waiting needed to be gifted at poetry, calligraphy, music, and clever genteel conversation. Being selected as a lady in waiting was considered a great honor for a woman's family and a recognition of her talent.

Murasaki Shikibu entered Empress Shōshi's service in 1006 when Shōshi was in her late teens and Murasaki was about thirty. Like any lady in waiting, she read aloud to the empress every night before the empress went to bed and would sometimes write poems on behalf of the empress. Considering the intense competition among Fujiwara fathers to place their daughters in the highest possible position in the court, it is not surprising that most celebrated Heian female writers were, at one point in their life, ladies in waiting. Sei Shonagon, author of *The Pillow Book*, for example, served Empress Teishi (976–1001). Akazome Emon (ca. 960–1041), lady in waiting to Empress Shōshi's mother, was the attributed author of *A Tale of Flowering Fortunes*, a historical tale that glorifies the deeds of Shōshi's father, Michinaga. As such, Akazome is often considered Japan's first vernacular historian and the first Japanese to treat historical materials in the *monogatari* (tale) style. Another famous lady in waiting was Izumi Shikibu (ca. 970–ca. 1030), the author of *The Izumi Shikibu Diary (Izumi Shikibu nikki)* and *The Izumi Shikibu Poetic Memoirs (Izumi Shikibu shu)*. Known for her extraordinarily gifted poetry, she was generally considered the most brilliant female poet in Heian Japan (**Document Five**). Murasaki knew all three of her celebrated contemporaries and her diary detailed professional and personal discord among them (**Document Six**).

Heian elite women commonly expressed their sense of beauty and uncertainty of the world through poems in the emerging Japanese tradition. Murasaki Shikibu's poetic memoirs, for example, contain 128 poems, touching on themes from music, ceremony, festival, shrine, court service, and court life to love, friendship, longing, melancholy, and bereavement to transience of life, acceptance of fate, and memories.[12] These poems reflect the strong individuality of the author,

12. Bowring, 1982, 210.

and the collection reflects how she would wish us to see her: "not as successful lover, warm, softhearted woman, distraught mother, but as a person who had simply lived a life that she believed had validity and that was worthy of recording for posterity"[13] (**Document Six**).

Finale

After Minamoto no Yoritomo established the Shogunate in Kamakura in 1192, the Bakufu (or "tent government") ruled Japan with absolute power in civil, military, and judicial matters. However, while the Heian court completely lost its political relevance, the Heian spirit and its unique percept of *mono no aware* were absorbed by the samurai and became a core element of Japanese culture. The fate of the fictional figure Genji and his remarkable creator foreshadows the continuity of the essence of Heian culture. In the novel, Genji's son becomes the Reizei emperor; his daughter becomes the Akashi empress; and his adopted daughter, Akikonomu, becomes the favored consort of the emperor. Thus, Genji succeeded in "rejoining the imperial and regental lines."[14]

As her death neared, Murasaki Shikibu often pondered her life as a female writer. At one point, she sighed over a letter sent to her by Lady Koshōshō: "Who will read it? Who will live forever in this world?" Nearly a thousand years have passed since after the birth of *Genji* and the death of its creator; the legacy of Murasaki Shikibu, as well as that of Heian literary women and Heian spirit, lives on and will continue to inspire generations to come.

13. Bowring, 1982, 216.
14. See Nickerson, 461.

Documents

DOCUMENT ONE

MURASAKI SHIKIBU

Genji in Exile
The Tale of Genji
(Early eleventh century)

The notes and poems exchanged between Genji and Murasaki during his exile in Suma and Akashi were among the most endearing ones the two wrote. In reading these excerpts, what themes are universal? What are uniquely Japanese?

As things gradually settled down and the rain season began, his thoughts turned to the capital, and to the many people he missed, especially Murasaki, whose grieving figure haunted his memory; also the crown prince, and the little son who had run from one person to another in innocent play. He decided to send a messenger to the city. When he tried to write to Murasaki and the Fujitsubo lady, blinding tears forced him to break off. . . .

Many people in the capital suffered great anguish as they read these messages. To the dismay of Murasaki's women, who tried in vain to comfort her, she lay prostrate with the letter in her hand, racked by passionate longing. She grieved for him as though for the dead, treasuring his personal belongings, the koto on which he had strummed a few notes, the scent from a discarded robe, and other such things. Her behavior seemed positively inauspicious; Shonagon asked the bishop to offer prayers. The Bishop performed esoteric rites for both Genji and Murasaki. Moved to compassion, he prayed that she might find surcease from her grief, and that he might return and be as he had been.

Murasaki prepared bedclothes and other necessities to send to the country. Saddened by the sight of informal cloaks and bloused trousers made of plain white taffeta, all so different from his usual attire, she remembered his poem about the mirror. The promised reflection appeared in her mind's eye, but it afforded small comfort. She choked up whenever she looked at an entrance he had used or a pillar he had leaned against. When we consider that such a parting would have saddened anyone, even a woman of mature years, profound discernment, and much experience in the ways of the world, her desperate longing seems only natural, for she had been torn apart from the one person with whom she was most comfortable, the one person who had cherished and reared her in the place of a father and mother. Nothing could have been done about it if he had died; she would probably have begun to forget as time went on. But she never ceased to agonize over the impossibility of telling how long this parting might last, even though he was apparently not very far away. . . .

Murasaki's letter, a response to his own loving message, contained much to stir his emotions. She had included this poem:

Compare it to the sleeve
  of the dweller by the shore
dipping salt water—
  the robe worn at night by one
  beyond the waves of the sea.

The bedclothes she sent were beautifully dyed and tailored. She did everything so well. How ideal it would be to live here quietly with her, free of other demands on his time and energy—and how frustrating to be denied that pleasure! Her face stayed with him day and night, a source of unbearable memories. Should he not, after all, bring her to Suma in secret? But no. In this world of sorrows, he must at least try to atone for his sins. He restricted himself to vegetarian fare and read the scriptures all day long.

DOCUMENT TWO

MURASAKI SHIKIBU

On Being a Learned Woman
The Diary of Lady Murasaki
(Early eleventh century)

Even though Murasaki was quite proud of her Chinese learning, the atmosphere of her time seemed to discourage women from learning Chinese classics or Japanese works that modeled after Chinese classics, such as the Chronicles of Japan. *In this entry, dated 1010, Murasaki criticized her peer, Saemon no Naishi, for showing off her ability in Chinese writing. In your opinion, were Heian diaries reflections of public discourse or private thoughts?*

There is a woman called Saemon no Naishi who, for some strange reason, took a dislike to me. I heard all sorts of malicious rumours about myself. His Majesty was listening to someone reading the *Tale of Genji* aloud. 'She must have read the *Chronicle of Japan!*' he said. 'She seems very learned.' Saemon no Naishi suddenly jumped to conclusions, spread it abroad among the senior courtiers that I was flaunting my learning. She gave me the nickname Lady Chronicle. How very comical! Would I, who hesitate to show my learning in front of my own servants at home, ever dream of doing so at court?

When my brother, Secretary at the Ministry of Ceremonial was a young boy learning the Chinese classics, I was in the habit of listening to him and I became unusually proficient at understanding those passages that he found too difficult to grasp. Father, a most learned man, was always regretting the fact: 'Just my luck!' he would say. 'What a pity she was not born a man!' But then I gradually realized that people were saying 'It's bad enough when a man flaunts his Chinese learning; she will come to no good,' and ever since then I have avoided writing the simplest character. My handwriting is appalling. And as for those 'classics' or whatever they are that I used to read, I gave them up entirely. Yet still I kept on hearing these malicious remarks; so in the end, worried what people would think if they heard such rumours, I pretended to be incapable of reading even the inscriptions on the screens. Then Her Majesty asked me to read with her here and there from the *Collected Works* of Po Chü-I,[1] and because

1. Po Chü-I (772–846) was a Tang dynasty Chinese poet who had the distinction of being well known and read in Japan during his own lifetime. In Murasaki's time his work still formed the foundation of a courtier's knowledge of Chinese poetry. (Bowring, 2005, 58)

she evinced a desire to know more about such things, to keep it secret we carefully chose times when the other women would not be present, and, from the summer before last, I started giving her informal lessons on the two volumes of 'New Ballads.' I hid this fact from others, as did Her Majesty, but somehow both His Excellency and His Majesty got wind of it and they had some beautiful copies made of various Chinese books, which His Excellency then presented to Her. That gossip Saemon no Naishi could never have found out that Her Majesty had actually asked me to study with her, for had she done so, I would never have heard the last of it. Ah, what a prattling, tiresome world it is!

DOCUMENT THREE

Murasaki Shikibu

On Buddhism
The Diary of Lady Murasaki
(Early eleventh century)

By Murasaki's time, Buddhism had taken hold and been immersed into everyday life in Japanese society. Murasaki's father and one of her brothers eventually chose to become Buddhists and Murasaki herself had contemplated such a path as well. In this entry, dated 1010, Murasaki reflects her identity as a female and a Buddhist believer. Why was Murasaki drawn to Buddhism? Did she completely embrace the Buddha's teaching?

Why should I hesitate to say what I want to? Whatever others might say, I intend to immerse myself in reading sūtras for Amida Buddha. Since I have lost what little attachment I ever had for the pains that that life has to offer, you might expect me to become a nun without delay. But even supposing I were to commit myself and turn my back on the world, I am certain there would be moments of irresolution before Amida came for me Riding on his clouds. And this I hesitate. I know the time is opportune. If I get much older my eyesight will surely weaken, I shall be unable to read the sūtras, and my spirits will fail. It may seem that I am merely going through the motions of being a true believer, but I assure you that now I think of little else. But then someone with as much to atone for as myself may not qualify for salvation; there are so many things that serve to remind one of the transgressions of a former existence.[1] Everything conspires to make me unhappy.

1. Murasaki may be thinking of the fact that she was born a woman and so might well have to go through at least one further rebirth as a man. In early Buddhism the female state was a major handicap to enlightenment, although by Murasaki's time, in Japan textual 'proof' was available, particularly in the *Lotus Sūtra*, that enlightenment was more or less attainable by women. (Bowring, 2005, 59). Ed.

DOCUMENT FOUR

Murasaki Shikibu

On the Birth of Prince Atsuhira
The Diary of Lady Murasaki
(Early eleventh century)

The entry details the Birth of Prince Atsuhira by Empress Shōshi ("Her Majesty" in the diary). It not only reflects Murasaki's amazing narrative capability but also presents a vivid picture of how Fujiwara Michinaga ("His Excellency" in the diary) made sure that such an important birth at his residence was highly publicized. What does this event tell you about Heian marriage practice?

At dawn on the eleventh, two sets of sliding screens on the north side were taken away and Her Majesty was moved into the back gallery. Since it was not possible to hang up blinds, she was surrounded by a series of overlapping curtains. The Archbishop, Bishop Jōjō and the Bishop for General Affairs were in attendance performing rites. Bishop Ingen, having added some portentous phrases to an invocation composed by His Excellency the day before, now read it out slowly in solemn and inspiring tones. It could not have been more impressive, especially when His Excellency himself decided to join in the prayers. Surely nothing could go wrong now, I thought; and yet such was the strain that none of us could hold back her tears. No matter how much we told ourselves how unlucky it might be to cry like this, it was impossible to refrain.

His Excellency, concerned that Her Majesty might feel even worse with so many people crowded around, made everyone move away to the south and east, only those whose presence was considered essential were allowed to remain. Her Excellency, Lady Saishō and Lady Kura were in attendance inside the curtains, as were the Bishop of the Ninnaji and the Palace Priest from the Miidera. His Excellency was shouting orders to all and sundry in such a loud voice that the priests were almost drowned out and could hardly be heard. In the remaining section of the back gallery sat Lady Dainagon, Lady Koshōshō, Miya no Naishi, Ben no Naishi, Lady Nakatsukasa, Lady Tayū, and Lady Ōshikibu—His Excellency's envoy, you know. It was only to be expected that they should seem distraught, for they had all been in service for so many years, but even I, who had not known Her Majesty for long, knew instinctively how very grave the situation was.

Another group of women, among them Nakatsukasa, Shōnagon and Koshikibu, who had been wet nurse to His Excellency's second, third, and youngest daughters, squeezed their way in front of the curtains that hung as a divider behind us, with the result that people could barely pass along the narrow passage at the rear of the two daises, and those who did manage to push their way through could hardly tell whom they were jostling.

Whenever the men felt like it, they looked over the curtains. Somehow, one expected this kind of behaviour from His Excellency's sons, and even from Kanetaka, Adviser of the Right, and Junior Captain Masamichi, but not from the Adviser of the Left or the Master of Her Majesty's Household; they were usually more circumspect. We lost all sense of shame being seen in such state, our eyes swollen with weeping. In retrospect it may have been amusing, I suppose, but at the time we must have presented a sorry sight, rice falling on our heads like snow and our clothes all crumpled and creased.[1]

When they started to snip Her Majesty's hair and make her take her vows, everyone was thrown into confusion and wondered what on earth was happening. Then in the midst of all this despair, she was safely delivered. Everyone, priests and laymen alike, who was crowded into that large area stretching all the way from the main room to the southern gallery and the balustrade, broke once more into chanting and prostrated themselves in prayer until the afterbirth appeared.

The women in the gallery to the east seem to have become mixed up with the senior courtiers with the result that Lady Kochūjō came face to face with First Chamberlain Yorisada. Her embarrassment later became the source of some amused comment. Very elegant and always more particular about her appearance, she had made herself up in the morning, but now her eyes were swollen with weeping and tears had made her powder run here and there; she was a dreadful sight and looked most odd. I remember what a shock I had when I saw how Lady Saishō's face had changed too. And I hate to think of how I must have looked. It was a relief that no one could actually recall how anyone else had looked on that occasion.

At the moment of birth what awful wails of anguish came from the evil spirits! Preceptor Shin'yo had been assigned to Gen no Kurōdo, a priest called Myōso to Hyōe no Kurōdo, and the Master of Discipline from the Hōjūji to Ukon no Kurōdo. Miya no Naishi's enclose was being overseen by Preceptor Chisan; he was thrown to the ground and a preceptor came to his aid with loud spells. Not that his powers were on the wane, it was just that the evil proved so very persistent. The priest Eikō, brought in to help Lady Saishō's exorcist, became hoarse from shouting spells all night. There was further chaos when not all of the women managed to accept the spirits to whom they had been assigned.

It was already midday, but we all felt just as if the morning sun had risen into a cloudless sky. Our delight on hearing Her Majesty had been safely delivered knew no bounds, and how could we have been anything but ecstatic that it was a boy. Those ladies who yesterday had wilted and this morning had been sunk in a mist of autumn tears all took their leave and retired to rest. The older women, who were best fitted for the task, were in attendance on Her Majesty.

1. The rice is being thrown in the air as part of the rituals to keep all evil influences at bay. See Bowring, 2005, 10. Ed.

Their excellencies moved through to another part of the mansion to distribute offerings of thanks both to those priests who had carried out rituals and chanted sūtras for months past and to those who had come in response to more recent demands. Gifts were also presented to those doctors and diviners who had shown special skill in their respective arts. I assume that preparations for the ceremony of the first bathing were already proceeding at the Palace.[2]

In the women's apartments servants brought in new dresses in large bundles and packages. Both the embroidery on the jackets and the hem-stitching with mother-of-pearl inlay on the trains had been grossly overdone, and the women tried to hide them from each other, concentrating on their powder and their dresses and fussing about why the fans they had ordered had not yet arrived.

Looking out as usual from my room at the end of the corridor, I noticed the Master of Her Majesty's Household waiting by the side door in the company of Yasuhira, Master of the Crown Prince's Household, and various other nobles. His Excellency emerged and gave orders that the stream be cleared of the leaves that had been blocking it for some days past. Everyone was in high spirits. In the general atmosphere, which must have allowed even those with private worries to forget their troubles for the time being, it was only natural that Tadanobu, as Master of Her Majesty's Household, should find it hard to hide his own particular delight, although he tried not to smile too broadly. Kanetaka was sitting on the veranda of the east wing exchanging jokes with Takaie, Middle Counselor Elect.

First Chamberlain Yorisada, who had brought the ceremonial sword from the Palace, was charged by his Excellency to return and report the safe birth to the Emperor. . . .

2. These preparations included making the bathtub and other ceremonial objects. Murasaki's assumption here is incorrect. The bathtub was made at the Tsuchimikado mansion rather than at the palace. See Bowring, 2005, 12. Ed.

DOCUMENT FIVE

Izumi Shikibu

The Izumi Shikibu Poetic Memoirs
(Late tenth century to early eleventh century)

Izumi Shikibu was considered the most gifted female poet in Heian Japan. The first poem selected for this chapter, "Which Is Worse," was said to be most representative of her work; the second poem, "Out of the Dark," was said to be her death verse. In what way do these poems reflect the precept of mono no aware?

Which Is Worse

Which should I think shouldn't exist in this world,
  those who neglect or those who are neglected?
Which is worse, to miss someone dead
  or to be unable to meet someone alive?
Which is worse, to love someone far away
  or to often see someone you don't love?

Out of the Dark

Out of the dark,
Into a dark path
I now must enter:
Moon of the mountain fringe![1]

1. The moon may refer to Buddha's teachings. Ed.

DOCUMENT SIX

Murasaki Shikibu

On Corresponding with Lady-in-Waiting Friends
The Diary of Lady Murasaki
(Early eleventh century)

The early writings in Japanese alphabets, authored by women, provided with modern readers a wonderful window to understand Heian women's endeavor in "defining the self in textual terms."[1] *In your opinion what themes does this passage convey? Is such self-expression a unique literary phenomenon in world history?*

Seeing the water birds on the lake increase in number day by day, I thought to myself how nice it would be if it snowed before we got back to the Palace—the garden would look so beautiful; and then, two days later, while I was away on a short visit, lo and behold, it did snow. As I watched the rather drab scene at home, I felt both depressed and confused. For some years now I had existed from day to day in listless fashion, taking note of the flowers, the birds in song, the way the skies change from season to season, the moon, the frost and snow,

1. Bowring, 2005, xvii.

doing little more than registering the passage of time. How would it all turn out? The thought of my continuing loneliness was unbearable, and yet, I had managed to exchange sympathetic letters with those of like mind—some contacted via fairly tenuous connections—who would discuss my trifling tales and other matters with me; but I was merely amusing myself with fictions, finding solace for my idleness in foolish words. Aware of my own insignificance, I had at least managed for the time being to avoid anything that might have been considered shameful or unbecoming; yet here I was tasting the bitterness of life to the very full.

DOCUMENT SEVEN

Murasaki Shikibu

Poems (Early eleventh century)

Before her death, Murasaki Shikibu compiled her own anthology of her poems. A total of 128 poems were selected by the author to represent her journey from a daughter of a governor to a renowned lady in waiting and much-admired writer. Would you be able to identify her mono no aware *at different stages of her life and on different occasions?*

1. I met someone I had known long ago as a child, but the moment was brief and I hardly recognized them. It was the tenth of the tenth month. They left hurriedly as if racing the moon.

Brief encounter;
Did we meet or did it hide
Behind the clouds
Before I recognized
The face of the midnight moon?[1]

2. When someone asked whether I was worried, I replied as follows; it was the end of the ninth month.

Dew that hides
In the plumes of autumn grass,
Why do you thus
Refuse to leave
The withered fields?
It was a time when I had much on my mind.

1. The moon represents the friend. Ed.

3. Fate itself
Is never subject to the whims
Of one's desire,
But subject to one's fate
Desire itself can change.

4. Not knowing
Where to put myself
Nor what to do,
I continue to exist
Despite the weariness.

QUESTIONS

1. What qualities were essential to be considered a refined and highborn man or woman during the Heian period? Why?
2. What is *mono no aware?* What role did this play in the Heian court and in everyday life during that time? Which document best reflects the *mono no aware* concept?
3. How would you characterize Heian gender relations and marriage practices? Were Genji's relationships with women and his marriages representative of Heian gender institutions or different, and how?
4. What factors contributed to the burgeoning of female literacy during the Heian period? In reading **Documents Five** to **Seven,** what are the most distinctive features of Heian women's writings?
5. Compare Murasaki Shikibu with Ban Zhao of the Han dynasty. What are the similarities and differences between these two women writers? What factors contributed to these similarities and differences?

SUGGESTED READINGS

Bowring, Richard. *Murasaki Shikibu, Her Diary and Poetic Memoirs: A Translation and Study*. Princeton, NJ: Princeton University Press, 1982.

Field, Norma. *The Splendor of Longing in the Tale of Genji*. Ann Arbor: University of Michigan Press, 2001.

The Pillow Book of Sei Shonagon. Trans. and ed. Ivan Morris. New York: Columbia University Press, 1991.

Shively, Donald H., and William H. McCullough, eds. *Cambridge History of Japan: Heian Japan*. Vol. 2. London: Cambridge University Press, 1988.

Source Materials

The Tale of the Genji (videocassette, 60 min.) Princeton, NJ: Films for the Humanities, 1993.

The Metropolitan Museum of Art has a site for the Heian period. http://www.metmuseum.org/toah/hd/heia/hd_heia.htm

PART

III

Regional Contests and Imperial Conquest, 1100–1600

The reintegration of western Europe into the complex web of cultural, political, and commercial networks of the Afro-Asian world system began with a call by the Roman Catholic pope Urban II for a holy war against the Muslims in 1095 (Chapter 11). This call had been prompted by a request by the Byzantine emperor for assistance against the Seljuk Turks who were quickly capturing Byzantine territories in Asia Minor and in the eastern Mediterranean. The network's linchpin was the Byzantine capital of

Constantinople, which controlled the land bridge between Europe and Asia.

At the same time that political and military conflicts transformed the westernmost borders of this world system, Mongol clans in the central Asian steppes began their expansion into China, Russia, and western Asia. As the first four chapters in this section (Chapters 11 to 14) demonstrate, the regional contests among and between Christians and Muslims in the west and Mongolian conquests across Eurasia resulted in transforming political, social, commercial, cultural, and religious structures throughout the known world. Social, cultural, and religious diffusion occurred at unprecedented rates and across vast distances.

Historians agree that Europe's maritime explorations between 1450 and 1550 eventually transformed regional interactions and connections into broader, more penetrating global contacts and conquest. However, the early period of European exploration and expansion occurred within existing regional power structures (Chapters 14 and 15). As the Europeans expanded outward from their Atlantic and Mediterranean ports, they encountered well-established trade networks; prosperous regional economies; powerful empires; long-standing social, cultural, religious institutions; and well-developed gender systems. In Europe's first 100 years on the world stage, its people happened on regional contests between Christians and Muslims in the Indian Ocean, the military and cultural hegemony of the Chinese state in east Asia, affluent imperial kingdoms in the Americas, diverse ethnic and religious kingdoms in sub-Saharan Africa, while closer to home, they encountered a powerful Islamic empire in North Africa and the eastern Mediterranean.

The final two chapters in this section, the exploration of the Atlantic world and the nature of contact between Europe and the Western Hemisphere (Chapter 15) and the expansion of the Ottoman Turkish Empire into north Africa and southeastern Europe (Chapter 16), examine the scope, breadth, and impact of imperial quest and conquest. The influence and impact of the Ottoman Empire in the Mediterranean is often overlooked and unexamined in favor of the rise of the Atlantic world. Contrasting the experiences and the nature of contact, contest, and conquest by the Spanish and the Ottoman states and their agents examines the ways in which each organized their societies for conquest, treated subjugated populations, and exploited their conquests, how each of these societies met the challenges of possessing far-flung territories, and the response of the conquered peoples to these encounters.

It is not enough to ponder how big structures, such as trade routes, markets, and political entities are impacted; we must also think about how individual men and women contributed to the diffusion of new social, cultural, religious, and gender norms. Highlighting men and women from these different regions "before European hegemony" reveals the ways in which individuals from different world systems encountered each other, as military conquerors, political overlords, chroniclers of history, religious leaders, believers and seekers, and merchants and as men and women.

Along with questions about the nature and use of sources, readers should attempt to answer the following as they read Chapters 11 to 16:

- How do encounters with other societies and peoples impact gender norms, definitions, and roles?
- What were the causes, motivations, and impact of the encounters and conquests in this period?
- How do the encounters and conquests of this time impact existing political systems, trade networks and economies, and cultural norms and practices?
- How do people of this time describe these encounters? How do later observers and historians?

CHAPTER

11

The Crusades: Raymond of Toulouse (1052–1105) and Anna Comnena (1083–1148)

Setting the Stage

The First Crusade (1095–1099) took place against the backdrop of the rapid changes roiling the Islamic and Christian Mediterranean worlds in the eleventh century. During this century, Western Christendom experienced the rise of powerful noble houses in France, Germany, and Spain, each of which sought to expand their territories. The dukes of Normandy led their armies south into Byzantine Italy, while the nobles of northern Spain fought wars of territorial expansion both among themselves and with the Muslim *taifa* kingdoms in Spain. In the midst of these wars and conflicts, the powerful Germanic (Eastern Frank) successors to Charlemagne disputed the power of the papacy. The Roman Church sought to expand both its spiritual and political influence in their states and in northern Italy.

Beyond Western Christendom lay the still powerful and expansive Eastern Roman Empire, the Byzantine Empire. In 1050, the Byzantine Empire straddled two continents (Europe and Asia) and four seas (the Mediterranean, Aegean, Adriatic, and Black). However, after a century and a half of successful offensives, the empire now faced challengers on every border. To the north along the Danube, a steppe tribe from Central Asia, the Pechenegs, penetrated into the Balkans. The Seljuk Turks, a Muslim tribe, moved through the Empire's eastern borders into Armenia and the Anatolian peninsula, and its western territories in Italy were being conquered by the Normans. According to an eleventh-century Byzantine courtier, Michael Psellos, such attacks constituted a "mighty deluge."[1]

How to meet the challenge of this mighty deluge was the political question of the day in mid-eleventh-century Byzantium. Throughout the eleventh century and beyond, Byzantine emperors lacked the reserves to defend their long borders. As a result, they relied on recruiting professional soldiers from foreign lands, traditionally employing Turkic tribesmen to fight for them. However, by the first half of the eleventh century, the threats advanced by the Turkic peoples themselves moved the Byzantines to seek a new pool of professional soldiers. They found promising recruits among the Western Christians who, by that time, were becoming an increasing presence in and around Constantinople.[2]

The presence of increasing numbers of western Europeans was the result of their growing interest in making pilgrimages. Pilgrimages to Palestine had become easier at the beginning of the eleventh century when the Byzantine Empire wrested Syria away from the Fatimid caliph of Egypt. They then negotiated with the Fatimids for access to Palestine and Jerusalem to allow European Christian pilgrims to visit the holy sites. The truce between the Byzantines and the Fatimids was increasingly beneficial to both sides as each came to fear the Seljuk Turks, who in 1055, overran Mesopotamia, conquered Baghdad, and became the ruling dynasty there.

By 1071, the Seljuk Turks were challenging both the Egyptian Fatimids and the Byzantines in the eastern Mediterranean. The Turks defeated a Byzantine army and its emperor at Manzikert in eastern Anatolia and then pushed the Fatimids out of Palestine and Jerusalem. They continued to expand further into Anatolia and along the eastern Mediterranean coast, bringing Syria and more and more of Asia Minor under their rule. Muslim encroachment and the fall of Jerusalem ended Christian pilgrimages to significant holy sites and

1. Michael Psellos, *Fourteen Byzantine Rulers*, trans. E. R. A. Sewter (Harmondsworth, UK: Penguin Books, 1966), 159. Quoted in Jonathan Harris, *Byzantium and the Crusades* (London: Hambledon and London, 2003), 33.

2. Harris, 35.

proved to be important rallying points and propaganda tools for Western Christians by the end of the century.

When the Byzantine emperor Alexius I (r. 1081–1118) asked Western Christians to help in the fight against the Seljuk Turks, Pope Urban II (1088–1099) saw an opportunity to assert real leadership in Latin Christendom. In spring 1095, Urban responded as his papal predecessor had and called on Western knights to "promise, by taking an oath, to aid the emperor most faithfully as far as they were able against the pagans."[3] Initially, both Alexius I and Urban II thought that individual Western knights would serve as mercenaries in the Byzantine army and swear allegiance to the emperor as they had done earlier. Eight months later in November 1095, even though no real threat loomed for the Byzantine Empire, Urban II altered papal tradition and called on all of Western Christendom, not just individual mercenaries, to march to the rescue of the Byzantines and liberate the Eastern churches. The ultimate goal was for Christians to retake the Holy Land, particularly Jerusalem, from the Turks[4] (**Document One**).

What motivated this change of papal strategy? This all-embracing papal call to arms was an expression of Urban II's ambition of asserting papal power over all of Christendom, both East and West. Relations between the Eastern and Western Christian churches had been strained by a schism over liturgical practice in 1054. Urban calculated that expanding Latin Christendom's influence into the eastern Mediterranean, uniting Christian knights, and redirecting their violence to a holy and papally sanctioned war would lead to papal preeminence in all of Christendom.[5]

Urban II did not make this decision hastily. From July to November 1095, Urban toured southern France, a region where he had both personal connections and a power base. He visited his former house of Cluny and conferred with Adhemar, bishop of Le Puy, a prominent churchman who had become an ally of Raymond of Toulouse, the most powerful secular ruler in the Midi. Urban knew that a campaign to the East would not be possible without designated spiritual and secular leaders, and these two men were good candidates for these positions. The day after Urban's sermon at Clermont, Raymond pledged his support and went on to become the most powerful First Crusader. It is his life, motivations for crusading, and experiences in the Holy Land that will be the focus of this chapter.

Urban II's crusade did bring Western and Eastern Christendom into close proximity and it provided opportunities for both Latin and Byzantine chroniclers to observe, evaluate, and opine about the other. One chronicler was Anna Comnena, daughter of Alexius Comnenus I (r. 1081–1118). Her biography of her father, *The Alexiad*, provides an account of the Crusades from the Byzantine perspective.

3. Fulcher of Chartres, *Chronicle of the First Crusade*, trans. Martha Evelyn McGinty (Philadelphia: University of Pennsylvania Press, 1941), 13.

4. Thomas Ashbridge, *The First Crusade: A New History* (New York: Oxford University Press, 2004), 33.

5. Ibid., 20.

Her works are full of details about daily life at court and the deeds of her father and family as well as her disdain for Western Christendom and ridicule of its people, its pope, and its Crusaders. In 1095, Anna Comnena saw Western Christendom, with its center in Rome, as "a hinterland, a place of barbarians, a supplier of raw materials, mercenaries, and slaves."[6] The *Alexiad*, like other medieval chronicles, depicts the Crusades as masculine endeavors.

The twelfth century was the zenith of historical writing in medieval England and France, prompted to a large degree by the First Crusade. Not only do we have a number of Crusade chronicles, year-by-year records of the events that the chronicler deemed noteworthy, but a number of biographies and biographical entries in the chronicles record the words and deeds of medieval kings, nobles, and religious leaders. The works of these chroniclers and early biographers must be approached cautiously. The authors were men of the elite, usually monastic or ecclesiastical, who generally came from noble and wealthy backgrounds. They saw nothing wrong with altering facts and information to reflect their own and their community's sensibilities, values, and political and social practices. In addition, some of the Western chroniclers were followers of the various nobles and religious leaders who participated in the events they recorded. These retainers presented their patrons in the best possible light, while depicting rivals as villainous, corrupt, and immoral. Muslim accounts of the First Crusade are few in comparison to Crusader sources.[7] Two Syrian chroniclers wrote accounts around 1160. and one Muslim historian, Ibn al-Jawsi (1160–1233), used earlier materials to narrate the history of the First Crusade. In Muslim accounts, Western Christians were referred to as Franks and Latins, designations that Anna Comnena used as well.

Women appear in the Crusade chronicles only episodically and are generally portrayed as wives, widows, or queens who may have influenced their male counterparts. Any other type of participation on the part of women is generally ignored or simply not seen by chroniclers because of the contemporary assumption that women had no contribution to make to the public world. By this time women were denied access to positions of spiritual, political, or intellectual authority in the Christian Church except as holy, sanctified women or leaders of women's communities. Of course, medieval European women often accompanied husbands, sons, and fathers to war, and this military adventure was no exception. During the First Crusade, women were nurses, cooks, prostitutes, washerwomen, and warriors, and sometimes chronicles did note the role played by women during battle. However, the Western chroniclers generally chose not to record women's heroism during battle because "Christians expected that good,

6. Lynda N. Shaffer and George J. Marcopoulos, "Murasaki and Comnena: Two Women and Two Themes in World History," *History Teacher* 19, no. 4 (August 1986): 493.

7. Carole Hillenbrand, *The Crusades: Islamic Perspectives* (Chicago: Dearborn, 1999), 54.

virtuous women would not normally fight."[8] Instead Crusader chroniclers identified women with "vulnerability, weakness, frailty, and motherhood."[9] The crusade was to be a "manly achievement" according to Robert the Monk who described the valiant Crusader soldiers as unhindered "by love of children, parents and wives."[10]

The events and personalities of the First Crusade demonstrate the religious, social, and political divisions that existed between the orthodox Christian Byzantine Empire and the Western Roman Church and its Holy Roman Empire, as well as the divisions within each empire. In addition, the experiences and actions of historian and biographer Anna Comnena and Crusader Raymond of Toulouse juxtapose the declining power of the Eastern Roman Empire with the development of powerful kingdoms and states in the West. Ultimately the reintegration of Europe into a broader Afro-Asian world system is among the major long-term effects of these military, cultural, and political interactions.

The Actors

Raymond of Toulouse and Anna Comnena

Raymond IV of Toulouse was born, ca. 1042, the second son of Count Pons of Toulouse and his third wife, Almodis. While details of Raymond's early life are scarce, we do know something of the social, political, and religious milieu into which he was born. Since imperial Roman times, the city of Toulouse, in the southeastern corner of France, had enjoyed political, economic, and religious prominence. It was a focal point for trade between the Pyrenees, the Mediterranean, and the Atlantic, and it capitalized on its key economic position during the Roman period when Rome controlled both seas. Toulouse was unscathed by the invasions which left most of Gaul occupied by Germanic tribes in the third century and became the fourth largest city in the Western Roman Empire and an important bishopric in what was left of Roman Gaul. After 508, Toulouse and its surrounding countryside were controlled by the Frankish kings who now ruled over much of western Europe. In 721, Toulouse withstood a three-month siege by the Muslim governor of al-Andalus, rallying with help, to defeat the Arab army at the Battle of Toulouse. Toulouse's geographical setting vis-à-vis Muslim Spain elevated the importance of the city and its surrounding territory, and by the tenth century it was one of the most important landholdings of the French crown.

Raymond's father was an important vassal of the king of France by

8. H. J. Nicholson, "Women on the Third Crusade," *Journal of Medieval History* 23 (1997), 340–41. Quoted in Michael R. Evans, "'Unfit to Bear Arms': The Gendering of Arms and Armour in Accounts of Women on Crusade," in *Gendering the Crusades*. Susan B. Edgington and Sarah Lambert, eds. (New York: Columbia University Press, 2002), 45.

9. Keren Caspi-Reisfeld, "Women Warriors during the Crusades," Ibid., 94.

10. Robert the Monk, "Speech of Urban II," quoted in *Translations and Reprints from the Original Sources of European History*, vol. 1, no. 2 (Philadelphia: University of Pennsylvania Press, 1895), 6.

virtue of receiving Toulouse as a fiefdom from the crown, but Raymond was the second son in a world where the eldest son usually was the single designated heir. Primogeniture (inheritance by first born) and patrilineal inheritance (tracing inheritance through the male line) not only affected younger sons but also daughters. Both lost power and status that came with inherited land. Without an inheritance, younger sons needed to find a place within medieval society, and this meant aligning themselves with a powerful noble as a retainer, that is, a knight, or joining the church as a cleric or monk. Knights lived in the household of their lords, were unmarried, and fought for the lord. Constituting a new class of individuals—youths or bachelors—these men could be counted on to fight to extend their lord's territory, to defend against invaders, or as we shall see, to take up the sword against infidels.

By mid–eleventh century, boys of Raymond's class and region were schooled in the art of warfare as well as in the basic subjects of the liberal arts in preparation for the life of either a warrior or a cleric. As the second son of a lord, Raymond probably received some early schooling. Most boys began their studies at the age of seven and were taught by a tutor specializing in Latin grammar. Grammar was one of the first three subjects of the liberal arts or the *trivium,* the others being logic and rhetoric. Raymond undoubtedly also had instruction in the elements of faith: the Lord's Prayer, the Apostles' Creed, the Athanasian Creed, selections from scriptures, and stories of the lives of the saints.

Raymond might not have inherited land, but his older brother died without male heirs in 1093. His brother's death, his ability to pursue familial claims to lands in southern France, three advantageous marriages, and the "occasional use of force,"[11] gave Raymond control of Toulouse and its surrounding counties, Provence, and Narbonne. He had become one of the most powerful nobles in Western Christendom and his power and wealth brought him to the attention of the Church and its leaders.

Raymond's family, notably his mother, had long been associated with the monastic order at Cluny. The Cluniac order had been a leader of Western Christendom's reform movement for over two centuries, and the reforming pope Gregory VII and his successor, Urban II, were members of this order. With his election to the papacy in 1073, Gregory VII set out to restore discipline within the church. Clerics were to remain celibate and to refrain from using their positions to enrich themselves or their families. In addition, the papacy was to be restored as the central authority in the Church. Powerful nobles often supported provincial bishops and clerics whose power was threatened by these reforms. Raymond was excommunicated twice in the 1070s because he did not support Gregory VII's efforts. A decade later, Raymond embraced the reform movement and found himself allied with one of Rome's favored sons, Adhemar, the Bishop of Le Puy.

The idea of fighting for Christendom was part of Gregory VII's reform

11. Ibid.

plans. Because the pope and his officers were forbidden to shed blood, Gregory realized that papal authority could not be effective unless the papacy could command the allegiance of Western Christendom's warriors. Gregory reconciled his ambitions with his limitations when he formulated the idea that "all of lay society had one overriding obligation: to defend the Latin Church as 'soldiers of Christ' through actual, physical warfare."[12] Gregory developed this concept by arguing that, because the pope was god's representative on Earth, lay society owed the pope a debt of military service. While not all nobles accepted this idea, Gregory attracted a number of nobles, like Raymond of Toulouse, who were willing to leave home and family and become faithful followers. Eventually many of them heeded Urban II's call for a crusade.[13]

Anna Comnena was born on December 1, 1083, the eldest of Emperor Alexius Comnenus and Irene Doukaina's seven children, four of whom lived to adulthood. Anna's mother was a member of the powerful Doukas clan that had placed one of its sons on the Byzantine throne thirty years earlier (**Document Two A**). Alexius I became emperor by deposing the existing ruler. He was able to do so because he was a respected member of Byzantium's military aristocracy and had familial alliances with the empire's powerful nobles. Marrying Irene helped to legitimize Alexius's claims to leadership in the eyes of the Byzantine elite. But Alexius's mother Anna Dalessena had her own ambitions, disliked her daughter-in-law, and did everything she could to weaken Irene's influence. Women like Anna Dalessena who wielded formal and informal imperial power were not unusual in Byzantium. Between 527 and 1204, seven empresses ruled as regents for young sons, while several others ruled in their own right. Yet other empresses exercised authority through their position as consort to the emperor, but this kind of authority depended on the willingness of the emperor to hand over some of his duties and powers. Long absences or military campaigns by an emperor meant that an empress could be required to exercise imperial authority.

Anna Dalessena held power at her daughter-in-law's expense and ruled jointly with her son until her voluntary retirement to a convent in 1100.[14] Despite what seems to be evidence to the contrary, Anna Comnena maintains that Alexius formally appointed his mother regent, even though Anna Dalessena was reluctant to take up these duties. Anna Comnena also portrayed her grandmother as being devoted and pious, a characterization which was much more acceptable to her readers than that of a woman seeking power and wielding authority (**Document Two B**).

Alexius's use of personal alliances and familial relationships to bolster his legitimacy and to guarantee a dynastic succession affected Anna directly. She was betrothed at birth to the seven-year-old Constantine, son of

12. Ashbridge, 27.

13. Ibid., 28

14. Rae Dalven, *Anna Comnena* (New York: Twayne, 1972), 51.

the former emperor, whom Alexius allowed to act as a junior or co-emperor, accompanying Alexius on public occasions and even signing state documents.[15] But in 1087 Alexius and Irene had a son, John, who would inherit the throne and Anna's engagement to Constantine was broken off and her chances of becoming empress diminished. Eventually she was married to Nicephorous Bryennios, a historian and scholar from another prominent family.

For Anna, as for many other elite women, the terrain of dynastic politics could be uneven and unpredictable. Many years later Anna wrote: "I was only eight when my misfortunes began."[16] Nevertheless, Anna received an extraordinary education for a girl, mostly through the use of tutors. As in Western Christendom, the basic curriculum rested on grammar, logic, and rhetoric with the goal of mastering Greek and the Greek classics. Anna states, "I fortified my mind with the *quadrivium* of the sciences."[17] The *quadrivium* comprised geometry, astronomy, arithmetic, and music. Anna's mastery of these subjects, especially her ability to draw on both classical and biblical allusions in her history, attracted the attention of contemporaries. One scholar concluded that Anna surpassed the education of most accomplished men in Byzantium, including that of her eventual husband, Nicephoros Bryennios. In addition, Anna's grounding in Greek, rather than Latin, gave her a wider base of erudition than is found in the writings of her Latin contemporaries. Sprinkled throughout the *Alexiad* are comments on her love of learning and respect for education, a respect she says she learned from her father.

Anna's position as the well-educated eldest child of the emperor, her well-developed intellect, and her physical and emotional proximity to her father and his activities allowed her unique access to and insight into her father's rule. Anna's husband, at the request of the empress Irene, wrote a history of Alexius up to his coronation. Anna, at the end of her life, continued the history and focused on the years of Alexius's rule, 1081–1118. This history, known as the *Alexiad*, is a narrative history that is grounded not only on her intimate knowledge of Byzantine politics, but also on a number of sources and eyewitness accounts.[18]

Much has been said of the familial relationship between Anna, the historian, and her subject, her father. Many historians see the text as nothing more than a panegyric to her father and her family. Others like the famous eighteenth-century historian of antiquity, Edward Gibbon, argue that it is "no more than an unreliable and prejudicial account written by a loving daughter, rather than an objective observer." He dismissed the text, concluding that the *Alexiad* "betrays in every page the vanity of the female author."[19] Anna had expected such

15. Lynda Garland, *Byzantine Empresses: Women and Power in Byzantium AD 527–1204* (London: Routledge, 1999), 185.

16. Anna Comnena, *The Alexiad*, trans. E. R. A. Sewter (New York: Penguin, 1969), 105.

17. Ibid., 17.

18. Peter Frankopan, "Perception and Projection of Prejudice," in *Gendering the Crusades*, 67.

19. Ibid., 61.

criticism. She stressed the extent to which she tried to be impartial, describing, for example, the plots against and the animus toward her father as well as some of his less than noble actions, such as the sacking of Constantinople by his troops at the time of his ascension. By contrast, the male Latin chroniclers who followed their lords on crusade unabashedly reported only the heroic and honorable deeds, ignoring the less noble and immoral ones and often seeking to discredit a rival. Unlike Anna, each seemed unaware of his biases and prejudices and none reflected on his position vis-à-vis the personages or events about which he wrote.[20]

The *Alexiad* is the only Byzantine text that provides a detailed account of the Crusades as well as an account of conflicts between the Western leaders of the Crusades and Alexius. One of the major themes running through Anna's commentary on the First Crusade is how the Normans, who had encroached on Byzantine lands in southern Italy and the Balkans during the 1080s, had become Alexius's nemeses.[21] As she wrote, she extended this perspective to include the Western crusaders who appeared outside the gates of Constantinople in 1096 and 1097.

Act I

Byzantines, Franks and Normans: An Uneasy Alliance

As we already know, Urban II called on Western Christians and their secular leaders to go to the aid of Eastern Christians against the infidels. This papal mandate sanctioned the use of violence by Western knights against Muslims, and unlike violence used against each other, this act of war served as penance. As one cleric wrote, "Until now you have waged wrongful wars, often hurling insane spears at each other, driven only by greed and pride, for which you deserved only death and damnation. Now we propose for you battles which offer the gift of glorious martyrdom."[22] After the sermon at Clermont, Urban II and others continued to tour and preach about the idea of a crusade for another six months. In order to ensure that the pope's interests were represented and his leadership asserted, Urban appointed Adhemar, the reforming bishop of Le Puy to plan the expedition, and Raymond of Toulouse immediately pledged his support. His age and wealth made him a logical candidate for overall military command, and his own ambition might have motivated him to pledge. According to several contemporary chroniclers, Raymond's decision to join the crusade rested on his piety and willingness to serve the church (**Document Three**). Along with Raymond, the who's who of Italian and French nobility volunteered to lead their retainers. Adhemar's plan called for the volunteers to be divided into

20. Ibid.
21. Ibid., 60.
22. Ibid., 52.

separate forces, each led by a different lord. These would travel separately to Constantinople, assemble there, and then a combined force would cross into Asia Minor and make its way toward Jerusalem, the ultimate goal of the First Crusade.

What really motivated the Crusaders is difficult to ascertain. While it is impossible to ascribe specific motives to any one individual, historians have generally come to accept that many Crusaders answered Urban's call because by "joining Christ's militia a knight could do what he was good at with the blessing of Christ."[23] Mixed in with piety were personal ambition, glory, and the promise of adventure. Greed and land acquisition were also powerful motivations even though equipping oneself or an entire army might cost more than what could be acquired.

The papally sanctioned armies, led by nobles, were not the first Crusaders to set out and reach Constantinople. Instead the first wave was made up of small bands of peasants and a few knights. Disparate groups of men, women, and children were inspired by popular preachers like Peter the Hermit who gathered his followers in Cologne. As this wave swept through central Europe, powerful local aristocrats joined, sectioned off, and established control of parts of the People's Crusade for their own purposes.[24] One nobleman, Emicho of Lenngen, made Jews the main target of his contingent of Crusaders. Fueled by ideas that Jews, like Muslims, were the enemies of Christianity and tapping into long simmering resentment and animosity toward this "alien" community, these pilgrims embarked on a frenzy of violence and extortion, and even forced conversions in central Europe's urban Jewish communities. Other groups, like those following Peter the Hermit, made their way to Constantinople, but not without earning a reputation for robbing and pillaging the communities and lands through which they passed. Anna Comnena commented specifically on this "army's" penchant for brutality and volatility. The officially sanctioned Crusader armies arrived in Constantinople in late 1096 and early 1097 (**Document Four**).

Alexius managed the situation with great skill. He required the armies to camp outside the city, despite their genuine curiosity and the desire of the Crusaders to explore the greatest Christian city on Earth. Fulcher of Chartres, who traveled with Stephen of Blois, was overwhelmed by Constantinople's exotic and opulent grandeur. Alexius used the grandeur of the city and the riches of the Byzantine court to dazzle and overawe the Latin nobles. By invitation, each lord and his entourage entered into the city for an audience. One chronicler described Alexius as "seated, as was his custom, looking powerful on the throne of his sovereignty, not getting up to offer kisses [of greeting] to the duke [Godfrey of Bouillon] or to anyone."[25]

23. *Chronicles of the Crusades: Eye-Witness Accounts of the Wars between Christianity and Islam*, ed. Elizabeth Hallam (New York: Salamander, 2000), 59–60.

24. Ashbridge, 86.

25. Albert of Aachen, *Historia Hierosolymitana, Recueil des historiens des croisades, Historeins occidentaux*, Vol. 4, ed. Academie des Inscriptions et Belles-Lettres (Paris, 1844–1895), Pt. 2, 16, quoted in Ashbridge, 110.

Alexius was able to exact two pledges from the Latin princes: first they had to agree that any territory conquered by the Latin armies had to be given to the Byzantines; and second, they took an oath of loyalty to Alexius. Only Raymond of Toulouse refused the pledges, but he did agree to respect the possessions of the emperor.[26] Immediately after receiving the pledges, Alexius lavished on his guests exquisite gifts as well as supplied much needed intelligence about Turkish positions in Asia Minor and their military tactics. The Crusaders were now ready to fight their way to Jerusalem.

ACT II

To Jerusalem

Raymond had come late to Constantinople, and this delayed his army's departure to Nicaea, the first city targeted and then captured by the Crusaders on their way to Jerusalem. Nicaea was a Byzantine fortified city that had been taken by a group of Seljuk Turks twenty-five years earlier. Its siege and subsequent capture was a collaborative effort among the Latin Crusaders and between the Latin and Byzantine forces. Alexius ordered the victory celebrated by a gift of food to every Crusader, and shared the wealth from Nicaea with the Latin nobles. Even at this early stage of the campaigns it was clear that the behavior, goals, and tactics of the Byzantine emperor might be quite different from those of his Western Latin allies. For example, the emperor allowed the Turkish captives to buy their freedom, and Alexius even returned one of the Sultan's daughters without ransom, much to the surprise of the Latins. For the Crusaders, Nicaea was simply a stop on the way to Jerusalem. For the Byzantines, however, this was a strategic campaign that removed the Turkish threat from Constantinople's doorstep and gave them a staging area from which to reconquer lost Byzantine territories.

The Byzantine army campaigned separately for the next several years in Anatolia, retaking key Byzantine cities and territories. The Latin Crusaders' desire to reach the Holy Land allowed Alexius to realize another of his goals, repossessing the city of Antioch. In order to reach Jerusalem, the Latin armies would have to capture Antioch. This city, an important trading center and frontier garrison for the Byzantines, had fallen to the Turks in 1085. Alexius wanted the Western Crusaders to take it back. In order to guarantee its return to him, he dispatched one of his generals, Taticius, and a modest detachment of troops to participate in the campaign.

Alexius was not the only leader with territorial ambitions. The Latin nobles had their own interests. In June 1097, the Crusader forces split. Baldwin, a son of Godfrey of Bouillon, and Tancred, the nephew of Bohemond of Taranto, were both younger sons without prospects to rule at home. They struck out on their own, hoping to find territories over which they could rule. Baldwin, putting aside his

26. John and Laurita Lyttleton Hill, *Raymond IV, Court of Toulouses* (Syracuse, NY: Syracuse University Press, 1962), 51.

vow to march to the Holy Land, accepted an invitation from the Armenian Christians of Edessa to be their duke. As Baldwin and his troops moved eastward, it became increasingly clear that he would not relinquish the territories that he conquered to Alexius, and Edessa and its surrounding land became the first crusader state. Later, reflecting on the events of the crusade, Anna reported her father's dismay and disappointment at the creation of crusader states and the eventual loss of Antioch.

The main armies of the Crusaders, led by Raymond of Toulouse and his Norman rivals, Robert of Normandy and Bohemond of Taranto, numbered close to 70,000 knights and camp followers. They marched and campaigned through Anatolia during the hot summer months of 1097 as they covered the hundreds of miles to Antioch. Slowed by the logistics of the march and harassed and attacked by the Seljuk Turks, by the time of their arrival in Antioch in October 1097, the Crusaders had lost half of their army to warfare, disease, and starvation.

Antioch guarded the route through Syria to Jerusalem, but in order to make their way safely, the Crusaders needed to capture the city. Yaghi Siyan, the Turkish governor of Antioch, had prepared his city for the attack by provisioning it well, but he needed military aid from other Muslim rulers in the cities of Damascus, Aleppo, and Mosul in southern Mesopotamia. Unfortunately for him, few responded to Antioch's call. Since the time of the Turkish conquests in Syria, its petty city-states had engaged in territorial struggles, and their rulers saw little advantage in supporting Antioch against the Crusaders.[27] They gave the Antioch governor little help, and Muslim disunity eventually allowed the Western Christians to control most of the seaports along the Mediterranean Sea.

On the Christian side, the siege of Antioch demonstrated the tensions among the Crusaders (**Document Five**). Raymond wanted to begin the battle immediately on the Crusaders' arrival. Bohemond and the others ignored Raymond's suggestion and took up separate positions around the city and waited. The decision by the different leaders of the First Crusade to establish separate encampments, especially those around the main gates into the city, had strategic importance for the individual princes because of the principle of "right by conquest." The first army and prince to enter the city had the right to rule it and distribute its spoils.[28] This was most likely the thinking of Bohemond of Taranto who had ambitions regarding Antioch. By fall 1097, he probably had no intention of handing Antioch over to the Byzantines. The Byzantines, on the other hand, appeared willing to let the Crusaders meet their fate without them. Alexius' general, Taticius, decamped in February 1098.

The siege of Antioch lasted over eight months, and the Crusaders suffered almost as heavily as the inhabitants of the city from food shortages, weather, and disease. During the siege, Bohemond proved to be a skillful commander.

27. Hillenbrand, 21.

28. Ashbridge, 163.

On June 3, 1098, he and his men were able to find a way into the outer city by scaling a secretly placed rope. Antioch's Christians supported the Crusaders and opened the city's gates to the Latin knights waiting outside. Entering the city, the hungry and harassed Crusaders engaged in an ugly, brutal melee. The Latin knights killed all in their paths and stripped houses, stores, and streets of anything valuable. The indiscriminate brutality and violence of this moment later worked in the Crusaders' favor as word of the massacre spread throughout Syria. Other cities on the way to Jerusalem would consider negotiating with the Latins rather than face a similar fate.[29]

At the moment when the Crusaders' victory looked certain, an army from Mosul, the only city to answer Antioch's call for help, arrived. Led by General Kerbogha, the army, numbering 35,000, surrounded Antioch, pinning the Crusaders inside. Meanwhile, the remaining Turkish troops in Antioch had retreated into the inner city, trapping the Crusaders between the outer walls and the citadel. Rescue from Byzantine forces was not coming since Alexius had heard from a retreating Crusader that Antioch was lost.

The Latin Crusaders were now themselves besieged. By the end of June, the desperate Latin princes realized that they would have to fight their way out or die trying. Bohemond devised a plan to do this. On June 28, 20,000 crusaders marched out of Antioch to face Kerbogha's well-equipped and cavalry-based army, and somehow they broke through the Turkish lines and routed Kerbogha's army.

Past historians tended to ignore Bohemond's ingenious military plan, its skillful execution, and Kerbogha's poor strategic decisions, emphasizing instead the religious inspiration and zeal of the Crusaders, key elements in the popular imagery of the First Crusaders. More recently, historians have come to the conclusion that "blind, ecstatic faith did not send the crusaders running into battle. Instead, with all other options exhausted, trapped in an intolerable predicament, their strength failing, they decided to place their trust in their god and risk everything in one last-ditch effort."[30] Luckily for them, Bohemond's plan and Kerbogha's indecision combined to bring them this seemingly miraculous victory, and Antioch fell in June 1098.

Soon after the siege of Antioch, Bohemond and Raymond finally broke with each other. Bitter enemies, each now pursued his own goals. Bohemond and his nephew, Tancred, spent the months after their victory subduing and conquering neighboring cities and, by 1099, created the second crusader state, the county of Antioch. After the breach from Bohemond, Raymond allied himself with Alexius. A failed campaign in southern Syria in spring 1099 and his pro-Byzantine stance caused Raymond's popularity with the troops to plummet. He no longer possessed the moral or military authority to lead the Crusaders to Jerusalem. Godfrey of Bouillon emerged as the new Latin leader.

29. Ibid., 210.

30. Ibid., 232.

During the late spring and early summer months the crusaders advanced toward Jerusalem, prepared for the siege, and captured the city. Their initial assault on July 14, 1099, was successful. The next day, the Crusaders entered the city and, as in Antioch, slaughtered Jerusalem's Muslim and Jewish inhabitants, sacked the city, and seized its riches and treasures (**Document Six**). Given their behavior, it is difficult to believe that the Crusaders were motivated by anything other than greed and avarice. However, as one modern historian notes, "in the mind of the crusaders, religious fervor, barbaric warfare and a self-serving desire for material gain were not mutually exclusive. . . . In a moment that is perhaps the most vivid distillation of the crusading experience, they came, still covered in their enemies' blood, weighed down with booty, 'rejoicing and weeping from excessive gladness to worship at the Sepulchre of our Savior Jesus.'"[31] These warriors for Christ had freed Jerusalem and delivered it to Western Christendom.

Finale

Since the initial appeal for Crusaders, Urban II and his successor, Paschel II, had continued to call for more and more Christian knights to reinforce the armies of the First Crusade. In a wave of enthusiasm that followed the news of Jerusalem's conquest, a new set of Crusaders set out and reached Constantinople. Known as the 1101 Crusade, this new force and its leaders also pledged themselves to Alexius. Alexius appointed the Byzantine general Tzitas and Raymond of Toulouse as his representatives to this new army. Raymond, like Alexius, was embittered by Bohemond's control of Antioch, and both hoped that the new army would unseat the Norman and return Antioch to Byzantine control. However, as this force marched through Asia Minor, it met heavy Turkish resistance and was defeated. Tzitas and Raymond luckily escaped, and Raymond stayed in the East and tried to carve out a crusader state from the Syrian city of Tripoli. In 1105, he died pursuing this goal. Only in 1109 did Tripoli fall to the Western Christians and the fourth crusader state was established.

Anna Comnena's access to Byzantine politics came to an end with the death of her father in 1118. When he died, Anna participated in a plot to stop her brother's ascension and to place her husband on the throne. The attempt failed and her brother demonstrated restraint, simply banishing his sister from court life. After her husband's death in 1138, she entered a monastery, renowned for its devotion to learning. From here, she sponsored and directed intellectual gatherings dedicated to Greek philosophy. She also wrote the *Alexiad*, the first Western history written by a woman.

In that work Anna described her father's plans, his fears of the creation of the crusader states, and the dilemmas he faced at the close of the First

31. Ibid., 318.

Crusade. While parts of the empire had been restored, Alexius now had to contend not only with the challenges of the Turks but also with the territorial ambitions of his erstwhile allies. The establishment of these Latin enclaves meant that Western Christendom, its rulers, warriors, and merchants, now had access to a world outside of Europe. Italian merchants had safe harbors all up and down the eastern Mediterranean, buying goods from Arabia and beyond and transporting them back to the West. But these enclaves had to be fortified, provisioned, and defended against an increasingly unified Muslim world. For the next two centuries, Latin knights set out for the East while their own secular and religious leaders took advantage of the opportunity to divert violence from their own lands to the eastern Mediterranean.

The First Crusade colored the relationships between the two Christendoms and between Western Chris- tendom and Islam. Latin propaganda emanating from this period depicted the Byzantines as deceitful, wily, treacherous, and immoral, referring to them as Greeks and never as Romans. In the minds of Western Christians, this designation stripped the Byzantines of their continuity with the Roman imperium and established Western Christendom's claim as Rome's heir.[32] Western chroniclers linked a fictional Byzantine opposition to the crusades with the religious schism between the churches. Betrayal of religion and the Crusaders became a dominant trope in Latin perceptions of Byzantium. The danger of such propaganda lay in its legitimization of the idea that Western Christendom was justified in making war on these traitors.[33]

The First Crusade introduced Western Christendom to both a real and imaginary Islam. Urban II painted a grossly distorted image of the Islamic world that demonized and dehumanized the Muslims to justify holy violence against them. In reality, the Crusaders' contact with Muslim rulers, soldiers, and communities was varied, ranging from explosive violence meted out by the Crusaders on Muslim communities to the pursuit of alliances with various Muslim rulers throughout the Levant.[34] Papal propaganda altered this reality. During the twelfth century, violence and brutality against Muslims was celebrated as much as the conquest of Jerusalem and its holy sites. The brutality of religious intolerance during the First Crusade also shaped the views of the Muslim world. Saladin, the powerful ruler of Egypt, in the mid–twelfth century seized on this imagery and sought to unify Muslims by demanding revenge for Christian violence committed during the First Crusade.[35]

32. Harris, 89.
33. Ibid., 90.
34. Ashbridge, 339.
35. Ibid., 338.

Documents

DOCUMENT ONE

Fulcher of Chartres

The Council of Clermont (November 27, 1095)

There are five different accounts of Pope Urban II's speech proclaiming a crusade. Most likely four of the five authors of these accounts were present. However, none claim to give an exact replica of the speech. Instead, each account highlights what each author thought was most significant. This one is from Fulcher of Chartres who was present at Clermont and then accompanied the leaders of the northern Norman kingdoms to the East. Eventually Fulcher became the chaplain to Baldwin of Boulogne, the second king of the Crusader state of Jerusalem. His chronicle is an invaluable eyewitness account of the First Crusade. What themes does the author stress?

. . . 2. "Now that you, O sons of God, have consecrated yourselves to God to maintain peace among yourselves more vigorously and to uphold the laws of the Church faithfully, there is work to do, for you must turn the strength of your sincerity, now that you are aroused by divine correction, to another affair that concerns you and God. Hastening to the way, you must help your brothers living in the Orient, who need your aid for which they have already cried out many times.

3. "For, as most of you have been told, the Turks, a race of Persians who have penetrated within the boundaries of Romania even to the Mediterranean to that point which they call the Arm of Saint George [Bosporus̄] in occupying more and more of the lands of the Christians, have overcome them, already victims of seven battles, and have killed and captured them, have overthrown churches, and have laid waste God's kingdom. If you permit this supinely for very long, God's faithful ones will be still further subjected.

4. "Concerning this affair, I, with suppliant prayer—not I, but the Lord—exhort you, heralds of Christ, to persuade all of whatever class, both knights and footmen, both rich and poor, in numerous edicts, to strive to help expel that wicked race from our Christian lands before it is too late.

5. "I speak to those present, I send word to those not here; moreover, Christ commands it. Remission of sins will be granted for those going thither, if they end a shackled life either on land or in crossing the sea, or in struggling against the heathen. I, being vested with that gift from God, grant this to those who go.

6. "O what a shame, if a people, so despised, degenerate, and enslaved by demons would thus overcome a people endowed with the trust of almighty God, and shining in the name of Christ! O how many evils will be imputed

to you by the Lord Himself, if you do not help those who, like you, profess Christianity!

7. "Let those," he said, "who are accustomed to wage private wars wastefully even against Believers, go forth against the Infidels in a battle worthy to be undertaken now and to be finished in victory. Now, let those, who until recently existed as plunderers, be soldiers of Christ: now, let those, who formerly contended against brothers and relations, rightly fight barbarians; now, let those, who recently were hired for a few pieces of silver, win their eternal reward. Let those, who wearied themselves to the detriment of body and soul, labor for a twofold honor. Nay, more, the sorrowful here will be glad there, the poor here will be rich there, and the enemies of the Lord here will be His friends there.

8. "Let no delay postpone the journey of those about to go, but when they have collected the money owed to them and the expenses for the journey, and when winter has ended and spring has come, let them enter the crossroads courageously with the Lord going on before."

DOCUMENT TWO

ANNA COMNENA

Her Family
The Alexiad

The nature of imperial rule was changing in the eleventh century as Byzantium faced numerous raiders and invaders on its borders. The Comneni family, members of the military elite, typified the new imperial virtues. Prior to this period, neither military prowess nor noble origins were essential qualities. Ideal qualities were those embodied in the classical and Christian worlds: righteousness, philanthropy, generosity, piety, love of truth and learning, and intelligence. In these excerpts Anna ascribes various qualities to her parents and to her grandmother. What are the ideal qualities for an emperor and empress? Do the qualities of Irene, her mother, have similarities to the qualities of her grandmother, Anna Dalessena? What impression of her parents and grandmother does Anna wish to convey to the reader? Why?

A. ON ALEXIUS AND IRENE

The physical appearance of the two rulers, Alexius and Irene, was remarkable, indeed quite incomparable. A painter could never reproduce the beauty of such an archetype, nor a sculptor mould his lifeless stone into such harmony.

Even the celebrated canon of Polyclitus would have seemed utterly inadequate, if one looked first at these living statues (the newly crowned rulers, I mean) and then at Polyclitus' masterpieces. Alexius was not a very tall man, but broad-shouldered and yet well proportioned. When standing he did not seem particularly striking to onlookers, but when one saw the grim flash of his eyes as he sat on the imperial throne, he reminded one of a fiery whirlwind, so overwhelming was the radiance that emanated from his countenance and his whole presence. His dark eyebrows were curved, and beneath them the gaze of his eyes was both terrible and kind. A quick glance, the brightness of his face, the noble cheeks suffused with red combined to inspire in the beholder both dread and confidence. His broad shoulders, mighty arms and deep chest, all on a heroic scale, invariably commanded the wonder and delight of the people. The man's person indeed radiated beauty and grace and dignity and an unapproachable majesty. When he came into a gathering and began to speak, at once you were conscious of the fiery eloquence of his tongue, for a torrent of argument won a universal hearing and captivated every heart; tongue and hand alike were unsurpassed and invincible, the one in hurling the spear, the other in devising fresh enchantments. The Empress Irene, my mother, was at that time only a young girl, not yet fifteen years old. . . . She stood upright like some young sapling, erect and evergreen, all her limbs and the other parts of her body absolutely symmetrical and in harmony one with another. With her lovely appearance and charming voice she never ceased to fascinate all who saw and heard her. Her face shone with the soft light of the moon; it was not the completely round face of an Assyrian woman, nor long, like the face of a Scyth, but just slightly oval in shape. There were rose blossoms on her cheeks, visible a long way off. Her light-blue eyes were both gay and stern: their charm and beauty attracted, but the fear they caused so dazzled the bystander that he could neither look nor turn away. Whether there really was an Athena in olden times, the Athena celebrated by poets and writers, I do not know, but I often hear the myth repeated and satirized. However, if someone in those times had said of this empress that she was Athena made manifest to the human race, or that she had descended suddenly from the sky in some heavenly glory and unapproachable splendour, his description would not have been so very inappropriate. What was rather surprising—and in this she differed from all other women—was the way she humbled swaggerers, but when they were subdued and fearful restored their courage by a single glance. For the most part her lips were closed and when thus silent she resembled a veritable statue of Beauty, a breathing monument of Harmony. Generally she accompanied her words with graceful gestures, her hands bare to the wrists, and you would say it (her hand) was ivory turned by some craftsman into the form of fingers and hand. The pupils of her eyes, with the brilliant blue of deep waves, recalled a calm, still sea, while the white surrounding them shone by contrast, so that the whole eye acquired a peculiar lustre and a charm which was inexpressible. So much for the physical characteristics of Irene and Alexius. . . .

B. On Anna Dalassena

. . . It was his desire that his mother should govern rather than himself, but so far the plan had been concealed for fear that she, if she knew of it, might leave the palace (Alexius was aware that she considered withdrawal to a monastery). Nevertheless, in all matters however ordinary he did nothing without her advice: she became his confidante and co-partner in government. Gradually and surreptitiously he involved her more and more in state affairs; on occasions he even declared openly that without her brains and good judgement the Empire would not survive. By these means he bound her more closely to himself, but prevented her from attaining her own goal and frustrated it. She had in mind the last stage of life and dreamed of monasteries in which she would drag out her remaining years in the contemplation of wisdom. Such was her intention, the constant aim of her prayers. Despite this longing in her heart, despite the total preoccupation with a higher life, she also loved her son to a quite exceptional degree and wished somehow to bear with him the storms that buffeted the Empire (if I may apply seafaring metaphor to the manifold troubles and tumults to which it was exposed). . . . The truth is that Anna Dalassena was in any case endowed with a fine intellect and possessed besides a really first-class aptitude for governing. On the other hand, she was distracted from it by her love for God. . . . In brief, nothing shall be reckoned invalid which she commands either in writing or by word of mouth, for her words and her decisions shall be reckoned as my own and none of them shall be annulled. In years to come they shall have the force of law permanently. . . .

The reader may be surprised by the honour conferred on his mother by the emperor in this matter, since he yielded her precedence in everything, relinquishing the reins of government, as it were, and running alongside as she drove the imperial chariot; only in the title of emperor did he share with her the privileges of his rank. . . . For my grandmother had an exceptional grasp of public affairs, with a genius for organization and government; she was capable, in fact, of managing not only the Roman Empire, but every other empire under the sun as well. She had vast experience and a wide understanding of the motives, ultimate consequences, interrelations good and bad of various courses of action, penetrating quickly to the right solution, adroitly and safely carrying it out. Her intellectual powers, moreover, were paralleled by her command of language. She was indeed a most persuasive orator, without being verbose or long-winded. She was already a woman of mature years when she was called upon to exercise imperial authority, at a time of life when one's mental powers are at their best, when one's judgement is fully developed and knowledge of affairs is widest—all qualities that lend force to good administration and government. It is natural that persons of this age should not merely speak with greater wisdom than the young (as the tragic playwright says), but also act in a more expedient way. In the past, when Anna Dalassena was still looked upon as a younger woman, she had impressed everyone as 'having an old head on young shoulders'; to the observant her face alone revealed Anna's inherent virtue and gravity. . . .

DOCUMENT THREE

Latin and Greek Chroniclers on Raymond of Toulouse

Many of the chroniclers followed their lords to the East and as a result their histories of the Crusades represent distinct points of view. Raymond of Toulouse, when he began the Crusade, was expected to lead, but at different points in time, his abilities, veracity, and morality were all questioned. Included are three different views of Raymond. The first is by Raymond d'Aguilers, Raymond's chaplain who accompanied him East and wrote Historia Francorum. *The second is found in the* Gesta Francorum, *written by a follower of Raymond's eventual rival, Bohemond. The third is a description from the* Alexiad. *Anna favors Raymond above all other Latins because of his eventual support for her father against Bohemond.*

A. Raymond d'Aguilers

Historia Francorum

. . . Accordingly, when the Count had been received most honorably by the Emperor and his princes, the Emperor demanded of the Count homage and the oath which the other princes had made to him. The Count replied that he had not come hither to make another his lord or to fight for any other than the One for whom he had left his country and his possessions. Nevertheless, if the Emperor would go to Jerusalem with the army, he would commit himself and his men and all his goods to him. But the Emperor excused himself from the journey by saying that he greatly feared lest the Germans, Hungarians, Cumans, and other wild peoples would devastate his empire, if he made the journey with the pilgrims. Meanwhile the Count, upon hearing of the flight and death of his men, believed that he had been betrayed, and through certain of our princes he vehemently charged the Emperor with having committed treason. But Alexius said that he did not know that our men had devastated his kingdom, and that he and his men had suffered many injuries; that there was nothing of which the Count could complain, except that while the army of the Count in its usual manner was devastating the villages and towns, it took to flight upon seeing his (the Emperor's) army. Nevertheless, he promised that he would give satisfaction to the Count and offered Bohemund as a hostage for the satisfaction. They went to trial; the Count, according to law, was compelled to give up his hostage.

B. *Gesta Francorum*

The Count of St. Gilles, however, was lodged outside the city in a suburb, and his force had remained behind. Accordingly, the Emperor bade the Count do homage and fealty to him, as the others had done. And while the Emperor was making these demands, the Count was meditating how he might take vengeance on the army of the Emperor. But Duke Godfrey and Robert, Count of Flanders, and the other princes said to him that it would be unjust to fight against Christians. The wise man, Bohemund, also said that if the Count should do the Emperor any injustice, and should refuse to do him fealty, he himself would take the part of the Emperor. Accordingly, the Count, after receiving the advice of his men, swore that he would not consent to have the life and honor of Alexius sullied either by himself or by anyone else. When he was called upon for homage, he answered that he would not do this at the risk of his head.

Then the host of Lord Bohemund approached Constantinople. Tancred, indeed, and Richard of Principati, and almost the whole of Bohemund's force with him, crossed the Strait by stealth, to avoid the oath to the Emperor. And now the army of the Count of St. Gilles approached Constantinople. The Count remained there with his own band. Therefore the illustrious man, Bohemund, stayed behind with the Emperor, in order to plan with him how they might provide a market for the people who were beyond the city of Nicaea.

C. Anna Comnena

The Alexiad

One of them especially, the Count of St. Gilles, he particularly favored because he saw in him superior prudence, tested sincerity, candor of bearing, and finally, such great zeal for truth that he never placed anything before it. He was as far superior to all the other Latins in all virtues as the sun is above the other stars. For this reason, therefore, the Emperor kept him near him for the time being.

When at the wish of the Emperor all had crossed over the Propontis and had arrived at *Damalium*, Alexius, thus relieved from care and trouble, had the Count of St. Gilles summoned and in talks showed him very distinctly what he thought might happen to the Latins on the way. At the same time, he disclosed to him what suspicions he was cherishing about the intentions and plans of the Gauls. He often spoke freely about them with the Count of St. Gilles, opening the doors of his heart to him, as it were, and making everything clearly known to him. He sometimes warned him, also, to keep close watch against the malice of Bohemund, so as to check him immediately if he should try to break his agreement, and to strive in every way to destroy his schemes. The Count of St. Gilles replied: "Since Bohemund has inherited perjury and deceit, as it were, it would be very surprising if he should be faithful to those promises which he has made under oath. However, I will try to carry out what you command, in so far as I can." Then at the wish of the Emperor he departed, joining himself to the forces of the united Gauls. . . .

DOCUMENT FOUR

Latin and Greek Chroniclers

Waves of Crusaders

The excerpts included convey the diversity of experience and motives of the Crusaders and their initial travels to Constantinople. How did the Byzantine elites see the arrival of the forces? What were Latin reactions to the journey to Constantinople and to the city itself?

A. Anna Comnena

The Alexiad, On the People's Crusade

. . . [Alexius] had no time to relax before he heard a rumour that countless Frankish armies were approaching. He dreaded their arrival, knowing as he did their uncontrollable passion, their erratic character and their irresolution, not to mention the other peculiar traits of the Kelt, with their inevitable consequences: their greed for money, for example, which always led them, it seemed, to break their own agreements without scruple for any chance reason. He had consistently heard this said of them and it was abundantly justified. So far from despairing, however, he made every effort to prepare for war if need arose. What actually happened was more far-reaching and terrible than rumour suggested, for the whole of the west and all the barbarians who lived between the Adriatic and the Straits of Gibraltar migrated in a body to Asia, marching across Europe country by country with all their households. The reason for this mass-movement is to be found more or less in the following events. A certain Kelt, called Peter, with the surname Koukoupetros, left to worship at the Holy Sepulchre and after suffering much ill-treatment at the hands of the Turks and Saracens who were plundering the whole of Asia, he returned home with difficulty. Unable to admit defeat, he wanted to make a second attempt by the same route, but realizing the folly of trying to do this alone (worse things might happen to him) he worked out a clever scheme. He decided to preach in all the Latin countries. A divine voice, he said, commanded him to proclaim to all the counts in France that all should depart from their homes, set out to worship at the Holy Shrine and with all their soul and might strive to liberate Jerusalem from the Agarenes. Surprisingly, he was successful. It was as if he had inspired every heart with some divine oracle. Kelts assembled from all parts, one after another, with arms and horses and all the other equipment for war. Full of enthusiasm and ardour they thronged every highway, and with these warriors came a host of civilians, outnumbering the sand of the sea shore or the stars of heaven, carrying palms and bearing crosses on their shoulders. There were women and children, too, who had left their own countries. Like tributaries joining a river from all directions they streamed towards us in full force, mostly through Dacia.

B. Raymond d'Aguilers

Historia Francorum, On the Provencals' March to the East

. . . We passed through Sclavonia without losses from starvation or open conflict largely through God's mercy, the hard work of the Count, and the counsel of Adhémar. This successful crossing of the barbarous lands leads us to believe that God wished His host of warriors to cross through Sclavonia in order that brutish, pagan men, by learning of the strength and long suffering of His soldiers, would at some time recover from their savageness or as unabsolved sinners be led to God's doom.

Upon our arrival at Scutari after our strenuous passage across Sclavonia, the Count affirmed brotherhood and bestowed many gifts upon the king of the Slavs so that the crusaders could buy in peace and look for the necessities of life. But this was only an illusion, for we sorely regretted our trust in the sham peace when the Slavs took advantage of the occasion, went berserk as was their custom, slew our people, and snatched what they could from the unarmed. You may well believe we prayed for a refuge and not for revenge; but why should we continue this dreary account of Sclavonia?

On our encampment at Durazzo we were confident that we were in our land, because we believed that Alexius and his followers were our Christian brothers and confederates. But truly, with the savagery of lions they rushed upon peaceful men who were oblivious of their need for self defense. These brigands, operating by night, slew our people in groves and places far from camp and stole what they could from them. While the Greeks acted thus without restraint, their leader, John Comnenus, promised peace; but during such a truce they killed Pontius Rainaud and fatally wounded his brother, Peter, two most noble princes. We had a chance for vengeance, but we renewed our march in preference to vindicating our injustices. En route, we had letters concerning security and brotherhood, and I may say of filiation, from the Emperor; but these were empty words, for before and behind, to the right and to the left Turks, Kumans, Uzes, and the tenacious peoples—Pechenegs and Bulgars—were lying in wait for us.

C. Fulcher of Chartres

Chronicle of the First Crusade, On the City of Constantinople

Oh, what an excellent and beautiful city! How many monasteries, and how many palaces there are in it, of wonderful work skilfully fashioned! How many marvelous works are to be seen in the streets and districts of the town! It is a great nuisance to recite what an opulence of all kinds of goods are found there; of gold, of silver, of many kinds of mantles, and of holy relics. In every season, merchants, in frequent sailings, bring to that place everything that man might need. Almost twenty thousand eunuchs, I judge, are kept there continuously. . . .

D. Anna Comnena

The Alexiad, On the Normans and Bohemond of Taranto

. . . Bohemond's appearance was, to put it briefly, unlike that of any other man seen in those days in the Roman world, whether Greek or barbarian. The sight of him inspired admiration, the mention of his name terror. I will describe in detail the barbarian's characteristics. His stature was such that he towered almost a full cubit over the tallest men. He was slender of waist and flanks, with broad shoulders and chest, strong in the arms; in general he was neither taper of form, nor heavily built and fleshy, but perfectly proportioned – one might say that he conformed to the Polyclitean ideal. His hands were large, he had a good firm stance, and his neck and back were compact. If to the accurate and meticulous observer he appeared to stoop slightly, that was not caused by any weakness of the vertebrae of the lower spine, but presumably there was some malformation there from birth. The skin all over his body was very white, except for his face which was both white and red. His hair was lightish-brown and not as long as that of other barbarians (that is, it did not hang on his shoulders); in fact, the man had no great predilection for long hair, but cut his short, to the ears. Whether his beard was red or of any other colour I cannot say, for the razor had attacked it, leaving his chin smoother than any marble. However, it *appeared* to be red. His eyes were light-blue and gave some hint of the man's spirit and dignity. He breathed freely through nostrils that were broad, worthy of his chest and a fine outlet for the breath that came in gusts from his lungs. There was a certain charm about him, but it was somewhat dimmed by the alarm his person as a whole inspired; there was a hard, savage quality in his whole aspect, due, I suppose, to his great stature and his eyes; even his laugh sounded like a threat to others. Such was his constitution, mental and physical, that in him both courage and love were armed, both ready for combat. His arrogance was everywhere manifest; he was cunning, too, taking refuge quickly in any opportunism. His words were carefully phrased and the replies he gave were regularly ambiguous. Only one man, the emperor, could defeat an adversary of such character, an adversary as great as Bohemond; he did it through luck, through eloquence, and through the other advantages that Nature had given him. . .

DOCUMENT FIVE

Latin Chroniclers

The Siege of Antioch

In the three years that it took the Crusaders to arrive in Jerusalem, they had to fight a variety of foes and conduct sieges of Antioch and Jerusalem. Excerpts from two of their accounts are presented. What are the circumstances and experiences of the

Muslims, Latins, and Greeks who found themselves caught up in the violence? Who are the heroes and villains in these accounts, and why draw such distinctions?

A. Stephen, Count of Blois and Chartres

To His Wife, Adele (Antioch, March 29, 1098)

Count Stephen to Adele, his sweetest and most amiable wife, to his dear children, and to all his vassals of all ranks—his greeting and blessing. . . .

We found the city of Antioch very extensive, fortified with incredible strength and almost impregnable. In addition, more than 5,000 bold Turkish soldiers had entered the city, not counting the Saracens, Publicans, Arabs, Turcopolitans, Syrians, Armenians and other different races of whom an infinite multitude had gathered together there. In fighting against these enemies of God and of our own we have, by God's grace, endured many sufferings and innumerable evils up to the present time. Many also have already exhausted all their resources in this very holy passion. Very many of our Franks, indeed, would have met a temporal death from starvation, if the clemency of God and our money had not succoured them. Before the above-mentioned city of Antioch indeed, throughout the whole winter we suffered for our Lord Christ from excessive cold and enormous torrents of rain. What some say about the impossibility of bearing the heat of the sun throughout Syria is untrue for the winter there is very similar to our winter in the west. . . .

I love to tell you, dearest, what happened to us during Lent. Our princes had caused a fortress to be built before a certain gate which was between our camp and the sea. For the Turks daily issuing from this gate, killed some of our men on their way to the sea. The city of Antioch is about five leagues' distance from the sea. For this reason they sent the excellent Bohemond and Raymond, count of St. Gilles, to the sea with only sixty horsemen, in order that they might bring mariners to aid in this work. When, however, they were returning to us with those mariners, the Turks collected an army, fell suddenly upon our two leaders and forced them to a perilous flight. In that unexpected flight we lost more than 500 of our foot-soldiers—to the glory of God. Of our horsemen, however, we lost only two, for certain.

B. Raymond d'Aguilers

Historia Francorum, On the Sufferings of the Crusaders

And so the poor began to leave [the siege], and many rich who feared poverty. If any for love of valor remained in camp, they suffered their horses to waste away by daily hunger. Indeed, straw did not abound; and fodder was so dear that seven or eight *solidi* were not sufficient to buy one night's food for a horse. Another calamity also befell the army, for Bohemund, who had become most distinguished in *Hispania* said that he would leave; that he had come for honor, and (now) beheld his men and horses perishing for want; and he (further) said that he was not a rich man whose private resources would suffice for so long a siege. We found out afterwards that he had said this for the reason that he was ambitiously longing to become head of the city of Antioch. . . .

There was, besides, in our army a certain member of the Emperor's household whom he had given to us in his place, *Taticius* by name, mangled in nose and all virtue. I had almost forgotten him, since he deserved to be abandoned to oblivion forever. This man, however, was daily whispering in the ears of the princes that they should scatter to the neighboring camp, and then assail the people of Antioch by frequent assaults and ambush. However, as all this was made clear to the Count (for he had been sick since the day when he was forced to flee at the bridge), he called his princes and the Bishop of Puy together. After holding a council, he gave them fifty marks of silver on this condition, truly, that if any of his knights lost a horse, it should be restored to him out of those fifty marks and other (resources) which had been given to the brotherhood. Moreover, this kind of cooperation was of great profit at that time, since the poor of our army, who wanted to cross the river to gather herbs, feared the frequent assaults of the enemy, and since very rarely did any care to go against the enemy, because their horses were starved and weak, and, in addition, so few that scarcely one hundred could be found in the whole army of the Count and Bishop. A similar lot had befallen Bohemund and the other princes. Accordingly, for this reason our knights were not afraid to meet the enemy, especially those who had bad or weak horses, since they knew that if they lost their horses they would obtain better ones. Moreover, something else occurred, namely that all the princes except the Count promised the city to Bohemund, provided it was taken. So Bohemund and the other princes swore to this agreement, that they would not withdraw from the siege of Antioch for seven years, unless the city was taken. . . .

DOCUMENT SIX

Muslim Chroniclers and Poets

The Fall of Jerusalem

Early Muslim chroniclers of the First Crusade briefly noted the fall of Jerusalem. However as time passed, the accounts changed. In what way and why did the accounts change? How can the chronicles be used as historical sources?

A. Al-Azimi, Syrian writer, written ca. 1160

Then they [the Franks] turned to Jerusalem and conquered it from the hands of the Egyptians. Godfrey took it. They burned the Church of the Jews.

B. Ibn al-Qalanisi, Syrian writer, written ca. 1160

The Franks stormed the town and gained possession of it. A number of the townsfolk fled to the sanctuary and a great host were killed. The Jews assembled in the synagogue, and the Franks burned it over their heads. The sanctuary was surrendered to them on the guarantee of safety on 22 Sha'ban [14 July] of this year, and they destroyed the shrines and the tomb of Abraham.

C. Ibn al-Jawzi, ca. 1200

Among the events in this year was the taking of Jerusalem by the Franks on Friday 13 Sha'ban [5 July]. They killed more than 70,000 Muslims there. They took forty-odd silver candelabra from the Dome of the Rock, each one worth 360,000 dirhams. They took a silver lamp weighing forty Syrian ratls. They took twenty-odd gold lamps, innumerable items of clothing and other things.

D. Ibn al-Athir, ca. 1233

The Franks killed more than 70,000 people in the Aqsa mosque, among them a large group of Muslim imams, religious scholars, devout men and ascetics from amongst those who left their homelands and lived in the vicinity of that Holy Palace.

E. Al-Abiwardi, ca. 1100, Lament for the Fall of Jerusalem

How can the eye sleep between the lids at a time of disasters that would waken any sleeper?
While your Syrian brothers can only sleep on the backs of their chargers, or in vultures' bellies . . . !
This is war, and the infidel's sword is naked in his hand, ready to be sheathed again in men's necks and skulls.
This is war, and he [the Prophet] who lies in the tomb at Medina seems to raise his voice and cry: "O sons of Hashim."

Questions

1. What types of primary sources are available to study the First Crusade? What types of prejudices and biases do medieval chroniclers have?
2. What were papal motivations in calling for a crusade to the Holy Land? Why did Latin princes go on the First Crusade? Who were their followers?
3. What was the relationship between Eastern and Western Christendom? How did the First Crusade alter the balance of power in the eastern Mediterranean?

4. What was the nature of imperial rule in the Byzantine state? How might women wield official and unofficial imperial authority and power?
5. What are the ideal masculine and feminine characteristics? How do the chroniclers use gender to depict a historic figure or a historic group?
6. How did the First Crusade transform Western Christendom's assessment of the Byzantine Empire and the Muslim states in the Near East?

Suggested Readings

Ashbridge, Thomas. *The First Crusade: A New History*. New York: Oxford University Press, 2004.

Edgington, Susan B., and Sarah Lambert, eds. *Gendering the Crusades*. New York: Columbia University Press, 2002.

Garland, Lynda. *Byzantine Empresses: Women and Power in Byzantium AD 527–1204*. London: Routledge, 1999.

Gouma Peterson, Thalia, ed. *Anna Komnene and Her Times*. New York: Garland, 2000.

Harris, Jonathan. *Byzantium and the Crusades*. London: Hambledon and London, 2003.

Hillenbrand, Carole. *The Crusades: Islamic Perspectives*. Chicago: Dearborn, 1999.

Shaffer, Lynda N., and George J. Marcopoulos. "Murasaki and Comnena: Two Women and Two Themes in World History." *History Teacher* 19, no. 4 (August 1986): 487–498.

Source Materials

The *Alexiad* in its entirety and other medieval texts can be accessed through *The Medieval Sourcebook, Full Texts*. http://www.fordham.edu/halsall/sbook2.html

CHAPTER

12

The Mongol Empire and World Conquest: Chinggis Khan (1162–1227)[1] *and Sorghaghtani Beki (?–1252)*

■ Setting the Stage

The Mongol conquest of much of the landmass of Eurasia has spawned many myths and legends and struck both terror and admiration in the hearts of the peoples of Eurasia. Separating fact from fiction has always been difficult for historians since much of

1. Chinggis Khan is normally referred to as Genghis Khan, and that is the more common spelling. In recent years, Chinggis has become the preferred spelling since it is closer to the Mongolian spelling and pronunciation than the more common usage.

the Mongol story is known through those who were conquered and subjected to Mongol rule. Yet, who were the Mongols, and how and why did they create the largest land empire in world history? The Mongols were nomadic people who originally lived on the steppes of central Asia. Prior to their explosion onto the world stage, the basic unit of their society was the tribe, which usually consisted of several patrilineal clans. Often these tribes were at odds with each other, fighting for pastures, animals, and sometimes women. However, they also found that alliances among clans and tribes were essential to surviving both the harsh semi-arid climate of the steppes and the constant attacks by neighboring nomadic groups. At times, the Mongols formed larger confederations of tribes. The leader of such a confederation was called *khan,* meaning "ruler," and his spouse was called *katun,* meaning "wife of *khan.*" Khans had absolute authority over the people in their confederation, and loyalty to the khans and the confederation's tribesmen were the most valued traits.

In a nomadic society, the work of all its members was critical to the success and survival of the tribe. As children, both boys and girls learned to ride, forage, fight, and manage scarce resources. As adults, men were expected to be herdsmen, hunters, and warriors. With their men constantly on the road, women were often caretakers of the herd and managers of children and the family economy. They had reserved key rights, including the right to own property and to divorce, and as a result they wielded authority within the family. Outside the family' Mongol princesses were included in the Great Assembly meetings, and Mongol women often fought in battles, proving themselves excellent riders and skilled archers. They were considered to be the equal of men in battle, in both prowess and cruelty. A Persian historian recorded the following incident during Chinggis Khan's conquest of western Asia in 1220, "A daughter of Chinggis Khan, who was the chief wife of Toghachar, now entered the town with her escort, and they slew all the survivors save only four hundred persons who were selected for their craftsmanship and carried off to Turkestan."[2]

What caused Mongol expansion? Scholars generally believe that, in addition to Chinggis Khan's military talent and ruthlessness, two other conditions contributed to this expansion.[3] First, during the late twelfth century and early thirteenth century, Mongolia experienced drastic climate and ecological changes; winters were prolonged and pastures were damaged. These changes forced the Mongols to seek new grasslands for their herds, often encroaching on other peoples' territories. Secondly, the emergence of more robust states in northern and northwestern China

2. Ala-ad-Din Ata-Malik Juvayni, *The History of the World-Conqueror,* trans. John Andrew Boyle (Cambridge, MA: Harvard University Press, 1958), 177.

3. See, for example, Leo de Hartog, *Chinggis Khan: Conqueror of the World* (New York: Tauris Parke, 2004).

at this time constricted trade between the Mongols and Chinese. The Mongols had relied heavily on the merchants of settled communities in these border regions for grains, tools, and daily necessities. Disruption of these well-established economic patterns in the early 1200s, not only in China but throughout central Asia, led Chinggis Khan and his followers to initiate raids, full-scale attacks, and even invasions in order to protect trade and the rights of Mongol merchants. The disunity of many of the Mongols' neighbors, the political vacuum in central Asia, and the Mongols' military advantage based on the horse and the bow contributed greatly to the Mongols' swift conquest of territories spanning Asia and Europe.

Given that the Mongols did not have a written language until the thirteenth century, sources for Mongol history as well as the lives of our protagonists are surprisingly abundant. Among these, three historical accounts produced during the thirteenth and fourteenth centuries provide historians with extremely detailed information. The *Secret History of the Mongols* was written by an anonymous author in Mongolian, using the Uyghur script, for the Mongol royal family several decades after Chinggis Khan's death. Scholars suspect the book was intended to serve as the official account of the Mongol ruling clan, from its origin to the rule of Chinggis's son, Ögödei Khan (r. 1229–1241), and so we can expect that it represents the Mongolian point of view. Even though the original version of the *Secret History of the Mongols* has been lost, the Chinese version, which first appeared during the early period of the Ming Dynasty (1368–1644), has survived.[4]

Much more was written by the Mongols' literate enemies. These contemporary chroniclers and their writings are from the perspective of peoples who were intimidated, invaded, and conquered by the Mongols. As a result, these documents give a very different point of view, emphasizing the barbarity of the attacks; the terrible, fiery sieges of towns and cities; and the exceptional skill of Mongol horsemen and -women and of the male and female archers who instilled fear in enemy soldiers and populations. The Persian historian Ala-ad-Din Ata-Malik Juvayni (?1226–1283) completed *The History of the World Conqueror* about 1260. Juvayni's account is undoubtedly the single most important source on the Mongols' conquest and their rule of western Asia. Juvayni was a middle-level bureaucrat in the Mongol government in western Asia and traveled widely in central Asia and Mongolia.[5] Rashid al-Din, a Jewish doctor and high-ranking official of the Mongol Il-khans of Persia, authored *The Successors of Chinggis Khan* at the

4. There are at least four credible translations of the *Secret History of the Mongols,* including the most recent and extensive annotated version by Igor de Rachewiltz, *The Secret History of the Mongols: A Mongolian Epic Chronicle of the Thirteenth Century* (Leiden, The Netherlands: Brill, 2004).

5. For a complete translation of Ala-ad-Din Ata-Malik Juvayni's work, see *The History of the World-Conqueror,* trans. John Andrew Boyle (Cambridge, MA: Harvard University Press, 1958).

behest of the Il-khan Ghazan (r. 1295–1304). In order to conduct his research, Rashid al-Din was allowed access to the sacred Mongol chronicle, *Altan debter,* a privilege usually reserved only for the Mongols, and to other documents in the court archives. In addition, information was gleaned from travelers, scholars, and envoys from East and West who journeyed across the steppes to Karakorum and wrote accounts of "the ways and customs of the Mongols"[6] and of their material world. The high visibility of noble Mongol women caused the chronicler of the *Secret History* and others to write at some length about women's roles in the development, rule, and disintegration of the Mongol Empire.

The Actors

Chinggis Khan and Sorghaghtani Beki

Chinggis Khan was born in 1162 into the Kiyad tribe. His father, Yesügei, was the leader of his tribe and a nephew of the founder of the Mongol tribal federation, Qabul Khan (r. 1125–1140). In 1162, Yesügei abducted a woman named Hö'elün from her fiancé, a Merkid tribesman. Hö'elün became Yesügei's principal wife and together they had four sons. Their firstborn was named Temüjin, because he was born about the time when Yesügei captured a Tatar chieftain of that name. The child would eventually be known as Chinggis Khan.

When Temüjin was eight, his father took him to his mother's tribe to find a future bride. The negotiation between the two potential fathers-in-law did not take long. Börte, the beautiful nine-year-old daughter of the chieftain, was betrothed to young Temüjin. Yesügei saw the betrothal as a strategic alliance between the two tribes and, as was the custom, placed Temüjin in the position to be of service to his father-in-law (**Document One**).

On his return trip, Yesügei was poisoned by a group of Tatars, who recognized him as one of the leaders who had raided their camps many times. After his father's death, Temüjin returned and sought the leadership of his family and tribe, but tribal rivals refused to follow such a young boy. The widowed Hö'elün and her sons were soon stripped of their herds and abandoned by their tribesmen. The *Secret History,* interweaving fact and legend, details how this exiled, impoverished family wandered from place to place, living by hunting and by gathering wild fruits and nuts, struggling to survive. In his teens, Temüjin survived a raid, kidnapping, and enslavement by his former tribe and was helped to escape by a young man who would become one of his future generals. Far from destroying Temüjin, the hardships helped forge him into a resourceful, brave, and ambitious young man.

His mother, an astute and practiced observer of Mongol tribal politics, schooled Temüjin in the art of alliance

6. Jeannine Davis-Kimball, "Katuns: The Mongolian Queens of the Genghis Khanite," in *Ancient Queens: Archaeological Explorations,* ed. Sarah Milledge Nelson (New York: Altamira, 2003), 152, 160, 169.

building which was the key to building power in the political climate of Mongolia. Temüjin also came to understand the need for his own alliance with a more powerful tribal leader. His future father-in-law honored his pledge to the deceased Yesügei, and in 1182 Temüjin took Börte as his first bride and principal wife, thus establishing an important alliance. She bore five daughters and four sons. Only the names of the sons are known, Jochi (1185–1217), Chaghadai (?–1241), Ögödei (1186–1248), and Tolui (?–1232). Over the course of his life, Temüjin took numerous concubines, almost one bride from every conquered territory,[7] but Börte was the only wife who held the title *katun.* Temüjin also pledged loyalty and service to Toghrul (Ong Khan), a sworn blood brother of his father and powerful leader of the *Kereyid.* In return Toghrul became Temüjin's sworn father. Temüjin proved himself in battle as leader of an army and a broker of alliances. Soon his growing stature brought challenges from other local tribal leaders seeking his power. Over the course of a decade, Temüjin met and defeated each of his challengers, including his sworn father. By 1206, he had united Mongol and Turkic tribes, large and small, into a single confederation under his rule. At the 1206 *khuriltai,* the governing body of the Mongol confederation that included all of the chiefs of the allied tribes and families, Temüjin was acknowledged as *khan.* He took the name Chinggis Khan, meaning "strong ruler" or "universal sovereign."

Among Chinggis Khan's most trusted advisers were his wife and mother whose "voices were ones of reason, calming the khan's volatile nature in the most treacherous of situations."[8] For example, his mother intervened when the predictions of a powerful and treacherous shaman turned Chinggis against one of his brothers, whom he perceived as a rival. According to the *Secret History,* she tore open her dress, revealed her breasts, and questioned, "'Have you seen them? The breasts that ye have sucked are these.' Passionately she declared that she had suckled [all] her sons and they had grown to strong manhood, then demanded of the khan, 'How could you destroy your brothers?'"[9] A contrite Chinggis not only released his brother but bestowed greater power and wealth on him. When the same shaman continued his intrigues, Chinggis Khan's wife intervened and convinced him to move against the shaman.

According to the *Secret History,* Mongolian gender customs and norms and the sage advice of the women around Chinggis set the stage for the emergence of powerful Mongol queens.[10] As the Mongol confederation expanded, the women of the royal family accrued greater and greater political and economic power.

7. A historical account of the Yuan dynasty produced by Chinese literati during the fourteenth century recorded the names of his twenty-three wives and sixteen concubines. See Song Lian et al., *History of the Yuan Dynasty* (Beijing: Zhonghua shuju, 1972).

8. Davis-Kimball, 161.

9. Ibid., 162.

10. Ibid., 160.

They held vast landholdings and herds, levied taxes on those who lived in their territories, and used this money for their own purposes. Probably the most successful Mongol imperial woman was Chinggis Khan's daughter-in-law, Sorghaghtani Beki.

Sorghaghtani Beki was married to the youngest of his four chief sons, Tolui. Sorghaghtani, meaning "she who has a birthmark," was the daughter of Jakha Gambu, brother of Ong Khan who was the leader of the *Kereyid* tribe and the sworn father of Chinggis Khan. According to Rashid al-Din, the marriage between Tolui and Sorghaghtani Beki was arranged when both were children.[11] There are no records of the exact year of the engagement or even their wedding. It seems the new couple did not spend too much time together, as Tolui was Chinggis Khan's most trusted son when it came to political and military strategies. He was "for the most part in attendance on his father," and Chinggis Khan "used to consult him on all occasions."[12] After the death of Chinggis Khan, Tolui helped his older brother Ögödei finish the plan of conquest laid out by their father. Returning from a long expedition, Tolui became seriously ill and died in 1232, only five years after his father.

According to Rashid al-Din, Tolui had begged God to take him instead of Ögödei. Soon after his prayer, Ögödei recovered, but Tolui became ill and died.[13] Therefore Ögödei felt personally responsible for Tolui's death and welcomed Sorghaghtani Beki and her four young sons into his palace. Sorghaghtani proved to be much more than just a hapless young widow. Rashid-al-Din wrote, "She was extremely intelligent and able and towered above all the women in the world, possessing in the fullest measure the qualities of steadfastness, virtue, modesty, and chastity." When Ögödei proposed the idea of her marriage to one of his own sons, which would guarantee the support of her four sons in any future power struggle, Sorghaghtani refused, saying, "My thought is only to bring up these children until they reach the stage of manhood and independence and to try to make them well mannered and not liable to go apart and hate each other so that, perhaps, some great thing may come of their unity"[14] (**Document Two**).

Modern historians, though, believe that she was far more ambitious than her contemporaries anticipated. Nineteen years later, her oldest son, Möngke, became the successor to the Mongol Empire (r. 1251–1259). Later, her second son, Khubilai, became the first emperor of Yuan China (r. 1260–1294), and her third son, Hülegü (1217–1265), became the il-Khan in Persia, conquered and destroyed the Abbasid caliphate in Baghdad, and then invaded Syria.

In addition to being an extremely capable mother, Sorghaghtani was

11. Rashid al-Din, *The Successors of Chinggis Khan*, trans. John Andrew Boyle (New York: Columbia University Press, 1971), 159.

12. Ibid., 163.

13. Ibid., 167.

14. Ibid.

known for her political acumen and tolerance. Herself a Nestorian Christian, she did not discriminate against other religions, but even patronized them in order to win the support of various subjects in the vast Mongol empire. In the *History of the World-Conqueror,* Juvayni wrote that Sorghaghtani commissioned one of the two major centers for Islamic studies in Baghdad. He wrote, "In each [center] every day a thousand students are engaged in profitable studies, while the professors are the greatest scholars of the age and the wonders of their day. And indeed these two buildings with their lofty pillars and trim courts at once adorn and dignify Baghdad, nay they are an ornament and delight to all Islam. Under these circumstances the people of Baghdad have regained some comfort as well as relief from subventions and similar burdens."[15]

Sorghaghtani fell suddenly ill in 1252. When the situation was extremely grave, the Mongols granted a one-day amnesty "as an almsgiving for her long life those who had that day been condemned to death all received their pardon."[16] But she never recovered.

Act I
The World Conqueror

The Mongol expansion was triggered by sudden changes in ecology and trade, but the success of this expansion was due to Chinggis Khan's political calculation, military talent, and ruthlessness. Chinggis Khan's political abilities were reflected in his consistent strategy of making alliances in any way possible, even if they were just temporary. The pledge of alliance between Chinggis Khan and Toghrul, for example, could be traced back to when Chinggis Khan was a child and went through repeated renewal. Throughout his military campaigns, Chinggis Khan rewarded the states and tribes that willingly submitted to his rule, but crushed those who put up resistance or dared to betray him.

When he was elected khan in 1206, Chinggis Khan believed that Tenggeri, the sky god of the Mongols, had given him the mission to bring the world under the shamanic umbrella. But he was well aware that his faith alone could not achieve this mission. With political and divine mandate in hand, Chinggis Khan worked on restructuring his now expanded military force in order to lessen tribal loyalties. He organized the warriors into groups of ten, then a hundred, and then a thousand. A total of 10,000 cavalry would be an army, called a *tumen.* Chinggis Khan made commanders at each level responsible for the training and discipline of their warriors. This military organization and governance proved to be extremely potent in the Mongol campaigns.

Chinggis Khan first attacked southward. In 1207 he ordered his troops to attack the Tanguts who

15. Ala-ad-Din Ata-Malik Juvayni, 108–9.

16. Ibid., 52–53.

had established the Xi Xia dynasty (1032–1227) in northern China. The campaigns lasted for several months, but the Mongol army eventually retreated due to a shortage of supplies. The Xi Xia state was located on the trade route between China and Mongolia and was strategically too important to pass up. Chinggis Khan personally led the second invasion in 1209, defeated the Tanguts, and forced them to pay tribute. His next target was the Jurchen, who had established the Jin dynasty (1115–1234) in northern China. The invasion of the Jin started in 1212 and ended in 1216, when the Mongols conquered the Jin's central capital, Zhongdu (today's Beijing). The invasion of the Jurchen was the first time that the Mongol force seemed unstoppable. The Mongol armies destroyed nearly a hundred cities in northern China. The central capital was set afire and burned for more than a month (**Document Three**).

Once the trade route with China was securely under Mongol control, Chinggis Khan began to seek economic benefits in trade to the west. Initially, he sent out merchants and envoys to central Asia, but they were captured and then executed by the Khwarazmian shah, Ala al-Din Muhammad. Enraged, Chinggis Khan led 200,000 troops on a punitive expedition against the shah in 1219. By 1220, Mongol troops had conquered Bukhara, in today's Uzbekistan. Here, for the first time, Chinggis Khan proclaimed himself a world conqueror who had divine sanction. According to Juvayni, the khan ordered the residents of Bukhara assembled and said to them, "O people, know that you have committed great sins, and that the great ones among you have committed these sins. If you ask me what proof I have for these words, I say it is because I am the punishment of God. If you had not committed great sins, God would not have sent a punishment like me upon you."[17]

The brutality and savagery unleashed during this expedition revealed Chinggis's modus operandi: the choice facing his enemies was to surrender and live under Mongol protection and authority or fight and suffer brutalities. Before each expedition, the *Secret History* states that Chinggis always asked for surrender, in which case no one would be harmed. When towns and populations resisted, as did the townspeople of Tirmiz, in today's Uzbekistan near the Afghan border, he ordered his troops to kill the inhabitants and to cut open "the bellies of all the slain" (**Document Four**).

Tales of Mongol brutality traveled quickly throughout central Asia and as a result, many towns immediately offered their surrender when the Mongols arrived. Mongol terror and brutality exceeded the norms of even the thirteenth century. Siege tactics, laying waste to towns and cities, and enslaving and executing populations were common at this time, but the Mongols went beyond these, incorporating a policy of deliberate terror into their military operations. It can be seen as a policy because the killing and brutality were not indiscriminate.

17. Ibid., 104–5.

For example, whenever the Mongols entered a town, they flushed out all residents and assembled them in a public place, separating artisans and engineers from the rest of the population in order to send them to Mongolia. A total of 30,000 Persian, Arabian, and Turkish artisans were said to be spared in this fashion.

By 1221, Chinggis Khan had completely subjugated central Asia and modern Afghanistan. While consolidating his rule in these areas, he sent out troops westward to the Crimea and eventually engaged the Russians in 1223 at the battle of Kalka River, during which the Mongols defeated 80,000 warriors led by Prince Mstitslav of Kiev. By the time Chinggis Khan returned from this expedition, he ruled everything between Kiev and Beijing.

In order to consolidate his authority over this vast territory, he provided lands and official positions of power to his family, relatives, and loyal supporters. Chinggis also allowed those who surrendered to him to be self-governing as long as they paid a tax of 10 percent on all the food, animals, and goods they produced. By the time of his death, the knowledge, technology, expertise, and wealth of the conquered peoples had greatly influenced Mongol society. His successor and son, Ögödei, commissioned the Uyghurs, a sedentary population, to develop a written Mongol script. Foreign envoys arrived to pay tribute, and leaders of various religions were invited to Karakorum. The royal court soon embraced Buddhism and declared it the official Mongol religion.

Chinggis ordered the compilation of the first Mongol legal code, the *Yasa,* which was a codification of ancestral traditions, customs, laws, and ideas of the Mongols. Throughout his lifetime he often added other laws in order to adapt to the new political and social order as the map of the Mongol empire expanded. It later became the legal code for all four khanates. Juvayni wrote:

> In accordance and agreement with his own mind he established a rule for every occasion and a regulation for every circumstance; while for every crime he fixed a penalty. And since the Tartar people had no script of their own, he gave orders that Mongol children should learn writing from the Uighur; and that these *yasas* and ordinances should be written down on rolls. These rolls are called the *Great book of Yasas* and are kept in the treasury of the chief princes. Wherever a khan ascends the throne, or a great army is mobilized, or the princes assemble and begin [to consult together] concerning affairs of state and the administration thereof, they produce these rolls and model their actions thereon; and proceed with the disposition of armies or destruction of provinces and cities in the manner therein prescribed.[18]

On his death in 1227, Chinggis Khan bequeathed the empire to his third son, Ögödei, who would be called the khagan, the khan of khans, or the great khan. His oldest son, Jochi, was granted jurisdiction over parts of present-day Russia, Ukraine, and

18. Ibid., 25.

Kazakhstan, or the Golden Horde; his second son, Chaghadai received the territory of central Asia; and Tolui, his youngest son, inherited Mongolia. Chinggis Khan instructed his sons to unite under the command of Ögödei. Not only had Chinggis created a vast empire, but he had also presided over the transformation of Mongol society from "a rudimentary nomadic tribal system to one that possessed the rudimentary principles of a moderately complex society."[19] Yet vestiges of earlier nomadic ways persisted; one of these was the public power of Mongol imperial women.

Act II

Kingmaking Among Imperial Women

Even though Mongol women did not have much say in choosing their husbands, once married, they nevertheless were considered the key player in the household. And when the husband died, the wife acted in his place and managed the household until the eldest son was in a position to do so. These traditions were codified in the *Yasa*. Chingghis Khan's mother, Hö'elün, as noted by the *Secret History*, successfully raised four capable sons and five daughters and led the household from poverty to power (**Document Five**). In the royal family, senior widows often ruled the empire as regents until the next khan could be elected by a *khuriltai*. The most notable of these were Töregene, who ruled from 1241 to 1246 in the name of her deceased husband Ögödei, and Oghul Khaimish, who ruled for Güyüg from 1249 to 1251.

This tradition, as well as her extraordinary intellect, made it possible for Sorghaghtani Beki to envision a grand future for her children; in implementing her vision, she became one of the best-known kingmakers in world history. Symbolic of this power was her title, beki, derived from the masculine bek, meaning "chieftain." After the death of her husband in 1232, Sorghaghtani became regent over the Mongol homeland that her husband had inherited. She also sought additional lands on her own account. According to Rashid al-Din, in 1236 Sorghaghtani requested from the khagan, Ögödei, two appanages in northwest China. Ögödei hesitated at first, but Sorghaghtani played on his guilt over the death of his brother, weeping and saying, "He [Tolui, her husband] that was my longing and desire, for whom did he sacrifice himself? For whose sake did he die?" Recalling Tolui's sacrifice, Ögödei was ashamed and immediately "begged her pardon and granted her request."[20]

19. Davis-Kimball, 168.

20. Bettine Birge, *Women, Property, and Confucian Reaction in Sung and Yüan China (960–1368)* (Cambridge, UK: Cambridge University Press, 2002), 200–5.

Historians believe that it was this land grant and her control over the Mongol homeland, where 2,000 to 2,500 Mongol noble families roamed with their great herds of animals, that laid the foundation for the future success of the Tolui family and turned the line of succession away from Ögödei to the Toluid line. The lands in northern China, an area called Zhending, had a population of over 8,000 households, largely composed of Chinese farmers. This possession provided the stable economic base for the development of Toluid authority.[21] The principle that Sorghaghtani used to manage and rule her lands was to support the local economy and local production, thus substantially increasing her tax revenues. Her sons followed her lead.

The second step in realizing her ambition was to provide for the education of her four sons. Illiterate herself, she devised a comprehensive and effective instructional program, which was made up of *yasas,* military training, language learning, and knowledge of various religious or cultural traditions, such as Buddhism, Islam, Christianity, and Confucianism. She provided support and protection, as did her sons, to each of the major religions within her lands. She also had her son Khubilai tutored in the Chinese language and traditions by Confucian scholars. Historians surmise that Sorghaghtani even encouraged her sons to marry women outside of Mongol shamanic belief. Both her oldest son, Möngke, and her third son, Hülegü, married Nestorian Christians. Her second son, Khubilai, married Chabui, a pious Buddhist.

Sorghaghtani was the most important force in Möngke's rise to the position of khaghan. Since Tolui died young, the chance that any of his children would reach such a high position was quite slim. Recognizing the seniority of Batu Khan (r. 1227–1255), the eldest son of Jochi, among the grandsons of Chinggis Khan, Sorghaghtani secretly allied with him in his power struggle with Ögödei's widow, Töregene. When the third khaghan, Güyüg, died in 1249, his son, Shirmün, was poised to succeed him. However, in order to legitimize the succession, the Güyüg family had to consult with Batu, who was the most powerful of the khans. At the time, Batu was ill and Sorghaghtani Beki instructed Möngke to pay proper respect to his cousin. She stated, "The others will not go to Batu, and yet he is the senior of them all and is ill. It is for thee to hasten to him as though upon a visit to a sick bed." This act of respect won Batu Khan's support for Möngke and the *kuriltai* elected him great khan. Beginning in 1251, Möngke ruled the greater Mongol Empire until his death in 1259. Afterward, Khubilai succeeded his brother and ruled China from 1260 to 1294. Sorghaghtani's other sons enjoyed similar successes, as noted above.

21. For a study of the life of Sorghaghtani, see Morris Rossabi "Khubilai Khan and the Women in His Family," in *Studia Sino-Mongolica: Festschrift für Herbert Franke,* ed. Wolfgang Bauer. (Wiesbaden, GER: Steiner, 1979), 153–180.

FINALE

After Khubilai became the fifth great khan, he concentrated his energies on ruling China and the rest of the Mongol Empire was divided into the four smaller empires: the Yüan dynasty of China (1279–1368); the Chaghadai khanate in central Asia, which eventually was reduced to a minor state and survived until the eighteenth century; the Golden Horde in Russia (1227–1480); and the Il-Khans, who ruled Persia from 1256 to 1353.

What is the legacy of Chinggis Khan, Mongol imperial women, and the Mongol conquest? The answers to this question are a matter of debate among students and scholars of world history. Recent studies, while citing the destructive force of the invasions, have examined how Chinggis and his immediate successors allowed those under their rule to conduct their own affairs, to travel trade routes unencumbered and unmolested, to bring the knowledge of the conquered to the Mongol steppes, and to expand the empire.[22] Scholars today who portray a positive image of the Great Khan might find a concurring voice from the thirteenth century. Ala-ad-Din Ata-Malik Juvayni, who recorded the bloodiest slaughters carried out by Chinggis's troops, nevertheless often praised the Great Khan in his *History of the World-Conqueror* (**Document Six**). Comparing him with ancient Egyptian pharaohs, Roman emperors, and Alexander the Great, Juvayni claimed that Chinggis Khan was "above all the kings of the world." He further claimed, "Alexander, who was so addicted to the devising of talismans and the solving of enigmas, had he lived in the age of Genghis Khan, would have been his pupil in craft and cunning, and of all the talismans for the taking of strongholds he would have found none better than blindly to follow in his footsteps."[23] Other contemporaries admired Mongol courage, discipline, loyalty, and strict adherence to tribal customs and laws.

Nevertheless, the enormous destruction and human suffering that accompanied the Mongol conquest is indisputable. After the Mongol invasion of China, for example, numerous cities were reduced to rubble; farmland was transformed back into steppe. The Chinese population plunged from about 120 million in 1215 to 58.8 million in 1290. As we shall see in the next chapter, the Mongol conquest of Mesopotamia resulted in the complete destruction of the center of Islamic civilization, Baghdad; the massacre of 800,000 of its city dwellers; the ruination of its extensive and sophisticated irrigation system; and the sack of its cultural and religious monuments and treasures. In time, much of what the Mongols destroyed was rebuilt. For example, in his remarks about the China of Khubilai Khan, Marco Polo noted the opulence and beauty of the palace in Beijing.

22. Jack Weatherford, *Genghis Khan and the Making of the Modern World* (New York: Crown, 2004).

23. Ala-ad-Din Ata-Malik Juvayni, 23.

Sorghaghtani Beki's legacy rested on her ability to build alliances, collaborate with powerful khans, and establish the house of her son Tolui as the line of succession for the Mongols. She was able to do so because of the status and authority that women possessed in this nomadic society and the powerful positions attained by other imperial women. Mongol imperial women's power rested on their acquisition of land and property and its management; loyalty to their clan and family line; and roles as wives, widows, or mothers of kings. As we have seen throughout this volume, the acquisition of power by imperial women is often based on these qualities and characteristics, and their contemporaries or later historians often portray these avenues as deceitful and devious, not as direct and admirable as conquest and warfare, the preserve of kings and emperors.[24]

24. Nelson, intro, 1–17.

Documents

DOCUMENT ONE

Author Unknown

The Secret History of the Mongols (Mid-thirteenth century)

The Secret History of the Mongols *was written several decades after Chinggis's death and most likely at the court of his son, Ödögei. This is the Mongols' version of their development, customs, and world conquests. Most of what is known about Chinggis Khan's life is from this history. Is there a foreshadowing of Temüjin's greatness? What is the importance of prophecy in establishing political legitimacy?*[1]

When Temüjin was nine years old, Yisügei Ba'atur set out to go to the Olqunu'ut people, relatives of Mother Höelün, taking Temüjin with him and saying, "I shall ask his maternal uncles for a girl in marriage for him." On the way, between Mount Čekčer and Mount Čiqurqu, he met Dei Sečen of the Onggirat.

Dei Sečen said, "Quda Yisügei, in whose direction are you going, coming this way?" Yisügei Ba'atur said, "I have come here on my way to the Olqunu'ut people, the maternal uncles of this my son, to ask for a girl in marriage for him." Dei Sečen said, "This son of yours is a boy

1. In this document, Yisügei Ba'atur is Yesügei, Chinggis Khan's father. Höelün is Hö'elün, Chinngis Khan's mother.

Who has fire in his eyes
Who has light in his face.

"Quda Yisügei, I had a dream last night, I did. A white gerfalcon clasping both sun and moon in its claws flew to me and perched on my hand. I told the people about this dream of mine, saying 'Before, when I looked, I could only see the sun and moon from afar; now this gerfalcon has brought them to me and has perched on my hand. He has alighted, all white. Just what sort of good thing does this show?' I had my dream, quda Yisügei, just as you were coming here bringing your son. I had a dream of good omen. What kind of dream is it? The august spirit of you, Kiyat people, has come in my dream and has announced your visit.

"With us, the Onggirat people, from old days,
To have the good looks of our granddaughters
And the beauty of our daughter is enough:
We do not strive for dominion.
For those of you who have become Khan,
We have our daughters with beautiful cheeks
Ride on a large cart to which we harness
A black male camel.
We trot them off to the Khan,
And *sent* them by him on the qatun's seat.
We do not strive for dominion, nor for people.
We lift our good-looking daughters,
We have them ride on a carriage with front seat;
We harness a dark camel,
We lead them off to the Khan,
And *sent* them on the throne, at his side.

From old days, the Onggirat people

Have the qatuns as shields,
Have their daughters as intercessors.
We live thanks to the good looks
Of our granddaughters
And the beauty of our daughters.
With our boys, when they seek a bride,
One looks at the wealth of our camp;
With our girls, when they are sought a brides,
One considers only their beauty.

Quda Yisügei, let us go to my tent. My daughter is still small, take a look at her, quda!" So said Dei Sečen, and having led him to his tent he made him dismount.

When Yisügei saw his daughter, he saw a girl
Who had light in her face,
Who had fire in her eyes.

He was pleased with her. She was ten years old, one year older than Temüjin, and her name was Börte. Yisügei spent the night there, and the following morning, when he requested his daughter for Temüjin, Dei Sečen said, "If I gave her away after much asking on your part, you would respect me; if I gave her away without much asking, you would despise me. But the fate of a girl is not to grow old in the family in which she was born. I will give you my daughter, and you, for your part, leave your son here as my son-in-law." So they both agreed and Yisügei Ba'atur said, "I will leave my son as your son-in-law, but my son is afraid of dogs. Quda, don't let him be frightened by dogs!" Then he gave him his spare horse as a pledge and went off, leaving Temüjin as his son-in-law.

DOCUMENT TWO

Rashid al-Din (1247–1318)

"History of Tolui's Wife, Sorghaghtani" *The Successors of Chinggis Khan* (ca. 1307)

Rashid al-Din was a man of multiple talents and faiths. He was born into a Jewish family and converted to Islam around the age of 30. He most likely served as a doctor, adviser, and historian at the Il-Khanate court in Persia. His history was commissioned by the Il-Khan, Mahmud Ghazan (r. 1295–1304), and details the early history not only of the Mongols but also the Il-Khanate in Persia. Not all portions survive.

After the death of Tolui Khan, his sons together with their mother were in attendance on Ögödei. He greatly honored and respected them and used to grant their petitions immediately. One day Sorghaghtani Beki asked Khan for one of the *ortoghs*. He made difficulties about it, and Sorghaghtani Beki wept and said: "He that was my longing and desire, for whom did he sacrifice himself? For whose sake did he die?" When these words reached Khan's ear he said, "Sorghaghtani Beki is right." And he begged her pardon and granted her request. She was extremely intelligent and able and towered above all the women in the world, possessing in the fullest measure the qualities of steadfastness, virtue, modesty, and chastity. Thanks to her ability, when her sons were left by their father, some of them still children, she went to great pains in their education, teaching them various accomplishments and good manners and never allowing the slightest sign of strife to appear amongst them. She caused their wives also to have love in their hearts for one another, and by her prudence and counsel [she] cherished and protected her sons, their children and grandchildren, and the great emirs and troops that had been left by Chinggis Khan and Tolui Khan and were not attached to them. And perceiving her to be extremely intelligent and able, they never swerved a hair's breadth from her command. And just as, when Chinggis Khan was left an orphan by his father, his mother, Hö'elün Eke, trained him and all the army, sometimes even going into battle herself and equipping and maintaining them until Chinggis Khan became independent and absolute, and attained to the degree of world-sovereignty, and accomplished great things thanks to his mother's endeavors, so too Sorghaghtani Beki followed the same path in the training of her children. It is said, however, that in one respect she was more long-suffering than the mother of Chinggis Khan and won the palm from her for constancy. After a time Chinggis Khan gathered from a cryptic remark of his mother that she wanted a husband and he gave her in marriage to Menglik Echige. [In the same way] Ögödei Khan sent for Sorghaghtani Beki to give her in marriage to his son Güyük and sent _____[1] as his ambassador in this affair. When he had delivered Khan's *yarlïgh,* she answered: "How is it possible to alter the terms of the *yarlïgh?* And yet my thought is only to bring up these children until they reach the stage of manhood and independence, and to try to make them well mannered and not liable to go apart and hate each other so that, perhaps, some great thing may come of their unity." Since she had no mind for Güyük Khan and had rejected that proposal by this excuse, no doubt was left that she did not wish to marry. On this account she was considered superior to Hö'elün Eke, the mother of Chinggis Khan.

. . .There is no doubt that it was through her intelligence and ability that she raised the station of her sons above that of their cousins and caused them to attain to the rank of *Khans* and emperors. The main reason that her sons became *Khans* was as follows. When Ögödei Khan died, Töregene Khatun did not allow Shiremün, who by virtue of his will was heir-apparent, to become *Khan,* but ruled for a while herself. When she set up her eldest son Güyük Khan as Emperor, Batu, who was the senior of them all, did not attend on the excuse that he was suffering from gout. Güyük Khan was offended at this and in his heart was meditating an act of treachery against Batu. On the pretext that the climate of Emil was good for his sickness, he set out in that direction. Sorghaghtani Beki, learning of his intention, secretly sent a message and warned Batu. Shortly afterward Güyük died, and the sons and kinsmen of Ögödei Khan wished to set up Shirmün as Khan, but first they sent to summon Batu. He said: "I am suffering from gout. It would be better for them to come to me." Töregene Khatun and the family of Ögödei Khan objected to this suggestion saying: "Chinggis Khan's capital is here: why should we go thither?" Now Batu was old and

1. Blank in all the manuscripts. Ed.

honored and the eldest of all the princes; and his was the right to nominate a new ruler. Sorghaghtani Beki said to her eldest son Möngke Khan: "The others will not go to Batu, and yet he is the senior of them all and is ill. It is for thee to hasten to him as though upon a visit to a sick bed." In obedience to his mother's command he proceeded thither and Batu, in gratitude for his gesture and in consideration of previous obligations, swore allegiance to him and set him up as Khan. Now as has already been mentioned, Sorghaghtani Beki, because of her ability, had not begrudged Köten and Süldüs troops, and he was in consequence on terms of friendship with them. When, therefore, the descendants of Ögödei Khan disputed the Khanate with Möngke Khan and meditated guile and treachery against him, Köten was in alliance with him and rendered him assistance. And when Köten died, Möngke Khan settled the troops that he had with him and the Tangqut country upon his sons, whom he always treated with respect and honor. The same arrangement continues till the present day, and these troops now belong to Öljeitü Khan.[2] These matters will be recounted in detail in the history of Möngke Khan, if God Almighty so wills.

Praise be to God, the Lord of the Worlds, and blessings and peace upon our Master Muhammad and all his holy family.

2. That is, Temür Öljeitü (1294–1307), the grandson and successor of Qubilai. Ed.

DOCUMENT THREE

Author Unknown

Chinggis Khan's Campaigns against the Tangut Xi Xia in 1211 and 1226
The Secret History of the Mongols
(Mid-thirteenth century)

Traditional evaluations of Mongol rule in China emphasize its destructive nature, yet the passages below emphasize Chinggis Khan's goodwill as well as his understanding of offense and betrayal. What type of homage do the Tanguts pay to Chinggis in 1211, and why doesn't Chinggis accept the gifts of Burqan in 1226? How does the author (unknown) justify Mongol violence against Burqan and the Tangut?

[The 1211 Campaign]

In the course of that military campaign (against the Jurchens), Chinggis Khan set out toward the Qašin people. When, moving in their direction, he reached their country, Burqan Khan of the Qašin people said, "I shall submit and, becoming your right wing, I shall serve you." And he offered his daughter, called Čaqa, to Chinggis Khan.

Further, Burqan Khan said, "Hearing of Chinggis Khan's fame we were in awe of you. Now your august person had arrived, you have come to us, and we are indeed awed by your majesty. Being awed, we the Tangut people have said, 'We shall become your right wing and we shall serve you.' When we served you, know that

We are the ones who live in permanent camps,
We are the ones who have towns with pounded-earth walls.

And so, when we become your companions,

In waging a swift campaign,
In fighting a deadly combat,
We shall not be able to hasten into a swift campaign,
We shall not be able to fight a deadly combat.

But if Chinggis Khan shows favor to us, we the Tangut people,

We shall bring forth many camels,
Reared in the shelter of the tall feather-grass:
We shall turn them into government property
And we shall give them to you.
We shall weave woolen material and make satin,
And we shall give them to you.
Training falcons to fly loose at game,
We shall gather them

And all the best ones we shall send to you." Thus he petitioned Chinggis Khan. And having spoken, he kept to his word. He levied camels from his Tangut people and, bringing so many that it was impossible to drive any more of them, he gave them to Chinggis Khan.

The 1226 Campaign

Chinggis Khan moved away from Časutu Mountain and set up camp at the city of Uraqai. After setting out from Dörmegei, Burqan came to pay homage to Chinggis Khan.

Burqan then paid homage, golden images of Buddha; then golden and silver bowls and vessels, nine of each kind; boys and girls, nine of each; geldings and camels, nine of each; and all sorts of other objects arranged in nines according to their color and form. Chinggis Khan kept the door closed and made Burqan pay homage outside the tent.

On that occasion, when Burqan paid homage, Chinggis Khan felt revulsion within his heart. On the third day, Chinggis Khan issued an order giving Iluqu BurKhan the name Šidurqu (Upright). Being *thus* visited by Iluqu BurKhan Šidurqu, Chinggis Khan then ordered that Iluqu be put to death and that Tolun Čerbi seize and execute him with his own hands.

Afterwards, when Tolun Čerbi reported that he had seized Iluqu and killed him, Chinggis Khan ordered as follows: "When I approached the Tangut people to call Iluqu BurKhan to account for his words, and on the way hunted the wild asses of Arbuqa, my body being in pain, it was indeed Tolun who, concerned about my life, spoke words of advice and said, "Let it heal!" We came here on account of the poisonous words of an enemy and with Our strength increased by Eternal Heaven, who gave him into Our hands, we took Our revenge. Tolun shall take for himself this movable palace brought by Iluqu, together with the bowls and vessels." So he ordered.

After he had plundered the Tangut people, and making Iluqu Burqan change his name to Šidurqu, had done away with him, and after having exterminated the Tangut people's mothers and fathers down to the offspring of their offspring, maiming and taming, Chinggis Khan gave the following order: "While I take my meals you must talk about the killing and destruction of the Tangut and say, "Maimed and tamed, they are no more."

DOCUMENT FOUR

Ala-ad-Din Ata-Malik Juvayni

The Siege of Samarkand
The History of the World-Conqueror (1259)

Ala-ad-Din Ata-Malik Juvayni (1226–1283) was a Persian historian who recorded the Mongol invasions and their impact on central Asia. This history is based on eyewitness accounts of the Mongol conquests along the Silk Road in central Asia and the sieges and capture of its cities such as Bukhara and Samarkand. Modern historians have noted how he exaggerates at times and overdramatizes the siege of the cities. Pick out examples of this dramatization and explain why Juvayni uses this literary device.

When Samarkand had been taken and he had dispatched his sons Chaghadai and Ögödei against Khorazm, he passed the spring of that year beside Samarkand and proceeded from thence to the meadows of Nakhshab.

When the summer had come to an end and the horses were fattened and the soldiers rested, he set out for Tirmiz. Upon arriving there he sent forward messengers to call upon the people to surrender and submit, and to destroy the fortress and citadel. But the inhabitants, encouraged by the strength of the fortress, half of whose walls were raised up in the middle of the Oxus, and rendered proud by the multitude of their troops, gear and equipment, would not accept submission but sallied forth to do battle. Mangonels were set up on either side, and they rested neither day nor night from strife and warfare until upon the eleventh day the Mongols took the place by storm. All the people, both men and women, were driven out on to the plain and divided proportionately among the soldiers in accordance with their usual custom; then they were all slain, none being spared.

When the Mongols had finished the slaughter they caught sight of a woman who said to them: "Spare my life and I will give you a great pearl which I have." But when they sought the pearl she said: "I have swallowed it." Whereupon they ripped open her belly and found several pearls. On this account Chinggis Khan commanded that they should rip open the bellies of all the slain.

When they had done with looting and slaying he departed to the region of Kangurt and Shuman, where he passed the winter. That region also he purged with slaying, and attacking, and sapping, and burning; and sent armies into the whole of Badakhshan and all that country, and conquered and subjugated the peoples, some by kindness, but most by severity; so that in all that region there was left no trace of his opponents. And when the season of winter drew to a close he made ready to cross the river.

All this occurred in the year 617/1220–1221.

DOCUMENT FIVE

Author Unknown

Hö'elün, *The Secret History of the Mongols* (Mid-thirteenth century)

The Secret History of the Mongols *sets out many examples of women's influence and courage. In the history, Chinggis often relates how his mother contributed to his and his clan's success. What are Hö'elün's qualities? Are these unique qualities for Mongol women? There is evidence that the Chinese translators of this work tried to downplay the influence of women. Why?*

Lady Hö'elün was born
A clever woman
And she nourished her small sons thus:
Pulling firmly her tall hat
Over her head,
Tying tightly her belt
To shorten her skirt,
Along the Onan River,
Running up and down,
She gathered crab apples and bird cherries,
Day and night she fed
Their hungry gullets.
Born brave, the noble mother
Nourished her sons who were favored
With heaven's good fortune.
With a pointed stick from a spruce
She dug for roots of the great burnet,
And for those of the silverweed,
And so she provided them with food.
The sons who were fed on wild garlic
And on wild onion by the noble mother,
In time became rulers;
The sons who were fed on wild lily bulbs
By the high-minded, noble mother
Became lawful and wise.
The hungry, nagging sons
Who were fed on wild leek
And on wild onion by the beautiful lady,
Became handsome and good
And grew up into fine men
Truly valiant and bold.
Saying to each other,
"Let us feed our mother!"
They set on the bank of Mother Onan,
They prepared their hooks and fished
Mean and paltry fish;
Bending needle into hook,
They fished for salmon and grayling.
They made seines and dragnets,
And caught fingerlings:
Then, with grateful heart,
They fed their mother.

DOCUMENT SIX

Ala-ad-Din Ata-Malik Juvayni

On Chinggis Khan
History of the World-Conqueror (1259)

In his history, Juvayni, a Persian official, details the atrocities of the Mongols, but he also was in the service of the Mongols and finds qualities to admire. According to Juvayni, how does the Khan treat those who resist? How does Chinggis compare with other world conquerors?

God Almighty in wisdom and intelligence distinguished Chinggis Khan from all his coevals and in alertness of mind and absoluteness of power exalted him above all the kings of the world; so that all that has been recorded touching the practice of the mighty Chosroes of old and all that has been written concerning the customs and usages of the Pharaohs and Caesars was by Chinggis Khan invented from the page of his own mind without the toil of perusing records or the trouble of conforming with tradition; while all that pertains to the method of subjugating countries and relates to the crushing of the power of enemies and the raising of the station of followers was the product of his own understanding and the compilation of his intellect. And indeed, Alexander, who was so addicted to the devising of talismans and the solving of enigmas, had he lived in the age of Chinggis Khan, would have been his pupil in craft and cunning, and of all the talismans for the taking of strongholds he would have found none better than blindly to follow in his footsteps: whereof there can be no clearer proof nor more certain evidence than that having such numerous and powerful foes and such mighty and well-accounted enemies, whereof each was the *faghfur*[1] of the time and the Chosroes of the age, he sallied forth, a single man, with few troops and no accoutrement, and reduced and subjugated the lords of the horizons from the East unto the West; and whoever presumed to oppose and resist him, that man, in enforcement of the *yasas* and ordinances which he imposed, he utterly destroyed, together with all his followers, children, partisans, armies, lands, and territories. There has been transmitted to us a tradition of the traditions of God which say: "*Those are my horsemen; through them shall I avenge me on those that rebelled against me,*" nor is there a shadow of doubt but that these words are a reference to the horsemen of Chinggis Khan and to his people. And so it was that when the world by reason of the variety of its creatures was become a raging sea, and the kings and nobles of every country by reason of the arrogance of pride and the insolence of vainglory had reached the very zenith of "*Vainglory in my tunic, and pride my clock,*" then did God, in accordance with the above-mentioned promise, endow Chinggis-Khan with the strength of

1. The Persian translation of one of the titles of the Emperor of China. Ed.

might and the victory of dominion—"*Verily, the might of the Lord is great indeed,*" and when through pride of wealth, and power, and station the greater part of the cities and countries of the world encountered him with rebellion and hatred and refused to yield allegiance (and especially the countries of Islam, from the frontiers of Turkestan to uttermost Syria), then wherever there was a king, or a ruler, or the governor of a city that offered him resistance, him he annihilated together with his family and followers, kinsmen and strangers; so that where there had been a hundred thousand people there remained, without exaggeration, not a hundred souls alive; as a proof of which statement may be cited the fate of the various cities, whereof mention has been made in the proper place.

Questions

1. What are the characteristics of nomadic society and what are the expected roles for men and women? How did they evolve during the imperial Mongol period?

2. What were the consequences of the Mongol invasions and dominance of Eurasia? Was Chinggis Khan a hero who initiated the first wave of globalization?

3. How did family, clan, and tribal relationships and alliances work in Mongol society? How did they contribute to the success of Chinggis Khan and his descendents? What role did women play in their creation, maintenance, and dissolution?

4. How have historians and chroniclers portrayed the Mongols, their rise, conquest, and creation ofempire?

Suggested Readings

Allsen, Thomas. *Mongol Imperialism: The Politic of the Grand Khan Möngke in China, Russia, and the Islamic Lands, 1251–1259*. Berkeley: University of California Press, 1987. Carboni, Stefano, and Linda Komaroff, eds. *The Legacy of Genghis Khan: Courtly Art and Culture in Western Asia, 1256–1353*. New York: Metropolitan Museum of Art/New Haven, CT: Yale University Press, 2002.

Ratchnevsky, Paul. *Chinggis Khan: His Life and Legacy*. Trans, and ed. Thomas Nivison Haining. Oxford, UK: Blackwell, 1991.

Rossabi, Morris. "Khubilai Khan and the Women in His Family." In *Studia Sino-Mongolica: Festschrift für Herbert Franke*, ed. Wolfgang Bauer. Wiesbaden, GER: Steiner, 1979, 153–80.

Rossabi, Morris. *Khubilai Khan: His Life and Times*. Berkeley: University of California Press, 1987.

Weatherford, Jack. Genghis *Khan and the Making of the Modern World*. New York: Crown, 2004.

Source Materials

"The Legacy of Genghis Khan" is available at an excellent website of the Metropolitan Museum in New York. http://www.metmuseum.org/toah/hd/khanl/hd_khanl.htm

CHAPTER

13

Egypt and the Foundation of a Slave Dynasty: Shajar al-durr (d. April 28, 1257) and Aybak (d. April 10, 1257)

Setting the Stage

Shajar al-durr, a Turkish slave concubine, and Aybak, a Turkish military slave of high rank, joined forces in a politically inspired marriage in the 1250s so that they could rule Egypt and Syria. Their short political careers are part of a recurring pattern of foreign rule in the medieval Middle East. The pair also exemplifies a very different understanding of slave status than that of agricultural slavery in the Americas.

Political volatility marked the eleventh through thirteenth centuries in the Islamic world, and this volatility made possible the unusual careers of Shajar al-durr and Aybak.[1] During these three centuries, the rulers of Islam were technically the Sunni Muslim Abbasid caliphs situated in Baghdad.[2] The title *caliph,* from the Arabic *khalifa* meaning "successor to" or "deputy for" the Prophet Muhammad, implied great authority. The Abbasid dynasty had exerted considerable though never complete control over conquered territories for several decades after its establishment in 750 CE. Soon, however, Muslim regional leaders in Persia, Syria, Egypt, Arabia, and finally Asia Minor, fragmented the empire into various kingdoms and principalities, representing a range of cultures and somewhat different understandings of Islam. The class of men educated in Islamic thought, the *ulama,* appropriated much of the religious authority associated earlier with the caliphs. Also, a series of foreigners entered the Middle East, further challenging the unity of the region.

The Abbasid regime still enjoyed prestige but, by the mid–eleventh century, had to share power even in Baghdad with outsiders. These foreigners were Turks of the Seljuk tribal confederation, who had migrated from central Asia and had become Sunni Muslim along the way. They pushed far into the politically fragmented Middle East. Between about 1050 and 1080, different segments of the Seljuk confederation established themselves in Persia, Baghdad, parts of northern Syria, and much of Asia Minor. Though the various Seljuk regimes were not under a central ruler, their collective existence did end the earlier pattern of fragmentation that had occurred in both the Arab and Persian cultural zones of the Middle East.

Seljuk presence in the Middle East marks the beginning of a reorganization based on a common style of rule often referred to as the military patronage state, a tradition with origins in the steppes of central Asia.[3] In such a state, the tribal army *was* the government. Power, wealth and land were distributed through the military ranks. The Seljuks found it necessary to compromise their steppe ideal in order to rule regions accustomed to *civilian* bureaucracy. Many Abbasid administrative institutions, such as public works and tax collection, persisted. No Seljuks or others, however, established effective unity in geographic Syria, leaving it vulnerable to the First Crusade.

At the very end of the eleventh century, European Crusaders appeared on the scene and stayed, off and on, well into the thirteenth. Middle Easterners lumped together all Europeans as Franks (Arabic *al-faranji* or Egyptian Arabic *al-farangi*), just as Europeans often categorized all Muslims as Turks. The first Muslim fighters that the Crusaders encountered in the Middle East were Seljuk Turks in Asia Minor and northern Syria, and the

1. Her name is pronounced "Shajar ad-durr," because the letter *d* is one of several consonants that overpower the *l* in the definite article *al.* In Egypt, the *j* in her name would be pronounced as a hard *g.*

2. Sunni Muslims were in the majority, and they generally accepted the validity of the succession of Islamic rulers since the time of Muhammad. They believed that the successor, or caliph, had no special divine knowledge and only temporal authority.

3. M. G. S. Hodgson, *Venture of Islam,* vol. 2 (Chicago: University of Chicago Press, 1974), 402–10.

Europeans generalized the Turkish ethnicity to all of Islam. Like the Seljuks who had entered the region just before them, the Europeans discovered in greater Syria a society more sophisticated than their own. Unlike the Seljuks who had converted to Islam, these foreigners differed not only in language but also in religion. The focus and symbol of dispute was Jerusalem, which passed back and forth between Muslim and European Christian control.

The last foreigners to arrive during this period were the Mongols, who wreaked havoc in the Middle East between about 1240 and 1260. They then ruled the Iranian cultural zone for nearly a century, combining their own version of military patronage from the central Asian steppe with some of the institutions of their Abbasid and Seljuk predecessors. They rebuilt much of the physical infrastructure that they had earlier destroyed, including irrigation systems and monuments. The Mongols play a role in the Finale of this chapter.

For the purposes of providing a stage for Shajar al-durr and Aybak, a good starting point is the 1160s, nearly a full century earlier than their own careers, with the establishment of the Ayyubid dynasty for whom they both would work. The transitional Ayyubid period illustrates the complexity of political and military alliances and the obstacles to unification of the Middle East against successive crusades. Shajar al-durr's and Aybak's generation would later hold the Ayyubid founder, Salah al-din ibn Ayyub, in high regard as a political and military hero.

Salah al-din, or Saladin, was a mercenary soldier of Kurdish ethnicity and a Sunni Muslim. He set in motion historical processes that would profoundly affect the thirteenth century. As ruler, Saladin used the title *sultan,* roughly translated as "holder of power," a title that did not challenge the religious authority of the Abbasid caliph. Saladin built up a large army of Turkish slave soldiers and used it to combine under one regime both Egypt and geographic Syria. By doing so, he united the two largest regional populations and economies of the Arabic-speaking cultural zone. Shajar al-durr and Aybak would later spend their careers trying to keep Egypt and Syria together.

Following the custom of the Syrian cities Aleppo and Damascus, Saladin ordered a protective wall to be built around Cairo, with various towers. Such a structure was also a highly visible sign of power and wealth. **Document One** describes a hospital that was also connected to the walls, an indication of the state's responsibilities toward the subject population.[4] In keeping with his new status, Saladin enlarged the citadel itself and used it as his primary residence. Later, it would be Shajar al-durr and Aybak's home.

Shajar al-durr and Aybak illustrate the complex and often violent transition from the Ayyubid dynasty to a new, quite different regime in geographic Syria and Egypt. Contemporary sources for the pair are almost all indirect. Sources for late Ayyubid history, including both Middle Eastern

4. K. A. C. Creswell, *The Muslim Architecture of Egypt*, vol. 2, *Ayyubids and Early Bahrite Mamluks A. D. 1171–1326* (New York: Hacker, 1978), chap. 1.

and European accounts of the Crusades, provide a general context but few specific references to the two individuals. One Muslim chronicler of the Crusader period was Ibn Wasil (d. 1298), who does give specific attention to Shajar al-durr and Aybak.

The relationship between Aybak and Shajar al-durr proved to be compelling to later chroniclers who embellished with numerous details, even conversations, in order to convey their particular slant on those turbulent times and also just to tell a good story. One of these chroniclers was the fifteenth-century al-Maqrizi (d. 1442). Modern historians must separate the historical wheat from the embellishment chaff in order to provide as reasonable a narrative as possible.

The Actors

Aybak al-Turkumani and Umm Khalil Shajar al-durr

When Saladin died in 1193, he left his family to continue a dynastic sultanate using the name Ayyub, Saladin's father. The Ayyubid successors continued to use the title *sultan* and also incorporated the word king *(malik)* into their throne names (e.g., al-Malik al-Salih, "the good or righteous king"), hoping it would add luster to their regime. The Arabic word for king, *malik,* suggests not only power but also appropriation, because the root of the word, *m-l-k,* denotes "property," "possessions." Despite the titles, the successors failed to measure up to the founder, Saladin. They lost territory and allowed their slave military commanders to assert their own political agendas. By 1250, slave commanders were acting independently, competing among themselves to see who could replace the Ayyubid regime. Among them was Aybak.

Aybak is a title rather than a personal name. The title is an Arabized version of the Turkish word *atabeg,* which means "a military mentor" or "military surrogate father." It referred to an accomplished officer whose superiors assigned him to train the sons of prominent men. The title suggests competence and prestige. Aybak did have a name, `Izz al-din, "esteem of religion." Later, when he became king, another form of the word *`izz* was incorporated into his royal title: al-Mu'izz, "the esteemed." We can distinguish this Aybak from other *aybaks* by his place of origin, Turkmenistan, then a traditional region of central Asia and currently a state formed after the demise of the Soviet Union. Aybak the Turkumani was a slave, a *mamluk.* The latter Arabic term for his status is a passive participle meaning "owned," from the same root (*m-l-k*) as the word *malik,* "one who owns" or "king."[5] The last Ayyubid ruler, al-Malik al-Salih, had personally selected Aybak for a position of authority in the royal slave army.

The institution of slavery, whether it was military (for Aybak), sexual (as we will see in the case of Shajar al-durr), domestic, or agricultural, was

5. Other common words for slave used in Arabic, Persian, and Turkish: *abd,* as in the name Abd Allah, "the slave of God," and *ghulam,* "slave boy," associated most with the Ottoman slave military system.

entrenched in Middle Eastern (as in most) societies. Slaves had to be procured from outside the Islamic religious fold, since it was illegal to enslave anyone who was already a Muslim or any Christian or Jew who lived within the Islamic state and had protected (*dhimmi*) status. Islam placed a spiritual value on manumission, the freeing of a slave. An owner who set a slave free or who allowed a slave to purchase his or her freedom would receive blessings.

Military application most distinguishes slavery in the context of Islamic history. The first instance was the Abbasid regime's slave army established in the ninth century. Adult Turks from central Asia were initially the preferred outsiders for military slavery because of their strong skills in horsemanship and archery and because they were likely to have been reared in shamanism or Buddhism, rendering them legal for enslavement by Muslims. The Turks were captured in battle or, when warfare diminished, purchased at slave markets. The officers were also Turkish slaves so that military communication would be clear. Once in service to someone like Saladin, the soldiers were totally cut off from their homeland and families. Conversion to Islam was part of their training and assimilation. They were not supposed to marry and produce legitimate offspring, although this sometimes happened. This restriction was meant to prevent new hereditary or family loyalties from competing with loyalty to the army and its rewards of booty, fiefs, and promotion. Avoiding hereditary privilege meant relying on merit for promotion and also dictated that an officer could obtain land only through a state-granted fief, not through inheritance. Starting in the late thirteenth century, it became increasingly common to free slave soldiers when they finished their training. This practice may have brought the blessings of manumission, but it also ensured that any sons of freed soldiers, born within or outside of marriage, would be deemed by law to be free and Muslim, and therefore could not participate in the privileged slave military system. Instead, replenishment for the ranks came with the constant introduction of new, outsider slave conscripts whose advancement still depended on merit rather than birth. Even though the practice of manumitting fully trained soldiers became common, for all practical purposes the system continued to "own" these soldiers and to command their loyalty.

Saladin built up a Turkish slave army, and his dynastic successors, down through al-Malik al-Salih, maintained it. Not only did each king have his own army, but high-ranking officers (*amir*s) with large, lucrative fiefs also purchased their own slave armies. These personal armies could act in concert, under a commander in chief, or independently, each under its own *amir.* When a sultan died and succession became the burning issue, *amir*s who owned large numbers of troops were in an advantageous position to fight their way to the throne.

By this time in the history of the slave military system, that is, the mid–thirteenth century, it was common to purchase young boys at the central Asian slave markets. Unlike captured adult soldiers, these boys had to be trained in the arts of war (some also in bureaucratic skills). This training was a considerable expense beyond the initial purchase price. There was an advantage, however, in the young age of recruits. The ideal age range was eight to twelve years, when the boys were malleable and would likely come to disdain or even forget their homes and backgrounds. The trained recruits would develop undiluted loyalty to their owner and to the slave system. Aybak's background was this very system.

Aybak appears in the chronicles of thirteenth-century events only after his peers selected him to be commander in chief of the *mamluk* armies. The title was *atabeg al-asakir,* literally, "military father of the armies." The lack of information about him previous to this promotion probably means that he was not famous or infamous, not outstanding in any particular way, and not involved in any particularly troublesome faction. For those very reasons, his *mamluk* peers probably thought he was a safe choice for commander in chief at a time of uncertainty. As we will see in Acts I and II, Aybak may have surprised his peers by his tenacious ambition. His future wife, Shajar al-durr, surprised them even more in the same regard.

Shajar al-durr is Arabic for "tree of pearls" or "spray of pearls." The woman with this name was a Turk, a slave, and a concubine to the last Ayyubid king, al-Malik al-Salih, the same king who owned the military services of Aybak. We know next to nothing about her until she appears in the chronicles as a royal concubine. Islam allows concubinage, cohabitation by a female, usually a slave, with a male, usually a man of wealth. Only a man's financial resources limited his use of concubines, and only wealthy men could afford the practice. Being the concubine of a king could mean a comfortable lifestyle and could even involve the brokerage of power, depending on the concubine's intelligence and her relationship with her master. Shajar al-durr was intelligent and was well liked by the king. In her case, status as a slave concubine was not overtly oppressive, though it certainly restricted her choices in life. She could be surrounded by comfort in the living quarters of Cairo's citadel, but that was her only option.

There is an incident early in her relationship with al-Malik al-Salih that suggests genuine affection. While on military campaign, al-Salih and his entourage were taken hostage by one of his rival male relatives. Shajar al-durr was the only woman with him at the time and had to suffer the temporary humiliation with him. Apart from that discomfort, the fact that al-Salih selected her as his only female partner while on campaign probably justifies the assumption that she was his favorite companion.[6]

As a Turk, Shajar al-durr had a linguistic tie with the slave soldiers, rather than with the Kurdish royal family. However, she also had a strong familial bond with al-Malik al-Salih because she had borne one of his sons,

6. R. Stephen Humphreys, *From Saladin to the Mongols: The Ayyubids of Damascus, 1193–1260* (Albany: State University of New York Press, 1977), 260.

Khalil. This son died very young, but even so, much of Shajar's status rested on being Umm Khalil, mother of Khalil. Being the mother of a prince was a way a woman could formally acquire high status. Her career reflects the nuances of her potentially conflicting loyalties. She tried to save the Kurdish Ayyubid succession but also supported Turkish *mamluk* aspirations.

In the story that follows, Shajar al-durr had an opportunity to rule, using the titles *sultana* and later *malika,* the feminine forms of the same titles used by the Ayyubids. First she ruled alone and then together with a *mamluk* king, Aybak. From the few available sources, we can extrapolate different reactions to her elevation to power: some people were simply negative and dismissive; others saw her reign as a temporary, legitimizing segue to either a continuation of Ayyubid kings or to a new regime of *mamluk* commanders. These reactions were somewhat dismissive, but Shajar al-durr was not a pawn in a male chess game. She took significant initiative and made consequential decisions. However, it must be said that there was and is in Islam, as in many other cultures, a fairly common bias against women rulers. Two sayings (*hadiths*) attributed to the Prophet Muhammad are "A people who place women in charge of their affairs will never prosper" and "Men perish if they obey women."[7]

ACT I

BECOMING QUEEN AND KING

Al-Malik al-Salih was the last effective Ayyubid ruler, from 1240 to 1249, and his reign was very difficult. By the time he attained the throne, the Ayyubid regime was splintering and faltering badly. Al-Salih had to fight against male relatives, first to secure Cairo and then to win back from rebels the cities of Damascus and Jerusalem. He and his rivals took turns making temporary alliances with crusader states in the region. His likely successor, a son named Turanshah by a woman other than Shajar al-durr, was a potential threat to his father. Al-Salih controlled this filial threat by sending Turanshah off to govern a principality in distant northern Mesopotamia (**Document Two**). In about 1245, al-Salih developed a serious chronic illness. In 1248, he faced a crusade, this one led by King Louis IX of France. Although he was unable personally to lead the defense, al-Salih had always been diligent about keeping up the numbers of his own *mamluk* army. Each Ayyubid army had a designation, usually a play on the name or title of the owner or some characteristic of the group. This king's *mamluks* had the collective nickname *bahriyya* (or *bahris*), meaning the "river" faction, because their main fortress was located on an island in the Nile.[8] Al-Salih did not live to see his soldiers successfully defend Egypt.

7. Denise A. Spellberg, *Politics, Gender and the Islamic Past: The legacy of `A'isha bint Abi Bakr* (New York: Columbia University Press, 1994), 139–49.

8. *Bahr* means "sea" or "river." The ending *-iyya* makes a noun abstract. This combination does not translate well into English, very roughly, "associated with the river."

When al-Salih died of his illness in November 1249, Crusaders were marching down the Nile delta toward Cairo. The concubine Shajar al-durr took it on herself to keep the death as secret as possible, in order to allow for a smooth succession. Reportedly, she signed the late sultan's name on documents and fooled enough people to buy time. Shajar al-durr and the Bahri inner circle summoned Turanshah from his provincial post, asking him to return and take the throne. The stability that Shajar al-durr provided in this time of crisis allowed the Bahri *mamluks* to focus on their successful defense of Cairo. King Louis was even captured for a time and then ransomed. Although fighting continued in Syria, Cairo was no longer directly threatened.

The Bahriyya had no time to savor the victory. The Ayyubid heir, Turanshah, reached Cairo with his own slave army. Reportedly, he snubbed his father's concubine, ungrateful to her for her stabilizing efforts. He immediately replaced three high-ranking Bahris with his own Turks (**Document Two**). The Bahriyya had been fiercely loyal to al-Salih and somewhat isolated from other *mamluk* groups. With al-Salih gone, they found themselves loyal only to their own best interests.[9] They turned against the son, Turanshah, and had him assassinated. Not only were they concerned for the honor of their late master and his insulted concubine, they were also making certain that Turanshah could not replace more Bahris at the top of the *mamluk* system with his own slave soldiers.

Shajar al-durr's son Khalil was long dead, and now so was Turanshah. Al-Malik al-Salih left no other son who was an obvious candidate. The Bahriyya selected (or perhaps allowed) Shajar al-durr to assume the throne, using the feminine title *sultana* and the honorific Umm Khalil ("mother of Khalil"), reinforcing her link to al-Salih. It is not entirely clear why the Bahris did this. As already noted, women rulers were uncommon and not likely to inspire confidence. The Abbasid caliph in Baghdad, himself under the political thumb of Seljuk Turks, used his remaining authority to denounce the *sultana*. The fifteenth-century historian al-Maqrizi gives these words to the caliph in a letter to the Bahriyya: "Indeed, if a man cannot be found among you, I will endeavor to send one to you."[10]

The likely Bahri motivation for backing Shajar al-durr was her closeness to her late husband, allowing her access to knowledge necessary for continuity. As mother of an Ayyubid son who, had he lived, might have succeeded his father, she had the closest legitimizing connection to the Ayyubids without actually being one of them. She was, after all, a Turk, like the soldiers. Many of them viewed her as an acceptable transitional leader while the leading Bahri commanders positioned themselves politically and militarily to compete for permanent power.

9. Humphreys, 304–5.

10. Ahmad ibn Ali al-Maqrizi, *Kitab al-suluk li ma`rifat duwal al-muluk,* vol. 1, ed. M. Mustafa Ziyada (Cairo, 1957), pt. 2, 368.

The Bahri leaders thought it appropriate to have a male consort for the *sultana,* since a general legal principle in Islam is that every female needs a male guardian. After unsuccessful offers of the male consort position to a prominent Ayyubid and at least one other man, they turned to the commander in chief of the late king's military, a fellow Bahri, Aybak the Turkumani (**Document Three**). With the blessing of the Bahriyya, he resigned as commander in chief, moved into the citadel, and became Esteemed King (*al-Malik al-Mu`izz*) Aybak, with Shajar al-durr the queen (*malika*). She continued to play a central political role. The marriage partly appeased Islamic sensibilities and partly established a strong common front. Almost immediately, the Bahriyya had second thoughts about the potentially powerful pair: the combination of Aybak and Shajar al-durr might not be the *temporary,* transitional solution for which many of the Bahriyya had hoped.

The new political arrangement in Cairo did not please Ayyubid supporters in the Syrian portion of the empire. Geographic Syria had been part of the Ayyubid polity since the time of Saladin, though it had never been fully in line with Egypt. Now, its local leaders were angry about Shajar al-durr's role and the marriage to Aybak. To express their displeasure, they forced out of their armies all the locally stationed Bahri Turks in favor of mercenary Kurds who shared ethnicity with the Ayyubid dynasty. A Kurdish Ayyubid prince, a great grandson of Saladin named al-Nasir Yusuf, became dominant over most of Syria and posed a real military threat to the ad hoc regime in Egypt. Aybak and Shajar al-durr now dropped their indirect link with the royal Ayyubid family; that is, they dropped Shajar al-durr's honorific, Umm Khalil. In Cairo, the government arrested men with known affiliations with the Ayyubid princes. Now the Turkish queen and king could hope that the Turkish *mamluks* still in service in Syria might choose sides on the basis of ethnicity. The continued presence of the Crusaders was a complicating factor in the balance of power. The ensuing skirmishes led to a not-so-decisive victory for Aybak and Shajar al-durr.

Aybak's commander in chief during all this was a man named Faris al-din Aktay, who was also the leader of the Bahriyya. He soon developed political ambitions of his own, and a rift grew between the two men and also between their respective *mamluks.* The story goes that Aktay demanded the installation of an Ayyubid family member on the throne, as a ploy to weaken Aybak's position. The agreed-on selection was curious: a ten-year-old Ayyubid prince who could not possibly rule alone without someone acting as regent. Clearly, Aktay was not willing to hold out for an *effective* Ayyubid succession. To counter any emerging challenge, al-Malik al-Mu`izz Aybak immediately increased the number in his own slave army, the Mu`izziyya, or Mu`izzi *mamluks,* further separating himself from his Bahri origins. Aktay married an Ayyubid princess and demanded that she, as a genuine royal, be allowed to live in the Cairo citadel, where Aybak and Shajar al-durr resided. That, reportedly, was the last straw: Aybak ordered

Aktay's murder, which was accomplished in September 1254. Due to Atkay's death, some Bahri *mamluks* of Cairo were frightened and fled to Syria while others stayed in Egypt to fight another day. The replacement for Atkay as leader of the now scattered Bahriyya was a fellow named Baybars, who for the time being stationed himself safely in Syria, out of Aybak's reach. He will reenter the story shortly.

The Bahris were scattered; Aktay was dead. The chronology of events here is disputed, but sometime close to the assassination of Aktay, Aybak and Shajar al-durr sent the ten-year-old Ayyubid prince off to the Byzantine city of Nicea for his schooling. All these circumstances meant that the new king and queen were as secure in power as they would ever be.

Act II

Jealousy, Intrigue, Murder, and Mayhem

Aybak was still concerned about al-Nasir Yusuf al-Ayyubi, the descendent of Saladin who ruled much of Syria. Aybak needed a strong military partner and so established an alliance with a powerful ruler in northern Mesopotamia, around the city of Mosul. To cement the alliance, Aybak married the Mesopotamian's daughter.

We do not know if Shajar al-durr, like Aybak, saw a potential threat in Syria or what she would have done about it. We do know that she regarded Aybak's new marriage as a problem. Shajar al-durr was probably not upset at the division of Aybak's affections since theirs was a political marriage. She did, however, view the new marriage as an immediate threat to her own position as queen. The father of the new bride had military and political power that trumped her faded, discarded Umm Khalil card. To redress the situation, Shajar al-durr recruited Bahri *mamluks* to kill Aybak in his bath at the citadel on April 10, 1257 (**Document Four**).

Aybak's death sparked struggles among the *mamluk* commanders and created even greater instability than had existed at the time of al-Malik al-Salih Ayyub's death. To make matters more complex, Aybak had a son, Ali, by an earlier marriage who was now fifteen years old. He sought revenge for his father's murder, and several powerful Mu`izzi *mamluks* rallied around him. They gave him a title, al-Malik al-Mansur ("the Victorious King"). From the point of view of the supporters of Ali, Shajar al-durr was clearly now expendable, and her dead body mysteriously appeared outside the citadel wall on April 28. She was buried in the brick mausoleum that she had commissioned early in her reign, when she ruled alone.[11]

In later versions of the *sultana*'s death, details were added to embellish the story. **Document Four** provides a selection of the best-known account, written in the fifteenth century by al-Maqrizi. In this version, Shajar al-durr was first imprisoned briefly in a tower of the citadel and then handed over to Ali's mother, the

11. Creswell, 139.

first wife of Aybak, who ordered her own slave girls to beat Shajar to death with their wooden clogs. This manner of death trivializes Shajar al-durr's political role and perhaps reaffirmed to later audiences the axiom that women really should not be allowed to rule.

The Bahri *mamluk* leader Baybars saw in these mutually contrived murders a potential opportunity to get himself and his men out of Syria and back to Cairo. Factions of Ayyubids still existed in Damascus and Aleppo, and they saw a different opportunity, the possibility of reestablishing their dynasty.

Finale

The potential rivalries among *mamluk* factions and between the *mamluks* collectively and the Ayyubids soon took a backseat to a new threat: the Mongols. Mongol troops had entered geographic Syria in 1248–1249, and over the next decade slowly made their way southward, razing Baghdad in 1258, capturing Aleppo in 1259, and soon after intimidating the inhabitants of Damascus into surrender.[12] The Mongol army's next objective was Egypt.

In November, 1259, a *mamluk* (neither Bahri nor Mu`izzi) named Kutuz set aside fifteen-year-old al-Malik al-Mansur Ali ibn Aybak and took the title sultan for himself, arguing that Ali was not experienced enough to defend Egypt. Kutuz began collecting a defensive army that included *mamluks* and ordinary Egyptian volunteers. By this point, a new regime without reference to the Ayyubids had emerged, that is, Mamluks with a capital *M*.

The Bahri leader Baybars was already strategically located in southern geographic Syria, biding his time before entering Egypt to reassert Bahri dominance. He was the logical commander of an advance guard to defend Mamluk territory. In September 1260, Baybars' Bahri forces were first to meet the Mongol army at a place called Ayn Jalut, near Nazareth. A bit later, the forces of Kutuz arrived and sealed a victory. For the first time in the Middle East, a contingent of Mongol forces was at a disadvantage. The Mongol general, Ket Buqa, was killed, and his surprised soldiers, not used to being on the defensive, fled.

Baybars became an instant hero and was able to translate the military victory into a political coup, arranging the death of Kutuz and taking over as the Mamluk sultan. His victory over a much-feared enemy gave him the legitimacy he needed to claim power. The Ayyubids of Aleppo and Damascus were either dead or disgraced for allowing themselves to fall under Mongol control, and so all of their territories came into the hands of Baybars as well. Egypt and geographic Syria were once again united under one ruler.

If the slave concubine Shajar al-durr had been alive, she might have been

12. As early as 1243, a Mongol general named Bayju Noyan had defeated the Seljuks of Asia Minor and demanded tribute from them. The Mongols did not occupy Asia Minor, but left it as a protectorate. The supply lines were too long and the distance from central Asia too great an obstacle for them to attempt direct rule.

well pleased by this outcome, that is, a new regime stronger than that of the late Ayyubids and under a Turkish Bahri Mamluk sultan. She might have detected an interesting comparison between Baybars and Saladin who had lived nearly a century earlier.

In the last quarter of the twelfth century, Saladin grew to heroic proportions for retaking Jerusalem and uniting Egyptian and Syrian territories. Baybars kept the Bahriyya alive, became a hero at Ayn Jalut, and reunited Egypt and Syria. The big difference was that the Mamluk ruler was *required* first to be a slave. The dynastic, free, Kurdish Ayyubids lost out to a nonhereditary, slave, Turkish regime. The old slave military system with roots in the Abbasid ninth century had finally crystallized into a governing institution that would last until 1517.

Documents

Document One

Ibn Jubayr

The Travels of Ibn Jubayr (Late twelfth century)

Needing a safe and prominent place to live, Saladin decided to enlarge the citadel of Cairo, lengthening its protective walls and enlarging its living spaces. A traveler named Ibn Jubayr, from Muslim Spain, visited Cairo in 1183, twelve years after Saladin had come to power and four years before Saladin retook Jerusalem from the Crusaders (1187–1192). He observed the construction on the citadel and its walls. This description is relevant here because the citadel was the home of Shajar al-durr and Aybak who wanted to maintain Saladin's state and its symbols.

We also observed new construction to the citadel, an impregnable fortress adjoining Cairo which the Sultan [Saladin] plans to take as his residence, extending its walls until it encompasses [the old garrison town of] Misr and [the newer city of] Cairo. The slave laborers on this construction, and those providing all the skilled services and technical preparations, such as sawing marble, cutting huge stones, and digging the trench that follows along the walls, . . . were prisoners [of war] from [East Roman] Asia Minor.

One of the buildings attached directly to the wall was a hospital, illustrating the long-standing tradition of Muslim rulers of taking responsibility for the health of their subject population. This description does not directly connect with the chapter, but does enrich one's understanding of Muslim rule.

Another of the things we saw that reflect honor on the Sultan, was the hospital. . . . It is palatial, notable for its beauty and spaciousness. [Saladin] constructed it so that he might deserve a heavenly reward and acquire merit. He appointed a man of science as the director, giving him a store of drugs and empowering him to use them. . . . In the rooms of this structure are placed beds, fully appointed, for patients. At the disposal of the director are servants whose duty it is, morning and evening, to examine the conditions of the sick, and to bring them the food and medicines appropriate for them.

DOCUMENT TWO

JEAN SIRE DE JOINVILLE

Histoire de Saint Louis (Thirteenth century)

Jean, Lord of Joinville, took part in the Seventh Crusade in the mid–thirteenth century, the Crusade led by King Louis IX, and was among those captured with Louis in Egypt. In this account of Jean's experiences, he indicates some knowledge of political events in Cairo. This selection is about al-Salih Ayyub's son, Turanshah, who made a start replacing Bahri mamluks *with his own slave soldiers. The selection also recounts the Bahri reaction. Despite the detail of this account, Jean de Joinville appears not to have known the unusual aftermath of Turanshah's assassination, Shajar al-durr's taking the throne as sultana. How close in time was the Lord of Joinville to the events he describes here?*

We return to the matter that we spoke of earlier: the sultan who was dead [al-Malik al-Salih Ayyub] had a son [Turanshah] twenty-five years old, wise, perceptive, and malicious; for this reason [the sultan] was concerned that [his son] would dispossess him, [and so the sultan] gave [Turanshah] a kingdom [i.e., a province in northern Mesopotamia] that [al-Salih] had in the East. Now that the sultan was dead, the amirs[1] sent for [Turanshah]. As soon as he arrived in Egypt, [Turanshah] took the gold staffs office from his father's chief steward, his constable, and his magistrate, and gave them to [slave soldiers of his own] who had traveled with him from the East. . . . [The amirs] approached those of the Halequa,[2] who . . . had the duty to protect the person of the sultan, and made a covenant that, upon the [*amirs'*] request, they would slay [the new sultan, Turanshah].

Weeks later, the amirs *made their request after a meal at the citadel to which they had been invited. When the meal was over, the* halqa *tried to kill Turanshah but*

1. *Amir* is a generic Arabic title suggesting both military and political power. In the slave military system, the *mamluks* who had the most lucrative fiefs were *amirs.* In this particular case, the powerful Bahri mamluk *amirs* are meant. Ed.

2. The Arabic word *halqa* means "circle," often of people. In this case, it is the circle of *mamluks* who guard the sultan, or the palace guard. Ed.

only wounded him. He fled and they cornered him in a tower. They launched Greek fire into the tower, forcing the sultan to flee to the Nile to try to escape.

And so they killed him in the river. One of the knights [i.e., one of the *halqa mamluks*] who had the name Faraquataye[3] cut the body open and removed the heart.

3. Faris al-din Atkay, the same man who later served as Aybak's commander in chief. Ed.

DOCUMENT THREE

Jamal al-Din Ibn Wasil

Mufarrij al-Kurrub fi Akhbar Bani Ayyub (Thirteenth century)

Ibn Wasil, who lived in Syria and who died in 1298 CE, was a near contemporary of Aybak and Shajar al-durr. The title of his book translates as Distressing Observations on the History of the Ayyubid Clan. *Ibn Wasil asserts that one of the men offered the job of being Shajar al-durr's king was a eunuch. What might that indicate? Another issue raised here is the significance of the* khutba, *the sermon at Friday congregational worship, being read in the name of the rightful ruler. What symbolism does the* khutba *carry?*

When [Turanshah] was killed the amirs and Bahrites assembled near the Sultan's palace and agreed that the functions of Sultan and ruler (of Egypt) should be assumed by Shajar ad-Durr, mother of Khalil and wife [sic] of al-Malik al-Salih Najm ad-Din Ayyub. The Sultan's decrees were to be issued at her command and in her name, and marked with her royal stamp. They [the Bahri mamluks] had already made [an offer of marriage with Shajar al-durr] to Husam ad-Din Muhammad ibn Abi `Ali, saying: "You were al-Malik al-Salih's most trusted statesman and so are the most worthy of this responsibility." But he declined and suggested that the more suitable man was the eunuch Shihab ad-Din Rashid al-Kabir. It was offered to him, but he too refused. So they agreed on the name of `Izz al-Din Aibek at-Turkumani al-Salihi, and all took the oath of loyalty to him. He came to Cairo, went up to the citadel and announced the news to al-Khalil's mother, the wife of al-Malik al-Salih. From that time she became titular head of the whole state; a royal stamp was issued in her name with the formula "mother of Khalil," and the *khutba* [Friday sermon] was pronounced in her name as Sultana of Cairo and all Egypt. This was an event without precedent throughout the Muslim world: that a woman should hold the effective power and govern a kingdom was indeed known; there was for example the case of Daifa Khatun, daughter of the Sultan al-Malik al-`Adil, who governed Aleppo and its province [as regent] after the death of her son al-Malik al-`Aziz for as long as she lived, but in this case the *khutba* was pronounced in the name of her grandson al-Malik an-Nasir.

After his death, [Turanshah's] body lay abandoned on the river bank and no one dared to approach it until some boatmen passing by on the west bank gave him a burial there.

DOCUMENT FOUR

Ahmad Ibn Ali al-Maqrizi

Kitab al-Suluk li Ma`rifat duwa (First half of the fifteenth century)

Writing in the fifteenth century, al-Maqrizi (d. 1442) was distant from the events he describes but obviously very familiar with previous accounts. Here he describes the assassinations of the king Mu`izz Aybak and the Queen Shajar al-durr, both in 1257 CE, equivalent to 655 in the Islamic hijri *calendar. Proper personal names have replaced many personal pronouns for the sake of clarity, and some parenthetical explanatory information has been provided. Why do you think a soothsayer is part of this account? What motive does al-Maqrizi assign to Shajar al-durr for her proposal to Nasr Yusuf?*

In the year 655, the estrangement between al-Malik al-Mu`izz Aybak and Shajar al-durr increased, and he resolved to kill her. He was informed [by a soothsayer or astrologer] that the cause of his own death would be a woman, and she was Shajar al-durr. Turning against her, he sent a message proposing marriage with the daughter of the ruler of Mosul. Meanwhile, Aybak arrested a number of Bahri *mamluks* [who were loyal to Shajar al-durr] and marched them to the citadel to imprison them. Among these men was Aydikin al-Salihi. When the *mamluks* were gathered under a latticed balcony where Shajar al-durr sat, Aydikin realized that she was there and made a sign to draw her attention. He said in Turkish: "It is the *mamluk* Aydikin, . . . By God, oh Lady, we do not know what offense brought us here, except that when Aybak sent a proposal of marriage with the daughter of the ruler of Mosul, we disapproved on your account. . . . When we reproved him, he turned against us and did to us what you see." Shajar al-durr signaled with a handkerchief, meaning, "I have heard your words." When he and the other Bahris were imprisoned, Aydikin said to them, "If Aybak will confine us, we will kill him." Shajar al-durr sent [a eunuch servant called] Nasr al-Azizi, with a gift, to al-Malik al-Nasir Yusuf [the Ayyubid who ruled much of Syria and who was Mu'izz Aybak's main enemy] and she informed him [via Nasr] that she planned to kill Mu'izz Aybak and to marry him [Nasir Yusuf] and make him king of Egypt. Nasir Yusuf feared treachery and did not reply.

Badr al-din Lulu, ruler of Mosul, sent a message warning Mu`izz Aybak against Shajar al-durr, saying that she conspired with al-Malik al-Nasir Yusuf. . . . Mu`izz Aybak forced her down from the citadel and to the palace of the grand vizir. Shajar al-durr had until then [truly] ruled the kingdom and had not informed Mu`izz Aybak about [her proposal to Nasir Yusuf]. . . . Shajar al-durr [had not disclosed] the treasures left by al-Malik al-Salih [i.e., the last Ayyubid sultan with whom she had had a close relationship]. Mu`izz Aybak stayed a number of days at al-Luq pavilion, until Shajar al-durr sent a message revoking her plot against him [and he believed her]. She arranged for five [assassins] in order that they kill him. . . . This occurred on the third day of the week, the twenty-fourth day of the month Rabi` al-Awwal [April 10]. At dusk, Mu`izz Aybak rode a horse from the hippodrome to the grounds of al-Luq, and went up to the citadel.

He went to the bathhouse after nightfall. [The main assassin, Muhsin] closed the door on him. A strong slave boy was with Muhsin, along with the rest of the [conspiratorial] group. They sought to kill him, some taking hold of his testicles and others choking him. Mu`izz Aybak appealed to Shajar al-durr, and she said, "Spare him." Muhsin rudely answered her, "When we spare him, he will spare neither you nor us." Then they killed him.

That same night, Shajar al-durr sent a finger of Mu`izz Aybak and his signet ring to the highest-ranking *mamluk amir* . . . and sent the message, "Arise as commander." He did not have the courage. Word spread that Mu`izz Aybak had died suddenly in the night, and professional mourners were brought to the citadel. Mu`izz Aybak's *mamluks* were not told the truth [but they suspected that Aybak's death had not been natural]. An *amir* called 'Ilm al-din Sanjar al-Ghatmi—he was at that time strongest of the Bahriyya—stood and he and the *mamluks* with him hurried to the sultan's apartments. They seized the servants and the women of the harem and induced them by force to speak. They determined what had happened. After that, Muhsin [and other named *mamluks*] seized Shajar al-durr, but the Salihiyya [i.e., remaining *mamluks* of the late Ayyubid, al-Malik al-Salih] protected her. She was removed to the Red Tower of the citadel. When the son of Mu`izz Aybak [i.e., Ali] was placed in the sultanate, Shajar al-durr was conveyed to Ali's mother on the day of communal prayer [Friday]. . . . The personal serving girls of Ali's mother beat Shajar al-durr with their wooden clogs to the point that she died the next day [28 April]. They threw her from the citadel wall into a ditch, and on her body there was nothing but knickers and a chemise. She remained in the ditch some days. A few vile men removed the waistband of her knickers. Then, she was buried after some days—the body was swollen and was carried in a basket—to her tomb near the shrine of Nafisi.

Questions

1. What variations in slavery and slave status can you describe that have existed throughout world history?
2. What roles do ethnic identity and language play in this chapter?
3. One of the major primary sources for this chapter is from the fifteenth century (**Document Four**). What questions would you ask about a source that postdates its topic by two centuries?

Suggested Readings

Creswell, K. A. C. *The Muslim Architecture of Egypt.* Vol. 2, *Ayyubids and Early Bahrite Mamluks A. D. 1171–1326.* New York: Hacker, 1978.

Humphreys, R. Stephen. *From Saladin to the Mongols: The Ayyubids of Damascus, 1193–1260.* Albany: State University of New York Press, 1977.

Ibn al-Furat, Muhammad ibn Abd al-Rahim. *Tarikh al-duwal wa al-Muluk,* selected extracts for the years 1244–1277. Trans. and ed. Ursula Lyons, M. C. Lyons, and J. S. C. Riley-Smith under the title *Ayyubids, Mamlukes and Crusaders: Selections from the Tarikh al-Duwal wal-Muluk.* 2 vols. Cambridge, UK: Heffer, 1971.

Mernissi, Fatima. *The Forgotten Queens of Islam.* Trans. Mary Jo Lakeland. Cambridge, UK: Polity, 1993.

CHAPTER

14

Christianity and State in Ethiopia: Emperor Zär'a Ya'qob (1399–1468) and Empress Eleni (?–1522)

Water of Conviction, from Gospels in Ethiopia, 1400. Photograph from The Pierpont Morgan Library, New York/Art Resource, New York.

SETTING THE STAGE

In 1493 the first Portuguese envoy reached the court of the Ethiopian Solomonic king.[1] The envoy confirmed for his king what European travelers had been reporting for centuries: a flourishing civilization and kingdom

1. Ethiopian Christians claim that the Queen of Sheba was an Ethiopian queen named Makeda. Around 1000 BCE, she traveled to the court of Solomon in Jerusalem and then returned to Ethiopia pregnant with Solomon's son, David. David became the first king of Ethiopia, ruling as Menelik I. The *Kebra Nagast* (*Glory of Kings*) details this story. Descendants of David, son of Solomon, are said to have continued to rule until the tenth century CE, when the Zagwe monarchs came to rule over Ethiopia. The Solomonic dynasty was restored in AD 1270.

existed astride one of the most prosperous and long-established trading routes in world history. Knowledge of such a place existed as early as the end of the first millennium BCE, when Egyptian, Greek, Arab, and possibly Indian merchants and their goods traveled between the Mediterranean Sea and the Indian Ocean. Ethiopia and the Horn of Africa were instrumental to these exchanges as caravan trade radiated from Ethiopia's interior to the coast, giving rise to city-states in northern Ethiopia. These trade routes supplied luxury products such as gold, ivory, precious skins, incense, agricultural goods, and slaves, but also provided avenues for the diffusion and exchange of religious and cultural ideas, traditions, and customs.

During the first millennium BCE, Egyptians and migrants from Arabia had mixed with local Kushites, producing an Ethiopian culture. Christian missionaries from Constantinople in the fourth century CE gradually converted the rulers of the northern Ethiopian city of Aksum, and then Christianity spread outward from there. Between the tenth and thirteenth centuries, the trade route along the Red Sea and Ethiopia's proximity to the Arabian Peninsula allowed for the gradual expansion of Islam to the coastal peoples of the Horn of Africa and then into central and southern Ethiopia. And European envoys, merchants, and adventurers, especially the Portuguese in the sixteenth century, traveled along these routes in order to forge alliances with Ethiopia's Christian rulers and to wrest the control of trade away from Muslim merchants.

Beginning in the thirteenth century, political disunity, fragmentation, and encirclement by Muslim sultanates to the east and south confronted Ethiopia's Christian kingdom. Over the next two centuries, successive Christian rulers from the Solomonic dynasty, founded in 1270, fought to establish control over their fragmented lands, expand outward, and campaign against key Muslim states. Slowly the central highlands came under the control of the dynasty. By the beginning of the fifteenth century, the Christian kingdom had greatly increased its trade routes through and influence on the Red Sea region, been able to spread Christianity into the southern highlands, and established a narrow Christian corridor, extending north of Aksum to Damot in the southwest.

The complex religious, political, and economic exchanges and conflicts of the Horn of Africa are embodied in the lives and experiences of the Ethiopian Christian emperor Zär'a Ya'qob (r. 1434–1468) and his wife, Eleni, a Muslim princess from Hadiya in southwestern Ethiopia, who converted to Christianity on her marriage. She was given in marriage to Zär'a Ya'qob, one of the most successful of the Solomonic rulers. Her firsthand knowledge about the internal relations of the eastern sultanates and the internal weakness and strong centrifugal forces which threatened Christian Ethiopia, along with her powerful backers at court, allowed her to influence and shape Ethiopia's political and economic life for three decades as adviser to her sons and grandsons. She played a decisive role in choosing her great-grandson, Lebna Dengel (r. 1506–1540), as emperor and acted as one of his regents. The lives of Zär'a

Ya'qob and Eleni coincided with the monarchy's struggle to maintain authority and stature as its nobility, church leaders, and foreign dignitaries sought to influence Ethiopia's domestic and foreign policies.

Knowledge about Ethiopia's early origins and developments is derived from a number of archeological and literary sources, including inscriptions. These sources establish, describe, and detail the ancient civilization emanating from Ethiopia. Early reference to the lands south of Egypt was found on the carved reliefs of Hatshepsut's funerary temple (see Chapter 2) as well as on other tomb reliefs. These reliefs show that this land, referred to as Punt, produced and traded gold, incense, exotic animals, and skins. Other archeological evidence such as inscriptions indicates a kingdom in northern Ethiopia existing as early as the fifth century BCE. From the first millennium to the sixteenth century CE much of our information is derived from Greek, Muslim, and European travelers. Written accounts about Ethiopia appear at the beginning of the common era when Greek merchants and scholars briefly noted the existence and the power of the city, Aksum, and its kingdom.

Ethiopia's conversion to Christianity in the fourth century brought it into the Byzantine sphere. Christian merchants, monks, and envoys wrote descriptions of the landscape, people, and cities of northern Ethiopia. Nonnosus, a late-sixth-century Byzantine ambassador visiting Aksum, wrote: "a considerable city, as if it were the metropolis of all Ethiopia."[2] As Aksum's power waned in the seventh century, the settlements in the highlands kept their Christian faith and the patriarchs of Alexandria continued to appoint Ethiopia's bishops; accounts of this period are preserved in the *History of the Patriarchs of Alexandria*. In addition, Aksum's proximity to the Arabian Peninsula brought it to the attention of Arab geographers and then, later, Muslim exiles, merchants, and converts. The fourteenth-century Egyptian geographer Makrisi used earlier descriptions to write about the Christian kingdoms of the Upper Nile. Extensive and numerous reports from European envoys, missionaries, and soldiers beginning in the sixteenth century provide much of what we know about the period.[3]

Inscriptions on Ethiopia's famed stone monuments and tombs, remains of Ethiopia's early-built environment, pottery, and coins provide insights about Aksumite Ethiopia. Ethiopian texts emerge during the fifth century as the Bible and other Christian texts were translated into Ge'ez, the classical language of Ethiopia. With the decline of Aksum, the literary outpouring of the previous two centuries appears to cease. Ge'ez literary, historical, ecclesiastical, and legal texts, chronicles, and hagiographies reappear with

2. Stuart Munro-Hay, *Ethiopia, The Unknown Land. A Cultural and Historical Guide* (New York: Tauris, 2001), 61.

3. The early Portuguese envoys called the king of Ethiopia Prester John. The legend of Prester John circulated throughout Europe in the twelfth to seventeenth centuries and told of a Christian king someplace in the East, perhaps India, ruling over a Christian kingdom surrounded by Muslims and pagans. By the fifteenth century, Europeans came to believe that the Ethiopian king was Prester John, thus the title of Father Francisco Alvares' memoir, *The Prester John of the Indies*.

the stabilization of rule in the northern Highlands and the rise of the Solomonic dynasty. The mythical and historical origins of the Solomonids are explained in the *Kebra Nagast* (*Glory of Kings*), written in the fourteenth century. A century later, the *Fetha Nagast* (*Laws of the Kings*) was compiled and remained the foundation for Ethiopian law until 1930. In addition, Emperor Zär'a Ya'qob commissioned a chronicler to document his rule. His son continued the practice.[4]

Difficulties still abound when trying to reconstruct Ethiopia's past and the place of individual men and women in it. Neither of our two individuals produced written sources, and as a result the student of history only knows them through the eyes of foreigners, court chroniclers, and the literate local elites, such as priests and monks, and their official royal correspondence. In addition, the spotlight on two royal Ethiopians inadequately addresses the experiences of the majority of Christian and Muslim men and women in the region. Nonetheless, highlighting the gendered experiences of Eleni and Zär'a Ya'qob provides a study of how Ethiopians adopted specific roles for and ideas about men and women in their society and what happened when their society and culture encountered others.[5]

The Actors

Zär'a Ya'qob and Eleni

In Ethiopia, succession to the throne was not clear. Any male blood relative to the emperor—brothers, sons, uncles, or cousins—could claim the throne, but brothers or sons of the emperor were preferred. As a result of this tradition, struggles for power between Ethiopia's nobility and Christian clergy revolved around who was to be the next emperor. Zär'a Ya'qob, the youngest son of King Dawit (r. 1380–1412), was born in 1399 and was prophesied to be destined for greatness. Zär'a Ya'qob's mother, Igzi-Kibra, feared that if her son were to remain at court, he would eventually become a victim in any succession crisis because of the prediction. So she entrusted her son to a monk, who spirited the youth away. The monk settled in Aksum with the young boy and gave him religious training.[6] The secret seclusion of a potential rival by one of the emperor's wives was not unusual and was an act of politics and an act of love. Mothers of princes, especially those who were underage, often played roles in the succession process and could serve as regents until their sons came of age. However, once an emperor was chosen, rivals were placed in detention or sent to inaccessible regions where they could not challenge the new monarch. Zär'a Ya'qob's older brother, Tewodros (r. 1413–1414),

4. Donald Crummey, *Land and Society in the Christian Ethiopian Kingdom of Ethiopia* (Urbana: University of Illinois Press, 2000), 7.

5. Iris Berger and E. Frances White, *Women in Sub-Saharan Africa: Restoring Women to History* (Bloomington: Indiana University Press, 1999), lxi. As part of a series, *Restoring Women to History*, edited by Cheryl Johnson-Odim and Margaret Strobel, the volume has an excellent thematic overview to the history of women in Africa, Asia, Latin America and the Caribbean, and the Middle East and North Africa.

6. Taddesse Tamrat, *Church and State in Ethiopia, 1270–1527* (Oxford, UK: Oxford University Press, 1972), 220–21.

probably imprisoned him when he became emperor.

Zär'a Ya'qob's brothers were born of a different mother, and they most likely lived at court until they were sent away to be educated. Usually royal sons were sent to one of the royal estates where a trusted official oversaw their training. This training included the arts of warfare and horsemanship and the art of governing. In addition, male royal children were educated and given religious instruction by prominent churchmen or sometimes a prince might be sent to a monastic school. Education for the Ethiopian elite consisted of reading and reciting religious texts written in Ge'ez, Ethiopia's classical language; warfare; and governance. The written word was used almost exclusively for religious matters.[7]

Each of Zär'a Ya'qob's three older brothers ruled briefly, as did their own sons. After twenty-two years and six monarchs, succession crises had severely weakened the Christian kingdom and a new successor had to be chosen. Careful consultation among senior officials at court, both secular and religious, resulted in the release of Zär'a Ya'qob from the royal prison and his accession to the throne.[8] The kingdom that Zär'a Ya'qob inherited was linguistically, religiously, and culturally diverse and was severely weakened by its rapid expansion in the thirteenth and early fourteenth centuries, the instability of governance, a powerful local nobility, warring religious orders, and the threat posed by powerful Islamic principalities on its borders.

Zär'a Ya'qob's first order of business was to secure the kingdom's borders and an outlet to the Red Sea. By the time of his marriage to Eleni, he had defeated the sultan of Adal and rendered that sultanate impotent for the next forty years, consolidated the kingdom's hold over its southern territories, strengthened its border defenses with new military colonies in the northeast, and developed relations with Europe's Christian kingdoms. His attempted rapprochement with Mamluk Egypt failed, as did his campaigns in the north to secure an outlet to the Red sea. Part of his strategy to cement alliances was through marriage. In 1445, Zär'a Ya'qob married Eleni, the daughter of one of his Muslim allies in the south.

Nothing is known of Eleni's life until she appears on the historical stage in 1445, married to King Zär'a Ya'qob. The chronicle of her husband noted that she was the daughter of a Muslim prince who ruled Hadiya, a state in southern Ethiopia. Once a center of Muslim influence and resistance, Hadiya had succumbed to the Solomonids a century earlier and became a tributary state.[9] An important source of gold and slaves, this dynastic marriage most likely strengthened Zär'a Ya'qob's control over this strategic and prosperous southern region and cemented an alliance with its ruler.

Marriages across religious or linguistic divisions were not at all uncommon among the dynasties of Ethiopia. In this fractured and diverse

7. Richard Pankhurst, *A Social History of Ethiopia* (Trenton, NJ: Red Sea, 1992), 5.

8. Tamrat, 221.

9. Mordechai Abir, *Ethiopia and the Red Sea* (London: Cass, 1980), 23.

region, the Solomonids often married more than one wife, breaking with Christian monogamy in order to resolve or minimize conflicts or to restrict the ambitions of a potential rival. The practice of a Christian ruler taking multiple wives and marrying across the Christian-Muslim divide struck Francisco Alvares, chaplain to a Portuguese diplomatic mission in 1520, as remarkable. Later, the Jesuit priest Father Manoel de Almeida, who traveled into the interior of Ethiopia in the early seventeenth century, condemned these practices when discussing emperor Lebna Dengel (r. 1508–1540), whom he noted "had heathen wives."[10] The two priests, a century apart, did not appreciate the political dimensions of these marriages.

Eleni converted to Christianity as commanded by the *Fetha Nagast* (*Law of the Kings*). It stated, "If a Christian marries an unbelieving woman, he must command her to the faith."[11] Once converted, marital relations between her and Zär'a Ya'qob were probably governed by Christian practice and duly codified in the *Fetha Nagast*. Marriage law referenced the writings of Paul of Tarsus regarding marriage and the obligations of husbands and wives and instructed women to be "subject to their husband as to the Lord."[12] Yet, not all was by "the book." Alvares noted that marriage among the Ethiopian elites could be easily dissolved and that spouses recognized that their marriage might be temporary[13] (**Document One**). The dissolution of marriage between elites did not necessarily leave women in a precarious position since it was customary among the elite for husbands and wives to retain their own property, possess their own slaves or servants, and goods. While Alvares and his earlier compatriot, Almeida, remarked on the dissolutions, Almeida noted that this practice was not common among the vast majority of Ethiopians.[14]

Most Ethiopians, as in the other societies mentioned in this volume, lived from what they themselves produced, grazed, traded, or gathered. "Corn of all kinds" and cattle were plentiful, and the productivity and the richness of cultivated land impressed the Europeans as they made their way into the interior of the country. Almeida, during his travels, saw "fine fields of very rich and fertile soil" and Alvares noted ten to twelve miles of fields that "were all cultivated" with "not a span" that was not made use of and were "sown with all sorts of seed" so that "fresh crops" were gathered "all the year round."[15] This abundance at times was plagued by excessive taxation or by locusts and other pandemics. Food preparation, cooking, water carrying, all were duties performed by women. Men tended the herds, constructed their houses, and

10. *Some Records of Ethiopia, 1593–1646, Being Extracts from* The History of High Ethiopia or Abassia *by Manoel de Almeida*, trans. and ed. C. F. Beckingham and G. W. B. Huntingford, quoted in Pankhurst, 26.

11. *The Fetha Nagast: The Law of Kings*, trans. Abba Paulos Tzadua and ed. Peter L. Strauss (Addis Ababa, ETH: Faculty of Law, Haile Selassie I University, 1968), 144.

12. Pankhurst, 68.

13. Ibid., 69.

14. Ibid., 70.

15. Ibid., 7.

made furniture and agriculture tools. While peasants produced most of what they needed, they depended on blacksmiths, potters, and weavers to augment their households.

There has been some debate about whether Eleni was the wife of Zär'a Ya'qob or the wife of his son and successor, Bär'idä-Maryam (r. 1468–1478).[16] In his examination of church and state in Ethiopia, Taddesse Tamrat scoured the royal chronicles of Zär'a Ya'qob and the travel journals of Alvares and concluded that she was in fact the wife of Zär'a Ya'qob and was held in great esteem by her husband and her stepson, Bär'idä-Maryam (**Document Two**). Her stepson permitted Eleni to retain the title of chief wife at his court. Perhaps the fact that she did not bear children and thus did not have a son to promote for succession won her some favor. Later, as Eleni aged, she was often referred to as Queen Mother. What is clear from this debate and the chronicle of Zär'a Ya'qob's reign is the esteem and influence that she wielded at her husband's and her stepson's courts. Her influence and political patronage extended into the reign of her other stepsons and grandsons but peaked when she became the regent (1508–1516) for her great-grandson, Lebna Dengel, who was not yet old enough to rule.

Act I

Imperial Rule and Its Decline

Zär'a Ya'qob, presided over the expansion of the Ethiopian kingdom and imperial authority. In 1445, he defeated the sultanate of Adal and its Muslim allies, who had threatened the Christian state for two centuries. Zär'a Ya'qob then set out to solidify royal control over the highly fragmented kingdom. As the Solomonids presided over the resurgence of the Christian northern highlands and the conquest of the regions to the south, these monarchs brought more and more land into the kingdom, and this land, in theory, was the king's to disperse as he wished. He had the right to recognize a noble family to govern a certain area, and in return, this family provided military service, collected taxes, and yielded to royal dictates. In fact, many of these nobles, far from the king, wielded considerable power, and if a king was weak and ineffectual, royal authority waned.

Zär'a Ya'qob has been called despotic because of his attempts to reassert royal authority. He created uniform religious practices among his subjects by expanding and reorganizing the Ethiopian Church, quashing theological disputes, mediating a truce between two warring monastic houses, and supporting the proselytization of the pagan populations recently incorporated into the kingdom. Politically, he stifled any opposition to his rule. He asserted control over wayward nobles by dismissing them and appointing his own daughters as court officials or as

16. Because she retained this title, later historians concluded that she was the chief wife of Bär'idä-Maryam.

heads of provinces.[17] At the same time, Zär'a Ya'qob created a group of loyal advisers and officials, which acted as a royal cabinet. Soon however, the emperor doubted their loyalty and abolished their positions. These political reforms and the heavy-handed tactics he used to implement them prompted an unsuccessful aristocratic revolt against him[18] (**Document Three**). When news of the revolt reached the Coptic patriarch in Cairo, he sent a letter of excommunication against "all the army, the chiefs and rulers, big and small, men and women. . . [who] desire to crown another."[19] Zär'a Ya'qob's attempts to consolidate royal power and erode the authority of local nobles were not long lasting. The recalcitrance of the local nobles as well as the reemergence of powerful Islamic principalities on Ethiopia's frontiers severely undermined the power of Zär'a Ya'qob's successors, including his great-grandson, Lebna Dengel, and his regent, the Queen Mother Eleni.

Zär'a Ya'qob struggled to bring unity to his kingdom and thought that creating and enforcing uniform religious practices would bind his subjects together and to him. "He sought to employ the symbols and institutions of Christianity as part of an ambitious attempt to forge loyalty in his large and varied empire."[20] To facilitate both ecclesiastical and political reform, he established a permanent capital and court in central Ethiopia and invited church leaders to establish a court church of Saint Mary. There, priests, monks, and scholars copied existing theological tracts, translated stories of Mary's miracles from foreign sources, and wrote down the homilies composed by the emperor in order to be distributed throughout the empire. Zär'a Ya'qob demanded from Ethiopian Christians that they prostrate themselves whenever Jesus's, Mary's, or his name was mentioned. The emperor facilitated Mary's veneration by creating thirty-two Marian feasts and ordered an annual celebration of "Our Lady Mary." The annual ritual was to include a procession with an icon of Mary, the recitation of Marian prayers, and the reading of three stories from the *Miracles of Mary*.

The emperor's allies in these reforms were the monasteries, which greatly increased their economic and political influence due to grants of sizable tracts of land to them. Land was the basis for reward in Ethiopia society, and monasteries used this wealth for political patronage. Their leaders became regular visitors at court, and Zär'a Ya'qob often consulted them about his programs of reform and literary development.[21] Eleni appears to have participated in this revival of the Ethiopian Christian Church and she is said to have written two religious works, one of which was on the purity of Mary.

17. Tamrat, 242.

18. Ibid., 241.

19. Ibid.

20. Steven Kaplan, "Review of *The Mariology of Emperor Zar'a Ya'eqob of Ethiopia: Texts and Translations*, trans. Getatchew Haile (Rome: Pontificium Institutum Studiorum Orientalium, 1992), in *Journal of Religion in Africa* 24, fasc. 3. (August 1994): 289–91.

21. Tamrat, 245.

During his three decades of rule, Zär'a Ya'qob initiated and implemented reforms, which if not entirely successful, undermined the power and authority of the local nobles. His ability to centralize power and banish detractors and challengers rested on a combination of coercion, persuasion, and personal despotic rule. The emperor even took action against his sons and his wives, whom he believed to be plotting against him. Zär'a Ya'qob had several of them beaten and his successor's mother died of such treatment. He planned to punish Bä'idä-Maryam in a similar fashion, but fear of a struggle over succession convinced Zär'a Ya'qob to designate this son as his successor. Bä'idä-Maryam (r. 1469–1478) could not match his father's steeliness, iron will, or despotic tendencies. Fragmentation caused by restive nobles, warring monastic houses, succession crises, and a revived Muslim kingdom of Adal returned.

Act II
Political Instability

Bä'idä-Maryam ruled only nine years as emperor before he died and left his young son, Iskindir (r. 1478–1494), age six, to govern. Over the next fifty years, the average age of princes at the time of their accession to the throne was eleven years old, and regents had to be appointed to help each youth rule. The constant intrigue and jockeying for power within the court to win appointment on the council of regents severely undermined the kingdom's unity, its ability to mediate conflict among elites, and its readiness to meet external threats. Eleni, until her death in 1522, was a key adviser to the young grandsons and great-grandsons of her husband. In 1508, after several years of being out of favor at court, Eleni engineered the accession of her step-great-grandson, Lebna Dengel. With help from influential court officials, she was appointed his regent (**Document Four**). The stage now belonged to her.

Lebna Dengel was the second son of Emperor Na'od (r. 1498–1508), Bär'idä-Maryam's second son. Lebna Dengel ascended the throne as a young boy when his father was killed while on a campaign against one of the southern Muslim kingdoms. In the first decade of the sixteenth century, Ottoman Turkish penetration in the Red Sea area and the growing power of its vassal Muslim states threatened vital trade routes to the sea and his kingdom. In addition, civil war and a resurgent sultanate of Adal threatened the kingdom and monarchical authority, and Eleni had to deal with these realities. In the ensuing decade, Eleni used her many years of experience to craft policy on the basis of the belief that Ethiopia's security and survival rested on devolution of authority to the nobles, compromise with Ethiopia's Muslim neighbors, and cooperation and alliances with the Portuguese and Western Christendom.[22] Compromise with its neighbors was necessary in order to facilitate the caravan trade that moved Ethiopia's wealth from its interior to the Red Sea. Following the

22. Abir, 37.

example of her own marriage to Zär'a Ya'qob, she arranged marriages with the ruling families of Adal and other Muslim sultanates.[23] Despite these compromises and arrangements, the internal weaknesses of the kingdom and lack of leadership from the monarch remained.

At the end of the fifteenth century, increased Portuguese influence in the Indian Ocean corresponded with Ottoman Turkish presence and influence in the Red Sea region. Strategically, it was feared that Christian Ethiopia and Europe might seek stronger ties with each other and challenge Muslim states and their merchants for supremacy in the Red Sea region and beyond. Such fears were exacerbated when a Portuguese armada defeated an Egyptian Mamluk fleet off the coast of India in 1508. This victory established Portuguese dominance in the Indian Ocean trade, and that the Portuguese would seek an alliance with Christian Ethiopia seemed a foregone conclusion.

Ethiopia had long been in contact with Christian Europe. Eleni had witnessed her husband's overtures to Christian Europe, which he saw as offering potential allies against the powerful Mamluk regime in Egypt and its Muslim allies in Red Sea trade. Zär'a Ya'qob had been interested not only in "Christian solidarity against the Muslim powers of the Near East" but also in European military technology and craftsmanship.[24] Depending on who ruled, interest varied in cultivating some type of Christian alliance between Ethiopia and Christian Europe. When the Portuguese began establishing their presence in the Indian Ocean, the Solomonids received them politely at court but did not seek aid from them until relations with their Muslim neighbors had descended into war.

In order to defend the kingdom, Eleni and Lebna Dengel had to rely on the armies of the nobility whose loyalty to the monarch was in question. The monarch's failure to repel border attacks and raids emanating from Adal further undermined aristocratic confidence in the monarchy. Large numbers of military colonists, who had been settled on the border to repel attacks, were killed or taken in slavery. The pressure being asserted by Adal and the understanding that the neighboring Muslim states were receiving assistance from the Ottomans compelled Eleni to seek Portuguese assistance.

In 1508, she sent Matthew, an Armenian, to Portugal with a dispatch proposing that marriage ties be established between the two royal families. In addition, when Matthew arrived at the court of King Emmanual in 1510, he relayed her strategic thinking. The Portugese navy, which had just defeated the Mamluk fleet off the coast of India, could challenge the Ottoman Turks for supremacy of the Red Sea and establish a Portuguese presence in this region with the help of Ethiopia. Eventually Matthew traveled to Rome to meet Pope Leo X and further explain the advantage of an alliance with Ethiopia. Together Matthew, the papacy, and the Portuguese arranged a delegation to travel to Ethiopia in 1515. Difficulties and tragedies beset

23. Ibid.

24. Tamrat, 265.

the delegation and only a few representatives survived the trip. By the time the remnants of the Portuguese and papal delegation arrived in 1520, Empress Eleni had been cloistered in a monastery for five years and her great-grandson, Lebna Dengel, had taken sole possession of the monarchy. The empress died two years later in 1522.

FINALE

When Christian Europe's delegation reached Lebna Dengel's capital in October 1520, they met an emperor flush with successes against Adal's border raiders. A member of the delegation, Francisco Alvares, was impressed with the bearing of the young emperor and wrote, "he is very much a man of breeding, of middling stature; they said that he was twenty-three years of age, and he looks like that, his face is round, the eyes large, the nose high in the middle, and his beard is beginning to grow. In presence and stature he fully looks like the great lord that he is."[25] Lebna Dengel, however, was less than impressed with the European delegation. He had expected that the Portuguese would bring military help. Instead, most of the delegation were priests and artisans.

Over his six-year stay in Ethiopia, Francisco Alvares observed Ethiopian society and wrote an account of his travels. Alvares reported admiration for Lebna Dengel among the court elders, who saw the young emperor as "so strong and valiant in the Christian faith and so resolved to destroy the Mourama [Islam]."[26] This assessment came on the heels of an important victory by Lebna Dengel against one of the kingdom's rebellious and hostile Muslim tribute states. At this point, it was believed that the Muslim threat to Ethiopia was over. When the Portuguese finally left three years later in 1526, they were confident that Lebna Dengel had secured his empire against the Muslim threat. Nonetheless, Lebna Dengel sent a request to the Portuguese crown to send artisans and technical assistance to his kingdom (**Document Five**). Ten years passed before the Portuguese again heard official news from the kingdom. During that decade, neighboring Muslim states had invaded and overrun Christian Ethiopia. By 1540, most of the Christian kingdom, its famed churches and monasteries, and its faithful had succumbed to the sultanate of Adal and its capable and ruthless leader, Ahmad ibn Ibrihim al-Ghazi, better known as Ahmad Gran. Under his authority, towns, villages, and religious sites were sacked and burned and many of their inhabitants converted to Islam. From this time forward, Christians and Muslims jockeyed for power in the Ethiopian highlands.

25. Alvares in Abir, 85.

26. Ibid.

Documents

DOCUMENT ONE

Ethiopians and Europeans
Ethiopian Marriage Customs

The marriage customs of the Ethiopian rulers merited passages in both Father Francisco Alvares's memoir about his travels to Ethiopia in 1520 and in Father Manoel de Almeida's the History of High Ethiopia or Abassia, *published a century later. These customs surprised both priests because the customs did not adhere to Christian principles about marriage. Ethiopian marriage law did however follow Christian teachings as evidenced below in the* Fetha Nagast (Law of Kings). *The* Fetha Nagast, *Ethiopia's legal code, was compiled around 1240 drawing partly from apostolic writings and partly from former legal codes of the Byzantine Empire. What are the specific behaviors required of husbands and wives in the* Fetha Nagast? *According to Alvares and Almeida, how are the Ethiopians deviating from apostolic teachings?*

A. *The Fetha Nagast*

. . . The second subdivision [of part two of family law] deals with the love of husbands for their wives and the obedience wives owe to their husbands.

Paul said in his letter to the Ephesians, 5: "Let women be subject to their husband as to the Lord, because the husband is the head of the wife, and husbands must love their wives as they love their own bodies. Let everyone of you love his wife as himself, and let the wife love and fear her husband." In his first letter, Peter said: "And so also you women be subject to your husbands, so that those who do not obey the word may be won without the word by the good manner of you, O wives, when they consider the purity of your heart and your turning to penance and justice. And you shall adorn yourselves thus: not with ephemeral ornaments or with plaiting of the hair or with rings of gold or with the putting on of fine dresses, but with the ornaments of man which are hidden, the true ornament which is found in a humble heart, an ornament that becomes not old, the ornament that is found in a peaceful mind, an ornament that is in God forever. The ancient holy women who trusted in God were so, and their ornament was to be in subjection to their own husbands. As Sara obeyed Abraham, calling him 'my lord,' so you, her daughters in doing good deeds, be not frightened by anything which causes fear. And you men, likewise dwell with them according to knowledge and purity; keep them as weak vessels and respect them, for they inherit with you the life everlasting."

At the beginning of the Didascalia Peter said: "O men, servants of God, every man among you shall bear the weight of his woman. He must not be haughty, nor deceitful, but shall be merciful and upright, one who hastens to do that which pleases his wife. He shall not adorn himself to make another woman desire him, lest she sin by looking at him." 3. Fear, O woman, your husband, and be respectful towards him; do, next to the Lord, only his pleasure; be vigilant to give him rest and to serve him. A wise woman does every good thing for her husband; she supervises the work of her servants and uses her hands for useful things. Her fingers are strong enough to weave clothing for the poor and to make two dresses, one for herself and the other for her husband. When she walks through the street, she veils her head with her cope; she veils herself with purity to defend herself from the looks of wicked men. She adorns neither her head nor her face, for there is nothing which renders her ugly and makes adornment necessary. Let her droop her head and look at the ground, and let her always remain veiled.

B. Father Francisco Alvares

The Prester John of the Indies

Chapter XXI. Of their marriages and benedictions, and of their contracts, and how they separate from their wives, and the wives from them, and it is not thought strange.

I saw the Abima Marcos, whom they call Pope[1] giving blessings in the church, that is to say, before the main door; the bride and bridegroom were also seated on a *catre*, and the Abima walked round them with incense and cross, and laid his hands on their heads, telling them to observe that which God had commanded in the Gospel; and that they were no longer two separate persons, but two in one flesh; and that so in like manner should their hearts and wills be. There they remained until mass had been said, and he gave them the communion, and bestowed on them the blessing. And this I saw done in the town of Dara, in the Kingdom of Xoa. I saw another performed in the town of Çequete, in the Kingdom of the Barnagais. When they make these marriages they enter into contracts, as for instance: If you leave me or I you, whichever causes the separation shall pay such and such a penalty. And they fix the penalty according to the persons, so much gold or silver, or so many mules, or cloth, or cows, or goats, or so many measures of corn. And if either of them separate, that one immediately seeks a cause of separation for such and such reasons, so that few incur the penalty, and so they separate when they please, both the husbands and the wives. If there are any that observe the marriage rule, they are the priests, who never can separate, and cultivators, who have an affection for their wives because they help them to bring up their [beasts and] sons, and to harrow

1. [*Abima* is a spelling of the word *abuna* (?"His Paternity"), the title of the head of the Church in Ethiopia]. Till 1950 the Abuna was always an Egyptian appointed by the Coptic Patriarch of Alexandria, and until 1936 he was the only bishop of the Ethiopian Church.

and weed their tillage, and at night when they come to their house they find something of a welcome: thus in effect or perforce they are married for the whole of their lives. As I said that they imposed penalties at marriages, the first Barnagais that we knew, whose name was Dori, separated from his wife, and paid her the penalty of a hundred *ouquias* of gold, which were a thousand *cruzados*, and he married another woman. And the wife that he separated from married a noble gentleman who was named Aaron, a brother of the said Barnagais. Both the brothers had sons, known to us, of this woman, and these were, or are, great lords; both are brothers of the mother of the Prester John, whom all of us know. All of us who were there knew Romana Orque, sister of the Prester John who is a noble lady married to a great lord, a noble young gentleman. In our time she separated from this husband and married a man more than forty years of age, who is one of the great lords of the court; the title of this one whom she married is Abuquer, and his father Çabeata. This is the greatest lord there is at Court. Thus I saw and knew many of these separations; I have named these because they are of great persons. . . .

C. Manoel de Almeida

The History of High Ethiopia or Abassia

Chapter 16. The women whom the Abyssinian emperors marry and the ceremonial they observe in receiving and proclaiming them as such.

In the first place one should know that the custom the Emperors of Ethiopia have always followed of having many wives who are held and considered to be legitimate, besides others who had no better title than concubine, is so ancient and inveterate that Menilehec[1] seems to have learnt it from his father Solomon. When they were converted to the faith of Christ our Lord, the people of this country did not abandon many Jewish customs. On the contrary they still keep them today with such obstinacy that it is one of the greatest difficulties that the holy Catholic faith has with them. . . . So it has happened that till this day they know of no Emperor who has abandoned the custom of having many wives. About the Emperor Onag Sagued, who was at first called David, in whose time Francisco Alvrez came to this country, he said he had not many. Either he was misinformed or if at first he did not have many, because he was a young man, he certainly had many afterwards. On the contrary I have sometimes heard from Ras Cellá Christos, brother of the Emperor Seltan Cagued, that he had some heathen wives and that, to please them he had, like his ancestor Solomon, gone so far as to have idols in his palace so that on one side was the church of God and Our Lady the Virgin and on the other the house of the idol.

1. Menilek, the supposed son of Solomon and the Queen of Sheba.

As for the Emperors' marrying daughters of Moorish and heathen Kings and lords after baptising them first, this was so common that even King Jacobo took the daughter of the Moorish King of Hadeâ in order to marry her, and was treating her as his wife already, but he died before he had gone as far as marrying her. Father Pero Paez who then frequented the court is witness of this.

The women they usually married were daughters of vassals, but of noble families, of which there are many in Tigrê and some other kingdoms, though sometimes they paid no attention to noble birth but only to good character and charm, for they say that the King gains nothing from his wife's noble birth while her great fortune in being chosen to be the Emperor's wife is sufficient nobility for her. When one of these ladies had been chosen, she was summoned to court. There she was placed in the house of one of the Emperor's female relatives so that he could inform himself more closely and positively about her good qualities. As soon as he was satisfied about them she and the Emperor used to go to church one Sunday to hear mass and communicate, for which the whole court was in fête. From the church they both came to the palace where the Abbuna[2] used to bless them. . . .

2. *Abuna*, the Metropolitan of Ethiopia, who is ordained by the Coptic Patriarch of Alexandria.

DOCUMENT TWO

The Chronicle of Zär'a Ya'qob (Sixteenth century)

The Chronicle of Zär'a Ya'qob *was written during the reign of Lebna Dengel and describes the reign of Zär'a Ya'qob and his son, Bär'idä-Maryam.*[1] *Written in Ge'ez, the chronicle was translated first into French in the late nineteenth century. How does the chronicler establish the legitimacy and authority of both Lebna Dengel and Queen Eleni?*

[Introduction]

In the name of the Trinity in three persons equal in glory and in majesty, the Father, the Son and the Holy Ghost, I herewith undertake to describe all the deeds of our king the Lord's annointed Zara Yaqob, who was named Quastantinos. May the glorious son of Mary, Jesus Christ, do him justice and admit him to his celestial kingdom, in order that he may enjoy it as much as he has desired and sought it, may he extend doubly His grace to his grandson Lebna Dengel, that he may surpass him in glory and in virtue—like Elisha, the disciple of Elijah, who received in double measure the spirit of his master, when he

1. In this document and the next, Zär'a Ya'qob is spelled Zara Yaqob. Eleni is spelled Iléni.

ascended to Heaven borne by the charges of the Spirit—and that he may prolong his days till heaven and earth disappear.—Amen.

[Description of Queen Eleni]

And as for the *Qägn-Bä'altéhat,* whose name was Iléni, the king loved her exceedingly, for she was accomplished in everything: in front of God, by practicing righteousness and having strong faith, by praying and receiving the Holy Communion; as regards worldly matters she was accomplished in the preparation of food [for the royal table], in her familiarity with books, in her knowledge of the law, and in her understanding of the affairs of state. For these qualities, the king loved our Queen Iléni very much, and he considered her like his own mother.

DOCUMENT THREE

Political and Administrative Reforms
The Chronicle of Zär'a Ya'qob
(Sixteenth century)

The Chronicle of Zär'a Ya'qob *details administrative changes implemented by Zär'a Ya'qob in order to control the provinces and centralize power in his kingdom. He initially appointed his own daughters as heads of the provinces. Why would the king appoint his daughters and what is the outcome? How does the chronicler justify the punishment meted out by Zär'a Ya'qob? Finally, how does Zär'a Ya'qob establish his authority?*

III. On the Organisation of the Administration of Ethiopia

Our King Zara Yaqob conferred on the princesses, his daughters, the government of Ethiopia and, during his reign, there had not been another *Belit Wadad* [highest-ranking military official] except for Amda Sayton, who was demoted soon after his nomination and condemned to exile for his crimes against the King. . . .

The government of Tigre was entrusted to Del Somera, that of Augot to Bahr Mangesha, that of Begander to Sabala Maryam, that of Amhara to Amata Mashili, that of Gedem to Sofya, that of the Shoa to Rom Ganayala, that of Gojam to Asnaf Samera, and Tewoderos was instituted Yojon Sabar Ras. But the *Gad Yestan* [local agent] of these princesses ravaged their provinces, for, at that time, there were no royal delegates, but they themselves were the delegates and Ethiopia was delivered up to pillage. It is at the instigation of these Gad Yestan that Amba Nahad, *shum* [governor] of Salamt, Sagey, shum of Samen and the shum Kantiba revolted. After having abandoned the faith of Christians, they embraced the Jewish religion, killed a great number of the inhabitants of the province of Amhara, and when the King came to do battle with them, they defeated his troops, drove them away and burned down all churches in their districts. This is how the Christians came to be ruined by these Gad Yestan who took away all their goods, pillaged their houses and did not even leave them the Mateb around their necks. Their ravages were not perpetrated solely against people in their part of the country, but extended to all the people of Ethiopia.

IV. How the Princesses and Several Other Persons Were Put to Death and Punished

At that time appeared evil men called Taowqa Berhan and Zara Seyon whose hearts Satan had filled with evil thoughts. They denounced to the King these princesses and other persons who they declared having prostrated themselves with the princesses before Dasak and Dino; they also brought up against them many other accusations known to the King only; the crime of idolatry is the only one which has been revealed to the public. The King punished severely these princes called Tewoderos, Galowdewos, Amde Seyon, Zara Abreham and others whose names I cannot recollect, as well as his daughters Asnaf Somera, Del Samere and others. He then summoned a great assembly, and showing those who composed it the pains and heavy punishment inflicted on his children, he said to them: "See how I have acted with my children; in my zeal for God, I have not spared them for having sinned against Him. Now, say whether you consider this calvary sufficient or if, for the glory of God, we should still increase it." Then all the people present burst into tears and replied: "What punishment could be added to this one, O King our Lord, for they are on the point of death." Some of the royal progeny died at the place of torture and others at their quarters. Besides there was a great number of Ethiopians whose names I do not know, who were put to death or condemned to other pains, for in these accusations brought by Zara Seyon, Taowqa Berhan and Gabre Krestos, these sons of Satan, were comprised judges, governors, monks, poor and rich; but afterwards the accusers were arrested themselves, punished severely for their evil deeds and condemned to imprisonment. . . .

V. How the King Reorganised the Administration of Ethiopia, Which He Had Previously Entrusted to His Daughters

The King named in each province an *Adagsh* [an official directly responsible to the King] to whom he gave, according to the district, the title of *Raq Masre* or of *Hagano*. Similarly he took in hand the administration of the clergy and nothing remained outside his authority. He directed to Dabra Libanos the revenues of Shoa, which had been granted to a Tsahafe Lam and those destined for the maintenance of some Tsewa, which had been granted to Baala Damo, Baala Diho, Jan Shanqa and Badel Dagan. As for other revenues of Ethiopia, he earmarked for himself alone and directed their yield for the maintenance of his table and for his personal needs.

Our King made also the following prescriptions: When you invoke the name of God, all you Christians, say at first: "I prostrate myself before the magnificence of his Kingship," then invoke his name. Likewise, when you will want to invoke the name of our Lady Mary, say: "It is meet to prostrate oneself before her virginity," then invoke it. Finally, when you hear our word or when you appear before us, say, always prostrating youselves: "We prostrate ourselves before the Father, the Son and the Holy Ghost, who gave us as King, Zara Yaqob." After a reign of thirty five years, during which he made all these prescriptions, fixed and strengthened institutions and had written new work, our King Zara Yaqob died in peace at Dabra Berhan. . . .

DOCUMENT FOUR

Father Francisco Alvares

The Prester John of the Indies

In the passage below, Father Alvares describes how Lebna Dengel (David or Dawit) became king and the practice of banishing other brothers and contenders for the throne to the highlands. Is Alvares critical? How have other world societies dealt with succession?

Chapter LX. Of the Size of the Mountain in Which They Put the Sons of the Prester John, and of its Guards, and How His Kingdoms are Inherited

The way they have of shutting up these sons of the Kings. Until this King David Prester John, all had five or six wives, and they had sons by them or by most of them. On the death of the Prester, the eldest born inherited; others say that he who appeared to the Prester the most apt and most prudent, inherited: others say that he inherited who had the most support. . . . So they set up as King this David [Lebna Dengel] who now reigns [who was the first to be born after his father had been made King], and who at that time was a boy of eleven years of age. The Abima [head of Ethiopian Church] Marcos told me that he and Queen Elena made him King, because they had all the great men [and all the treasure] in their hands. Thus it appears to me that besides primogeniture supporters [friendships and treasure] enter into the question. The other sons of Nahu, who were infants, remained with the eldest who had come from the mountain with his father, and they took them all back to the said mountain, and so they do with all the sons of the Prester from the time of that King Abraham until now. They say that this mountain is cold and big, and they also say that it is round on top, and that it takes fifteen days to go round it and it seems to me that may be so, because on this side, where our road lay, we travelled at the foot of it for two days [and then left it]; and so it reaches to the kingdoms of Amara and of Bogrimidi which is on the Nile, and a long way from here. They say that there are on the top of this mountain yet other mountains which are very high and form valleys [and rivers, and innumerable springs and fields which the inhabitants cultivate]: and they say that there is a valley there between two very steep mountains, and that it is by no means possible to get out of it, because it is closed by two [very strong] gates, and that in this valley [,which is very big and has innumerable houses and dwellings,] they place those who are nearest to the King, that is to say, those who are still of his own blood, and who have been there a short time, because they keep them with more care. Those who are sons of sons, and descendants, and already almost forgotten are not so much watched over. Still, this mountain is generally guarded by great guards, and great Captains; and a quarter of the people who always live at the Court are among the guards of this mountain and Captains over it. . . .

DOCUMENT FIVE

Father Francisco Alvares

Letter of Lebna Dengel to King of Portugal
The Prester John of the Indies

In his account of the Portuguese mission to Ethiopia, Father Alvares provides a translation of the letter that Lebna Dengel sent to the King of Portugal in 1526. In this letter, Lebna Dengel discusses the enemies facing each ruler. Who are these enemies? What does Lebna Dengel offer to the Portuguese king and what does Lebna Dengel need from the Portuguese?

. . . 'I, Incense of the Virgin, King of Ethiopia, send you this letter and embassy, the son of Nahu, son of the King of the Hand of Mary, son of the King of the Seed of Jacob, these are those who were born of the house of David and Solomon, who were Kings in Jerusalem. May this reach the King Dom Joam, King of Portugal, Son of the King Dom Manoel. Peace be with you, and the grace of our Lord Jesus Christ be with you for ever. When they gave us news of the power of the King your father, how he broke the power of Mourama,[1] sons of the dirty Mafamede,[2] I gave thanks and praise to the Lord God for the raising

1. Moors.
2. Muhammad.

up and greatness and crown of salvation in the house of Christendom. I also greatly rejoiced when the speech of your embassy reached me, which came to make love and friendship and knowledge between the King and me; so we might tear out and cast forth the evil Moors, Jews, and heathens from his kingdoms and mine. While I was pleased at this, I heard news that the King your father had died. . . . Lord brother, from the beginning of my kingdoms until now no Ambassador had come from the Christian Kings and kingdoms of Portugal; only we heard of the dangers of those who go of their own desire to those parts in pilgrimage to Jerusalem and to Rome, and they scatter through those kingdoms and countries and provinces, and I never had any certain news, only in the lifetime of the King your father, who sent his Captains and lords with many people and priests and deacons, who bring all things necessary for saying mass, and on that account I was very joyful, and ordered them to be received, and I received them with great honour. . . . I send them to you, and those that I sent to your and my father, to give you my embassy; and that which I send to the Pope. Lord King and brother, fulfil the friendship and love which the King your father opened between us, and always send me your embassies, which I much desire as from a brother, and such is reason, since we are Christians, for the Moors, who are dirty and bad, concert together in their sect; and now I do not wish for Ambassadors from the Kings of Egypt, nor from other Kings who used to send them, but only from Your Highness, which I much desire, because the Moorish Kings do not hold me as a friend on account of the faith, but only on account of their trade and merchandise, out of which much profit accrues to them from me, and they take away from my kingdoms much gold, of which they are great friends, and of me little; and their pleasures do not rejoice me, only I trade with them because it was the custom of my predecessors. And if I omit to make war upon them, and to destroy them, it is that they should not destroy the Holy House of Jerusalem, in which is the tomb of Jesus Christ, which God has left in the possession of the dirty Moors; and so they would destroy all the churches which are in the land of Egypt and Syria; and for this reason I omit to destroy them. For which I feel my heart somewhat angry and sad; and from not having near me any Christian King to help me and rejoice my heart. And I, Lord brother, am not pleased with the Kings of Frankland, who, being Christian, are not of one heart, and are always fighting with one another. If I had a Christian King for a neighbour, I would never separate from him for an hour. As to this, I do not know what to say or what to do, since these are things which God ordains. Lord King and brother, always send me your embassy and write to me, because seeing your letters it seems to me that I see your face, for much more love exists between those who are distant than between those that are near, on account of the desires they feel, as is mine, who do not see your treasures and love you well always in my heart. As Our Lord Jesus Christ said in the Gospel: "Where the treasure is, there is thy heart." Such is my heart for you, and you are my treasure; and do you make me your treasure, and join your heart to mine. Lord brother, keep this word, for you know a great deal, and also I dare to say that you know more than your father, and for this which I thus know, I give thanks to God, and leave sadness and take pleasure and say, "Blessed be the learned son of great understanding of the King Dom Manoel, who has sat on the seat of his kingdoms." Look, Lord, and do not weary against the Moors and heathens, for, with the help of the Lord God, you will destroy them; do not say that you have less strength than your father, because it is great and God will help you. I have got men, gold, and provisions like the sands of the sea and the stars of heaven. Both of us together we will destroy all the Mourisma. Neither do I want anything from you except people to set in order and arm our people, and you are a complete man. The King Solomon reigned at twelve years, and had great strength and had more knowledge than his father. I also, when my father Nahu died, was very little, and succeeded to his seat, and God gave me greater strength than my father, and I have got all the people of my kingdoms and provinces under my hand, and I am at rest. For this let us together give thanks to God for such great favour. Lord brother, hear another word now: I want you to send me men, artificers, to make images, and printed books, and swords and arms for all sorts for fighting; and also masons and carpenters, and men who make medicines, and physicians, and surgeons to cure illnesses; also artificers to beat out gold and set it, and goldsmiths and silversmiths, and men who know how to extract gold and silver and also copper from the veins, and men who can make sheet lead and earthenware; and craftsmen of any trades which are necessary in kingdoms, also gunsmiths. Assist me in this which I beg of you, as a brother does to a brother, and may God help you, and save you from evil things. . . . So, Lord, God will receive your sacrifices and prayers, and will help you to go forward against evil adversaries in all times and all days. Peace be with you, and I embrace you with the embraces of holiness, and so I embrace those of your holy council of the kingdom of Portugal, and the Archbishops, and Bishops, and priests, and deacons, men and women. The grace of God, and the blessing of Our Lady, Mother of God, be with you and with all. Amen.'

Questions

1. What type of sources are available for studying the Solomonic dynasty of Ethiopia? How do these sources depict the reign of the Solomonids, their policies, and their encounters with other societies and religions?
2. What are the sources of legitimacy for the Solomonids, and more specifically for Zär'a Ya'qob, Lebna Dengel, and Queen Eleni? How did each justify his or her rule or authority?
3. Describe and explain the types of roles that royal women played in the kingdom of Ethiopia. How and why did they exercise religious or political authority?
4. Describe Christian Ethiopia's relationship with their Muslim neighbors. Did contact with the Portuguese alter Ethiopia's policy toward their neighbors? Why or why not?

Suggested Readings

Almeida, Manoel. *Some Records of Ethiopia, 1593–1646, Being Extracts from The History of High Ethiopia or Abassia by Manoel de Almeida.* Trans. and ed. by C. F. Beckingham and G. W. B. Huntingford.

Alvares, Francisco. *The Prester John of the Indies.* Trans. and ed. C. F. Beckingham and G. W. B. Huntingford. Second Series, no. CXIV. Cambridge, UK: Cambridge University Press (published for the Hakluyt Society), 1961.

Pankhurst, Richard. *A Social History of Ethiopia.* Trenton, NJ: Red Sea, 1992.

Tamrat, Taddesse. *Church and State in Ethiopia,* 1270–1527. Oxford, UK: Oxford University Press, 1972.

Source Materials

The Chronicle of the Emperor Zara Yaqob (1434–1468). Trans. Louis Haber. http://tezeta.org/16/the-chronicle-of-the-emperor-zara-yaqob-1434–1468 (accessed September 26, 2006).

The Fetha Nagast (*The Law of Kings*). Trans. from the Ge'ez by Abba Paulos Tzadua and ed. Peter L. Strauss. Addis Ababa, ETH: Faculty of Law, Haile Selassie I University, 1968.

CHAPTER 15

Hemispheres Collide: The Spanish Conquest and Colonization of Mexico: Hernán Cortés (1485–1547) and Malintzin, or Doña Marina (ca. 1505–ca. 1529)

Setting the Stage

By the start of the sixteenth century, the Mexica, a large ethnic group inhabiting the island capital of the Aztec Empire in central Mexico, were led by King Moctezuma II.[1] Within the first decade of his rule, he received reports of strangers coming from the sea and

1. Moctezuma is the Spanish form of the name, which is frequently used in recent scholarship. Other versions of the name are the perhaps better-known English Montezuma and various alphabetical renderings of the name in the original Mexica language, Nahuatl, such as Moteuccoma or Motecuhzoma. Other Indian names that appear in this chapter might also have multiple spellings.

information of happenings on the eastern coast of what is today Mexico and the nations of Central America. By 1518, Moctezuma sent agents to the coast to investigate these happenings. They returned to the capital and informed their leader that indeed a group of people they could not identify had come ashore. They were "white men, their faces white, their hands white. They have long thick beards and their clothing is of all colors. . . . On their heads they wear round coverings" (**Document One**). Moctezuma certainly had no idea of the existence of a Spanish kingdom across the waters, nor could he have known that these strange white men were a tiny part of what were Europe's maritime explorations, which had become global by the late fifteenth century.

Other Europeans had launched expeditions to the west before Christopher Columbus sailed west to Asia in 1492, but following his explorations in the Caribbean, settlements in Puerto Rico, Cuba, and Hispaniola appeared. By the time Moctezuma ruled, the Spanish had laid claim to large territories in the Western Hemisphere. They did not do so without competition. Other European monarchies were equally interested in the possibilities of trade, land, people, and gold that accompanied the stories of exploration. While the Portuguese had traditionally focused on ventures to Asia along the eastern route, they also became interested in the west, and a diplomatic dispute between Spain and Portugal was resolved in 1494 when the papacy rather arrogantly divided the "uncharted" regions of the world between Portugal and Spain in the Treaty of Tordesillas (**Document Two**). International relations among the powerful dynastic monarchies of Europe are a factor to consider in understanding the history of conquest and colonization. But in order to grasp the full dimensions of this historical experience, it is critical to remember that the establishment of European colonial empires was a slow and uneven process; the political worlds being invaded were complex and sophisticated; and the whole process was one of interaction and exchange in which both European and indigenous actors played a role.

Spain's conquest and settlement of Mexico are ideally suited to illustrate conquest and colonization for a number of reasons. First, the territory of the Mexica was an empire that, like Spain, had been created out of conquest and diplomatic negotiations. It boasted a large population, a complex economy, great wealth, an extensive bureaucracy, and a wide array of tributary states that had varying relations with the capital, Tenochtitlán, which in certain cases worked to the advantage of the European conquerors. Second, while Spain certainly had a mission for its expansion, there was little long-range or strategic planning to guide the process, in part because they did not know what they were facing, and even when orders and guidance were provided, communication between Spain and the "new world" was slow. The result was often plans that were pragmatic, creative, and not always tested, and equally as important, there were frequent contests among the men who emerged or were appointed as leaders of the various expeditions. Finally, moving away from an institutional, top-down view of conquest and colonization requires that we ask different kinds of questions, and to do that, we need sources that describe diverse experiences. For Mexico, such sources are available.

Spanish government sources, from the monarchy down to the town level, are extensive, and an equal array of Spanish church records adds to the richness of the documentation. The law and careful recordings of a very large number of judicial procedures provide invaluable detail on a wide range of personal issues, rights, and behaviors. Additionally, letters and diaries from a heterogeneous Spanish population, including many of the conquistadors and their supporters, provide a different dimension. These records, as well as those of the clergy, do report on the day-to-day lives of indigenous peoples and on interactions between the strangers and the local communities. Obviously there are problems with such sources since they had a bias and purpose. Traditional Nahua sources and those of other peoples in the region are pictorial and oral. "Before the conquest, the Nahuas painted . . . on bark or animal skins or paper made of maguey fiber. They produced foldout books as well as individual maps or sheets of records."[2] Some of these survive, as do similar depictions of the events of the conquest. In addition to the visual record, we also have available a very large collection of documents or manuscripts written in Nahuatl. Most of these were probably produced sometime after the 1540s when a generation of young people were "taught to read and write and to be good Christians" by the Franciscan and Dominican friars who had started to arrive in 1523 and 1524.[3] Thus, young male children, both Spanish and Mexican-born, could learn Nahuatl and Spanish and become important scribes, collectors of narrative accounts, and translators. Few of these accounts are written by women. If women are mentioned in other sources, the focus is usually on elite women; nevertheless, they do provide details of everyday life that include both men's and women's experiences. The existence of such rich records has encouraged scholars to produce complex, detailed, and nuanced histories of the conquest of Mexico.

We are also fortunate to be able to identify and describe the experiences of a Spanish man and an Indian woman who moved together through the early period of conquest and colonization. Hernán Cortés and Malintzin, or Doña Marina (or La Malinche, as she became known later), met in April 1519 and together participated in the

2. Camilla Townsend, *Malintzin's Choices: An Indian Woman in the Conquest of Mexico* (Albuquerque: University of New Mexico Press, 2007), 63. This unique and excellent biography of Malintzin contains good examples of the pictorials, pp. 64–75. Additional information on the Indian sources comes from the authority on the subject, James Lockhart, trans. and ed., *We People Here: Nahuatl Accounts of the Conquest of Mexico* (Berkeley: University of California Press, 1993). Volume 1 contains Nahuatl in European alphabetic form with translations into Spanish and then into English.

3. Susan Schroeder, Stephanie Wood, and Robert Haskett, eds., *Indian Women of Early Mexico* (Norman: University of Oklahoma Press, 1997), 5. Schoeder also points to the gendered dimension of the educational enterprise and thus the viewpoint of the sources produced.

difficult and often violent events of the conquest. We have extensive records about and by Cortés but not one word written by Malintzin. In his letters, Cortés refers to her only once by name, but does acknowledge her important role as translator and negotiator. Both of them are rewarded by subsequent generations with conflicting stereotypes and images. He is described as a hero or a villain; she is a victim or a traitor. We will return to those legacies at the end of this chapter, but first we must consider what we do know about these two people, their lives, and their actions.

The Actors

Hernán Cortés and Malintzin

We do not know the exact date of Malintzin's birth, but references to her age at other times indicate she was probably born around 1505. Her birthplace was in an *altepetl,* a local ethnic state, affiliated with the larger state called Coatzacoalcos that was located on the eastern coast near the southernmost point of the Gulf of Mexico. This region lay between lands held by the Maya and the area dominated by the Aztec Empire centered at Tenochtitlán. Some assume her altepetl may have been a tributary state to the Mexica because later, Malintzin showed good knowledge of quite formal Nahuatl.[4] Some have speculated that her father was a member of the nobility, but we have no idea of her mother's status or if her mother and father were married.

By the time Malintzin was growing up, the Mexica and their predecessors had developed a legal and political system that was complex and involved numerous officials and bureaucrats. They had built dams, causeways, aqueducts, canals, irrigation works, terracing for agriculture, and impressive towns and cities. The staple of Indian life, maize, was highly nutritional, hardy, and resilient and, along with other food products and cotton, was part of an extensive tribute and trading network. The craftspeople and artists of the Mexica and other groups, including the Maya, produced artwork and artifacts of gold, silver, and jewels, intricate mosaics, woodcarvings, and delicate featherwork. The woven cotton cloth produced by women was important for daily life, and weavings were also pieces of art that had ritual significance.

Marriage was expected of all members of society, and normally individuals married people of the same social rank. However, in political marriages arranged to strengthen ties between altepetl or ruling families or perhaps to gain claims to territory, a king's daughter might have been married to someone of a lesser rank. There is no evidence in Malintzin's story that this was the case, so perhaps her mother was a secondary wife to an important man in the community. It was not

4. For biographical information and interpretations of Malintzin's early life, see Townsend, *Malintzin,* 11–25; see also another important source, Frances Karttunen, *Between Worlds: Interpreters, Guides and Survivors* (New Brunswick, NJ: Rutgers University Press, 1994), 1–23.

uncommon for wealthy and powerful men to have more than one wife, and polygyny probably served multiple social functions as women worked collectively and shared many important household tasks and was viable if the wealth of the household could sustain more than one wife and her children. A woman might end up in such a household if she were related to a defeated enemy and thus given up to the victor as a sort of peace offering. Women were also a high proportion of the slaves and were kept as domestic servants. All children, even those of slave women, were born free, but their fate was clearly tied to the status of their mother, and "Nahua women occupied a range of social and political positions and often had to jockey for their place."[5] If the ideal man was a warrior, the woman was the mainstay and protector of hearth and home, and, in fact, both the spindle and the broom, tools used in the household, had symbolic significance as weapons with which a woman fought and protected her home, family, and community.[6]

When the Spanish landed on the eastern coast, the Mexica Empire had reached its limits. Some of the largest altepetls, like Tlaxcala, were never completely subdued, and the empire had not conquered their neighbors to the east, the Maya. At some time in her early youth, Malintzin was either taken by or given to traders who in turn sold her to the Chontal Maya living to the east toward the region of Yucatan. We know little of her life with those people, except that she did learn both Chontal and Yucatec Maya, which later proved beneficial to her and to Cortés. As a slave in that society, she might have been involved in the production of textiles as well as in planting, harvesting, and storing food. It was the Chontal Maya who in April 1519, after defeat by Cortés, gave him twenty young women, one of whom was Malintzin. It is likely that she was used sexually in this period of her life, but since the Maya did not separate mothers from their children if they were given away or sold, we can assume that the adolescent Malintzin was childless when the Spanish arrived.

Tracing the early life of Hernán Cortés, a powerful Spanish conquistador, is a much easier task than trying to identify the events of Malintzin's youth. Cortés was born in Medellín in Extremadura at a time when conflict and contest characterized politics at all levels of life in Iberia. The Spanish monarchs Isabella of Castile (1451–1504) and Ferdinand of Aragon (1452–1516) spent their energies in efforts to unify Spain and carry the banner of the Catholic Church. During the year 1492 they reconquered Granada, the last of the Moorish kingdoms in Iberia, expelled the Jews, and authorized the voyage of Christopher Columbus.

Cortés's father, Martín, was the illegitimate son of a minor noble, or *hidalgo,* who had granted his son a

5. Townsend, p. 21.

6. For a detailed discussion of Indian women's roles and images, see especially Louise Burkhart, "Mexica Women on the Home Front: Housework and Religion in Aztec Mexico," in Schroeder, Wood, and Haskett, 25–34; and Karen Vieira Powers, *Women in the Crucible of Conquest: The Gendered Genesis of Spanish American Society, 1500–1800* (Albuquerque: University of New Mexico Press, 2005), 15–38.

minimum income, thereby ensuring his rank as well. Martín served as a town councilor, and the family had some land but not great wealth. His grandfather on his mother Catalina's side was trained in law and was a notary and magistrate in Medellín. Cortés grew to be an excellent horseman and learned something of artillery. He also spent time in Salamanca, the site of an important university. There he learned Latin and grammar, probably preparing for a law degree that he never finished, much to the disappointment of his family. Apparently he liked to read, but he enjoyed arms and gambling even more and early on expressed a desire to live a life of action. By 1501, he was back in Medellín to decide whether he should go to fight in the Spanish wars in Italy or join an expedition headed for the Indies. He chose the latter, but not until he had done some traveling to several other Spanish cities and gained a more sophisticated sense of the world of wealth and politics at the time. Cortés insisted that he wanted not only to be rich but "to live as a king, to give away presents, to have a title," but later in his life, in 1526, he wrote to his father, "I look on it as better to be rich in fame than in goods."[7]

In the summer of 1506, he sailed for Hispaniola, where he was favored by the governor (probably a distant relative) and worked as a notary. He certainly felt he was destined for greater things, and finally in 1511 he joined Diego de Velázquez in his conquest of Cuba, considered by many to be a particularly brutal episode that apparently had an impact on how Cortés would treat the Indian people in Mexico. Was Cortés the typical Spaniard involved in these adventures? Most of the leaders were of the minor nobility, not wealthy but not workers either; they were often younger sons who needed to find a career, were anxious to become rich and famous and to expand the influence of Christianity. A fairly large number of them were from Extremadura, including 200 of Cortés's 530 volunteers who eventually sailed to Mexico.[8]

In Cuba, Cortés first served as Velázquez's secretary and was awarded an *encomienda,* a grant of land not owned outright by the recipient or necessarily heritable, from which the recipient could extract tribute and labor. In the "new world," this became an increasingly common arrangement that supported the conquerors and exploited new colonies. While in Cuba Cortés had a daughter by a young Indian woman, and then in 1515 married Catalina Suarez who had come with her sisters to serve as ladies in waiting for the governor's wife. Cortés was successful politically and economically. He had a solid religious upbringing and was a sincere Christian, but he also was able to use his beliefs for pragmatic goals.[9]

7. Quoted in Hugh Thomas, *Conquest: Montezuma, Cortés, and the Fall of Old Mexico* (New York: Simon and Schuster, 1993), 128, 129. For Cortés, also see José Luis Martinez, *Hernán Cortés* (Mexico, DF: UNAM, Fondo de Cultura Economica, Mexico, 1990), including a very useful and detailed chronology; and Juan Miralles Ostos, *Hernán Cortés: Inventor de Mexico* (Barcelona: Tusquets Editores, 2001).

8. Thomas, 123.

9. For a discussion of Cortés's religious convictions, see Thomas, 123, 156–57.

In 1517 and 1518 Velázquez sent two expeditions to explore the "islands" to the west. (At that time, the Yucatan Peninsula was thought to be another string of islands.) Those expeditions were the ones that had prompted Moctezuma's investigation mentioned earlier. When the expeditions returned with tales of gold, Cortés decided he should seize the opportunity and lead an expedition, even though at that point he had never held a military command. Although he and Velázquez had begun to part ways by that time, the governor eventually gave him a commission to go to the "islands" and outfitted several ships. Cortés had to finance other vessels and people to accompany him. Velázquez tried to contain Cortés's ambition in this venture by providing specific instructions that included that no one was to "sleep on shore," Cortés should catalog what wealth he saw, and he should try to find out what had happened to the expeditions that preceded him. Velázquez considered this a limited and intermediary venture; Cortés clearly had other plans. He persuaded Pedro de Alvarado, who had been on an earlier expedition, to join him.

Cortés left his home, his wife, and his wealth and eventually left Cuba with eleven ships in February 1519. He had with him 530 Europeans, thirty crossbows, twelve guns, and fourteen pieces of artillery plus some cannon. He also took along sixteen horses and some fighting dogs that proved to be formidable tools of conquest.[10] As historian Hugh Thomas points out, you don't take horses and cannon if your only goal is to carry out an inventory, engage in trade, and acquire information. Cortés certainly had more in mind than trade!

Act I

Contact and Negotiation, 1519

The expedition landed on the island of Cozumel in late February, and there on the eastern coast of the Yucatan they found several Spaniards who had been shipwrecked eight years before. One of them, Gerónimo Aguilar, had learned the Mayan language and so could translate for Cortés. Aguilar also told Cortés what he knew of the indigenous populations and gave detailed accounts of the human sacrifice that constituted parts of their ritual practices. The Maya in the area had seen a number of Spanish excursions land in their area and each time hoped they would not return. By now, they were convinced that they should do battle in order to keep the strangers out. Cortés and his men continued around the coast of the Yucatan area and down the shores of the Gulf, eventually in March 1519 engaging the Maya in a battle at Cintla, not too far from the place where Malintzin was a slave. The battle was a resounding victory for the Spanish, as they suffered no casualties in contrast to fairly significant losses by the Maya. The Maya decided they had no choice but to submit and make peace. As part of the peace offering, they gave Cortés

10. Thomas, 150–52.

twenty young women, among them Malintzin. As was common practice, the young women were immediately baptized, although that could have meant little for them given language obstacles.

After their baptism, Cortés gave the women to some of his more prominent leaders. Malintzin was given to Alonso Hernández Portocarrero, one of his Medellín comrades and among his most important colleagues. Some have speculated that Cortés chose her to give to Portocarrero because she had "grown into a beautiful and self-assured young woman."[11] Cortés learned several important things in this first foray into indigenous territory. He had unloaded several of his horses from the ships during the battle, and he quickly discovered how intimidating they were to his enemies. He also learned that given the nature of his opponents' weapons, the Spaniards did not have to wear heavy metal armor but could use the quilted cotton armor of his adversaries. And finally, he learned that the people he had bested could become some of his most consistent allies.

After the battle at Cintla, the Spanish forces continued their passage along the coast of the Gulf of Mexico. Several evenings later, when they dropped anchor, two large canoes approached Cortés's ship. Aboard were emissaries from the king of the Mexica at Tenochtitlán, Moctezuma. At this juncture, Cortés learned that Gerónimo Aguilar could not speak Nahuatl but that Malintzin could. This discovery dramatically altered her status and importance in the expedition and gave Cortés another crucial resource in his plans for conquest. Cortés immediately took her from Portocarrero, who was given a replacement, and promised her riches if she would translate for him. Malintzin became Cortés's constant and visible companion, a position she would maintain for the next two years or more. She learned Spanish and thus became even more valuable, but equally important was the respect she inspired among the Spaniards, who often referred to her as Doña Marina (**Document Three**). Similarly, the indigenous populations were accustomed to seeing speakers or spokespersons for influential people, particularly when that person was a "'a lady of power' [who] spoke rhetorically, formally, high-handedly." But Malintzin's translations were not just to gain directions, military information, or basic necessities on their travels; she was "needed for the conquest itself." It was she who explained symbols and cultural practices to and negotiated for Cortés, and it was she who conveyed the meaning of the events and the expectations of the conquerors to those who were conquered.[12]

For the next month or so, more emissaries arrived from Moctezuma. They usually brought gifts to the Spanish, and although they were cordial and welcoming, they made it clear that Moctezuma did not want to see Cortés. At this time, back in the

11. Townsend, *Malintzin* 37.

12. Townsend, 59. See p. 58 for her evaluation of the importance of Malintzin as a translator. A similar assessment can be found in Karttunen, "Rethinking Malinche," in Schroeder, Wood, and Haskett, 302–3.

capital city Moctezuma had been receiving reports of the activities of the newcomers. He had even heard about their dogs, who went about barking and "panting, tongues hanging out."[13] Moctezuma, who had the responsibility of protecting his people, was indeed worried about the future.

Who were these invaders and what did they want? Were they simply new invaders from the north come to rob and conquer? A new and powerful enemy? Perhaps they were ambassadors from some far-off kingdom come to observe, trade, and learn. Or, perhaps they were gods, either new ones or long-lost gods returning to their home. Many scholars argue that the belief that the intruders were led by Quetzalcoatl or his emissaries had some resonance with Moctezuma, as Quetzalcoatl was a legendary deity, a half-man, half-god who had at one time been powerful in the valley of Mexico. At the same time, the elaborate stories of multiple omens of the gods' return and impending disaster more likely came from narratives developed as explanations for defeat in the postconquest period. After discussions with his family and important political and religious figures, Moctezuma decided that the best course would be to "appease the mysterious visitors whether or not they were gods."[14] For the next five or six months, he continued to send his agents to meet with Cortés, carrying gifts but also trying to persuade him not to try to approach Tenochtitlán, and even warning him of the difficulties and obstacles he would encounter on such a journey.

In the meantime, perhaps encouraged by his successes, Cortés continued to press forward. His goals and plans, although he did not share them with many, seemed more solid as he realized the wealth and power to be gained with conquest and saw that he had some real advantages in the contest. Certainly his technology and metal weapons and armor were major assets, as was the knowledge he had of the broader world and the general ability of the conquerors to "share information across time and space."[15] His translators, Malintzin in particular, have to be given considerable weight in the tally of his assets. Even though he had problems with his patron Velázquez, who sent forces to try to contain Cortés and to limit his authority in the new region, these same forces in some cases proved to be reinforcements. There were others who came to join Cortés once stories of his exploits reached nearby Spanish settlements. As already noted, the Spanish success definitely depended on their ability to find allies among the different altepetls. Cortés himself reported on this situation in one of his letters. He had discovered that the people of Tlaxcala, a large center midway between the Gulf coast and Tenochtitlán, were not Moctezuma's vassals, and when he "saw the

13. Thomas, 180. He provides a most interesting account and interpretation of the discussions among the Mexica and Moctezuma's dilemma in deciding what to do. 180–87.

14. Ibid., 188.

15. Townsend, 118. She argues convincingly for the successful Spanish strategy of dealing with their enemies and creating allies, pp.112–14.

discord and animosity between these two people I [Cortés] was not a little pleased, for it seemed to further my purpose considerably."[16] The Tlaxcalans became his largest and most consistent ally.

ACT II

ENCOUNTER AND CAPTURE, 1519–1521

In April and May 1519, Cortés established a new settlement, at Villa Rica della Vera Cruz. Knowing Spanish law helped him at this point as he created an independent political community with its own council, made up mostly of his closest associates who in turn elected him their captain general. With this support, Cortés began to plan his march inland to the capital of the Aztec Empire. He would have to cover about 250 miles over rough terrain and to secure the rear areas as he advanced. On July 26, he put his plan into motion. First, he grounded most of his ships, making it impossible for disgruntled soldiers to leave. Then, with about 300 hundred men, Indian allies, servants, and of course, Malintzin, he set off on his mission. As they moved inland, Cortés was able to establish alliances with important centers like Tlaxcala and to force other cities into submission. An infamous massacre at the large city of Cholula demonstrates that Cortés was willing to use the threat of violence as a means of intimidation, and he picked off smaller, weaker opponents to eliminate the possibility that they might join the Mexica.

In the fall of 1519, the Spanish arrived on the southern shores of the lakes that dominated the valley of Mexico. They could finally look at Tenochtitlán, one of the most spectacular cities in the world at the time, with a population of between 200,000 and 250,000 people. As Cortés and his entourage moved onto the broad causeway that would take them to the city, they too were impressive with their armor, weapons, horses, and dogs, all as if on parade. On November 8, Cortés and Moctezuma met on this causeway. For the first time, two key figures from two of the world's hemispheres came face to face.

Moctezuma and his nobility cordially welcomed Cortés and his followers to their city and provided housing for them in the palace of the former emperor. For the next few months, Cortés and his contingent had a chance to tour the city, and Cortés and Malintzin, in particular, had numerous conversations with their host about matters that concerned them. Cortés insisted that Moctezuma should accept the sovereignty of the new king of Spain, Charles I, and spoke about Christianity and the dangerous devils being worshipped by the Mexica and others. The Spanish also were interested in gold and were given quite substantial amounts of precious metals and jewels (**Document Four**). The Mexica were not entirely taken with their visitors, and as time passed, tensions

16. From his Second Letter in Hernán Cortés, *Letters from Mexico*, trans. and ed. A. R. Pagden (New York: Grossman, 1971), 69.

between the groups emerged. While Cortés and his followers could marvel at the city and its marketplace (**Document Five**), they were much less pleased with the indigenous beliefs and the local temples, which were sometimes sites for human sacrifice.

Tension mounted as Cortés and his army remained in the city. Perhaps Moctezuma and the Mexica grew tired of hearing about Christianity and the attacks on and disparagement of their deities. Certainly Cortés's efforts to end human sacrifice and eradicate any evidence of it in the city would not have been welcomed. Moctezuma had to continue to lead a functioning government and also to try to provide the resources to support his visitors. His major questions were probably what else Cortés wanted and when would he leave. Cortés, for his part, realized that they were in a vulnerable position in the city and also had begun to hear of the possibility of new Spanish forces arriving to replace him. In this unsettled situation, Cortés took Moctezuma hostage and placed him under house arrest. Perhaps Cortés hoped to show any new arrivals from Spain that he was indeed in control of the situation. In May 1520, an expedition from Cuba, led by Panfilo Narváez, landed at Villa Rica della Vera Cruz. On hearing of this landing, Cortés felt he had to return to the coast to protect his own interests, and so he set off with a number of his men and Malintzin, leaving his trusted lieutenant Pedro de Alvarado in charge of Tenochtitlán. The events of the next year would be both tragic and decisive for those whose lives we are following.

Act III

Defeat and Victory, 1520–1521

On his return to his settlement, Cortés reestablished authority, captured Narváez, and persuaded many of those who had come with Narváez to join his own ranks. But bad news came when he learned that his lieutenant, Alvarado, had killed large numbers of the Mexica population at a major religious festival and that in turn this massacre provoked a revolt against the Spanish. Cortés rushed back to the city in mid-June 1520 with additional men. Even with Malintzin trying to negotiate a settlement, tensions escalated. On June 27 or 28, Moctezuma was killed. Why, exactly how, and by whom remains uncertain, and the circumstances of his death are still debated. The Spanish were dissatisfied with him, and no doubt Moctezuma felt he had failed his people; the Mexica, in turn, sought another leader.

With Moctezuma's death, the Spanish were in an untenable position and tried to flee into the night. Many were killed or drowned as bridges and causeways were blocked and destroyed. Cortés, Malintzin, and most of their close associates did escape and retreated to their coastal center for a time. The Mexica celebrated, thinking they had driven out their enemies. Unfortunately, they were wrong on two counts. First, the expedition led by Narváez had brought smallpox to the area and it swept through the city and to other centers of the empire. While population loss from disease alone would not predict defeat, it weakened the Mexica and their allies.[17] Second, Cortés spent the next nine months planning what he probably thought of as a reconquest of the city. This time there would be no negotiation, only capitulation. The new ruler of the empire, young Cuauhtemoc, was resolute, smart, and popular; his warriors were brave, adaptable, and determined.

The battle for Tenochtitlán, which began in May 1521, lasted almost three months. As the siege drew to a close, Cortés ordered the city razed and burned, and few inhabitants were left when Cuauhtemoc surrendered and was taken captive on August 13, 1521. Cortés's dispatch to Spain, which tells of the close of the war and their victory, is quite sterile considering the death and destruction that had occurred: "We gathered up all the spoils we could find and returned to our camp, giving thanks to Our Lord for such a favor and the much desired victory which He had granted us. I spent three or four days in the camp attending to many items of business [and then moved on to the concerns of] the good order, government and pacification of these parts."[18]

Cortés had served God, country, and king, and now he awaited his rewards and planned further excursions. Was Malintzin as pleased with their victory? She had been involved intimately in all the planning and negotiations, had witnessed the violence of the conquest, and would be remembered as a conqueror and condemned for her participation.[19] The words of one of the Mexica nobles at the end of the conflict might typify what she and others were thinking: "O Mexica, o Tlatelolca, is there nothing left of the way it was in Mexico, of the way the Mexican state was?" Actually there was a great deal that was left, and, in the turbulent 1520s, as the Spanish rebuilt Tenochtitlán with the help of the remaining Mexica and before full-blown Spanish administration, law, and religion could be transported to the area, the regional political structures continued to operate and day-to-day economic and social relations were sustained. Even in more settled times, "Spanish administration relied on the organization of the altepetl, and Spanish authorities negotiated tribute with altepetl rulers."[20]

Cortés had always insisted that the Indians must accept Christianity, and baptisms had been performed on a regular basis, but the actual impact of the

17. The impact of disease on colonial peoples is the subject of considerable literature, and some disagreement about the political and economic effects of epidemics. Scholars ranging from Alfred Crosby to Jared Diamond have covered this subject in depth. For the area we are considering, see especially Suzanne A. Alchon, *A Pest in the Land: New World Epidemics in a Global Perspective* (Albuquerque: University of New Mexico Press, 2003).

18. From his Third Letter in Cortés, 265.

19. Townsend suggests this in her chapter on the end of the struggle, pp. 109–25. The Nahuatl account is in the Florentine Codex, bk. 12, ch. 38. See Lockhart, 240.

20. Rebecca Horn, *Postconquest Coyoacan: Nahua-Spanish Relations in Central Mexico, 1519–1650* (Stanford, CA: Stanford University Press, 1997), 2.

new religion was fairly superficial at the time. The arrival of Franciscans and Dominicans expanded the conversion efforts, but those too had mixed results and often failed "to make understandable the basic Christian abstractions of virtue and sin. . . . The Christian God was admitted, but not as an exclusive or omnipotent deity. . . . Indians accepted the concept of the soul, but they extended it to animals and inanimate objects."[21] While in many places traditional aspects of everyday life continued, profound disruptions and transformations in individual lives also occurred. A final look at Cortés and Malintzin gives us an idea of the impact and legacies of the conquest.

Finale

Cortés ordered the rebuilding of the Mexica capital, but that would take several years. In the meantime, he lived in Coyoacan, southeast of the capital, a region that was given to him as an encomienda several years later in recognition of his service to the crown. Malintzin lived there with him, continuing to help in negotiations with the altepetl about the organization of labor and collection of tribute.[22] But the pattern of their lives and their public personas changed in the postconquest world. Sometime in August 1522, Catalina Suarez, Cortés's wife, arrived from Cuba where she had been living. Malintzin probably resided in a separate house at that time. She was pregnant and gave birth to a boy, Cortés's son, to whom he gave his father's name, Martín.

In May 1523, Cortés was officially appointed captain general and governor, and sometime in 1524–1525, he led an expedition to the Caribbean coast and south into Honduras. As always, he took Malintzin with him because of her language skills. Before they left, she married one of Cortés's most seasoned captains, Juan Jaramillo, who also accompanied Cortés on this expedition. Juan and Malintzin had a daughter, Maria, born fairly soon after they returned.

We do not know how she felt about this marriage, but Jaramillo was not a stranger to her, and perhaps she realized in the postconquest world she would fare better as the wife of a respectable and successful Spaniard than as the highly visible but always vulnerable companion to the conqueror. Her earlier life had not been typical of that of most Indian women. The centers of home and community that marked their lives were not ones she could claim. Now that she was a wife and a mother and less connected to Cortés's fame (or notoriety), her life was more the norm. She let her son go to Spain with Cortés in 1528 and never saw him again. Martín was made legitimate there, entered the Order of Santiago, and was poised to assume a respectable social position. Malintzin died by 1529, although the actual circumstances and date of her death are not known.

21. Charles Gibson, *The Aztecs Under Spanish Rule* (Stanford, CA: Stanford University Press, 1964), 100–1.

22. Townsend, 133–41, discusses this period of her life.

Cortés faced struggles over power in the years after 1523. His enemies joined against him in a variety of legal challenges, beginning with a commission of inquiry in 1526 that questioned whether he was guilty of rebellion against Governor Velázquez of Cuba. That investigation dragged on, but in the process the public heard what a great man he was and the decision eventually went in his favor. Ongoing resentment, envy, and even anger against him, however, produced a whole spate of other accusations. His wife Catalina had died shortly after coming to Mexico in suspicious circumstances, and Cortés was accused of mistreating her. He also was charged with not sending the king the appropriate portion of the wealth that had been accumulated in the conquest and with establishing encomiendas illegally. Some people wondered whether he had mistreated the Indians, and many questions were raised about some of the more tragic events of the conquest, including the death of Moctezuma, the flight out of Tenochtitlán in 1520, and even the deaths at Cholula. In 1529, the emperor made Cortés the marques of the valley of Oaxaca and captain general of New Spain and the Mar del Sur. That same year in Spain Cortés married noblewoman Juana de Zuñiga; they had six children. But until his death in 1547, Cortés still had to defend his honor and his actions in the conquest of Mexico. When he died in Sevilla in 1547, he was overwhelmed by debt and forced to pawn gold, jewels, and clothing to survive. He was buried in Sevilla, leaving his and Juana's son, also named Martín, as his legitimate heir.

Historical memory took its turn with Cortés. His remains were moved nine times, most often by his descendants: from Spain to Tezcoco in 1566; to a convent chapel in Mexico City in 1629; to a different site in the same city in 1794. Then in 1822, as Mexico became independent of Spain, the new Chamber of Deputies recommended that the remains be exhumed and burned. But several people saved the day, and he was secretly buried in a church in the capital and the word was spread that his remains were taken to Italy. An excavation in 1946–1947 discovered the secret burial place, and he was reburied in the same church, but this time with a public plaque that reads simply, "Hernán Cortés, 1485–1547."[23]

We have no idea where Malintzin is buried or whether there were any speeches given in her honor or any sorts of commemorations at the time to recognize her contributions to those historic events. The earliest written accounts, like that of the Spaniard Bernal Díaz, do applaud her role and praise her character, even at times seeing her as a force that saved them all. Quite quickly, her life was "enclosed in an edifice of myth. . . . [By 1821 when Mexico became independent from Spain,] she became the scapegoat for three centuries of colonial rule."[24] As Cortés's "mistress" she is the mother of the mixed race, the *mestizo,* and she becomes the tragic

23. Martinez, *Cortés,* 778–94.

24. Karttunen, in Schroeder, Wood, and Haskett, 291, 297. The other piece that deals with these images and is subsequently quoted is Analisa Taylor, "Malinche and Matriarchal Utopia: Gendered Visions of Indigeneity in Mexico," *Signs* 31, no, 3 (spring 2006): 824–34.

symbol of a race born out of subjugation and even rape. She is also seen as a traitor to the Indian people because she willingly gave herself to Cortés and helped him in his conquest.

Cortés is also a figure of some controversy, and some of the same questions about national identity, race, and gender can be raised about him. But Cortés left a record of self-defense in his letters and many other documents. Malintzin never had a chance to defend herself or even to know that she should do so, and we have only begun to do the historical sleuthing necessary to tell the story of a strong and intelligent woman surviving the collision of the hemispheres.

Documents

DOCUMENT ONE

Fray Diego Durán

History of the Indies of New Spain

Diego de Durán was born in Spain, but came to Mexico after 1530, was raised in Mexico City, and joined the Dominican Order. He based his account both on narratives collected after midcentury, and also on a Nahuatl chronicle written by a Mexica but later lost. His account first appeared in 1579–1581. The portion that follows describes the response of Moctezuma to the arrival on the coast of the first Spanish explorers.

What surprises the indigenous people the most about the strange newcomers? How does Moctezuma react to this news?

Which treats of how a ship from Cuba arrived in this land and how Motecuhzoma, having been notified of this, sent emissaries to investigate what people had come. With a description of the events that followed.

. . . [A]t that time a man came before him. Having greeted the king with reverence, he said he wished to speak to him. Motecuhzoma observed him and saw that he lacked ears, thumbs, and big toes. He hardly looked like a human being. When he was asked who had sent him, he answered that he had come of his own will in order to serve the king and narrate the things he had seen. The king asked what these had been. The stranger described how, while he had been walking next to the seashore, he had seen a round hill or house moving from one side to another until it had anchored next to some rocks on the beach. He had never seen anything like this, which was both wondrous and terrifying. Motecuhzoma told the man to rest while he sent someone to see if this story were true. Meanwhile he called his jailers, who threw the man into jail.

Motecuhzoma then called one of his officials, who was named Teuctlamacazqui, giving him orders to go the sea and take along a slave of his whose name was Cuitlalpitoc. He was told to find out the truth or falseness of what had been told to him. He was also to reprimand the rulers and governors of the province of Cuetlaxtla and the coastal region because of their carelessness in not being alert and not watching for things he had recommended to them. The official and the slave left Tenochtitlan and soon arrived at Cuetlaxtla, where they presented themselves to Pinotl, the governor there. Teuctlamacazqui chided Pinotl for his negligence and ordered him, in the name of Motecuhzoma, to send some men to see if truly a hill had appeared upon the waters near the rocks on the coast.

The lord of Cuetlaxtla sent messengers to the seashore to see if there were truth in this. They soon returned, greatly frightened, saying they had seen a terrible large round thing in the midst of the waters. It moved to and fro and within it there were men who appeared from time to time. Teuctlamacazqui and his companion Cuitlalpitoc said they wanted to go see for themselves in order to give an account to their master, Motecuhzoma. Having arrived at the rocks on the beach, they concealed themselves so that the Spaniards could not see them, and soon they realized that everything that had been said was true. In order to observe the strangers better the two men climbed a large tree and from there they saw a boat being lowered into the water. Men entered it and went fishing near the shore. Later the boat returned to the ship, carrying the fish that had been caught. When the Aztec emissaries had seen these things, they departed for Tenochtitlan with great haste to tell their lord what they had observed.

On reaching Motecuhzoma's presence, Teuctlamacazqui said, "O powerful lord, you may kill us or have us put in jail to die, but what the man who is your prisoner said to you is the truth. I myself, O lord, with my own eyes wished to find this out, and with your slave Cuitlalpitoc I climbed a great tree in order to see better. This we saw: in the middle of the water a house from which appeared white men, their faces white, their hands white. They have long thick beards and their clothing is of all colors—white, yellow, red, green, blue, and purple. On their heads they wear round coverings. They put a rather large canoe in the water, some of them jump into it, and they fish all day near the rocks. At dusk they return to the house into which they are gathered. This is all we can tell you concerning which you queried us."

Motecuhzoma lowered his head and, without answering a word, placed a hand over his mouth. In this way he remained for a long time. He appeared to be mute or dead since he was unable to give any answer. After a long time had passed, he gave a mournful sigh, saying to the official who had brought him the news, "Whom shall I believe if not you? Why should I send another envoy if with your own eyes you have beheld the things you have described to me? The best thing to do now is to decide what measures must be taken." . . .

. . . Motecuhzoma then called one of his officers and told them to bring two goldsmiths, two lapidaries, and two feather workers. This was to be done in utmost secrecy, under pain of death, and that of the official's wife, children, and kinsmen, and the destruction of all his possessions.

The official took care in carrying out these orders. When the artisans arrived, they were given gold, stones, and feathers. They were told to create jewels of gold in different forms as swiftly as possible. The lapidaries were told to cut all kinds of precious stones, while the feather workers were ordered to make splendid ornaments. All of these were for a certain purpose and had to be done in secret, without anyone hearing a word about it. So, all precautions having been taken, in the very palace the goldsmiths made many jewels of gold—bracelets, leg ornaments, labrets, and ear pendants. The lapidaries worked green stones into many forms and cut other stones, and the feather workers made some fine ornaments. Motecuhzoma was satisfied with these splendid things and paid the artisans with mantles, food, and other basic items, which was the way he always remunerated those people who served him satisfactorily. He reminded them that all this was being done in secret. Then he called Teuctlamacazqui, who had returned from his trip to the coast where he had verified the coming of the Spaniards, and spoke to him thus:

"I have had jewels, precious stones, and featherwork made and I wish you to carry them as gifts to those men who have arrived in our land. I want you to find out who their commander is, since he is the one to whom you must give all these presents. . . .

DOCUMENT TWO

Treaty between Spain and Portugal Concluded at Tordesillas, June 7, 1494

This treaty was negotiated largely through the offices of Pope Alexander VI in an attempt to resolve disputed claims to territory by the Spanish and Portuguese rulers. What is the solution for their competing interests? What things about this treaty can you see as problematic in subsequent years?

. . . Thereupon it was declared by the above-mentioned representatives of the aforesaid King and Queen of Castile, Leon, Aragon, Sicily, Granada, etc., and of the aforesaid King of Portugal and the Algarves, etc.:

[1.] That, whereas a certain controversy exists between the said lords, their constituents, as to what lands, of all those discovered in the ocean sea up to the present day, the date of this treaty, pertain to each one of the said parts respectively; therefore, for the sake of peace and concord, and for the preservation of the relationship and love of the said King of Portugal for the said King and Queen of Castile, Aragon, etc., it being the pleasure of their Highnesses, they, their said representatives, acting in their name and by virtue of their powers herein described, covenanted and agreed that a boundary or straight line be determined and drawn north and south, from pole to pole, on the said ocean sea, from the Arctic to the Antarctic pole. This boundary or line shall be drawn straight, as aforesaid, at a distance of three hundred and seventy leagues west of the Cape Verde Islands, being calculated by degrees, or by any other manner as may be considered the best and readiest, provided the distance shall be no greater than abovesaid. And all lands, both islands and mainlands, found and discovered already, or to be found and discovered hereafter, by the said King of Portugal and by his vessels on this side of the said line and bound determined as above, toward the east, in either north or south latitude, on the eastern side of the said bound provided the said bound is not crossed, shall belong to, and remain in the possession of, and pertain forever to, the said King of Portugal and his successors. And all other lands, both islands and mainlands, found or to be found hereafter, discovered or to be discovered hereafter, which have been discovered or shall be discovered by the said King and Queen of Castile, Aragon, etc., and by their vessels, on the western side of the said bound, determined as above, after having passed the said bound toward the west, in either its north or south latitude, shall belong to, and remain in the possession of, and pertain forever to, the said King and Queen of Castile, Leon, etc., and to their successors.

[2.] Item, the said representatives promise and affirm by virtue of the powers aforesaid, that from this date no ships shall be dispatched—namely as follows: the said King and Queen of Castile, Leon, Aragon, etc., for this part of the bound, and its eastern side, on this side the said bound, which pertains to the said King of Portugal and the Algarves, etc.; nor the said King of Portugal to the other part of the said bound which pertains to the said King and Queen of Castile, Aragon, etc.—for the purpose of discovering and seeking any mainlands or islands, or for the purpose of trade, barter, or conquest of any kind. But should it come to pass that the said ships of the said King and Queen of Castile, Leon, Aragon, etc., on sailing thus on this side of the said bound, should discover any mainlands or islands in the region pertaining, as abovesaid, to the said King of Portugal, such mainlands or islands shall pertain to and belong forever to the said King of Portugal and his heirs, and their Highnesses shall order them to be surrendered to him immediately. And if the said ships of the said King of Portugal discover any islands and mainlands in the regions of the said King and Queen of Castile, Leon, Aragon, etc., all such lands shall belong to and remain forever in the possession of the said King and Queen of Castile, Leon, Aragon, etc., and their heirs, and the said King of Portugal shall cause such lands to be surrendered immediately.

[3.] Item, in order that the said line or bound of the said division may be made straight and as nearly as possible the said distance of three hundred and seventy leagues west of the Cape Verde Islands, as hereinbefore stated, the said representatives of both the said parties agree and assent that within the ten months immediately following the date of this treaty their said constituent lords shall despatch two or four caravels, namely, one or two by each one of them, a greater or less number, as they may mutually consider necessary. These vessels shall meet at the Grand Canary Island during this time, and each one of the said parties shall send certain persons in them, to wit, pilots, astrologers, sailors, and any others they may deem desirable. But there must be as many on one side as on the other, and certain of the said pilots, astrologers, sailors, and others of those sent by the said King and Queen of Castile, Aragon, etc., and who are experienced, shall embark in the ships of the said King of Portugal and the Algarves; in like manner certain of the said persons sent by the said King of Portugal shall embark in the ship or ships of the said King and Queen of Castile, Aragon, etc.; a like number in each case, so that they may jointly study and examine to better advantage the sea, courses, winds, and the degrees of the sun or of north latitude, and lay out the leagues aforesaid, in order that, in determining the line and boundary, all sent and empowered by both the said parties in the said vessels, shall jointly concur. These said vessels shall continue their course together to the said Cape Verde Islands, from whence they shall lay a direct course to the west, to the distance of the said three hundred and seventy degrees, measured as the said persons shall agree, and measured without prejudice to the said parties. When this point is reached, such point will constitute the place and mark for measuring degrees of the sun or of north latitude either by daily runs measured in leagues, or in any other manner that shall mutually be deemed better. This said line shall be drawn north and south as aforesaid, from the said Arctic pole to the said Antarctic pole. And when this line has been determined as abovesaid, those sent by each of the aforesaid parties, to whom each one of the said parties must delegate his own authority and power, to determine the said mark and bound, shall draw up a writing concerning it and affix thereto their signatures. And when determined by the mutual consent of all of them, this line shall be considered as a perpetual mark and bound, in such wise that the said parties, or either of them, or their future successors, shall be unable to deny it, or erase or remove it, at any time or in any manner whatsoever. And should, perchance, the said line and bound from pole to pole, as aforesaid, intersect any island or mainland, at the first point of such intersection of such island or mainland by the said line, some kind of mark or tower shall be erected, and a succession of similar marks shall be erected in a straight line from such mark or tower, in a line identical with the above-mentioned bound. These marks shall separate those portions of such land belonging to each one of the said parties; and the subjects of the said parties shall not dare, on either side, to enter the territory of the other, by crossing the said mark or bound in such island or mainland.

[4.] Item, inasmuch as the said ships of the said King and Queen of Castile, Leon, Aragon, etc., sailing as before declared, from their kingdoms and seigniories to their said possessions on the other side of the said line, must cross the seas on this side of the line, pertaining to the said King of Portugal, it is therefore concerted and agreed that the said ships of the said King and Queen of Castile, Leon,

Aragon, etc., shall, at any time and without any hindrance, sail in either direction, freely, securely, and peacefully, over the said seas of the said King of Portugal, and within the said line. And whenever their Highnesses and their successors wish to do so, and deem it expedient, their said ships may take their courses and routes direct from their kingdoms to any region within their line and bound to which they desire to despatch expeditions of discovery, conquest, and trade. They shall take their courses direct to the desired region and for any purpose desired therein, and shall not leave their course, unless compelled to do so by contrary weather. They shall do this provided that, before crossing the said line, they shall not seize or take possession of anything discovered in his said region by the said King of Portugal; and should their said ships find anything before crossing the said line, as aforesaid, it shall belong to the said King of Portugal, and their Highnesses shall order it surrendered immediately. . . .

DOCUMENT THREE

Bernal Díaz del Castillo

The Discovery and Conquest of Mexico, 1517–1521

Soldier-chronicler Bernal Díaz was born in Spain c. 1494 and left there seeking his fortune to go to Panama by 1513. He then went to Cuba and was on one of the earliest expeditions to the Yucatan; eventually he joined Cortés's expedition. His account was written after 1550 while he was retired and living in Guatemala. Considered by many as one of the most readable of the memoirs of the conquest, his account includes fascinating detail, but often he is considered naive and even inaccurate. In this portion of his narrative he gives the history of Doña Marina. How does his account differ from descriptions in the text that cover Malintzin's life? How would you describe his feelings and his memory of this Indian woman?

. . . Before telling about the great Montezuma and his famous City of Mexico and the Mexicans, I wish to give some account of Doña Marina, who from her childhood had been the mistress and Cacica of towns and vassals. It happened in this way:

Her father and mother were chiefs and Caciques of a town called Paynala, which had other towns subject to it, and stood about eight leagues from the town of Coatzacoalcos. Her father died while she was still a little child, and her mother married another Cacique, a young man, and bore him a son. It seems that the father and mother had a great affection for this son and it was agreed between them that he should succeed to their honours when their days were done. So that there should be no impediment to this, they gave the little girl, Doña Marina, to some Indians from Xicalango, and this they did by night so as to escape observation, and they then spread the report that she had died, and as it happened at this time that a child of one of their Indian slaves died they gave out that it was their daughter and the heiress who was dead.

The Indians of Xicalango gave the child to the people of Tabasco and the Tabasco people gave her to Cortés. I myself knew her mother, and the old woman's son and her half-brother, when he was already grown up and ruled the town jointly with his mother, for the second husband of the old lady was dead. When they became Christians, the old lady was called Marta and the son Lázaro. I knew all this very well because in the year 1523 after the conquest of Mexico and the other provinces, when Cristóbal de Olid revolted in Honduras, and Cortés was on his way there, he passed through Coatzacoalcos and I and the greater number of the settlers of that town accompanied him on that expedition as I shall relate in the proper time and place. As Doña Marina proved herself such an excellent woman and good interpreter throughout the wars in New Spain, Tlaxcala and Mexico (as I shall show later on) Cortés always took her with him, and during that expedition she was married to a gentleman named Juan Jaramillo at the town of Orizaba.

Doña Marina was a person of the greatest importance and was obeyed without question by the Indians throughout New Spain.

When Cortés was in the town of Coatzacoalcos he sent to summon to his presence all the Caciques of that province in order to make them a speech about our holy religion, and about their good treatment, and among the Caciques who assembled was the mother of Doña Marina and her half-brother, Lázaro.

Some time before this Doña Marina had told me that she belonged to that province and that she was the mistress of vassals, and Cortés also knew it well, as did Aguilar, the interpreter. In such a manner it was that mother, daughter and son came together, and it was easy enough to see that she was the daughter from the strong likeness she bore to her mother.

These relations were in great fear of Doña Marina, for they thought that she had sent for them to put them to death, and they were weeping.

When Doña Marina saw them in tears, she consoled them and told them to have no fear, that when they had given her over to the men from Xicalango, they knew not what they were doing, and she forgave them for doing it, and she gave them many jewels of gold and raiment, and told them to return to their town, and said that God had been very gracious to her in freeing her from the worship of idols and making her a Christian, and letting her bear a son to her lord and master Cortés and in marrying her to such a gentleman as Juan Jaramillo, who was now her husband. That she would rather serve her husband and Cortés than anything else in the world, and would not exchange her place to be Cacica of all the provinces in New Spain.

Doña Marina knew the language of Coatzacoalcos, which is that common to Mexico, and she knew the language of Tabasco, as did also Jerónimo de Aguilar, who spoke the language of Yucatan and Tabasco, which is one and the same. So that these two could understand one another clearly, and Aguilar translated into Castilian for Cortés.

This was the great beginning of our conquests and thus, thanks be to God, things prospered with us. I have made a point of explaining this matter, because without the help of Doña Marina we could not have understood the language of New Spain and Mexico.

DOCUMENT FOUR

The Seventeenth Chapter of Book Twelve of the *Florentine Codex*

This account comes from the General History of the Things of New Spain *organized by Franciscan friar Bernardino de Sahagún. According to the historian James Lockhart who has translated the documents, somewhere around 1547 Sahagún and aides he had trained began to collect statements from indigenous people who could describe the events of the previous half-century. Although the famous Book Twelve was drafted around 1555, another twenty years or more passed before the document appeared publicly. The portion of the document which follows describes the first meeting between Cortés and Moctezuma in the palace at Tenochtitlán. How would you describe the Spaniards' behavior and Moctezuma's situation? Compare this account with what Cortés has to say of the meeting in his Second Letter, a portion of which follows in* ***Document Five.***

. . . Seventeenth chapter, where it is said how the Spaniards went with Moteucçoma to enter the great palace, and what happened there.

And when they had reached the palace and gone in, immediately they seized Moteucçoma and kept close watch over him, not letting him out of their sight, and Itzquauhtzin along with him. But the others were just [allowed to] come back out.

And when this had happened, then the various guns were fired. It seemed that everything became confused; people went this way and that, scattering and darting about. It was as though everyone's tongue were out, everyone were preoccupied, everyone had been taking mushrooms, as though who knows what had been shown to everyone. Fear reigned, as though everyone had swallowed his heart. It was still that way at night; everyone was terrified, taken aback, thunderstruck, stunned.

And when it dawned, everything [the Spaniards] needed was proclaimed: white tortillas, roast turkeys, eggs, fresh water, wood, firewood, charcoal, earthen tubs, polished bowls, water jars, large clay pitchers, vessels for frying, all kinds of earthenware. Moteucçoma himself ordered it. But when he summoned the noblemen, they would no longer obey him, but grew angry. They no longer performed their duty to him, no longer went to him; no longer was he heeded. But he was not therefore forsaken; he was given all he needed to eat and drink, and water and deer fodder [for the Spaniards].

And when [the Spaniards] were well settled, right away they interrogated Moteucçoma about all the stored treasure of the altepetl, the devices and shields. They greatly prodded him, they eagerly sought gold as a thing of esteem. And then Moteucçoma went along leading the Spaniards. They gathered around him, bunched around him; he went in their midst, leading the way. They went along taking hold of him, grasping him. And when they reached the storehouse, the place called Teocalco, then all the <shininag things> were brought out: the quetzal-feather head fan, the devices, the shields, the golden disks, the necklaces of the devils, the golden nose crescents, the golden leg bands, the golden arm bands, the golden sheets for the forehead.

Thereupon the gold on the shields and on all the devices was taken off. And when all the gold had been detached, right away they set on fire, set fire to, ignited all the different precious things; they all burned. And the Spaniards made the gold into bricks. And they took as much of the green-stone as pleased them; as to the rest of the green-stone, the Tlaxcalans just snatched it up. And [the Spaniards] went everywhere, scratching about in the hiding places, storehouses, places of storage all around. They took everything they saw that pleased them.

DOCUMENT FIVE

Hernán Cortés

Letters from Mexico

Between 1519 and 1526 Hernán Cortés wrote a series of very long letters or reports to the Hapsburg Emperor Charles V (who was also Charles I of Spain). Portions of the Second and the Third Letters are included here (probably written in 1520 and 1522). Multiple versions and copies of these letters are in existence. What do you think Cortés hoped to accomplish in writing these letters to the emperor? In what ways do you think Cortés colored and even altered the events that he describes?

Cortés, The Second Letter (1520)

. . . Here as many as a thousand men came out to see and speak with me, important persons from that city, all dressed very richly after their own fashion. When they reached me, each one performed a ceremony which they practice among themselves; each placed his hand on the ground and kissed it. And so I stood there waiting for nearly an hour until everyone had performed his ceremony. Close to the city there is a wooden bridge ten paces wide across a breach in the causeway to allow the water to flow, as it rises and falls. The bridge is also for the defense of the city, because whenever they so wish they can remove some very long broad beams of which this bridge is made. There are many such bridges throughout the city as later Your Majesty will see in the account I give of it.

After we had crossed this bridge, Mutezuma came to greet us and with him some two hundred lords, all barefoot and dressed in a different costume, but also very rich in their way and more so than the others. They came in two columns, pressed very close to the walls of the street, which is very wide and beautiful and so straight that you can see from one end to the other. It is two-thirds of a league long and has on both sides very good and big houses, both dwellings and temples.

Mutezuma came down the middle of this street with two chiefs, one on his right hand and the other on his left. One of these was that great chief who had come on a litter to speak with me, and the other was Mutezuma's brother, chief of the city of Yztapalapa which I had left that day. And they were all dressed alike except that Mutezuma wore sandals whereas the others went barefoot; and they held his arm on either side. When we met I dismounted and stepped forward to embrace him, but the two lords who were with him stopped me with their hands so that I should not touch him; and they likewise all performed the ceremony of kissing the earth. When this was over Mutezuma requested his brother to remain with me and to take me by the arm while he went a little way ahead with the other; and after he had spoken to me all the others in the two columns came and spoke with me, one after another, and then each returned to his column.

When at last I came to speak to Mutezuma himself I took off a necklace of pearls and cut glass that I was wearing and placed it round his neck; after we had walked a little way up the street a servant of his came with two necklaces, wrapped in a cloth, made from red snails' shells, which they hold in great esteem; and from each necklace hung eight shrimps of refined gold almost a span in length. When they had been brought he turned to me and placed them about my neck, and then continued up the street in the manner already described until we reached a very large and beautiful house which had been very well prepared to accommodate us. There he took me by the hand and led me to a great room facing the courtyard through which we entered. And he bade me sit on a very rich throne, which he had had built for him and then left saying that I should wait for him. After a short while, when all those of my company had been quartered, he returned with many and various treasures of gold and silver and featherwork, and as many as five or six thousand cotton garments, all very rich and woven and embroidered in various ways. And after he had given me these things he sat on another throne which they placed there next to the one on which I was sitting. . . .

. . . They had confessed that Mutezuma had ordered them to kill those Spaniards, I ordered him to be put in irons, from which he received no small fright, although later that same day, after having spoken with him, I had them removed, and he was very pleased.

From then on I did all I could to please him, especially by announcing publicly to all the natives, the chiefs as well as those who came to see me, that it was Your Majesty's wish that Mutezuma should remain in power, acknowledging the sovereignty which Your Highness held over him, and that they could best serve Your Highness by obeying him and holding him for their lord, as they had before I came to this land. So well did I treat him and so much satisfaction did he receive from me that many times I offered him his liberty, begging him to return to his house, and each time he told me that he was pleased to be where he was and he did not wish to go, for he lacked nothing, just as if he were in his own home. Also, his going might permit certain chiefs, his vassals, to induce or oblige him to do something against his will and prejudicial to the service of Your Highness; for he had resolved to serve Your Majesty in all that he could. As long as these chiefs were informed of all he wanted he was content to remain there, as he might excuse himself, should they wish to demand anything of him, by replying that he was not at liberty. Many times he asked my permission to go and spend some time at certain residences which he owned both inside and outside the city, and not once did I refuse him. Many times he went with five or six Spaniards to entertain himself one or two leagues beyond the city, and he always returned very happy and content to the quarters where I held him. Whenever he went out he gave many gifts of jewels and clothing, both to the Spaniards who escorted him and to the natives by whom he was always so well attended. . . .

. . . This province is circular and encompassed by very high and very steep mountains, and the plain is some seventy leagues in circumference: in this plain there are two lakes which cover almost all of it, for a canoe may travel fifty leagues around the edges. One of these lakes is of fresh water and the other, which is the larger, is of salt water. A small chain of very high hills which cuts across the middle of the plain separates these two lakes. At the end of this chain a narrow channel which is no wider than a bowshot between these hills and the mountains joins the lakes. They travel between one lake and the other and between the different settlements which are on the lakes in their canoes without needing to go by land. As the salt lake rises and falls with its tides as does the sea, whenever it rises, the salt water flows into the fresh as swiftly as a powerful river, and on the ebb the fresh water passes to the salt.

This great city of Temixtitan is built on the salt lake, and no matter by what road you travel there are two leagues from the main body of the city to the mainland. There are four artificial causeways leading to it, and each is as wide as two cavalry lances. The city itself is as big as Seville or Córdoba. The main streets are very wide and very straight; some of these are on the land, but the rest and all the smaller ones are half on land, half canals where they paddle their canoes. All the streets have openings in places so that the water may pass from one canal to another. Over all these openings, and some of them are very wide, there are bridges made of long and wide beams joined together very firmly and so well made that on some of them ten horsemen may ride abreast.

Seeing that if the inhabitants of this city wished to betray us they were very well equipped for it by the design of the city, for once the bridges had been removed they could starve us to death without our being able to reach the mainland, as soon as I entered the city I made great haste to build four brigantines, and completed them in a very short time. They were such as could carry three hundred men to the land and transport the horses whenever we might need them.

This city has many squares where trading is done and markets are held continuously. There is also one square twice as big as that of Salamanca, with arcades all around, where more than sixty thousand people come each day to buy and sell, and where every kind of merchandise produced in these lands is found; provisions as well as ornaments of gold and silver, lead, brass, copper, tin, stones, shells, bones, and feathers. They also sell lime, hewn and unhewn stone, adobe bricks, tiles, and cut and uncut woods of various kinds. There is a street where they sell game and birds of every species found in this land: chickens, partridges and quails, wild ducks, flycatchers, widgeons, turtledoves, pigeons, cane birds, parrots, eagles and eagle owls, falcons, sparrow hawks and kestrels, and they sell the skins of some of these birds of prey with their feathers, heads and claws. They sell rabbits and hares, and stags and small gelded dogs which they breed for eating.

There are streets of herbalists where all the medicinal herbs and roots found in the land are sold. There are shops like apothecaries', where they sell ready-made medicines as well as liquid ointments and plasters. There are shops like barbers' where they have their hair washed and shaved, and shops where they sell food and drink. There are also men like porters to carry loads. There is much firewood and charcoal, earthenware braziers and mats of various kinds like mattresses for beds, and other, finer ones, for seats and for covering rooms and hallways. There is every sort of vegetable, especially onions, leeks, garlic, common cress and watercress, borage, sorrel, teasels and artichokes; and there are many sorts of fruit, among which are cherries and plums like those in Spain.

They sell honey, wax and a syrup made from maize canes, which is as sweet and syrupy as that made from the sugar cane. They also make syrup from a plant which in the islands is called *maguey*, which is much better than most syrups and from this plant they also make sugar and wine, which they likewise sell. There are many sorts of spun cotton, in hanks of every color, and it seems like the silk market at Granada, except here there is a much greater quantity. They sell as many colors for painters as may be found in Spain and all of excellent hues. They sell deerskins, with and without the hair, and some are dyed white or in various colors. They sell much earthenware, which for the most part is very good; there are both large and small pitchers, jugs, pots, tiles, and many other sorts of vessel, all of good clay and most of them glazed and painted. They sell maize both as grain and as bread and it is better both in appearance and in taste than any found in the islands or on the mainland. They sell chicken and fish pies, and much fresh and salted fish, as well as raw and cooked fish. They sell hen and goose eggs, and eggs of all the other birds I have mentioned, in great number, and they sell *tortillas* made from eggs. . . .

Cortés, The Third Letter (1522)

. . . For no race, however savage, has ever practiced such fierce and unnatural cruelty as the natives of these parts. Our allies also took many spoils that day, which we were unable to prevent, as they numbered more than 150,000 and we Spaniards were only some nine hundred. Neither our precautions nor our warnings could stop their looting, though we did all we could. One of the reasons why I had avoided entering the city in force during the past days was the fear that if we attempted to storm them they would throw all they possessed into the water, and, even if they did not, our allies would take all they could find. For this reason I was much afraid that Your Majesty would receive only a small part of the great wealth this city once had, in comparison with all that I once held for Your Highness. Because it was now late, and we could no longer endure the stench of the dead bodies that had lain in those streets for many days, which was the most loathsome thing in all the world, we returned to our camps.

That evening I arranged that when we entered the city on the following day three heavy guns should be prepared and taken into the city with us, for I feared that the enemy, who were so massed together that they had no room to turn around, might crush us as we attacked, without actually fighting. I wished, therefore, to do them some harm with the guns, and so induce them to come out to meet us. I also ordered the alguacil mayor to make ready the brigantines, so that they might sail into a large lake between the houses, where all the canoes had gathered; for they now had so few houses left that the lord of the city lived in a canoe with certain of his chieftains, not knowing where else to go. Thus we made our plans for the morrow.

When it was light I had all the men made ready and the guns brought out. On the previous day I had ordered Pedro de Alvarado to wait for me in the market square and not to attack before I arrived. When all the men were mustered and all the brigantines were lying in wait behind those houses where the enemy was gathered, I gave orders that when a harquebus was fired they should enter the little of the city that was still left to win and drive the defenders into the water where the brigantines were waiting. I warned them, however, to look with care for Guatimucín,[1] and to make every effort to take him alive, for once that had been done the war would cease. I myself climbed onto a roof top, and before the fight began I spoke with certain chieftains of the city whom I knew, and asked them for what reason their lord would not appear before me; for, although they were in the direst straits, they need not all perish; I asked them to call him, for

1. Guatimucín – Cuauhtemoc. Ed.

he had no cause to be afraid. Two of those chieftains then appeared to go to speak with him. After a while they returned, bringing with them one of the most important persons in the city, and he was captain and governor of them all and directed all matters concerning the war. I welcomed him openly, so that he should not be afraid; but at last he told me that his sovereign would prefer to die where he was rather than on any account appear before me, and that he personally was much grieved by this, but now I might do as I pleased. I now saw by this how determined he was, and so I told him to return to his people and to prepare them, for I intended to attack and slay them all; and so he departed after having spent five hours in such discussions.

The people of the city had to walk upon their dead while others swam or drowned in the waters of that wide lake where they had their canoes; indeed, so great was their suffering that it was beyond our understanding how they could endure it. Countless numbers of men, women and children came out toward us, and in their eagerness to escape many were pushed into the water where they drowned amid that multitude of corpses; and it seemed that more than fifty thousand had perished from the salt water they had drunk, their hunger and the vile stench. . . .

Questions

1. What motivated men like Hernán Cortés to undertake exploration and conquest?
2. What things about the Spaniards were most fascinating or frightening to the indigenous populations? What things about the Aztec Empire and its peoples were of greatest interest or most foreign to the Spaniards?
3. Why was Malintzin so important in the conquest of Mexico? Can you think of any other situation that would call for someone with her sorts of skills?
4. How did the conquest of Mexico affect men and women differently in both its process and its results?
5. How has history treated Cortés and Malintzin?

Suggested Readings

Glendinnen, Inga. *The Aztecs*. New York: Cambridge University Press, 1991.

Kellogg, Susan, and Matthew Restall, eds. *Dead Giveaways: Indigenous Testaments of Colonial Mesoamerica and the Andes*. Salt Lake City: University of Utah Press, 1998.

Paz, Octavio. *The Labyrinth of Solitude: Life and Thought in Mexico*. New York: Grove, 1961.

Restall, Matthew. *Seven Myths of the Spanish Conquest*. New York: Oxford University Press, 2003.

Socolow, Susan. *The Women of Colonial Latin America*. New York: Cambridge University Press, 2000.

CHAPTER

16

The Ottoman Empire: Hurrem Sultan (d. 1558) and Ibrahim Pasha (d. 1535)

Setting the Stage

Hurrem was the beloved wife of one of the most powerful men in world history, Suleyman, ruler of the Ottoman Empire from 1520 until his death in 1566. Ibrahim Pasha was his close friend and prime minister. Hurrem and Ibrahim illustrate the significance of the family and the inner circle of officials in relation to imperial power. Both strongly influenced Suleyman and thereby helped shape the course of Ottoman history during their own sixteenth century and well into the seventeenth.

The stage itself belonged to Suleyman. He exercised personal control over the policies and ambitions of a huge empire, although he also accepted advice from close advisers and delegated significant responsibility. In a famous 1538 inscription on the citadel in Istanbul, these words are attributed to him and demonstrate the extent of his geographic and political authority:

> I am God's slave and sultan [holder of power] of this world. By the Grace of God I am head of Muhammad's community. God's might and Muhammad's miracles are my companions. I am Suleyman, in whose name the *hutbe* [Arabic *khutba,* means "sermon"] is read in Mecca and Medina. In Baghdad I am the shah [Persian: king], in Byzantine realms the Caesar, and in Egypt the sultan; who sends his fleets to the seas of Europe, the Maghrib [western North Africa] and India. I am the sultan who took the crown and throne of Hungary.[1]

Much empire building was due to Suleyman's father, Selim I (r. 1512–1520), who during his reign stopped Persian Safavid advances into his territory and, in the short space of two years (1516–1517), conquered Mamluk Syria and Egypt. The victory also entitled him to the Mamluk province of the Hijaz in Arabia, location of the holy cities of Makka and Madina. Holding these two cities gave Selim and his successors responsibility for the security of the Muslim pilgrimage and sufficient prestige to claim the title *khalifa* (anglicized as "caliph"), "successor" or "deputy" to the Prophet Muhammad.

Selim had come to the throne only after defeating his own brothers in battle. Toward the end of his life, he did not want his competitive sons to break apart his huge empire in a civil war after his death. The succession process was, theoretically, left to the will of God, and the Ottomans saw God's will in the outcome of battles between claimants to the throne. Selim, however, decided to execute all but the son he wanted to succeed him, an option that had legally existed since the fifteenth century.[2] A number of religious leaders justified the practice as saving many innocent lives that would otherwise be lost in a civil war. In this way, Suleyman took the throne in 1520 without opposition, an enormous practical advantage. He built directly on his father's success, adding to the empire southern Iraq and greater Hungary, which brings us back to the inscription in Istanbul.

Suleyman's empire was immense and abutted much of the world. To the east, it shared a mutually hostile border with the Safavid rulers of Persia. Far beyond Persia lay Ming China, with which the Ottomans had some trade. To the south, Suleyman

1. Halil Inalcik, *The Ottoman Empire: The Classical Age 1300–1600*, trans. (from the Turkish) Norman Itzkowitz and Colin Imber (London: Weidenfeld and Nicolson, 1973), 41.

2. Mehmed II, conqueror of Constantinople, left the option to the successful son, postponing it: "For the welfare of the state, the one of my sons to whom God grants the sultanate may lawfully put his brothers to death. A majority of the ulema [religious authorities] consider this permissible." Ibid., 59.

faced the challenge of incorporating the recently conquered Arabic-speaking populations of Syria, Egypt, and North Africa. To the north, czarist Russia under Ivan IV (d. 1584) formed a barrier. To the west, there was the Hapsburg Empire centered in Vienna, a city that Suleyman tried but failed to conquer. Further west was a French monarchy that was hostile to the Hapsburgs, and the French king half-heartedly sought an Ottoman alliance against them. On Suleyman's mental political map, the England of Henry VIII (d. 1547) was very marginal and obscure and the Americas were nearly mythic. Still, the extent of Ottoman interests and concerns was very broad.

During Suleyman's reign, the empire constituted a first-class world power, confident of continuing success. Geographic expansion brought with it new taxable populations and land to distribute as military fiefs (*timar*s). Suleyman and his early ministers expanded the reach of Ottoman bureaucratic institutions. For example, the government took responsibility for selecting the heads of important guilds that collectively dominated commerce and the production of goods and services. The government chose guild leaders who were loyal to the regime and who would support Ottoman policies that affected taxation and both local and long-distance trade. Suleyman also augmented the body of Islamic law (the *shari'a*) with secular law (*kanun*; Arabic *qanun*) consisting of his own imperial decrees. Religious leaders expected these decrees not to contradict the *shari'a*, but otherwise the sultan's law was unfettered. The *kanun* allowed more flexibility in imperial administration and also in trade and diplomacy with foreigners.

In the sixteenth century, the sources for Ottoman history proliferate, both in the Ottoman archives themselves and in the reports, letters, and journals of Europeans who increasingly visited and lived in the empire. Even so, sources for Ibrahim and Hurrem are thin. Ibrahim was certainly literate but left no autobiographical material. It is difficult to recount details of his early life with confidence. The Ottoman chroniclers, paid by the ruler, consistently put Suleyman first at the expense of all others. European sources, sometimes hostile and often wary, depict Ibrahim as competent but arrogant. Ottoman chroniclers give us virtually no information on Hurrem, as they typically avoided mention of women, considering it impolite and intrusive to do so. Foreigners in Istanbul tell us something of her, but what they say must be taken with several grains of salt, because they had no access to her.

An interesting detail about Hurrem is that she was literate in her birth language as well as her adopted Ottoman Turkish. For the first fifteen years or so that she lived in the capital city, her Ottoman Turkish was imperfect, and scribes wrote her letters for her, but by about 1535, she wrote on her own. Many of her letters were addressed to her absent husband, who was frequently away on military campaigns, political shows of force, or public relations tours.

THE ACTORS

IBRAHIM PASHA AND HURREM SULTAN

Ibrahim most likely came from the vicinity of Venetian-controlled Parga, a town on the west coast of mainland Greece. He was captured as a youth in an Ottoman raid and then was channeled into a slave system that provided well-trained military and bureaucratic personnel for the empire. The system of slave recruitment was well in place by the time of the Ottoman conquest of East Roman Constantinople in 1453 (**Document One**). The Ottomans viewed the system as taxation or tribute, called a harvest (Turkish *devshirme*). Technically, the Ottomans could not call the practice enslavement because the "recruits" were Christian and technically among the protected, or *dhimmi*, population of the empire, and thus exempt from enslavement. Approximately every four years, Ottoman officials assessed Balkan towns and villages a tribute in boys, ideally between about eight and twelve years of age. The boys went off to Istanbul to be trained, primarily to fill the ranks of a new regular army. They grew into young men who knew no other home or family than the Ottoman military. There was still an important Turkish tribal cavalry, based on the old tradition of military patronage, but the cavalry was not content with the emerging centralized tendencies of the royal family. Now there was also this "new army" (Turkish *yeni çeri*), the Janissary corps, that was largely infantry, and loyal directly to the sultan and to the military system itself.

Some of the brighter *devşirme* youth were not only given military training but also became pages in the palace and learned bureaucratic skills as well. The best of these could hope for high political office. Surrounded now by people of slave status, the free, dynastic royal family monopolized the top job of sultan, but a man with *devshirme* roots could aspire to the second-highest office in the empire, that of prime minister, on the basis of merit. Ibrahim Pasha was one of these *devshirme* men.

When Ibrahim was placed into the slave system, he went with the Balkan tribute boys to the palace school in Istanbul to learn military skills, Turkish, and some Arabic and become converted to Islam. His high aptitude led him to become a page, which meant further training with a view to a bureaucratic future. The pages served as apprentices in various palace services and were taught scribal skills, Islamic studies, and a craft or fine art.[3] Ibrahim met young Suleyman, his future sultan, in the palace environment. They were close in age and temperament and became fast friends.

Hurrem (Persian *khurrem*) means "cheerful," while the added "Sultan" identified her as a member of the royal family. She was also called *Haseki*, "favorite" of the ruler. Hurrem was from what is now western Ukraine, the daughter of an Orthodox Christian priest, although Europeans of the time often assumed that she was Russian. Her real name may have

3. Ibid., ch. 9.

been Aleksandra, but she is better known as Roxelana. Tatars captured the village of her youth, taking the inhabitants prisoner. They sold her into slavery as a concubine. How she got to Istanbul is not clear, but probably a master, wishing to curry favor at court, gave her to Suleyman as a gift. She soon became part of the royal family.

Ottoman family politics played out largely in the main palace, a huge complex where hundreds of people ran the core of the empire. In 1453, Sultan Mehmed II (r. 1444–1446; 1451–1481) conquered the fortified capital city of Constantinople, all that remained of the East Roman Empire. In 1454, Mehmed ordered a palace to be built; just as it was completed, four years later, he ordered yet another much larger palace in a more defensible position. The earlier, smaller complex was then dubbed the Old Palace and the large new one, eventually called Topkapi,[4] was symbolically, and also in a practical sense, the center of the Ottoman Empire. The palace was nearly a city within a city, enclosing gardens and playing fields. The administration was divided into two parts, the Inner (Turkish *enderun*) and Outer (Turkish *birun*) Services, and the sultan headed both. The Inner Service included public administration, the treasury, and the palace school for the *devshirme* boys. It also included the harem (Arabic *harim*), the inviolable living spaces of the women and younger children of the sultan, located outside Topkapi. The Outer Service included diplomatic functions and the military administration (**Document Two A**). A palace portal, the Gate of Felicity, gave access to foreign diplomats. The French referred to it as the gate or door (*la porte*), a term that became a European synonym for the Ottoman government.

Until the time of Hurrem, the harem was located in Mehmed II's Old Palace, rather than in the much larger Topkapi. Royal women of the harem had their own wealth and typically used it to sponsor the construction of mosques, schools, and hospitals.[5] Their financial means gave them some public clout. Women's influence in and beyond the harem was, however, mainly based on their degree of closeness to the ruler. The women, especially the sultan's mother (*valide sultan*), who officially ran the harem, and the slave concubine currently in favor, could promise officials and military officers the ear of the sultan in exchange for political support for the succession of a particular prince. Succession was critical to these women. Once a new sultan took the throne, the previous *valide sultan* was shuffled off to a third-rate mansion with her retinue. The mother of the new sultan took over the harem, and her retinue was elevated along with her. The status of each royal woman was at stake every time a sultan died, not to mention the survival of sons not chosen for the

4. The final vowel is pronounced like that in the English word *it*.

5. Suraiya Faroqhi, *Subjects of the Sultan: Culture and Daily Life in the Ottoman Empire* (London: Taurus, 1995), 118.

throne, who legally could be executed. Competition over succession meant that the harem had its own factions, and each faction sought support from outside the palace walls.

Underlying the factions of the harem were the politics of reproduction. Prior to the mid-fifteenth century, when the Ottoman polity was still a tribal state, the reigning sultan usually married off his sons to young female royals of neighboring states, Christian or Muslim, in order to cement alliances. One of those sons would eventually become the next sultan and bring his foreign wife along as consort. His harem might also include any number of concubines. Either as the result of abstinence or proactive birth control methods, these foreign, legal wives seldom gave birth, leaving reproduction to the concubines. This practice precluded a situation in which an Ottoman heir would have royal blood ties—and perhaps political affinity—with his mother's home regime. By about 1400, when the Ottoman tribal state had absorbed neighbors that had provided royal, legal wives, the dynasty felt it no longer needed politically inspired marriages. Nearly without exception, Ottoman princes no longer married anyone, with the new justification that no women were good enough for them except as concubines. There was also the consideration that wives were more of a legal encumbrance than concubines because the former enjoyed rights of inheritance. Each concubine was allowed to give the sultan *only one son*, a custom that had the effect of limiting her influence with the sultan. Most Ottoman sultans were sons of female slaves whose backgrounds were not even carefully recorded.[6] Only the paternal lineage mattered for the descendents of Osman, founder of the dynasty. Hurrem and Suleyman would defy all of these conventions.

When the royal son of a concubine reached young manhood (typically, age eighteen), his father sent him on provincial assignment so that the prince might gain administrative and military experience.[7] By custom, the concubine mother of the prince went with him, a mild, polite form of exile that put her out of central political range. Hurrem, as we will see, defied this custom as well.

Act I

The Prime Minister's Career

Three years into his reign, in 1523, Suleyman appointed his long-time friend Ibrahim prime minister (grand *vizir,* the chief of three *vizir*s at the capital), choosing him over a Turkish candidate, Ahmed Pasha, who had expected to get the job. Ibrahim's elevation over Ahmed not only demonstrates the importance of the sultan's

6. Leslie P. Peirce, *The Imperial Harem: Women and Sovereignty in the Ottoman Empire* (New York: Oxford University Press, 1993), 42–50. This is an excellent study for further reading.

7. By the late sixteenth century, when controlled succession became the norm, theoretically it was no longer necessary to provide provincial experience to all the royal sons, only to the son chosen to succeed, but that choice might come too late to allow time for proper training. Even worse, during the seventeenth century, *none* of the sons received such training and instead grew up in the harem, waiting for the death of their father when one of them would succeed to the throne as an ill-prepared sultan.

personal friendship but also exemplifies a trend beginning with Mehmed II to favor *devshirme* men over the traditional Turkish elite for important appointments. *Devshirme* men were supportive of the central governing institutions of which they were part, while the Turkish elite tried to maintain old, central Asian ideals of military-political institutions. Since the time of Mehmed II, most grand *vizir*s had been *devshirme* men, and from Suleyman's time on, they would have more power.

The grand *vizir* was responsible for the management of government departments and ministries. Next to the sultan, he was the highest-ranking member of the government's council which consisted also of two other lesser *vizir*s and a number of high-ranking bureaucratic and military officials as well as some lower-level administrators. Suleyman usually allowed the grand *vizir* to conduct council meetings and the day-to-day business of the empire. As we will see, Ibrahim took on several other types of responsibilities and exceeded this basic job description.

One of Ibrahim's first assignments was to oversee the refurbishing and enlargement of Topkapi Palace.[8] Suleyman broke with custom and allowed his prime minister, a member of the *Outer* Service, to have an apartment in the Inner Service space of Topkapi. Simply by virtue of being prime minister, Ibrahim had his own, separate palace as well. An apartment in Topkapi indicated an expansion of the *vizir*'s visibility and authority.

In 1524, Suleyman arranged for Ibrahim to marry one of his half-sisters, Hadije (Arabic Khadija), a union that brought him into the royal family and its politics. Ibrahim enjoyed also the support of the *valide sultan,* who ran the harem in the Old Palace. She and Ibrahim both favored a particular prince for succession, Mustafa, Suleyman's son born in 1515 of the then-favorite concubine, Mehideran Khatun.

A revolt soon distracted Suleyman and Ibrahim from concerns in the palace. Later on in 1524, a group of people in the Ottoman province of Egypt staged a revolt against Istanbul. The main instigator was Ahmed Pasha, the very Turk that Ibrahim had edged out for the office of prime minister the year before. Among Ahmad's co-conspirators were a number of Mamluks whose power and wealth had been limited by Ottoman conquest of Egypt in 1517. After suppressing the rebels with military force, Suleyman entrusted Ibrahim to bring Egypt back into line. Ibrahim implemented new policies to prevent the same sort of thing from happening again. He executed many of the rebels and confiscated their property. He installed a Janissary garrison but diplomatically did not allow the officers to engage in tax farming, which could have led to tensions between the Arab population and the foreign *devshirme* men. He revitalized the shipyard at Suez, creating work and strengthening the Ottoman navy. Ibrahim also implemented new laws allowing for the reimbursement of

8. Gulru Necipoglu, *Architecture, Ceremonial, and Power: The Topkapi Palace in the Fifteenth and Sixteenth Centuries* (Cambridge: MIT Press, 1991), 22.

some Egyptians, including Mamluks, who had lost property during the Ottoman conquest in 1517. The new laws represented generosity on the part of the empire. Suleyman, in his capacity as lawgiver, had decreed the new statutes, but they reflected well on Ibrahim, too, in his capacity as administrator.

Ibrahim's next major assignment was to join Ottoman campaigns into Hapsburg Hungary as *serdar,* top general. The first such campaign, in 1526, resulted in the conquest of greater Hungary at the battle of Mohacs, but stopped short of Vienna. Other Ottoman attempts to take the Hapsburg capital during the next several years were unsuccessful but confirmed Ottoman dominance of Hungary, exercised through cooperative local administrators.

In 1533, Ibrahim led the Ottoman army east toward the Iranian Empire of the Safavids, and Suleyman joined him later, indicating again that Suleyman was willing to place great responsibility in his prime minister's hands. Together they invaded and eventually conquered southern Iraq. Then, on his own initiative, Ibrahim invaded Azerbayjan, and this seems to be the point at which Suleyman's confidence in his servant waned. A contemporary chronicler says that Ibrahim fell into "tyranny and error," appropriating the title *serasker sultan* ("sultan-general"), which enraged Suleyman, who had already returned home.[9] On Ibrahim's return from the east to Istanbul in 1535, Suleyman ordered that his grand *vizir* be strangled, an order promptly carried out.

The punishment, many believed, did not fit Ibrahim's crime. What was usual in such a case was dismissal and possibly exile. Officials speculated that execution was far too severe, leading some to credit Hurrem with the sentence since Ibrahim's death permanently eliminated a powerful supporter of the heir apparent, Mustafa. A letter Hurrem wrote to her husband indicates that her dislike of Ibrahim was no secret, but the reason for her antipathy remains unclear (**Document Three**). It was also the case, however, that Suleyman independently viewed Ibrahim's recent behavior as a very serious threat.[10] Hurrem's role, if any, in the execution of Ibrahim remains unresolved.

Act II

A Royal Wedding

Suleyman met the slave concubine called Hurrem soon after he took the throne in 1520. She was somewhat attractive and very intelligent. Early in their relationship, Suleyman fell in love with Hurrem and often wrote ardent poetry to her and about her (**Document Four**). He respected her intelligence and sought her advice. Their close relationship contributed to changes in the evolution of Ottoman institutional elements, specifically

9. Christine Woodhead, "Perspectives on Suleyman," in *Suleyman the Magnificant and His Age: The Ottoman Empire in the Early Modern World,* ed. Metin Kunt and Christine Woodhead (London: Longmans, 1995), 176.

10. Ibid., 177.

the harem and succession. The role of royal women in sixteenth- and seventeenth-centuries Ottoman history appears far more active than in other periods, a situation explained partly by the precedents set by Hurrem, as described in Acts II and III.

Hurrem's first son, Mehmed, was born in 1521 and immediately became a potential rival for succession to Mustafa, son of the older concubine Mehideran Khatun. The well-entrenched custom was for a concubine to bear only *one* son with the ruler. Hurrem, however, defied the limit; she had several children with Suleyman, including five sons and at least one daughter. Suleyman obviously consented to this break with custom, probably because Hurrem remained his favorite. By all accounts, he took no other women as sexual partners after committing himself to her. One son died very young and another was disabled, still leaving three qualifying princes of the same mother, with Mehmed preferred by his mother for the succession. The other two were Selim and Bayezid.

In 1534, Suleyman and Hurrem broke with custom yet again. The two contracted a marriage, and Suleyman supplied her with a dowry, in accordance with Islamic law. As indicated above, royal Ottoman marriage had been rare since about 1440 and royal marriage to a slave concubine was unprecedented. The couple waited until after the death of the *valide sultan* earlier that year, because she would have been seriously opposed. Still, there was great scandal. Ordinary Ottoman subjects were very angry and even demonstrated in the streets of Istanbul. Suleyman rose above the fray by virtue of his awesome power, and Hurrem bore the brunt of disapproval. The deaths of the *valide sultan* and Ibrahim, in 1534 and 1535, respectively, left Hurrem as the sole close adviser to the sultan and strong enough to endure public resentment.

Act III
Moving to Topkapi

The Topkapi Palace was by far the largest and most elaborate of Ottoman royal residences. Prior to Hurrem's time, it housed the sultan and his male servants and retainers. Also in the palace were a large number of female slaves, some of whom became concubines to the sultan.

The official harem was in the Old Palace. This was home for the mother of the sultan and those concubines who had given birth, the children themselves, and servants and eunuch guards.[11] When the sons reached eighteen years of age, they and their mothers were sent off to a provincial city where the princes would learn administrative and military skills. Use of the Old Palace for the women's harem and the custom of provincial assignments kept physical distance between Topkapi and succession politics. Hurrem declined to move to

11. In 1475, there were said to be 400 female slaves at Topkapi and 250 at the Old Palace. Inalcik, 85.

the location of any of her sons' provincial training assignments, although she did visit her sons in these locations.[12]

Hurrem scandalized Istanbul yet again by moving from the Old Palace into Topkapi, probably shortly after her marriage in 1534. Some women of the Old Palace joined her and together they set a precedent for the future, housing women in the physical center of power. The sultan enlarged Topkapi yet again with a harem complex in order to accommodate the women.

After the execution of Ibrahim, the new grand *vizir* was Rustam Pasha. It was not a coincidence that he was married to Mihrimah, Hurrem and Suleyman's daughter. A Hapsburg diplomat, Ogier de Busbecq, recounts a discussion he had with the grand *vizir* (**Document Two B**). Rustam told Busbecq that he himself, along with his wife Mihrimah and his mother-in-law Hurrem, had been successful in dissuading the sultan from launching a new military campaign into Hapsburg territory, a dissuasion that constituted a significant impact on imperial policy.

During and after Hurrem's time, the women's Topkapi harem was an important political institution, particularly in succession maneuvering and in advancing (or blocking) individual petitions. Topkapi was the *working* palace where most discussions and decision making occurred, and the women there enjoyed influence and access to power. The women's harem also became famous. European artists and courtiers who never laid eyes on the harem space or its occupants depicted them nonetheless, creating a false impression of rampant sexuality (**Document Five**). Some European captives and diplomats who actually stayed in Istanbul for years at a time more accurately assessed the significance of royal women's power, but were never able to provide firsthand accounts of life in the harem.[13]

The Inner and Outer Services of the Ottoman government were not the same as private and public categories familiar from Euro-American social history, although the Inner Service did include the harem, a domestic equivalent to private. Inner and Outer Service administrations had some horizontal linkage. For example, the treasury was part of the Inner Service but had budgetary leverage over the military, part of the Outer Service. Ibrahim's apartment in Topkapi also blurred the lines of demarcation.

FINALE

In 1530, Mustafa, son of Suleyman by Mehideran Khatun, and Mehmed and Selim, two of Hurrem Sultan's five sons, all celebrated their circumcisions together in a massive ceremony and festival that lasted about two weeks. The festivities were *not* a sign of familial unity, as is evident from the succession struggle that followed. Hurrem's first choice as heir, Mehmed,

12. Peirce, 61.

13. Ibid., 113–118.

died of natural causes in 1543. Mustafa, the candidate favored by most of the powerful *devshirme* men, was caught up in rumors that he planned to unseat his aging father. Suleyman responded in haste, ordering the immediate execution of Mustafa. The *devshirme* men were aghast, and blamed Prime Minister Rustam Pasha for the rumors and Hurrem for having the idea in the first place (**Document Two A**). With his beloved Mehmed gone, Suleyman supported Selim, another of his sons with Hurrem. He loaned this son soldiers from his own personal guard so that Selim could defeat his younger brother, Bayezid.

Selim ascended the throne when his father died in 1566. Selim II, named for his grandfather, ruled until 1574. It was not an illustrious reign, and the sultan was nicknamed "the sallow" and "the drunkard." Hurrem did not live to see this unhappy outcome. She had become ill and died in 1558, before her husband's death and well before Selim earned his unflattering reputation. Her death had elicited from the sultan new poetry of sorrow and despair. His unhappiness was only increased by the succession conflicts.

Some Ottoman analysts who lived in the late seventeenth and eighteenth centuries, seeking an easy explanation for the imperial weakness of their own time, scornfully referred to the period from the 1530s through the 1650s as "the rule of women." The context and tone of this phrase implied pettiness and intrigue. Yet, men shared with women similar aspirations with regard to controlling succession. The great difference was that men close to the center of power had many *more* aspirations, often in regard to their own careers and wealth, and they had a far larger portion of the stage on which to play their parts, in some cases, major administrative provinces of the empire. The view from the palace harem was necessarily limited and women had to use the only tactics available to them to advance their interests.

Both Ibrahim and Hurrem affected the central governing institutions. The legacy of Ibrahim rests in his advancing the power and prestige of the office of prime minister, evident in his own tenure as grand *vizir* and also in that of Rustam Pasha. Ibrahim also contributed to the prestige of the *devshirme* men over the traditional Turkish elites. By acting on his own initiative in conquest and by aspiring to the title *serasker sultan,* he also rendered the relationship between sultan and prime minister more problematic. The legacy of Hurrem lay in her flaunting of existing customs governing reproduction and thus affecting succession. Her move to Topkapi forever changed the institution of the harem by bringing it physically close to the center of power.

Documents

DOCUMENT ONE

Konstantin

Memoirs of a Janissary

Konstantin was a fifteenth-century Serb who witnessed firsthand the expansion of the Ottoman Turks into Europe. While probably not a genuine devshirme *man, Konstantin was captured by the Ottomans and served in some capacity in the Janissary corps and participated in the conquest of Constantinople in 1453. Here is his description of Ottoman expansion. Why might he refer to the Ottomans as heathens?*

Turkish or heathen expansion is like the sea, which never increases nor decreases, and it is of such nature: it never has peace but always rolls. If it falls calm in one region, in another it crashes against the shores. Sea water is dense and salty, so that in some regions they make salt of it; nevertheless, without adding a portion of fresh water to the salt water, salt cannot be made. Likewise all the streams which flow about the world wind here and there: the waters are fresh and good and useful for all things, but when they fall into the sea and are mixed with the sea water, all their freshness and goodness are lost and they become dense and salty like the sea water. The Turks are also of such a nature as the sea: they never have peace, but always carry on a struggle from year to year from some lands to others. If they make a truce somewhere, it is better for them, and in other regions they perpetrate evils: they take people into bondage, and whoever cannot walk they kill. And this happens many times every year: they round up and bring several thousand good Christians amongst the heathens; having been mixed they are spoiled, like the above-mentioned water. Having forgotten their good Christian faith they accept and extol the heathen faith. And such heathenized Christians are much worse than true-born heathens. This, then, adds to the expansion of the Turks. Some have served their terms, others are serving, while a third group is newly brought in and they ride [out] for a fourth time, striving so that their number would never diminish, in accordance with the word of Mohammed.

And so for those above that who voluntarily become heathen, every year there is a considerable number; as it happened in a city called Galata or Pera during the time when I was in Turkey, that a certain noted monk of the order of St. Bernard through his ignobility deprived a good man of his life, for the heathens had him burned without [proof of] guilt, and his wife was left a widow. Now then this same monk took Mohammed's faith and insulted Christ's and asked the heathens for this same woman, and they gave her to him against her will. Later more than forty Catalan and Italian sailors accepted the heathen faith, insulting the Christian faith. The heathens, however, did not praise the monk for his deeds. And that happened in Constantinople.

And thus the heathens expand, as was said of the abovementioned sea. And this you can know yourselves, that the Turks capture people and not livestock. Who then can prevent them? Having taken [captives] they swiftly ride away with them, and before the Christians are ready they are already where they ought to be. And the more men you maintain, wanting to prevent this, the greater the expense and torment you will bear. And further, you understand the rest by yourselves. Until you smash a snake's head it is always worse. Likewise you also: [even] if you defeat them sometime on a foray they will do just the same damage as before.

DOCUMENT TWO

Ogier De Busbecq

His First and Third Letters

Busbecq's four letters were written in Vienna from notes he had taken during his recent stay in Istanbul as ambassador representing the Hapsburgs. He addressed the letters to a fellow diplomat as private correspondence, but this was a literary device; the letters were meant for publication and a public audience.

A. First Letter, dated September 1, 1555

In this first letter, Busbecq describes a royal audience in which the Safavid ambassador and he sought peace agreements with the Ottomans. Does his description of Suleyman match with the information you have about the sultan in this chapter?

. . . The Persian ambassador had arrived on the 10th of May and had brought with him many splendid presents—carpets of the finest texture, Babylonian tent-hangings embroidered on the inner side in various colours, harness and trappings of exquisite workmanship, scimitars from Damascus adorned with jewels, and shields of wonderful beauty. But all these presents were eclipsed by a copy of the Koran, the book which contains their ceremonies and laws, which the Turks believe to have been composed by Mahomet under divine inspiration. A gift of this kind is very highly esteemed among them.

Peace was granted on the spot to the Persian representative, in order that greater attention might be paid to us, with whom it seemed likely that there would be more trouble. No possible honour towards the Persian was omitted, that we might have no doubt about the genuineness of the peace which had been made with him. In all matters, as I have already said, the Turks are in the habit of going to extremes, whether in paying honour to their friends or in showing their contempt by humiliating their foes. Ali Pasha, the second Vizier, gave a dinner to the Persians in a garden, which, though it was at some distance and separated from us by a river, was visible from our quarters; for, as I have said, the situation of the town on sloping ground is such that there is scarcely a spot which one cannot see and in which one cannot be seen. Ali Pasha, a Dalmatian by birth, is a delightfully intelligent person, and (what is surprising in a Turk) by no means lacking in humanity. The Pashas reclined with the ambassador under an awning which shaded the table. A hundred youths, all clad alike, served the meal, bringing the dishes to the table in the following manner. They first advanced, drawn up at equal distances from one another, towards the table where the guests were reclining, with their hands empty, so as not to hinder their salutations, which consisted of placing their hands on their thighs and bowing their heads to the earth. After they had performed this salutation, the attendant who had taken up his position nearest to the kitchen received the dishes and handed them on to the man next to him, who passed them on to a third; the latter then handed them on to a fourth, and so on, until they reached the attendant who stood nearest to the table, from whose hands the chief butler received them and placed them on the table. In this manner a hundred or more plates streamed, so to speak, on to the table without any confusion. When this was accomplished, the attendants again saluted the guests and returned in the same order as they had come, except that those who had been last when they came were the first to withdraw, and those who were nearest to the table now brought up the rear. The other courses were brought to the table in the same manner. Thus in matters of small moment the Turks like to observe due order, whereas we neglect to do so in matters of the gravest importance. The ambassador's suite was entertained by some Turks not far from their master's table.

Peace having been, as I have said, ratified with the Persians, we could obtain from the Turks no terms which had even the semblance of justice. All that could be arranged between us was a truce for six months, during which an answer might be sent to Vienna and a further reply brought back. I had come to assume the functions of an ambassador in ordinary, but, since nothing had been arranged about a peace, the Pashas were resolved that I should depart to my royal master with a letter from Soleiman and bring back a reply if the King were pleased to send it. I was, therefore, again introduced into the Sultan's presence. Two ample embroidered robes reaching to my ankles were thrown about me, which were as much as I could carry. My attendants were also presented with silken robes of various colours and, clad in these, accompanied me. I thus proceeded in a stately procession, as though I were going to play the part of Agamemnon or some similar hero in a tragedy, and bade farewell to the Sultan after receiving his dispatch wrapped up in cloth of gold and sealed. The more distinguished of my suite were also admitted to salute the Sultan. Having afterwards paid my respects to the Pashas in like manner, I left Amasia with my colleagues on June the 2nd. It is customary to offer a breakfast to ambassadors who are on the point of departing in the Divan, as they call the place where the Pashas administer justice; but this is only done when they are friendly, and our relations had not yet been placed on a footing of peace. . . .

B. Third Letter, dated June 1, 1560

This third letter concerns Busbecq's negotiations with the Ottoman administration and others involved in an attempt to forestall or preclude a contemplated Ottoman campaign against the Hapsburgs, whom Busbecq represented. According to Busbecq, the negotiations finally came down to himself and the Ottoman prime minister, Rustam Pasha. Embedded in this account is a reference to the influence that Rustam had with his sultan, and also the influence of two women: the sultan's wife Hurrem, who was mother-in-law to Rustam, and Mihrimah, who was the daughter of Suleyman and Hurrem and wife to Rustam.

. . . When my colleagues, with whom you are acquainted from my former letters, saw that we had already spent three years here in vain and that no arrangements had been made for peace or a truce of any duration, and there seemed only a vague and distant hope of making any progress in the future, they began to exert all their efforts to obtain leave to depart. When Soleiman had with great difficulty been induced to consent to their departure—for when a man has arrived here it is no easy matter for him to return when he wishes to do so—one question still remained, whether the others should leave without me, since they had been here longer than I, or whether we should all depart; for Soleiman, desirous of not appearing too eager for peace by detaining any of us himself, left the choice to us. My colleagues were of opinion that it was greatly to the Emperor's interest that one of us should remain. This was obvious (and I agreed with them), but I thought it well to dissemble and hide my intention from the Turks. And so, whenever the question was mentioned in their presence, I expressed a strong aversion to remaining. I admitted that I had come as an ambassador in ordinary, but pointed out that such a position was only possible when peace had been arranged; as long as peace was uncertain, I did not see how I could remain without disobeying, or at any rate going outside, my master's instructions, which would be best carried out if we all departed. I argued thus in order that, if I remained at the request of the Turks, I might be in a better position than if I offered to do so and forced my presence upon them. I fully realized that, if we all departed, it meant not merely throwing open a window whereby war might enter, but throwing wide the gates of the Temple of Janus; whereas, if I stayed, the prospect of peace was unimpaired. Before dispatches could be exchanged between the two capitals, a long time would elapse during which much might happen to render our position more favourable. Finally, anything was better than needlessly to make a terrible war inevitable. I was, however, well aware how little I was consulting my own interests, since I was only preparing trouble for myself and should have to support alone a vast weight of responsibility; and many various and unforeseen circumstances were to be anticipated, especially if my action resulted in a declaration of war. But those who undertake such onerous duties must think lightly of them in comparison with the public interest, and must only look to what is for the advantage of the State. Roostem, by showing himself very eager that I should remain, gave me greater freedom of action; he naturally realized how much it would promote the outbreak of hostilities if we all departed and the peace negotiations already begun were broken off. He was particularly opposed to war at this time with a foreign power, because, being a man of foresight, he anticipated that, if Soleiman made an expedition into Hungary, his sons were sure to seize the opportunity for some fresh attempt. He, therefore, summoned us to his house and detailed to my colleagues at great length the arguments which he wished them to place before the Emperor with a view to the conclusion of peace. He exhorted me to remain behind and not to abandon the task which I had undertaken, but to persevere until I had brought it to a successful conclusion. He expressed his conviction that the Emperor, who had never shown himself averse to peace, would approve of my remaining at my post. I, on my part, raised objections and refused to comply as far as I could conveniently and safely do so. My remarks spurred on Roostem to further efforts and, to prevent my putting an end to all hopes of peace, he insisted that his master was very eager to lead an army into Hungary, and would have done so long ago but for the fact that he himself with the support and help of the women (meaning his wife and his mother-in-law) held him back, to use his own expression, by clinging to the hem of his raiment [cloak]. He begged us not to provoke the sleeping lion and irritate him against us. I, thereupon, became less vehement in my refusal, and said that I would no longer refuse to remain, were it not that I feared that they would immediately lay the blame on me if anything occurred against their wishes, though it was not in my power to prevent this, and would vent their wrath on me. Roostem bade me have no fear, whatever happened, that I should be held responsible; if I would but remain, he would protect me 'as though I was his own brother'. I said that I would consider the matter, and so we parted.

The next day we were summoned to the Divan, which is their Council of State, where practically the same scene occurred, except that Roostem, in view of the presence of the other Pashas, spoke somewhat less openly. I eventually consented to remain, after depositing with the Pashas a written document in which I recorded that I was remaining without any knowledge of my master's wishes and therefore reserved every question free and unprejudiced for his decision; I took nothing upon myself and denied responsibility for any result which Heaven might be pleased to ordain. This document proved afterwards of great service to me in times of difficulty, when anything happened to give the Pashas an excuse for dealing hardly with me. Such were the reason and the manner of my remaining behind. . . .

DOCUMENT THREE

Hurrem

A Letter to the Absent Suleyman (ca. 1534)

These portions of a longer letter may have been penned by Hurrem herself. In the second portion, she alludes to a disagreement between her and the prime minister, Ibrahim. Her lack of further explanation is intriguing. If she ever gave Suleyman an explanation, it is lost to us. What does this letter suggest about Hurrem's relationship with Suleyman?

[First Portion]

My sultan, there is no limit to the burning anguish of separation. Now spare this miserable one and do not withhold your noble letters. Let my soul gain at least some comfort from a letter. . . . When your noble letters are read, your servant [i.e., Hurrem] and son Mir Mehmed and your slave and daughter Mihrimah weep and wail from missing you. Their weeping has driven me mad, it is as if we were in mourning. My sultan, your son Mir Mehmed and your daughter Mihrimah and Selim Khan and Abdullah [two other sons] send you many greetings and rub their faces in the dust at your feet [a common expression of respect and devotion toward the ruler].

[Second Portion]

You ask why I am angry at [Ibrahim] Pasha. God willing, when we are able to be together again, you will hear. For now, we send our regards to the Pasha—may he accept them.

DOCUMENT FOUR

Suleyman

A Poem

Under the pen name Beloved, Suleyman wrote a number of poems to and about Hurrem. By all accounts, she was the love of his life. Because Suleyman spent long periods away from Istanbul, and from Hurrem, on state business and to lead military campaigns, they often had to sustain their relationship with the letters and poems that passed between them. Note the indirect reference to Hurrem's Christian background. It is not certain that she ever formally converted to Islam; while conversion was part of the devşhirme *program for boys, it was not required of female slaves. What does the poem tell you about their relationship?*

Your presence castes a shadow over me like a bird of paradise.
I have become emperor of the world by being a beggar at your door.
Let world events rage like the turbulent sea; I will not set sail.
The ship of your love is an anchor for me.
My intimate companion, my elixir of paradise, my Eden;
My Istanbul, my Karaman, and all the Anatolian lands that are mine.
If I die, yours is the guilt. Help, I beg of you my love from a different religion.

DOCUMENT FIVE

Paul Rycaut

The Present State of the Ottoman Empire (1686)

Paul Rycaut was secretary to the English ambassador to the Ottoman Empire in the 1660s. Since access to the harem was strictly limited, his account of harem life could not have been based on his own observations but rather had to be based on second- or thirdhand accounts that hold no assurance of being accurate. Rycaut did go to great lengths to try to understand Islamic doctrines, gleaned from discussions with Ottoman men. He appears to be genuinely curious about his foreign surroundings and eager to learn. If this eager curiosity extended to the harem, then perhaps he talked with informants who wanted to exaggerate and titillate. The account below suggests that the sultan went through an elaborate ceremony to choose a bedmate whenever the mood struck him. In fact, most sultans were loyal to a favorite woman for months or years at a time. The custom of allowing a concubine to have only one son was more of an obstacle to lengthy relationships than the sultan's lust. Does Rycaut's account match stereotypes of the Ottoman harem?

When the Grand Signior is pleased to dally with a certain number of these Ladies [of the harem] in the Garden; *Helvet* [Arabic *khalwa*, an appeal for privacy] is cryed, which rings through all the Seraglio [i.e., the harem], at which word all people withdraw themselves at a distance, and Eunuchs are placed at every avenue [or entrance] it being at that time death to approach near those walls. Here the Women strive with their Dances, Songs and Discourse to make themselves Mistresses of the Grand Signior[']s affection, and then let themselves loose to all kind of lasciviousness and wanton carriage, acquitting Themselves as much of all respect to Majesty as they do to modesty. When the Grand Signior resolves to choose himself a Bed-fellow, he retires into the Lodgings of his Women, where according to the story in every place reported, when the Turkish Seraglio falls into discourse: the Damsels being ranged in order by the Mother of the Maids [that is, the mature woman tutor], he throws his handkerchief to her, where his eye and fancy best directs, it being a token of her election to his bed. The surprized [sic] Virgin snatches at this prize and good fortune with that eagerness, that she is ravished with joy before she is defloured [sic] by the Sultan, and kneeling down first kisses the handkerchief, and then puts it in her bosom, when immediately she is congratulated by all the Ladies of the court, for the great honour and favour she hath received.

Questions

1. Hurrem and Ibrahim, two people of slave origin, both came into an inner circle of power. How did their experiences differ?
2. What is an institution? Do you agree that the Ottoman harem was an institution? Why or why not?
3. Two of the documents are personal, a poem and a letter. Are they good historical sources? Why or why not?

Suggested Readings

de Busbecq, Ogier Ghislen. *Turkish Letters*. Trans. Edward Seymour Forster from the Latin. 3d ed. repr. London: Sickle Moon, 2001.

Faroqhi, Suraiya. *Subjects of the Sultan: Culture and Daily Life in the Ottoman Empire*. London: Taurus, 1995.

Inalcik, Halil. *The Ottoman Empire: The Classical Age* 1300–1600. Trans. Norman Itzkowitz and Colin Imber from the Turkish. London: Weidenfeld and Nicolson, 1973.

Kunt, Metin, and Christine Woodhead, eds. *Suleyman the Magnificent and His Age: The Ottoman Empire in the Early Modern World*. London: Longman, 1995.

Necipoglu, Gulru. *Architecture, Ceremonial, and Power: The Topkapi Palace in the Fifteenth and Sixteenth Centuries*. Cambridge, MA: MIT Press, 1991.

Peirce, Leslie P. *The Imperial Harem: Women and Sovereignty in the Ottoman Empire*. New York: Oxford University Press, 1993.

CREDITS

Text Credits

CHAPTER 1 Document 1, A-C, page 16: Documents 4, 5, 6, page 20: J. Smith, *Origin and History of Hebrew Law*. Excerpts from "Law Code of Hammurabi," translated by D. Luckenbill, pp. 181–182 and 221–222. Copyright © 1931 by the University of Chicago Press. Reprinted by permission of the University of Chicago Press.

CHAPTER 2 Document 1, page 42: Document 4, page 47: The Victorious King from William Kelly Simpson (eds.), *The Literature of Ancient Egypt* (New Haven, CT: Yale University Press, 1972), pp. 285, 286, 287, 288. Copyright © 1972 Yale University Press. Reprinted by permission of Yale University Press.

CHAPTER 3 Document 1, page 62: The Dark Bird from *The Book of Songs*, trans. Arthur Waley. New York: Grove Press, 1996, p. 320. Copyright © 1996 by Grove Press, Inc. Reprinted by permission.

CHAPTER 4 Document 1, page 83: Suetonius, Augustus 68, 69 and 70 from *The Twelve Caesars,* trans. Robert Graves, (London: Penguin Books, 1957), 88–90. Reprinted by permission of Carcanet Press Limited. **Document 2, page 85:** Reprinted by permission of the publishers and the Trustees of the Loeb Classical Library from *Plutarch – The Parallel Lives: Volume IX,* Loeb Classical Library Volume 101, translated by B. Perrin, pp. 257, 259, Cambridge, Mass.: Harvard University Press, 1920. The Loeb Classical Library® is a registered trademark of the President and Fellows of Harvard College. **After document 2, page 86:** Alexander, Sidney: *The Complete Odes and Satires of Horace.* © 1999 Princeton University Press. Reprinted by permission of Princeton University Press. **Documents 3, 5, pages 88, 93:** From *The Complete Works of Tacitus* by Tacitus, edited by Moses Hadas, translated by Alfred John Church & William Jackson Brodribb, copyright 1942 and renewed 1970 by Random House, Inc. Used by permission of Random House, Inc. **Documents 4, 5, pages 90, 95:** Reprinted by permission of the publishers and the Trustees of the Loeb Classical Library from *Dio Cassius – Roman History: Volume VII,* Loeb Classical Library® Volume 175, translated by Earnest Cary, Cambridge, Mass.: Harvard University Press, Copyright © 1924 by the President and Fellows of Harvard College. The Loeb Classical Library® is a registered trademark of the President and Fellows of Harvard College. pp. 5, 7, 9, 13, 17, 19.

CHAPTER 5 Document 2, page 108: Source: *The History of the Former Han Dynasty,* trans. and ed., Homer H. Dubs with the collaboration of Jen T'ai and P'an Lo-chi (Baltimore: Waverly Press, 1938), pp. 99–102. Modified by Ping Yao. **Document 4, page 110:** Ban Gu: "Lady Li, Concubine of Emperor Wu" from *Courtier and Commoner in Ancient China: Selections from the History of The Former Han* by Pan Ku, trans. Burton Watson, pp. 247–251, © 1974 Columbia University Press. Reprinted with the permission of the publisher. **Documents 5, 6, pages 112, 114:** *Pan Chao: Foremost Woman Scholar of China,* trans., Nancy Lee Swann (Ann Arbor: Center for Chinese Studies, The University of Michigan, 2001), pp. 83–86, 113–116. Originally published 1932, copyright renewed 1960. © East Asian Library and the Gest Collection, Princeton University.

CHAPTER 6 Documents 1, 4, pages 131, 136: Goldman, Robert P., *The Ramayana of Valmiki.* © 1984 Princeton University Press. Reprinted by permission of Princeton University Press. **Document-2, page 134:** Excerpt from *The Laws of Manu,* translated with an introduction and notes by Wendy

Doniger with Brian K. Smith (Penguin Classics, 1991), p. 115 and pp. 197–198. Copyright © Wendy Doniger and Brian K. Smith, 1991. Reproduced by permission of Penguin Books Ltd. **Document 5, page 138:** Swami Venkatesananda, *The Concise Ramayana of Valmiki* (Albany, NY: State University of New York Press, copyright 1988), pp. 341–342.

CHAPTER 7 Document 1, page 156: From "A Letter from Gregory, Bishop of Nyssa, on the Life of Saint Macrina" (his sister, c. 380), in Petersen, Joan M., trans. and ed., *Handmaids of the Lord: Contemporary Descriptions of Feminine Asceticism in the First Six Christian Centuries* (Kalamazoo, Michigan: Cistercian Publications, Inc., 1996), pp. 54–57. © Cistercian Publications, Kalamazoo, Michigan. All rights reserved. **Document 2, page 158:** From Petersen, Joan M., trans. and ed., *Handmaids of the Lord: Contemporary Descriptions of Feminine Asceticism in the First Six Christian Centuries* (Kalamazoo, Michigan: Cistercian Publications, Inc., 1996), pp. 128-31, 146–49. © Cistercian Publications, Kalamazoo, Michigan. All rights reserved. **Document 4, page 165:** John Chrysostom from Clark, Elizabeth A., Jerome, Chrysostom, and Friends: *Essays and Translations* (New York: The Edwin Mellen Press, © 1979), pp. 164–65, 177–79, 220–23, 228–31. Reprinted by permission. **Page 167:** Reprinted by permission of the publishers and the Trustees of the Loeb Classical Library from *St. Jerome: Select Letters*, Loeb Classical Library Volume L 262, translated by F. A. Wright, pp. 67–69, 125–127, 343–351, 357–361, Cambridge, Mass.: Harvard University Press, 1933. The Loeb Classical Library® is a registered trademark of the President and Fellows of Harvard College.

CHAPTER 8 Document 2, page 184: Source: *Ennin's Travels in T'ang China.* Translated by Edwin O. Reischauer. New York: The Ronald Press Company, 1955. Pp. 221–224. Reprinted by permission of Robert D. Reischauer. **Document 3, page 186:** Source: *Ennin's diary: the record of a pilgrimage to China in search of the law,* translated from the Chinese by Edwin O. Reischauer. New York: Ronald Press 1955. Pp. 242–243. Reprinted by permission of Robert D. Reischauer. **Documents-4, 5, 6, page 187, 188:** Sources: Suzanne Cahill, "Resenting the Silk Robes that Hide Their Poems: Female Voices in the Poetry of Tang Dynasty Taoist Nuns." In Deng Xiaonan, Gao Shiyu and Rong Xinjiang, eds. *Women and Society in Tang-Song China (Tang Song nüxing yu shehui),* Shanghai: Shanghai cishu chubanshe, 2003. Pp. 548–549, 550–552, 541. Reprinted by permission of Suzanne Cahill.

CHAPTER 9 Documents 1, 3, pages 201, 203: Extract from Ibn Ishaq, *The Life of Muhammad, Apostle of Allah,* translated by Edward Rehatsek and edited by Michael Edwardes (London: The Folio Society, 1964), pp. 39–41 and pp. 115–119. Reproduced by permission of The Folio Society, Ltd. and the Royal Asiatic Society.

CHAPTER 10 Document 1, page 217: From McCullough, Helen Crag, translator. *Genji and Heike: Selections from "The Tale of Genji" and "The Tale of the Heike."* Copyright © 1994 by the Board of Trustees of the Leland Stanford Junior University. All rights reserved. Used with the permission of Stanford University Press, www.sup.org. **Documents 2, 3, 4, 6, pages 219, 220, 221, 224:** Excerpts from *The Diary of Lady Murasaki by Lady Murasaki* translated by Richard Bowring (Penguin Books, 1996). Translation copyright © Richard Bowring, 1996. Reproduced by permission of Penguin Books Ltd. **Document 5, page 223:** Matters I want settled from *The Ink Dark Moon: Love Poems* by Ono no Komachi and Izumi Shikibu translated by Mariko Aratani and Jane Hirshfield, copyright © 1990 by Jane Hirschfield. Used by permission of Vintage Books, a division of Random House, Inc. **Page 224:** Out of the Dark from Donald Keene, *Anthology of Japanese Literature from the Earliest Era to the Mid-nineteenth Century,* New York: Grove Press, 1955, p. 92). Copyright © 1955 by Grove Press, Inc. Reprinted by permission. **Document 7, page 225:** Source: Richard Bowring, *Murasaki Shikibu, Her Diary and Poetic Memoirs: A Translation and Study.* Princeton: Princeton University Press, 1982, pp. 217, 247, 234, 254. Reprinted by permission of the author.

CHAPTER 11 Documents 1A, 4C, pages 247, 254: Fulcher of Chartres, *Chronicle of the First Crusade,* trans. Martha Evelyn McGinty (Philadelphia: University of Pennsylvania Press, 1941), 15–17, 28. Reprinted by permission of the University of Pennsylvania Press. **Documents 2A, 2B, 4A, 4D, pages 248, 250, 253, 255:** Excerpts from *The Alexiad of Anna Comnena* translated by E.R.A. Sewter (Penguin Classics, 1969). Copyright © E.R.A. Sewter, 1969. Reproduced by permission of Penguin Books Ltd. **Document** 6, page 257: *Crusades: Islamic Perspectives* by Carole Hillenbrand. Copyright 1999 by Routledge Publishing Inc.-Books. Reproduced with permission of Routledge Publishing Inc.-Books in the format Textbook via Copyright Clearance Center.

CHAPTER 12 Document 2, page 274: From Rashid al-Din, *The Successors of Chinggis Khan,* trans. John Andrew Boyle, © 1971 by Columbia University Press. Reprinted with the permission of the publisher. **Document 3, page 276:** *Arab Historians of the Crusades* by Francesco Gabrieli. Copyright 1969 by University of California Press - Books. Reproduced with permission of University of California Press - Books in the format Textbook via Copyright Clearance Center. **Document 4, page 278:** Reprinted by permission of the publisher from 'Ala ad-Din 'Ata Malik Juvaini's, *The History of the World-Conqueror,* translated by John Andrew Boyle, pp. 23–25, 128–130, Cambridge, Mass.: Harvard University Press, copyright © 1958 by Manchester University Press.

CHAPTER 14 Documents 1B, 4, 5, pages 312, 317, 318: From *Father Francisco Alvares, The Prester John of the Indies.* Trans. and edited by C. F. Beckingham and G.W. B. Huntingford. Second Series, no. CXIV. Cambridge University Press (published for the Hakluyt Society), 1961, pp. 106–108, 240, 41, 243, 244. Reprinted by permission of David Higham Associates, London. The Hakluyt Society was established in 1846 for the purpose of printing rare or unpublished Voyages and Travels. For further information please see their website at: www.hakluyt.com. **Document 1C, page 313:** From *Some Records of Ethiopia, 1593-1646, Being Extracts from The History of High Ethiopia or Abassia* by Manoel de Almeida, trans. and edited by C. F. Beckingham and G.W.B. Huntingford. Second Series, no. CVII. Cambridge University Press (published for the Hakluyt Society), 1954. Reprinted by permission of David Higham Associates, London. The Hakluyt Society was established in 1846 for the purpose of printing rare or unpublished Voyages and Travels. For further information please see their web site at: www.hakluyt.com. **Document 2, page 314**: Source: The Chronicle of the Emperor Zara Yaqob (1434 1468), translated by Richard Pankhurst http://tezeta.org/16/the chronicle of the emperor zara yaqob 1434 1468. Accessed September 26, 2006. Reprinted by permission of Richard Pankhurst.

CHAPTER 15 Document 2, page 338: From Fray Diego Duran, *The History of the Indies of New Spain,* translated, annotated and with an introduction by Doris Heyden. Copyright © 1994 by the University of Oklahoma Press, Norman. Reprinted by permission. **Document 3, page 341**: Source: From Bernal Diāz Del Castillo, *The Discovery and Conquest of Mexico, 1517–1521* edited by Genaro Garcia; translated by A. P. Maudslay, Farrar, Straus and Cudahy Publishers, 1956, pp. 66, 67, 68. **Document 4, page 343**: From James Lockhart, (ed. and translator), *We People Here: Nahuatl Account of the Conquest of Mexico, Vol. 1* (Berkeley: University of California Press, 1993), pp. 120, 122. Reprinted by permission of the author. **Document 5, page 344**: Source: From Hernán Cortés, *Letters from Mexico*, Translated and edited by A. R. Pagden, pp. 84, 85, 91, 102, 103, 104, 262, 263. Copyright © Anthony Pagden 1971. Reprinted by permission of Yale University Press. **Document 1, page 336**: Constantin Mihailovic: *Memoirs of a Janissary,* translated by Benjamin Stolz, commentary and notes by Svat Soucek (Ann Arbor, MI: Michigan Slavic Publications, University of Michigan, 197, p. 191 and p. 193. Reprinted with permission. **Document 2, page 338:** Ogier Ghislen de Busbecq, Turkish Letters, reprint of 3rd edition, translated from the Latin by Edward Seymour Forster (London: Sickle Moon Press, 2001), pp. 41–43. Reprinted by permission of Oxford University Press, London.

Photo Credits

CHAPTER 1 Page 4: *(Left)* head of Hammurabi, King of Babylon, 18th Century BC Mesopotamian from Susa. The Art Archive/Musee du Louvre Paris/Gianna Daglis Orti. *(Right)* head of a prince or princess of Mari, ivory and gold, c. 2000–1500 B.C. National Museum, Damascus, Syria. Photograph from The Bridgeman Art Library/Getty Images.

CHAPTER 2 Page 29: *(Left)* Sphinx of Pharaoh Hatshepsut, one of a pair from her funerary temple at Deir Bahari, 18th Dynasty 1473–1458 B.C. Photograph from The Art Archive / Egyptian Museum, Cairo/Dagli Orti (A), Ref AA326331. *(Right)* Bust of Tuthmosis III, Deir El Bahari. Photograph © John P. Stephens/Ancient Art and Architecture Collection, Ltd.

CHAPTER 3 Pages 51 and 63: Tomb of Lady Hao, China. Photograph from The Art and Architecture Collection, Ltd.

CHAPTER 4 Page 70: *(Left)* Antique bust of Roman date. Photograph from The Granger Collection, New York. *(Right)* Roman bust, from Glypotek Museum, Copenhagen. Photograph by G.T. Garvey/Ancient Art and Architecture Collection, Ltd.

CHAPTER 5 Page 98: *(Left)* Ban Gu, The Art and Architecture Collection, Ltd. *(Right)* Ban Zhao, The Art and Architecture Collection, Ltd.

CHAPTER 6 Page 122: *(Left)* 11th Century Chola period bronze sculpture of Rama. Photograph © Philadelphia Museum of Art/Corbis. *(Right) Sita Answers with a Smile*, Indian miniature, gouache on paper, Pahari School, Basohli style, 1665, Dogra Art Gallery. Photograph from akg-images/Jean-Louis Nou.

CHAPTER 7 Page 141: *(Left) Saint Jerome*, by Fiorenzo di Lorenzo, 15th Century. Photograph © Arte and Immagini sri / Corbis. *(Right)* mosaic pavement from Basilican Aquileia, 4th Century A.D. Photograph from The Art Archive / Basilica Aquileia, Italy/Gianna Dagli Orti (A), Ref. AA325473.

CHAPTER 8 Page 171: Yu Xuanji, The Art and Architecture Collection, Ltd. **Page 183:** Diagram of Capital Chang'an, Tang Dynasty, reprinted with permission from *Sui-Tang Chang'an: A Study in the Urban History of Medieval China* (Michigan Monographs in Chinese Studies, 2000), U-M Center for Chinese Studies ISBN 0-8264-137-1 (diagram 9.1. Distribution of Religious Establishments in Chang'an).

CHAPTER 9 Page 190: 9th Century leaf from a Koran written in kufic script, Abbasid Dynasty, Iraq. Collection of Mrs. Bashir Mohamed, London, UK. Photograph by Werner Forman/Art Resource, New York.

CHAPTER 10 Page 208: *(Left) Prince Genji watching at the Suma Beach* (detail), Leeds Museum and Art Galleries (City Museum), UK. Photograph by Hiroshige, The Bridgeman Art Library / Getty Images. *(Right)* Murasaki Shikibu, 11th Century. Photograph from The Art Archive.

CHAPTER 11 Page 232: *(Left) Departure of the Barons for the First Crusade*, preceded by the Bishop of Puy, from *Histoire d'outremer*, 1280. Photograph from Bibliotheque Municipale, Lyon, France, Snark/Art Resource, New York. *(Right)* Empress Irene, detail of Byzantine mosaic, photograph © Paul H. Kulper/Corbis.

CHAPTER 12 Page 260: Genghis Khan on the Throne, 14th Century Persian book illumination. Photograph Bibliotheque Nationale, Paris/akg-images.

CHAPTER 13 **Page 283:** 1935 photograph of the Cairo Citadel from *Glimpses of the East.* Photograph from the Mary Evans Picture Library/The Image Works.

CHAPTER 14 **Page 300:** *Water of Conviction*, from Gospels in Ethiopia, 1400. Photograph from The Pierpont Morgan Library, New York/Art Resource, New York.

CHAPTER 15 **Page 322:** Contemporary Aztec drawing of Dona Marina (right) interpreting during meeting of Montezuma II (seated, left) and Cortés (seated, right), November 1519.

CHAPTER 16 **Page 350:** *(Left)* Roxelana, wife of Ottoman Sultan Suleiman I, the Magnificent, 1557 woodcut. Photograph © Mary Evans Picture Library/The Image Works. *(Right)* Ibrahim Pasha, detail from *Arrival of the Austrian Ambassadors,* folio 328a, Painter B, Topkapi Palace Museum, Istanbul.

INDEX